The Sound of Silence

Also by Michael G. Ankerich

Broken Silence: Conversations with 23 Silent Film Stars (McFarland, 1993)

The Sound of Silence

Conversations with 16 Film and Stage Personalities Who Bridged the Gap Between Silents and Talkies

by MICHAEL G. ANKERICH

McFarland & Company, Inc., Publishers
Jefferson, North Carolina, and London

British Library Cataloguing-in-Publication data are available

Library of Congress Cataloguing-in-Publication Data

Ankerich, Michael G., 1962–
The sound of silence : conversations with 16 film and stage personalities who bridged the gap between silents and talkies / by Michael G. Ankerich.
p. cm.
Includes index.
ISBN 0-7864-0504-X (library binding : 50# alkaline paper) ∞
1. Silent films — United States — History and criticism. 2. Sound motion pictures — United States. 3. Motion picture actors and actresses — United States — Interviews. I. Title
PN1998.2.A66 1998
791.43'0973 — dc21 98-20085
CIP

Manufactured in the United States of America

McFarland & Company, Inc., Publishers
Box 611, Jefferson, North Carolina 28640

To Billie, Mary and Anita,
and the 13 others
who trusted me with their memories.
And to Charlie, who trusted me with his life.

Contents

Acknowledgments

Film historian Roi Uselton tops the list of those to whom I wish to express my deepest appreciation. He was a source of support from the inception to the completion of *The Sound of Silence*. He introduced me to four of the subjects included within these covers, and he made himself available to edit the finished manuscript. I am grateful for his advice, his encouragement and his inspiration.

Thanks also go to Pat H. Broeske, Juan Camacho, Jean Porter Dmytryk, Lenore Foote, Leatrice Gilbert Fountain, Eve Golden, Doris Heath, Bob King, Robert Klepper, Pancho Kohner, Donald Ludwin, Erik Madden, Randal Malone, Pat "Vilma" Marsh, Margaret O'Brien, Jim Parish and Michael W. Schwibs.

—Michael G. Ankerich
Columbus, Georgia
Spring 1998

Foreword

It was a rainy afternoon in San Francisco—lights glistening in the mist, a tingle in the air in a favorite restaurant high above Union Square, everyone eager to be seated. I had a date with Michael Ankerich, whom I had never met personally and knew only through his book *Broken Silence,* his magazine articles, and an exchange of letters. However, I had seen his picture accompanying his articles and soon recognized him.

We greeted each other with a hug and then sat down to one of the most delightful luncheon-visits I've ever enjoyed. So much to talk about—mutual friends, and then the movies, movies, movies...

At that time, he was interviewing for the volume you're reading now, *The Sound of Silence.* I was more than happy to pass along my Hollywood experiences to him.

With the passing of years, more visits followed. Whenever Michael is in California, he shares some of his precious time with my family and me. How we look forward to his visits. He brings fun and interest to every moment for each one of us, from chatting with my 95-year-old husband to drawing pictures—sometimes stretched out on the floor—with our nine-year-old granddaughter Tammy Frances, who adores Michael.

Michael's presence never fails to generate excitement. Our telephone is ringing constantly when he's here, usually with calls from celebrities. One I recall with particular fondness. When I answered, a woman asked for Michael. I pictured a lovely face to match that low, velvety voice. My assumption was not unwarranted. I later learned the voice belonged to Billie Dove, the idol of my youthful days. And I had actually talked with her.

Michael often mentions Anita Page, another subject included in *The Sound of Silence.* I share his enthusiasm for this star of silent and early talking pictures. When I was under contract to MGM in 1929, Anita was the darling of the lot, MGM's young glamour girl. She was everyone's favorite, and I shall never forget her kindness to me. Warm and outgoing from my first introduction to her, she invited me to her birthday party at the Hollywood Roosevelt Hotel — a dinner-dance on the famous Roof Garden. For one starry-eyed guest, it was some enchanted evening.

I knew many of those featured in this book so many years ago — (I was a Wampas Baby Star with Barbara Weeks in 1931.) Through Michael's writing, however, I learned much about my contemporaries I never knew.

Michael once told me his philosophy of relating to people and writing about their lives. He said, "It's not what they achieved or didn't achieve in their careers; it's [how] they got there that counts." That's in tune with his straightforward, uncluttered, forceful, pure style. He has a magic way with words.

I feel fortunate that Michael has focused his interest on my era of Hollywood. The choice of films of that period brought a higher dimension to our lives, an enchantment. The wholesome values of those movies, their spiritual uplift, are ever-widening in their influences.

The 16 people featured in this book contributed so much to the art of motion pictures as we know it today. I am pleased to have shared my memories and experiences of what was the finest era of filmmaking. It is often called the Golden Age of Hollywood, and it was. I know for a fact — I was there!

— Marion Shilling

Introduction

The Sound of Silence is a companion volume to *Broken Silence: Conversations with 23 Film Stars* (McFarland, 1993), a collection of interviews I conducted with silent film players.

Contained in this book are the stories of 16 film players, compiled from exclusive interviews I conducted by phone, through the mail or in person from 1987 to 1997. The quotes are from those conversations; the other text draws from my research into their lives and careers.

Scattered throughout are photographs from the personal collections of the subjects as well as from my own collection. A filmography of feature film appearances for each subject follows each chapter.

Most of these actors began their careers in silent films or in early talkies (some did most of their work in sound). Most of them have never before spoken this extensively about their work in motion pictures. All the subjects tell honest and fascinating stories about themselves and the Hollywood they lived, worked and played in.

For this volume, I approached a group of film players as diversified as the many roles they played in Tinseltown. Billie Dove was one of the last silent stars and, aside from Mary Brian, the most reluctant interview in *The Sound of Silence.* Brian and Anita Page started out as ingenues in silent films and soon graduated to leads.

Pauline Curley began her career in the early 1910s and later appeared opposite such silent heartthrobs as Antonio Moreno (in two serials), Harold Lockwood, John Gilbert and Douglas Fairbanks. She retired from the screen at the advent of sound after a decade of appearing in Westerns. Marion Shilling, who began her career as an ingenue at MGM in the late 1920s, later became one of the screen's most dependable Western heroines of the 1930s.

Barbara Barondess, Rose Hobart, Barbara Weeks and Esther Muir were on the New York stage before breaking into films at the beginning of sound.

Barondess and Hobart developed reputations as character actresses, and Muir was a screen comedienne and vamp. Lupita Tovar, an exotic Mexican beauty, is a film legend in Mexico and is remembered among film fans for her role in the Spanish version of *Dracula* and for several Westerns with Gene Autry and George O'Brien.

Barbara Kent reluctantly began her career in silents in 1925 and was soon appearing with Greta Garbo and John Gilbert. She was a popular leading lady for the remainder of the silent era and made an easy transition to talkies with Harold Lloyd.

Of the actors interviewed for *The Sound of Silence*, William Janney and Thomas Beck were stage actors before being wooed into films. Hugh Allan played leads during the last years of the silent era.

Marcia Mae Jones and Edith Fellows had strong careers throughout the 1930s as child actresses. Like many of their contemporaries, however, they did not make successful, nor particularly happy, transitions into adult roles.

I still feel a sense of urgency about capturing the memories of our early film players. It is indeed sobering to realize that, of the 23 silent film players interviewed for *Broken Silence*, only six now remain.

In just a few short years no one who worked in films when motion pictures were in their infancy will be around to tell the stories, and the era of silent films will fade farther into the past. When there is no one left to remember, it is my hope that books like *Broken Silence* and *The Sound of Silence* will serve as a bridge to the past, to the days that made up the most illustrious period in the history of Hollywood.

1

Hugh Allan

"I found it. Here it is," he said, pulling the yellowed memento from its hiding place among a stack of old newspaper clippings, studio contracts and stills.

From his home in Memphis, Tennessee, Hugh Allan had spent the greater part of a Saturday morning in late summer 1992 remembering the details of his brief adventure in the movies. Lunch at a nearby fast food joint was over, and now, early afternoon, he had pulled out boxes of memorabilia which, like his memories of that period, had long since been put away.

The newly discovered artifact was a Western Union telegraph from July 1928. It read, "I am giving a dance for Our Girl's Club* at Pickfair Tuesday night, July 24, and we would like to have you join us at 9:30 P.M. It will be formal. Please reply to me at the studio. Mary Pickford Fairbanks."

The invitation was important then, proof he rubbed shoulders with major figures in the movie industry. His memories of Pickford, however, were always bittersweet. In the mid–1920s, she plucked Allan from the ranks of an extra to play her leading man, only to replace him after his inexperience came through in the rushes.

Disappointing, yes, but he took advantage of the situation, enrolled in acting classes, sharpened his skills, and for the next four years, worked steadily in about 15 features, two serials and some comedy shorts. His uncertainty about talkies, his disgust over studio politics and his outrage over a producer whose breach of contract left him stranded in Hawaii prompted his departure from Hollywood in 1930.

Leaving town with little more than the clothes on his back, he rebuilt his life. Over the years, he became the head of a corporation, owned his own

**Mary Pickford formed "Our Girls" as an informal social club for prominent female stars in the mid–1920s.*

Hugh Allan in the late 1920s. (Courtesy of Hugh Allan.)

businesses and gave little thought to his disappointing Hollywood experience. That is, until the day he agreed to sit for the first extensive interview he'd given on his film career.

The 88-year-old didn't dodge questions, whitewash the truth or put on airs. After a lengthy conversation, the only thing I found phony about Hugh Allan was his name, which he acquired shortly after arriving in Hollywood.

He was born Allan Abram Hughes on Nov. 5, 1903, in a small community near Oakland, CA. He was the oldest of four sons born to Enoch (a contract painter) and Jane Hillam Hughes.

Because the family was rather poor, Hugh was introduced to the labor market at an early age. First, like many kids in those days, he delivered newspapers. This led to a job as a route inspector. While in high school, he carried golf clubs at the Sequoia Country Club.

While he had time for little else, he did go to the movies from time to time. "I thought Tom Mix, Hoot Gibson, Francis X. Bushman and Mary Pickford were pretty great," he said. While in school, he excelled in swimming. During his last year of high school, he had some training under Hawaiian Olympic swimming champion Duke Kahanamoku* and became East Bay High School's champion in freestyle swimming.

When he graduated from high school in 1921, Hugh's uncle, who was vice-president of Folger & Company, had two jobs lined up for his nephew. One was with the Southern Pacific Railroad, the other with the Cunard Steamship Company.

"You know what a kid at that age is going to take," he said. "He wouldn't go with an old railroad. Cunard was much more romantic."

**Duke Kahanamoku (1890–1968) appeared in both silent and sound films, most often as a native chief.*

Allan started at Cunard as an office boy at $60 a month. His innate business sense surfaced, and in less than six months, he was promoted to file clerk. When he developed a communication code for the company, he was promoted to foreign exchange clerk.

Then, because he had studied and was familiar with the different trade routes and shipping lines, he was placed behind the counter selling tickets to passengers going from San Francisco to Europe on the Cunard line.

After six months selling tickets, Allan's supervisor asked the company to raise his wages to $275 a month. When the request was turned down (they gave his single status and age as reasons) the supervisor told Allan he was too smart for the job and urged him to find one that would take fuller advantage of his abilities.

About a week later, San Francisco socialite Leland Stanford Ramsdale, a frequent passenger on the Cunard line, approached Allan with an idea for making two-reel collegiate comedies in Hollywood. He had never produced a motion picture and said he could benefit from Allan's business sense.

Disillusioned by his career direction at Cunard, Allan accepted his offer of $250 a month and, in February 1924, signed a one-year contract.

In Hollywood that March, Ramsdale and Allan made the two short films. Gordon White, an unknown actor, was hired as the lead, and Frank Capra— "a wonderful gentleman," Hugh said, was brought in to direct one of the shorts.

With the finished films in hand, Ramsdale and Allan went to New York and ran them for Pathé and several other motion picture producers. There was some interest in Ramsdale's efforts, but the producers felt the $10,000 he was asking for each of the films was high. Knowing they could produce the comedies for half the price, the producers declined and showed the two men to the door.

They returned to Hollywood empty-handed except for the two films they thought would get them into the movie business. They were disappointed and broke, especially Ramsdale, who had sold a home to float the deal.

Allan, who was seven months into the contract, told his boss to terminate the agreement. Said Allan, "I felt sorry for him, so I told him to tear it up, that I could always make a living. I didn't sue like they do today."

Out of work Allan followed in the footsteps of many young, good-looking hopefuls in Hollywood: He went to the movie studios and registered for bit parts and extra work.

"Everybody in the acting phase said I could get in by going as an extra and that it paid pretty good money. You couldn't make any better money doing anything else. I was a nice-looking, athletic, young man, so I tried it," he said.

After Allan did bits in several Milton Sills pictures, First National made several screen tests of him and added them to their library. Once they realized the young actor had potential, they offered him a year's contract.

During the negotiations, the studio told him he needed a new name for the movies. With actor Lloyd Hughes and director Rupert Hughes already working in the business, there was no room for another Hughes.

"The big thing in those days was to look Spanish. Ricardo Cortez, Ramon Novarro, Antonio Moreno and Rudolph Valentino were doing great," said Allan, "but I didn't look very Spanish. I was an all–American boy."

It was scenarist June Mathis* who, over cocktails at her home one evening, used the study of numerology to decide on the name Hugh Allan. "She suggested we just switch the names around, that Hugh Allan suited me better anyway."

While Allan was negotiating a contract with First National, he also caught the eye of the most powerful woman in films. Mary Pickford, looking for a leading man for her next picture, *Little Annie Rooney* (1925), spotted him in one of his screen tests.

Acting fast, while Allan was free of any contractual obligations, Pickford offered him the role of Joe Kelly at $100 a week. He accepted. Pickford's contract, dated April 7, 1925, read, "The employee agrees that his contract with First National will not become effective until the completion of this production." The clause enabled Pickford to avoid paying any loan-out to First National for Allan's services. Later that month (April 22), Allan with the Pickford deal under his belt, agreed to First National's terms and signed a year's contract for $250 a week.

He considered himself lucky. Many in the film industry believed in him and his ability. While he was confident in himself, Hugh Allan had a lot to prove.

To have been handpicked by Mary Pickford as her leading man was "overwhelming," he said. "I was absolutely flabbergasted." The two met on set of *Little Annie Rooney* in mid–April 1925. "Here was the goddess of the world. That's why I was so frightened."

His fear, coupled with his inexperience, provided the pin than burst his bubble of hope and enthusiasm. About ten days into the production, Allan, Pickford and director William Beaudine† realized a serious casting mistake had been made.

"They started filming some scenes and just found out I couldn't do them," the actor admitted. "I was as stiff as a wooden soldier. I couldn't even walk straight."

While Pickford tried to put the struggling actor at ease, her younger

**June Mathis (1892–1927) played an important part in launching Rudolph Valentino to popularity by writing some of his early vehicles:* The Four Horsemen of the Apocalypse *(1921),* Camille *(1921),* The Young Rajah *(1922) and* Blood and Sand *(1922). She wrote the screen adaptation of* Ben-Hur *(1926) and was charged with the tedious task of re-editing Erich von Stroheim's* Greed *(1922) from three hours to one hour and 50 minutes.*

†William Beaudine (1892–1970) also directed Pickford in Sparrows *(1926).*

brother Jack did everything he could to antagonize him. "Jack Pickford* was a real son of a bitch. He was on the set making wisecracks while I was trying to do a scene. I finally got a little annoyed and said to him, 'One more wisecrack out of you and I'll put the nose on the front of your face on the back of your face.' He got his ass out of there. By that time, I realized I couldn't do it, and his wisecracking didn't help at all."

The publicity would have devastated Allan's budding career if he had been fired, yet Pickford had to protect the studio's investment in the picture. The solution concocted was executed in true Hollywood style. The story went out that he was being replaced after he broke an arm in a fall from a roof. A photograph of Allan with his arm in a sling, sitting on the set with Pickford, was distributed to newspapers and fan magazines.

Although he was reluctant to pose for the photos and thought the whole episode a "little unethical," the studio had the last word. Did they do him a favor? "Of course they did," he said. "It was a favor for them and for me."†

Allan never saw the finished picture. "No, I didn't want to see it. I had better things to do," he said.

After his release from the picture, Allan immediately left Hollywood for Tijuana, a Mexican border town full of "howling, drinking and prostitutes," he said. While it was a rambunctious place in those days, it was no more so than Hollywood in the mid–1920s.

"Serge Mdivani§ was a great dancer and a wild son of a bitch," Allan reminisced. "He invited me down to his house on Sunset for a party one weekend. I didn't have much of an acquaintance with booze — I had only been drunk once in my life. Anyway, there were all these motion picture people around and they were serving this amber-colored liquid, which Serge told me was vodka brought from Russia. After about five of those things, I decided I'd better get up and go home. I was getting a bit bored. I tried to get up and couldn't. I fell back. I finally got up and waddled home. A day or two later, I awoke with the phone ringing and this guy identified himself as the police and informed me that my car had been parked on Sunset for two nights. 'Are you kidding?' was all I could say."

During those early years, Allan lived at the Hollywood Athletic Club. He was a member of the Santa Monica Swimming Club, where he played volleyball with George O'Brien, another friend, and watched Charlie Chaplin and others play cards in the sand.

It was at the beach club that he was introduced to Rudolph Valentino. The first time I saw him, I was actually in the shower, and he came in to take a

**Jack Pickford (1896–1933) became a star in his own right and co-directed a couple of films. A notorious playboy, he was married to actresses Olive Thomas, Marilyn Miller and Mary Mulhern.*

†William Haines replaced Hugh in the part of Joe Kelly.

§Prince Serge Mdivani of the Republic of Georgia was married to actress Pola Negri (1894–1987) from 1927–31. His brother David was married to silent film actress Mae Murray.

Hugh Allan, Barbara Bedford, Lewis Stone and Shirley Mason in *What Fools Men* (1925). (Courtesy of Hugh Allan.)

shower. He was a beautiful physical specimen, a muscular, fine-looking man. He was very quiet, not too bright, just typical."

Back in Hollywood after three weeks in Mexico, the actor was ready to make the best of his disappointing experience with Mary Pickford. He enrolled in acting classes and concentrated on his First National contract.

He was cast as Shirley Mason's chauffeur in *What Fools Men* (1925). While he enjoyed working with Mason and fellow First National contract player Joyce Compton, his experience with director George Archainbaud* was unpleasant. "I didn't think he was worth a damn. He was a poor director, and personally, he was kind of a jackass. He just didn't know how to work with young people."

Allan was also turned off by Lewis Stone's† acting style in the picture. "He was very stilted, with all these gestures. He wasn't a great actor, but he had a good reputation. I personally believed in realism. I didn't have any phony gestures. I

**George Archainbaud (1890–1959) worked on the European stage (he was French) as an actor and assistant stage manager before coming to Hollywood to direct films in 1915.*

†Lewis Stone (1879–1953) was a popular leading man in silent films, the epitome of the dignified, romantic hero. He graduated to mature leads and spent his entire sound career at MGM (he was Judge Hardy in the Andy Hardy *film series). He was a veteran of almost 200 films.*

was no John Barrymore, a phony character all the time. I wore very little makeup and thought I should look natural."

Allan's one-year contract with First National ended in April 1926. That July, now freelancing, he appeared with Ralph Lewis and Jean Arthur* in *The Block Signal.* "I was crazy about Jean Arthur," he said. "She was a nice, freckle-faced little girl."

In *Birds of Prey* (1927), Allan played the boyfriend of Priscilla Dean.† His memories of working on the picture revolved around the love scenes he had with her. "She was a good-looking woman with a good-looking figure," he recalled. "The crew would kid us a lot about our kissing scenes. We made them very realistic." Although Allan found working with Dean satisfying, the filming was exhausting thanks to the extreme demands of studio boss Harry Cohn, who was frequently on the set.

"We made that picture in about a week," he said. "They worked us to death. On the fourth day, Priscilla got hold of Harry Cohn and said, 'Now look, we're not coming back tomorrow to make this thing. I'm worn out; Hugh's worn out. He has to shave twice a day so he won't look like an Indian in the picture. We're going home.' She raised hell with him and he gave us the next day off. He was a real hotshot."

Allan found himself squiring both mother and daughter in *The Cruel Truth* (1927). Hedda Hopper, years before she became a gossip columnist, plays the mother, who, in the course of courting a much younger man (Allan), keeps her daughter (Constance Howard) in the background. Allan saves Constance from drowning and the two fall in love, leaving Hopper to first seethe with anger before giving in to young love. "Hedda Hopper was articulate, bright, attractive, sophisticated—so much more sophisticated than I was," Allan said.

Allan had been riding horses all his life, so he had little trouble with the filming of his first Western, *Wild Beauty* (1927), a film in which he enters a horse race to save the fortune of his girlfriend's (June Marlowe) father. "The film was a very rugged picture to make because we herded about 1,200 wild horses almost every day for 12 days. Once they got going and turning up the dust, I had a devil of a time knowing where I was riding and whether or not I was in danger. The prairie-dog holes into which a horse could step and break a leg added to the risk."

Stuntmen could have been used for the potentially dangerous scenes; however, the film's director, Henry McRae, didn't believe in using doubles. "What a jerk he was, a slave driver who wanted his actors to do everything. He'd try to get us to do really dangerous scenes, and he'd even do them himself. He was goofy."

**Jean Arthur (1900–1991) had been in films since 1923 and would pay her dues in many low-budget films and comedy shorts before reaching a career turning point in John Ford's* The Whole Town's Talking *(1935).*

†Priscilla Dean (1896–1987) began at Biograph in 1910 and rose to stardom after she joined Universal in 1916. Her popularity continued into the 1920s, but when talkies came in, she slipped into minor films.

Hugh Allan (left) and John Mack Brown in *Annapolis* (1928). (Courtesy of Hugh Allan.)

Allan had similar gripes with his next director, Michael Curtiz,* during the filming of his love scenes with Helene Costello in *Good Time Charley* (1927). Curtiz, who was Hungarian, had a European style of showing affection on film. "I was supposed to make love to Helene Costello and we had a little argument about it. Helene finally told him, 'Now look, we're not foreign over here. Hugh's right. We do pat women, we don't rub them.' Curtiz was a real jerk. Why the hell they had him directing the picture I don't know."

Allan and John Mack Brown vie for the affections of Jeanette Loff in *Annapolis* (1928), a film shot on location at the Naval Academy in Maryland. It was Allan's finest film performance. He was so good that when the picture was previewed in Santa Monica, the majority of the audience commented on their cards that producers should have had him in the leading role, not Brown.

In *Sin Town* (1929), Allan plays a rancher who goes West with Jack Oakie. Accused of a crime, he escapes and joins another rancher determined to burn Sin Town to the ground. The buildings burned during the scenes were actually

**Michael Curtiz (1888–1962) had a prolific career as a stage and screen actor and director in Europe before being brought to the United States in 1924 by Harry Warner, who kept him at Warner Bros. for 25 years. His work in* Casablanca *(1943) earned him an Oscar for Best Director.*

Gladys McConnell and Hugh Allan in *The Fire Detective* (1929). (Courtesy of Hugh Allan.)

part of the Harold Lloyd studios that were destroyed to make room for the University of California at Los Angeles.

Allan's most enjoyable roles came soon after *Sin Town* in his two serials with Gladys McConnell, *The Tiger's Shadow* and *The Fire Detective.* "I enjoyed making those serials because of their athletic action and all the other exciting things involved. They made us do our own stunts, and once I got all my eyebrows burned off, but they were awfully fun to make."

Allan found the director, Spencer Bennet, known for his action serials, a "wonderful gentleman and a damned good director," and McConnell* "a lady. She always had her mother along. She was not a promiscuous female and had a high opinion of herself."

Since the work was fun and his experiences with McConnell pleasant, Hugh hoped there would be other serials in his future, and that he and McConnell would be a team. However, his agent discouraged further serials. "You're going

**Gladys McConnell (1907–1979) was a Wampas Baby Star in 1927. She made a number of features during the 1920s and retired from the screen to marry after* Parade of the West *(1930).*

to be typecast and you're too good an actor to be making serials," the agent told him.

"How stupid could you get?" Allan said. "I remember that Bill Boyd got typecast as Hopalong Cassidy and went on to make a tremendous success. It was a bad piece of advice. After that, I never got a good part."

His agent's insistence that he stop making serials bred disillusionment in the young actor; the final straw came later in 1929 when that same agent negotiated a contract with an independent producer/director for Allan to appear in a film (*The Goddess of Pele*) to be shot in Hawaii. His co-star would be Gladys McConnell.

While the cast and crew were on their way to Hawaii, the stock market crashed, causing the producer's assets to be frozen. Allan, who then didn't understand the workings of the stock market, didn't realize that there was now no money to film the picture nor pay the actors. He caught on about ten days into the production. "I realized he was cranking the camera in front of us, but there was no film in the camera," said Allan. "He was putting on a show for the local people in hopes of raising money for the picture."

When the plot was uncovered, the charade stopped and the actors wondered how they would find the money to get back to California. "I told the producer that I didn't care about myself or the rest of the people here, but that he was going to take Gladys and her mother home. Well, he gave everyone a ticket but me."

Allan borrowed money from a friend to get back to the States. He arrived in Hollywood disgusted over the Hawaiian fiasco and concerned about the changing environment in the movie business: talkies.

To help develop his voice for sound, Allen did two shows at the Egan Theater in Los Angeles. He got good reviews, and hired a singing teacher for the musicals he felt would come his way. She coached him for about five months on "The Pagan Love Song," which at that time was a big hit for Ramon Novarro. The results were disastrous. "She told me I was wasting my time, that I didn't have a real talent for singing," Allan said. "That was all I needed to hear. I quit."

The actor needed advice, but didn't know where to turn. "I didn't have enough sense to know what to do, and I didn't have any real close friends to advise me. I tended to be a loner. I would have made a good director because I have a sensitive feel for people. I wouldn't have made them look stupid."

He moved out of Hollywood into a tiny apartment in the San Fernando Valley. For almost two months, he waited by the phone. One night at 2 A.M., he got a call. It wasn't an agent or a studio offering him a movie part, but a friend asking him to join him as his vice-president and general manager in his Texas automobile firm. Allan, sick of "this movie business," jumped at the offer.

Because he had no money for gasoline and tires to take him to Texas,

Allan placed an ad in a Los Angeles paper offering a ride to Texas to anyone who would pay him. A Filipino chauffeur and a lady with a Pekinese dog responded and accepted his offer. A couple of days later, with a full tank of gas, a set of new tires and two new friends, Allan crossed the desert towards Texas, leaving Hollywood and his foundering career in the dust. He never looked back.

For a year, he worked in the car business, making a decent living, but "not doing too well." Then he joined Rotary Lift Company in Memphis, as their distributor for Texas, Arkansas and Louisiana. It was while on business in Texas in 1931 that he met his wife, the former Lou Williamson. They were married in April 1932. A daughter, Carita, was born in 1935, and a son, Hugh, Jr., in 1938.

Allan and his family lived in New York City for a couple of years in the 1930s while he was sales manager for Rotary Lift. He was named company president in 1947. The operation expanded over the next five years, and the Dover Corporation was organized, with Rotary as a division. In 1955, Dover separated from the group and Allan remained president of both Dover and Rotary until his retirement in 1968.

Allan was not satisfied with retirement. He bought interests in various businesses and started his own — he was chief executive officer for over 20 companies in his long career. His vast business ventures once prompted a local newspaper to dub him Memphis' Howard Hughes.

At the time of our interview, he still owned one company, followed the movement of his stocks by computer and played golf (he enjoyed the sport for over 40 years and played in numerous tournaments). He was also intensely interested and involved in the lives of his grandchildren.

Hugh Allan died February 12, 1997, of an apparent self-inflicted gunshot wound at his home. He was said to have been concerned about his health. He was survived by his wife of 63 years, his daughter, seven grandchildren and four great-grandchildren.

During our interview, Allan admitted his short career in films taught him a valuable lesson. "I thought after I got into regular business that I had wasted six years of my life in Hollywood," he said. "But, after I went along, maybe seven or eight years later, I realized that the movie business gave me a tremendous insight into people and the way they think. That's a valuable quality."

Taking a glimpse back to his Hollywood days was a rare occurrence for Hugh Allan. "I don't dwell on it and it never crosses my mind at all. You see, the future always looks exciting to me. I spend my time working on things to be done, not things that have already happened."

FILMOGRAPHY

1925: ***What Fools Men.*** First National. Director: George Archainbaud. Cast: Lewis Stone, Shirley Mason, Ethel Grey Terry, Barbara Bedford, John Patrick, David Torrence, Hugh Allan, Joyce Compton. **1926:** ***The Block Signal.*** Lumas-Gotham. Director: Frank O'Connor. Cast: Ralph Lewis, Jean Arthur, Hugh Allan, Sidney Franklin, George Chesebro. **1927:** ***Birds of Prey.*** Columbia. Director: William J. Craft. Cast: Priscilla Dean, Hugh Allan, Gustav von Seyffertitz, Sidney Bracy, Ben Hendricks, Jr. ***What Happened to Father.*** Warner Brothers. Director: John Adolphi. Cast: Warner Oland, Flobelle Fairbanks, Hugh Allan, William Demarest, Vera Lewis, John Miljan. ***The Cruel Truth.*** Sterling. Director: Philip Rosen. Cast: Hedda Hopper, Constance Howard, Hugh Allan, Frances Raymond, Ruth Handforth. ***Dress Parade.*** Pathé. Director: Donald Crisp. Cast: William Boyd, Bessie Love, Hugh Allan, Walter Tennyson, Maurice Ryan, Louis Natheaux, Clarence Geldert. ***Wild Beauty.*** Universal. Director: Henry McRae. Cast: Rex (Horse), Hugh Allan, June Marlowe, Scott Seaton, William Bailey. ***Good Time Charley.*** Warner Brothers. Director: Michael Curtiz. Cast: Warner Oland, Hugh Allan, Helene Costello, Clyde Cook, Montagu Love, Julanne Johnston. **1928:** ***Beware of Married Men.*** Warner Brothers. Director: Archie Mayo. Cast: Irene Rich, Audrey Ferris, Hugh Allan, Clyde Cook, Richard Tucker, Stuart Holmes, Myrna Loy. ***Hold 'Em Yale.*** Pathé. Director: Edward H. Griffith. Cast: Rod La Rocque, Hugh Allan, Jeanette Loff, Joseph Cawthorn, Tom Kennedy, Jerry Mandy. ***Plastered in Paris.*** Fox. Director: Benjamin Stoloff. Cast: Sammy Cohen, Hugh Allan, Jack Pennick, Marion Byron, Lola Salvi, Albert Conti, Ivan Linow, Michael Visaroff. ***Annapolis.*** Pathé. Director: Christy Cabanne. Cast: John Mack Brown, Jeanette Loff, Hobart Bosworth, William Bakewell, Charlotte Walker. ***The Tiger's Shadow.*** Pathé (serial). Director: Spencer Bennet. Cast: Hugh Allan, Gladys McConnell, Frank Lackteen. ***Object—Matrimony.*** Columbia. Director: Scott R. Dunlap. Cast: Lois Wilson, Hugh Allan, Ethel Grey Terry, Douglas Gilmore, Roscoe Karns, Carmelita Geraghty, Dickie Moore. **1929:** ***Sin Town.*** Pathé. Director: J. Gordon Cooper. Cast: Jack Oakie, Hugh Allan, Elinor Fair, Ivan Lebedeff, Robert Perry. ***The Voice of the Storm.*** FBO. Director: Lynn Shores. Cast: Karl Dane, Hugh Allan, Theodore von Eltz, Martha Sleeper, Brandon Hurst, Warner Richmond, Lydia Yeamans Titus. ***The Fire Detective.*** Pathé (serial). Director: Spencer Bennet. Cast: Hugh Allan, Gladys McConnell, Leo Maloney, John Cossar, Frank Lackteen, Larry Steers.

2

Barbara Barondess

Where does one begin to sort out the full and busy life of Barbara Barondess? Which of her four careers does one ask about first? With so much to talk about, just where does one start?

One could mention her work in films with Garbo, Harlow or the Barrymores, her million dollar fashion and interior design businesses or her budding writing career.

Barondess and I set aside an entire afternoon in mid–October 1995 to talk about how she managed to cram so much living into one lifetime. Her apartment on Park Avenue in New York City was evidence the lady of the house had been busy for most of her almost 90 years.

It appeared she never threw anything away. She admitted she purposely saved everything from her careers because she believed when she "got to be an old lady, no one would believe I had done this much."

Somewhere in a box out in the kitchen was a newsreel of Barondess when she won the Miss Greater New York Modern Venus beauty contest — it paved her way to the stage in the 1920s. Stills of her films covered the dining room table where she was busy on the second volume of her autobiography. Racks of her own line of clothing practically filled one bedroom. In another corner of the room were stacks of film canisters holding husband Douglas MacLean's films of the 1920s. Her marriage to him in the late 1930s, she said, was the only one of her four that meant anything.

When talking about her career as an interior designer (Marilyn Monroe, Errol Flynn and Norma Shearer were some of her clients), she pointed to a photo of herself in the White House, where she worked during the Kennedy Administration on a committee to remodel one of the rooms.

If one doubted her claims she had done so much, if one thought she was only boasting, the proof was there. She had saved it all.

Pointing out the relics surrounding her, however, only gave hints about

Clarence Bull's 1932 photograph of Barbara Barondess shortly after her arrival at MGM. (Courtesy of Barbara Barondess MacLean.)

her life. They only told part of the story, the successful side of her life. It was only when we sat together in conversation that it all came together, her triumphs and tragedies, her accomplishments and her disappointments.

She was quick to point out her successes and failures were her own. She blamed no one but herself for her mistakes along the way, while she credited no one but herself for her achievements. "I lived my life the way I decided to live it," she said. "I was the captain of my ship."

For instance, she plotted the course of her ten-year career in show business, working on the stage during the 1920s and appearing in character parts (often as sluts or rebels) in a dozen Hollywood films of the 1930s. She was determined that her rise or fall in films be based on her own talent as an actress.

"I'll give you an example," she said. "I never cultivated the heads of studios where I worked. I kept very exclusive, polite with it. I didn't want any connection, any reputation.

"I always said there are the starlets who dance on one leg and then the other, and manage to make a living in between them. I was never one of them."

Barondess discussed her failed marriages and other unfortunate experiences in her life without hesitation, but the mention of the United States of America brought tears to her eyes as she expressed love for her country. They share the same birthday, July 4. Barbara was born Mary Barondess in 1907 to Russian parents living in New York—her father was from a wealthy Russian-Jewish lumber family.

When she was six months old, the family journeyed to her parents' homeland for what was to be a brief visit. Surrounded by the family wealth, her parents decided to stay longer and raise their family. Two other daughters were born.

When the Russian Revolution broke out, the family, being Jewish and wealthy, found themselves enemies of the rising Bolsheviks. During the revolution, her father, a capitalist, was fired upon. The first bullet missed; just before the second shot, Barbara threw her arms around her father and caught the other bullet in her shoulder.

The family finally escaped in a hay wagon into neighboring Poland, where they were jailed as suspected spies. If they were returned to Russia, it would have meant the firing squad. After many months, the family located a copy of Barbara's birth certificate. Because of Barbara's American citizenship, they were allowed to return to the United States. It didn't prevent them, however, from being detained for two weeks upon their arrival in the U. S. Barbara claimed to have been the only United States citizen detained at Ellis Island.

The Barondess family faced hardships in New York like nothing they had seen in Russia. They scraped for a living in a tiny candy store in Brooklyn.

For as long as she could remember, Barondess wanted to be an actress. The only spanking she ever received from her father came when she, against his wishes, appeared in a play in Russia. "His main objection was that it wasn't safe for us to be out in the streets during the revolution," said Barondess. "I was determined to be in the play anyway. I was going to play a boy. I told the school I couldn't rehearse much. On the night of the play, I asked my father to take me to the show. When we got there, I said I was going to the powder room, but I actually went backstage and got into my costume. Fifteen minutes later, the curtain went up and there I was on stage. After it was over, my father was very silent. He told me I should not have lied to him and gave me a spanking for it."

That's when her father gave her a board and 100 nails to teach her a lesson about lying. After she nailed them into the board, he asked her to take them out. "'Look,' I said, 'the board is full of holes.' My father said, 'Those never go away.' I learned a lesson, the most important one of my life, to think twice about something I was going to do. Your mistakes never go away."

In June 1922, only seven months after entering school in New York, Barondess graduated from public school. The next year, she enrolled in Erasmus High School, where she was considered an outcast because of her background. She graduated within two years and then went to work full time in a bank. She worked during the day and attended night classes at New York University.

After a while, she quit the bank to work in Russek's Department Store. Through her work, she became acquainted with Russek's personal secretary, who invited her one evening on a double date. Barondess' escort was Eugene Zukor, son of Paramount executive Adolph Zukor. They went to a dance at the Astor Hotel to celebrate the opening of the Paramount Theater.

During the evening, Zukor introduced Barondess to director Herbert Brenon, who asked her if she would be interested in playing one of the bridesmaids in his upcoming picture *A Kiss for Cinderella* (1926). The next morning, Barondess turned in her resignation at the department store and reported to the Paramount studios in Astoria, where she made her motion picture debut.

After only a week on the set, Barondess said she fell under the acting spell. One of the first changes she made on her way to being an actress was her name. "I decided that my name, Mary, was not good for the movies," she said. "I wanted my father's initials (his name was Benjamin) and I had once seen Barbara La Marr on the screen and thought she had a certain dignity. So that's how I became Barbara Barondess, instead of Mary."

Registered as a bit player, Barondess made the rounds of the studios. In 1926 she had parts in D. W. Griffith's *The Sorrows of Satan*—"Griffith was polite but impersonal"—and *The Reckless Lady* with Lois Moran and Belle Bennett.

While appearing in *All Aboard* (1927), filmed in Coney Island, New York, Barondess was given a season's pass to Steeplechase Park. During an August 1926 return visit, she entered and won the Miss Greater New York Modern Venus beauty contest. Her photo appeared in newspapers everywhere the next morning, the day she was to report to Fox Studios to begin work on *Summer Bachelors* (1926), a Madge Bellamy feature. Because of the publicity surrounding the contest, director Allan Dwan decided to enlarge her part, and the studio put out information on "their" newest film player.

Barondess said she should have been elated over the publicity, but knew the studio was only using her to promote the picture. She used the opportunity to get her name in print, but decided that once the excitement of the contest was over, she would have progressed little professionally. She plotted another course.

A month after the contest, Barondess was back at the beach, where she met theatrical agents Louis Shurr and Harry Bestry. They gave her a card and urged her to get in touch. The next morning, she was in their office, where she learned they intended to put her on the road in Al Jolson's *Artists and Models*. She informed them she did not intend to start her career as a showgirl. Impressed with her candor, they cast her in a New York show, *Gay Paree*. The show opened in New Haven, Connecticut, after four weeks of rehearsal, and soon made its Broadway debut (October 1926). The show's star, Winnie Lightner, took Barondess under her wing and made her an understudy.

While still appearing in *Gay Paree*, Barondess began rehearsals for a new play, *The Spider*, which was to be her first straight part. Then along came *Crime*, which offered her the chance to play two parts: a black girl and a night club singer. She quit both plays and signed with *Crime*, which opened in January 1927.

Barondess was impressed with the cast which included Sylvia Sidney, Kay Francis, Chester Morris, James Rennie, Kay Johnson and Douglass Montgomery. She was captivated by Sidney's beauty, talent and sophistication and knew the actress was destined for stardom. Kay Francis, she said, behaved like a "snobbish loner" toward the rest of the cast. Douglass Montgomery became a lifelong friend.

After six months in *Crime*, Barondess' restlessness prompted her to quit the production. She got her own radio show and gathered a repertoire of torch songs. When she appeared in a second-rate vaudeville house, George Gershwin, unbeknownst to the audience, accompanied her on piano. "I was delirious with joy," recalled Barondess. "Our friendship remained close until I left for Hollywood in 1932."

While visiting casting agents and theatrical producers, Barondess secured an appointment with Broadway producer Jed Harris. It was through him that she experienced her first taste of love and heartache.

It wasn't long after their introduction that Barondess fell hopelessly in love with the producer. At that first meeting, he invited her for dinner and drinks, after which he took her back to his apartment, where she lost her virginity. Barondess said it would be easy to blame the situation on the amount of liquor they consumed that evening, but that was only part of the story. She was hypnotized by Harris' charm.

They went out several times over the next couple of months. The young love she was experiencing took precedence over her career ambitions. One afternoon before a date, Barondess called his apartment to confirm the evening. The operator put her on hold as Harris was on another line. However, the lines crossed and Barondess listened to Harris' conversation. She recognized the other voice as that of actress Ruth Gordon. As Barondess listened quietly, Harris told Gordon he would meet her that evening, that he had another date, but it was not as important as rendezvousing with her. Barbara replaced the receiver in disappointment.*

Barondess tried to put the affair behind her, and get on with her life. She was hired to appear in *The Garden of Eden*, which she was to join in Washington, D. C. Not long before she was to leave, Barondess learned she was pregnant with Harris' child. Motherhood, at this stage, was not in her plans. She rode alone in a taxi to an abortionist's office, where she gave up her unborn child.

Doubled over in pain from the procedure, Barondess said she stretched out on the back seat of the taxi for the ride back to the city. "It was a horror, the most shameful experience of my life."

She never told Harris of the love child they shared or the pain she had over their affair. "I saw him later in New York in 1948 walking up Fifth Avenue. We stopped and had a cup of coffee at a counter. At that time, he was broke, forgotten and being supported by his sister, a woman he treated shamelessly. He asked what happened to us way back then. 'I don't know,' I said. 'Circumstances, I suppose.'"

**Ruth Gordon's affair with Harris resulted in the birth of a son, Jones Harris, on October 16, 1929, in Paris, France.*

Looking back, Barondess believed Harris suffered from what appeared to be a split personality. When he was kind, she said, he was "irresistible," but the darker side of his personality bordered on the sadistic. "An overly sensitive person, Jed left Yale many years before after a couple of snobs there gave him a few push-offs. He hated everyone after that, so he got even with the people he starred. He knew talent and would give them a chance. He also knew plays, but he lost his balance, his judgment along the way."

Barondess joined the cast of *The Garden of Eden*, which consisted of Miriam Hopkins and Robert Montgomery, in Washington D. C. It was the perfect way to mend her broken heart, not only because it was a good role, but because her old pal, Douglass Montgomery, was also in the cast. A pleasant experience for her, the play closed in March 1928 after 20 performances.

After appearing in a musical, *Rain or Shine*, with Joe Cook, Barondess began making a series of screen tests for scouts who had come to New York searching for talent. Most of them led nowhere and she concentrated her efforts on the stage. "I came to the conclusion I was not the type for the movies. I was bigger that most of the girls."

In 1929, Barondess met and married Irving Jacobs, then working on Wall Street (he later became a film producer and distributor). They lived at the Des Artistes apartments, whose famous tenants included Fannie Hurst and Natacha Rambova, the ex-wife of Rudolph Valentino. The marriage was not a particularly happy one. Barondess said she supported the two while her husband, who lost his job on Wall Street after the stock market crash, became a "professional job-hunter" who rarely found work.*

Barondess, on the other hand, had little trouble professionally. In January 1930, she stepped into the ingenue role in *Topaze*, replacing an actress who became pregnant. The play, which starred Frank Morgan, ran through the summer. In October, the production was taken on the road.

Barondess said she was enlightened to the devastating effects of alcohol while on the tour. Morgan,† an alcoholic, often played his part intoxicated and had trouble catching the train the next morning due to hangovers. In Chicago, they crossed paths with Helen Morgan, appearing there in *Sweet Adeline*. The actress invited Barondess to stay in her apartment during the month they were in Chicago. There, Barondess witnessed binge after binge and the wasting of talent.

"She was so very lovely," Barondess said, "but very insecure. That's true of many in the arts. I often wondered what was haunting her, but I never got around to asking."

Barondess returned to New York in the spring of 1931, exhausted from the tour that had taken her through Kansas City, Milwaukee, Minneapolis, Boston

**Barbara eventually divorced Irving Jacobs in 1934.*

†Frank Morgan (1890–1949) is best known for the title role in The Wizard of Oz *(1939).*

and Philadelphia. In June, she joined the Robert McLaughlin stock company and toured that season. She also continued her nightclub engagements and radio program.

She was getting ready to leave for Cleveland, Ohio, to do some stock work, when interest in her developed in Hollywood. Through her frequent screen tests with MGM, Barondess had gotten friendly with the talent scout's secretary. The secretary informed Barondess that Irving Thalberg had seen one of the tests and was interested, but wanted her to make a "silent" test.

When the contacts were made, Barondess agreed to make another test, but with conditions. This time, she wanted the test to be made at MGM in Hollywood, to be photographed by William Daniels and to have the studio pay her expenses. MGM agreed, and in the summer of 1932, Barondess left for Hollywood. She was met at the train station by director William Wyler, a friend since the mid–1920s. The tests were made as promised. At one screening where Barondess was present, there were several men she later learned were Richard Boleslavsky, Charles MacArthur and Ben Hecht, all of whom were associated with an upcoming MGM film, *Rasputin and the Empress* (1932). After viewing the test again, Barondess was cast in a small role as one of Rasputin's (Lionel Barrymore) girlfriends.

"Lionel was in great pain," she said. "He had running sores on his legs and spent part of his time sitting in a wheelchair. He was a fine actor and gentleman. Ethel [Barrymore] stuck much to herself and tried to be as sober as possible."

Because MGM brought Barondess to Hollywood for a screen test, she said the studio considered her under contract. (In reality, she never officially signed with them.) Barondess kept quiet, continuing to earn the salary of a new contract player. It wasn't long before she was introduced to the stars of the lot. "Marion Davies couldn't have been sweeter to me, but I thought William Randolph Hearst was a bore. Joan Crawford tried to be decent to everyone. She did not seem quite the horror her daughter wrote about, but she was a very unhappy woman."

It was through MGM producer Bernard (Bernie) Hyman, a Thalberg assistant, that Barondess became involved in a studio cover-up which remained a mystery for over 60 years. On September 4, 1932, Hyman told Barondess it would be a favor to him if she would accompany him on a dinner date with MGM producer Paul Bern. "Bernie said he was tired of listening to Bern talk about his inadequacies with Jean Harlow. Two months before, he had married Jean, a sex symbol who really didn't care that much for sex. Still, he felt inadequate."

Barondess told Hyman she had an early call at the studio the next morning, but he assured her she would be home by ten. "I thought our dinner would be at the Cocoanut Grove, but it turned out to be in one of the bungalows there. I was furious, but went through with it. The three of us talked about the differences between movies and the theater. I was watching the clock, and when it got to be a quarter of ten, I reminded Bernie of his promise to have me home by ten."

The next morning, Barondess was awakened by a call from Hyman. "Bernie said not to say a word—just listen. He told me to get the newspaper and said goodbye. The headlines read, 'Paul Bern Commits Suicide.' The story went on to question who the two people were who had dinner with him the night before. I needed this publicity like I needed a hole in the head."*

The only other person who knew the identity of the mystery couple was Howard Strickling, MGM's head of publicity, who silenced any potential scandal involving Barondess. "I learned a great lesson through this. It taught me never to go out alone with a married man."

In early 1933, Barondess was sent to Columbia to meet with Harry Cohn. She had been warned about Cohn's "hot seat," a chair he had wired to send electrical shocks through unsuspecting starlets, and was ready for his trick. She arrived for the meeting wearing a rubber girdle. As she suspected, Cohn invited her to sit in the chair. He pressed the hidden button and nothing happened. He pressed again—nothing. Finally, he said, "You must have an ass made of lead." She said, "No, just rubber." Cohn, amused at Barondess' wit, hired her for two Columbia pictures, *Soldiers of the Storm* and *When Stranges Marry.*

After six months in Hollywood, Barondess still had serious doubts about her future in films. She felt she had no control over the direction in which her life was going. Her instincts were to return to New York, but she decided to stay if the right part came along. The perfect roles, she thought, were solid character parts.

Such a role came her way when Hyman cast her (at $275 a week) in *Hold Your Man* (1933) as one of the inmates (the rebel) in a girls' reformatory. In the picture, Jean Harlow, pregnant by Clark Gable, is sentenced to two years in the institution following the death of a former boyfriend. "The part of 'Sadie' was the best of my movie roles that was allowed to stay in the picture. It didn't end up, like many of them, on the cutting room floor," she said.

Barondess enjoyed working with Harlow and said she never disclosed to her that she was one of the last to see her husband alive. "There was never any need for that. I liked Jean very much. She was a gentle, educated lady, not the harlot she often played on the screen." Gable, on the other hand, was a different story. "I thought he was a whore. He only went with older women who could

**Samuel Marx, a story editor at MGM at the time of the incident, told a different account of the story in his book* Deadly Illusions: Jean Harlow and the Murder of Paul Bern *(Random House, 1990). He wrote that Hyman was enamored of Barondess and had asked Bern to suggest a place where they might have an intimate dinner while Hyman's wife was out of town. Bern suggested a bungalow at the Ambassador Hotel rather than the Cocoanut Grove where they might be recognized. Bern, at Hyman's suggestion, met them for a drink; then, as they agreed, he made a hasty exit, allowing Hyman and Barondess to be alone. Barondess refuted the account, saying there was no affair going on between them. "If Sam Marx had just called me before he printed that, I could have set him straight," she said.*

Muriel Kirkland and Barbara Barondess (second from left) witness the marriage of Jean Harlow and Clark Gable by Henry B. Walthall in *Hold Your Man* (1933). Walthall appeared in the southern-released version, George Reed in the general release. (Courtesy of Roi Uselton.)

do him some good in the business. He used to sleep with everything on the MGM lot. He used Josephine Dillon, who really loved him.*

When director Rouben Mamoulian approached Barondess with the offer of a role as a maid in *Queen Christina* (1933), she refused, thinking the part insignificant. "It was little more than a bit, and I thought I had graduated from bits," she said. The director and Johnny Hyde† (who sometimes acted as

**Clark Gable was married to Josephine Dillon, a veteran actress and acting coach, from 1924 to 1930.*
†Johnny Hyde is the agent credited with discovering Marilyn Monroe.

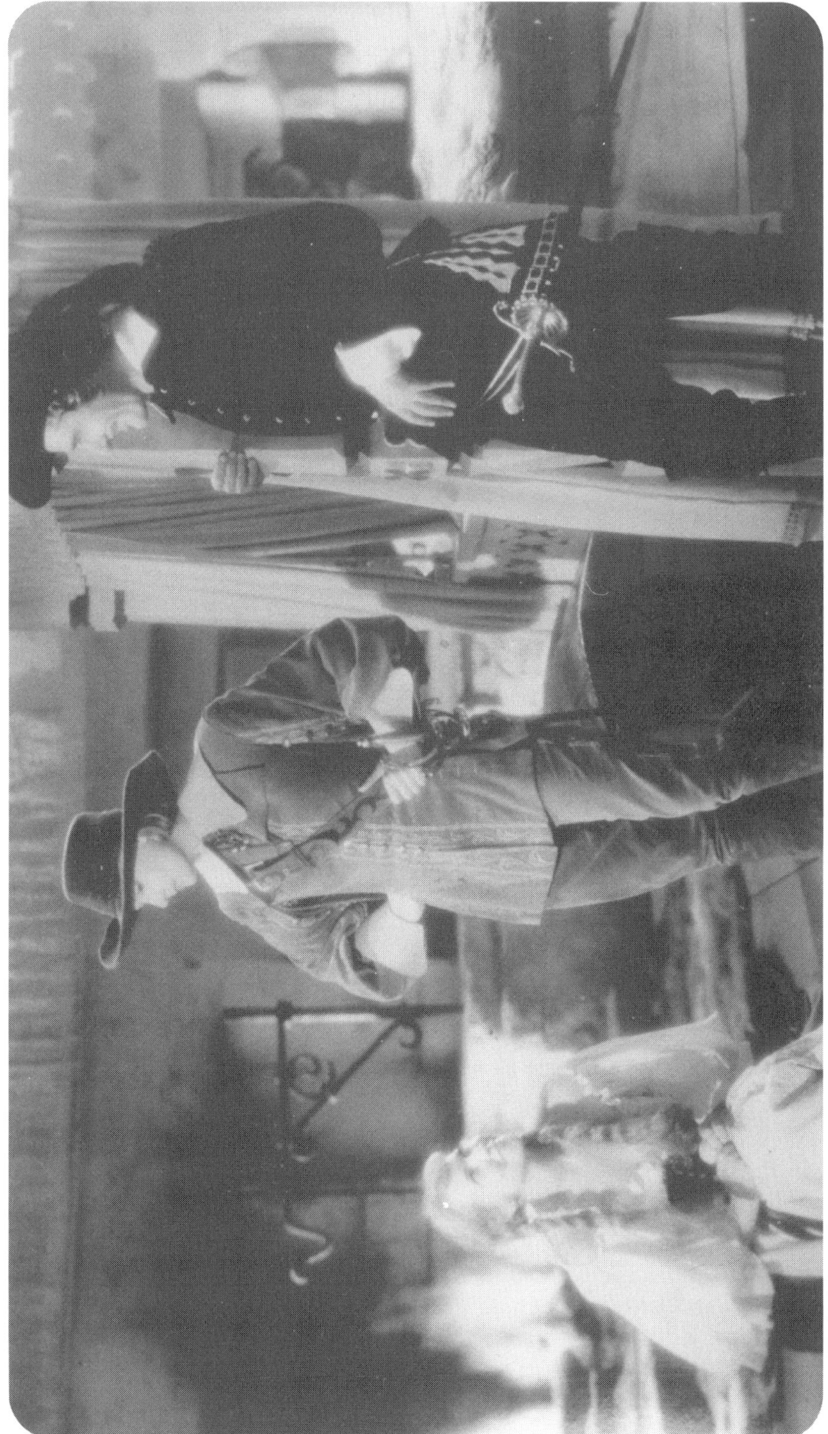

a contact for Barondess) intervened. Mamoulian told her that although it was a small part, it was a significant one, the only laugh in the picture. Then Hyde, working with the studio, negotiated a salary increase for her. MGM, still believing that she was under contract, doubled her weekly salary from $750 to $1,500 with a six-week guarantee. She made $9,000 for her small role.

"That was not too bad for 1933 Hollywood for an actress who had no picture released and who had only been in Hollywood for four or five months. I took the part."

In the picture, Garbo, disguised as a man, arrives at an inn with John Gilbert. Barondess (as Elsa) is fooled and begins making advances to Garbo. In a scene that was deleted from the final cut, Barondess, assisting Garbo in dressing, runs her hands up her legs, and is still rejected. Giving up, Barondess leaves the room, only to return saying, "If you change your mind, my room's at the end of the hall."

After the picture, Barondess sold her story "I Act with Garbo" to one of the movie magazines. Garbo refused to speak to her for a month. The two later became friendly and began an acquaintance that lasted a lifetime.

"As a matter of fact, I never got rid of her," Barondess said of Garbo. "As an interior designer later on, I did her house. She used to come into my shop and talk. I think she was the dullest woman I have ever met. I bought her first Renoirs. She begged me to take her to the auction sale where they were selling the paintings. She sat next to me and when I bid over $30,000 for the two paintings, she almost had a heart attack. She was the tightest, most miserly figure who ever lived. She paid for the paintings that day, but never paid me my commission. I never asked for it. I knew she was a tightwad. She used people and rarely gave anything back."

During this time, Barondess saw a lot of Douglass Montgomery.* In her autobiography *One Life Is Not Enough*, Barondess described the relationship: "It was a unique bond—with affection, tenderness and no strings—between two people who enjoyed each other's company and could talk about anything together, do whatever they felt like doing without inhibition, and completely get rid of their frustrations. We liked each other, without ever falling in love ... We knew we had something unique and precious without ever discussing it."

Over the years, Montgomery drifted in and out of her life. The two were very close, yet the relationship never developed romantically. "I suspected that

**Douglass Montgomery (1907–1966) made his Broadway debut in 1926 in* God Loves Us. *He worked in New York until he was awarded an MGM contract and left for Hollywood in 1930. His first film was* Paid *(1930) as Kent Douglass. He continued in films and on the stage, later using his real name, throughout the 1930s. He made several British films in the 1940s and worked both on stage and in television in the 1950s. He was married to actress Kay Young, formerly the wife of Michael Wilding.*

***Opposite:* Barbara Barondess, Greta Garbo and John Gilbert in *Queen Christina* (1934). (Courtesy of Leatrice Gilbert Fountain.)**

Barbara Barondess and Maurice Chevalier in *The Merry Widow* (1934). (Courtesy of Barbara Barondess MacLean.)

he was bisexual. At that time, his friend was Tom Wanamaker. They, along with Judith Anderson, would invite me to go on trips with them because I was the sober one who drove the car. It was a foursome, but I soon learned it was not the kind of foursome I thought it was. I went on two or three trips, but I soon tired of it. All that drinking bored me."

Eight Girls in a Boat (1934) was Barondess' only film appearance with Montgomery. The film, about a girls' boarding school, was shot on location in Lake Arrowhead. Since much of the cast consisted of teenage beauty contest winners, director Richard Wallace set a 10 P.M. curfew for the crew. It was bad enough that Barondess, then 27, was playing a 17-year-old schoolgirl, but being treated like one bordered on the extreme. "Douglass, Kay Johnson and I used to sneak off from Lake Arrowhead at night to meet Ramon Novarro and all the other boys at their parties. After three or four times of doing that, I stopped going, because I couldn't stand all that drinking."

She had a small role as one of "Maxim's girls" in *The Merry Widow* (1934). Although the part called for her to do little more than stand around and look pretty, she got along well with the director, Ernst Lubitsch. "He gave me a lot of respect. Lubitsch never went on the make per se," Barondess said, "but he invited me to all his parties."

Barondess was becoming increasingly frustrated that her career wasn't advancing. She appeared in small roles for pictures at major studios such as Paramount, Universal and RKO, and in bigger parts for independent studio releases. (One of her best roles was as a hooker in Majestic's *Unknown Blonde* [1934].) She thought the roles offered little challenge and that most of her best scenes were cut from the final releases, her best example being *A Tale of Two Cities* (1935), her final film for MGM.

"I had a great part in it, but it ended up being one line because they overshot. I played a revolutionary who had a death scene by falling off a drawbridge. My double was actually hanging from the bridge and he's the one who fell. My mother, after seeing the picture, called me from New York and said, 'Barbara, I didn't know you had hair on your arms. When did you grow hair on them?' The whole picture was a big disappointment for me."

The lack of control over her career was one of the reasons Barondess retired from the business. "You couldn't control your life. You had no say over the way you were photographed until you went to a preview to see how much was left of your part. The parts I ended up playing had no beginning or end. They were nothing."

She stressed during our interview that she plotted the course of her career based on her own talents as an actress, not relying on sexual favors for advancement. Did she believe she might have been more successful had she offered herself to producers and studio heads?

"I don't know. How would you know unless an important producer had chosen me as a lead in a play or a movie and it made me a star. He would be stupid to discard me because I would be bringing in the tickets. There were so many games to play in Hollywood that I wasn't willing to play. You were always required to be charming and amusing. After a while, I wasn't willing to go along with it."

Leaving the film business also coincided with her marriage to actor-producer Douglas MacLean in February 1938.* "I didn't want anyone saying that I married MacLean to continue in films. If he wanted to marry me, I had to quit the movies. He was amazed that I wanted to give it up. He asked what I was going to do with my time. I told him I was going to learn about all the things I never had time for."

Barondess decided she wanted to be an interior decorator. MacLean bought her a house and said, 'Okay, you want to be a decorator, now decorate. I'm going on my boat and will come back when you're finished.' A friend of mine, Irene Lee, a story editor at Warner Brothers, came over when I was doing it. When I finished, she had me do her home. She gave a party, and before I knew it, I was in the decorating business."

**Douglas MacLean (1890–1967) was a popular silent film star who made his screen debut in 1914. After the coming of sound, he quit acting and became a screenwriter and producer. MacLean is remembered, along with his wife Faith Cole, as the neighbors of director William Desmond Taylor who was murdered in February 1922. "Douglas always told me that he and his wife heard shots and walked over to the window in time to see a woman dressed in men's clothing leaving Taylor's apartment," said Barondess. "They recognized the person as Mary Miles Minter's mother."*

After completing some college courses, Barondess opened her own designing and antique business in Beverly Hills. She was soon decorating the homes of Norma Shearer, Gracie Fields, Gail Patrick, Errol Flynn and Gary Cooper. The home she decorated for Ronald Reagan and Jane Wyman in 1942 appeared on the cover of *House Beautiful* magazine, as well as in the pages of *Architectural Digest*. She was decorating Marilyn Monroe's home at the time of her death in 1962.

"Three days after she died, she was supposed to have gone away for a week to a spa so I could complete the project," said Barondess. "She would return and walk into it when it was finished. I did that with all my clients. I asked them to leave the house for a week.

"Marilyn didn't know what she wanted in the house, but I did, because she lived in my house in Beverly Hills for a time with Joe DiMaggio. I knew her for 17 years. I was her big sister."

Her business continued to prosper, allowing her to eventually open a branch in New York. By the mid–1940s, she was doing an annual business of $3 million, had four personal assistants and 65 on her payroll. In the 1940s, Barondess added a dress factory to her decorating business and became a fashion designer, creating a sensation with the highly successful "New Look" bolero skirt.

While Barondess prospered professionally, MacLean struggled to maintain his own identity at home. By the time of their marriage, projects in the movie industry were scarce.

"He wasn't working and was going crazy from the inactivity. It was a comedown for him, because he had done very well in movies," she said. "He stayed home, got sick and went into hospitals. This went on until he became a hypochondriac. It never mattered to me who made more or less money. I wanted to be a wife and a partner. I thought that was what marriage was supposed to be about."

One thing missing from their lives were children. "Douglas never had nor wanted any. That was to my great sorrow, but evidently I wasn't meant to have any either. That abortion I had took care of my having them. They scraped my whole uterus so after six months of pregnancy, my unborn child gave up holding on. I had three miscarriages with Douglas. That was a shame."

Barondess thought getting MacLean back to work would boost his spirits. She hired Florence Barton as his secretary to assist him in his writing and scouting for locations. Barton had been the secretary to MGM casting director Ben Piazza and had been especially helpful and encouraging to Barondess when she arrived on the MGM lot in 1932.

"They went on trips for inspiration for stories; they went to San Francisco for the weekend. He was busy with her. I came home exhausted, had dinner and went to bed. I never paid any attention to them. Finally, after several years, she began to poison his mind against me. She told him I was having affairs with my clients. He believed her and walked out on me. I had the rug pulled out from what I thought was the perfect marriage. Finally, I thought to hell with it." The couple divorced in 1949.

MacLean married Barton, who died in 1959. Barondess said he later found out the accusations Barton made against her were false. "He told me she had wanted to be in my shoes but ended up in my grave, because Douglas had bought two plots next to his mother, one of which was meant for me."

Barondess said MacLean was on his way to his lawyer's office to change his will, leaving her his estate, when he swerved to miss an animal and skidded into a post. The trauma caused a stroke from which he never recovered. "He never came to and spent the rest of his life in a wheelchair without being able to speak. I flew to him to make sure his real estate holdings would be enough to take care of him. The money—he never signed the will—went to Florence Barton's relatives, who hated his guts."

In March 1952, Barondess married lawyer Nathaniel Ruvell. The marriage lasted three days. "I found out he had a temper, and I couldn't live with a man who threw things. I think he's grown up now—he's 89."

Her almost 20-year marriage to Leonard Knaster was also an empty one, she said. "We had absolutely no marriage or relationship except for a polite 'how do you do.' He lived in whatever house I chose to live in—I had homes in California, New York and Palm Beach. I paid for everything. He lived like a king until I had enough of it. I told him that everything with his initials on it was his and that I didn't want anything he had and he didn't want anything of mine."

Barondess ran her interior design firm until her retirement in 1978. In 1981, she established the Barbara Barondess Theater Lab, a non-profit foundation supporting professional performers and providing an arena to practice new scripts. The foundation gives an annual Torch of Hope award to honor contributors to the art of acting. Past winners have included Morgan Freeman, Estelle Parsons, Geraldine Page, John Beal, Tony Randall and others.

In 1986, Barondess penned the first volume of her memoirs, *One Life Is Not Enough*.* At the time of her interview for this book, she had completed the second book, *Coincidence or Fate?: A Game Called Fame*. "Fame is a game," she said. "It's the no business called show business. It's a disease, an incurable infection."

Her survival, she said, has come from being able to accept credit for and learn from both her successes and mistakes. "People tell me I don't have a wrinkle in my face. That's not true. I have wrinkles under my eyes and a couple are sneaking above my upper lip. The reason I don't show my age in my late 80s—let's fact it, in a year and a half I'll be 90 years old—is my brain and my enthusiasm. My mind is a little affected. It's because my brain is full of so much stuff that some of it gets pushed around."

**Published by Future Press, New York, 1986.*

Late in the afternoon when our interview was wrapping up, Barondess tried to pull together almost 90 years of living that included four marriages and careers. She sat quietly for a few moments pondering the idea, completely shutting out the piercing sirens of ambulances and police cars, the honking of horns and other noises of a busy world going by below us.

"Life is not meant to be a rose garden, and it has not been for me. I realize my choice in husbands wasn't very good, but my choice in careers was," she said. "It's the hits, the runs and the errors that make us who we are."

FILMOGRAPHY

1926: *A Kiss for Cinderella.* Famous Players-Lasky. Director: Herbert Brenon. Cast: Betty Bronson, Tom Moore, Esther Ralston, Henry Vibart, Dorothy Cumming, Ivan Simpson, Dorothy Walters, Flora Finch, Anita Page, Barbara Barondess. ***The Sorrows of Satan.*** Famous Players-Lasky. Director: D. W. Griffith. Cast: Adolphe Menjou, Ricardo Cortez, Lya De Putti, Carol Dempster, Ivan Lebedeff, Marcia Harris, Lawrence D'Orsay, Nellie Savage, Dorothy Hughes, Josephine Dunn, Dorothy Nourse, Jeanne Morgan, Barbara Barondess. ***The Reckless Lady.*** First National. Director: Howard Higgin. Cast: Belle Bennett, James Kirkwood, Lois Moran, Lowell Sherman, Ben Lyon, Marcia Harris, Charlie Murray, Barbara Barondess. ***Summer Bachelors.*** Fox. Director: Allan Dwan. Cast: Madge Bellamy, Allan Forrest, Matt Moore, Hale Hamilton, Leila Hyams, Charles Winninger, Clifford Holland, Olive Tell, Walter Catlett, James F. Cullen, Cosmo Kyrle Bellew, Charles Esdale, Barbara Barondess. **1927: *All Aboard.*** First National. Director: Charles Hines. Cast: Johnny Hines, Edna Murphy, Dot Farley, Henry Barrows, Frank Hagney, Babe London, Sojin, James Leonard, Barbara Barondess. **1932: *Rasputin and the Empress.*** MGM. Director: Richard Boleslavsky. Cast: John Barrymore, Ethel Barrymore, Lionel Barrymore, Ralph Morgan, Diana Wynyard, Tad Alexander, C. Henry Gordon, Edward Arnold, Mischa Auer, Sara Padden, Jean Parker, Dawn O'Day, Henry Kolker, Gustav von Seyffertitz, Helen Robinson, Mary Marden, Purnell Pratt, Louise Closser Hale, Dale Fuller, Brandon Hurst, Nigel de Brulier, Otto Lederer, Charlotte Henry, Barbara Barondess, Mary Alden, Oscar Apfel. ***Luxury Liner.*** Paramount. Director: Lothar Mendes. Cast: George Brent, Zita Johann, Vivienne Osborne, Alice White, Verree Teasdale, Frank Morgan, C. Aubrey Smith, Henry Wadsworth, Wallis Clark, Billy Bevan, Theodor von Eltz, Barry Norton, Edith Yorke, Barbara Barondess. ***Devil's Mate.*** Monogram. Director: Phil Rosen. Cast: Peggy Shannon, Preston Foster, Ray Walker, Hobart Cavanaugh, Barbara Barondess, Paul Porcasi, Harold Waldridge, Jason Robards, Harry Holman, Bryant Washburn, George Hayes, Paul Fix. ***Hold Your Man.*** MGM. Director: Sam Wood. Cast: Jean Harlow, Clark Gable, Stuart Erwin, Dorothy Burgess, Muriel Kirkland, Garry Owen, Barbara Barondess, Elizabeth

Patterson, Inez Courtney, Blanche Friderici, Helen Freeman, Paul Hurst, Louise Beavers, Lillian Harmer, Theresa Harris, George Reed, Wade Boteler. ***Soldiers of the Storm.*** Columbia. Director: D. Ross Lederman. Cast: Anita Page, Regis Toomey, Barbara Weeks, Robert Ellis, Wheeler Oakman, Barbara Barondess, George Cooper, Dewey Robinson, Henry Wadsworth. ***When Strangers Marry.*** Columbia. Director: Clarence Badger. Cast: Jack Holt, Lilian Bond, Arthur Vinton, Barbara Barondess, Ward Bond, Gustav von Seyffertitz, Harry Stubbs, Rudolph Amendt [Anders], Charles Stevens, Paul Porcasi. ***Queen Christina.*** MGM. Director: Rouben Mamoulian. Cast: Greta Garbo, John Gilbert, Ian Keith, Lewis Stone, Elizabeth Young, C. Aubrey Smith, Reginald Owen, Georges Renavent, David Torrence, Gustav von Seyffertitz, Ferdinand Munier, Akim Tamiroff, Paul Hurst, Cora Sue Collins, Barbara Barondess, Fred Kohler, Edward Norris, Lawrence Grant. **1934: *Eight Girls in a Boat.*** Paramount. Director: Richard Wallace. Cast: Dorothy Wilson, Douglass Montgomery, Kay Johnson, Walter Connelly, Ferike Boros, James Bush, Barbara Barondess, Colin Campbell, Peggy Montgomery, Dorothy Drake, James Ellison. ***Beggar's Holiday.*** Tower Productions. Director: Sam Newfield. Cast: Hardie Albright, J. Farrell MacDonald, Sally O'Neil, Barbara Barondess, George Grandee, William Franklin. ***Unknown Blonde.*** Majestic. Director: Hobart Henley. Cast: Edward Arnold, Barbara Barondess, Barry Norton, John Miljan, Dorothy Revier, Leila Bennett, Walter Catlett, Helen Jerome Eddy, Claude Gillingwater, Esther Muir, Clarence Wilson, Arthur Hoyt. ***Change of Heart.*** Fox. Director: John G. Blystone. Cast: Janet Gaynor, Charles Farrell, James Dunn, Ginger Rogers, Nick [Dick] Foran, Beryl Mercer, Gustav von Seyffertitz, Kenneth Thomson, Theodor von Eltz, Drue Leyton, Nella Walker, Shirley Temple, Barbara Barondess, Fiske O'Hara, Jane Darwell, Mary Carr, James Gleason. ***The Fountain.*** RKO. Director: John Cromwell. Cast: Ann Harding, Brian Aherne, Paul Lukas, Jean Hersholt, Ralph Forbes, Violet Kemble-Cooper, Sara Haden, Ian Wolfe, Frank Reicher, Ferike Boros, Richard Abbott, Barbara Barondess, Rudolph Amendt [Anders], Betty Alden, Douglas Wood. ***The Merry Widow.*** MGM. Director: Ernst Lubitsch. Cast: Maurice Chevalier, Jeanette MacDonald, Edward Everett Horton, Una Merkel, George Barbier, Minna Gombell, Ruth Channing, Sterling Holloway, Henry Armetta, Barbara Leonard, Donald Meek, Akim Tamiroff, Herman Bing, Lucien Prival, Luana Walters, Sheila Mannors, Caryl Lincoln, Edna Waldron, Lona Andre, Barbara Barondess, Patricia Farley, Shirley Chambers, Maria Troubetskoy, Eleanor Hunt, Dorothy Granger, George Lewis, Cosmo Kyrle Bellew, Gino Corrado, Paul Ellis, Leonid Kinskey, Jason Robards. ***The Pursuit of Happiness.*** Paramount. Director: Alexander Hall. Cast: Francis Lederer, Joan Bennett, Charles Ruggles, Mary Boland, Walter Kingsford, Minor Watson, Adrian Morris, Barbara Barondess, Duke York, Burr Caruth, Jules Cowles, Irving Bacon, Spencer Charters, Henry Mowbray, Boyd Irwin, Holmes Herbert. **1935: *Life Begins at 40.*** Fox. Director: George Marshall. Cast: Will Rogers, Richard Cromwell, George Barbier, Rochelle

Hudson, Jane Darwell, Slim Summerville, Sterling Holloway, Thomas Beck, Roger Imhof, Charles Sellon, John Bradford, Ruth Gillette, Jed Prouty, T. Roy Barnes, Claire Du Brey, John Ince, Creighton Hale, Barbara Barondess, Gloria Roy. ***Diamond Jim.*** Universal. Director: A. Edward Sutherland. Cast: Edward Arnold, Jean Arthur, Binnie Barnes, Cesar Romero, Eric Blore, Hugh O'Connell, George Sidney, Robert McWade, Charles Sellon, Henry Kolker, William Demarest, Albert Conti, Armand Kaliz, Tully Marshall, Purnell Pratt, Helen Brown, Dorothy Granger, Patricia Farley, Robert Burns, Barbara Barondess, Addie McPhail, King Baggott. ***A Tale of Two Cities.*** MGM. Director: Jack Conway. Cast: Ronald Colman, Elizabeth Allan, Edna May Oliver, Reginald Owen, Basil Rathbone, Blanche Yurka, Henry B. Walthall, Donald Woods, Walter Catlett, Claude Gillingwater, H. B. Warner, Lucille LaVerne, Mitchell Lewis, Isabel Jewell, Tully Marshall, Ralf Harolde, John Davidson, Dale Fuller, Barbara Barondess, Brandon Hurst. **1936: *Lady Be Careful.*** Paramount. Director: Theodore Reed. Cast: Lew Ayres, May Carlisle, Benny Baker, Larry [Buster] Crabbe, Grant Withers, Irving Bacon, Barbara Barondess, Sheila Bromley, Wilma Francis, Ethel Sykes, Murray Alper, Jack Chapin, Wesley Barry, Purnell Pratt. ***Easy Money.*** Chesterfiled. Director: Phil Rosen. Cast: Onslow Stevens, Kay Linaker, Noel Madison, Allen Vincent, Barbara Barondess, Wallis Clark, Selmer Jackson, Robert Homans, Robert Graves, John Kelly, Allan Wood, John Dilson, Robert Frazer, Broderick O'Farrell, Barbara Bedford. ***The Plot Thickens.*** RKO. Director: Ben Holmes. Cast: James Gleason, ZaSu Pitts, Owen Davis, Jr., Louise Latimer, Arthur Aylesworth, Paul Fix, Richard Tucker, Barbara Barondess, James Donlan, Agnes Anderson, Oscar Apfel. **1937: *Make a Wish.*** RKO. Director: Kurt Neumann. Cast: Bobby Breen, Basil Rathbone, Marion Claire, Henry Armetta, Leon Errol, Donald Meek, Billy Lee, Ralph Forbes, Herbert Rawlinson, Spencer Charters, Johnny Arthur, Lew Kelly, Charles Richman, Fred Scott, Barbara Barondess, Dorothy Appleby, Richard Tucker. ***Fit for a King.*** RKO. Director: Edward Sedgwick. Cast: Joe E. Brown, Helen Mack, Paul Kelly, Harry Davenport, Halliwell Hobbes, John Qualen, Donald Briggs, Robert Warwick, Frank Reicher, Russell Hicks, Charles Trowbridge, Charles Lane, Barbara Barondess. **1940: *Emergency Squad.*** Paramount. Director: Edward Dmytryk. Cast: William Henry, Louise Campbell, Richard Denning, Robert Paige, Anthony Quinn, John Miljan, John Marston, Joseph Crehan, Barbara Barondess, Darryl Hickman, Maude Fealey, Georgia Simmons.

3

Thomas Beck

While he had never been one of the boss' favorite contract players, Thomas Beck never intended to offend his boss at a party somewhere in the late 1930s. Yet it happened.

Tom and his date were mingling among the guests, working their way through the crowd. As they approached 20th Century–Fox production head Darryl F. Zanuck, his date said (within earshot of Zanuck) she wanted to meet the man. Tom said, "Meeting him won't be the difficult part, getting away from him will be." After they said their hellos, Tom continued, "Now that we've met the man, can we go home?"

Almost 60 years after making the comments, Beck chuckled at his boldness. "I remember Zanuck just froze over at what I said. I figured I had nothing to lose. Needless to say, it was my last studio party."

It also wasn't long before the studio dropped Beck, who had shown much promise in films.

Beck came to Hollywood in 1934 from the New York stage on the advice of his doctor, who said he needed to recuperate from an illness in a warmer climate. He signed with Fox Films that year and began a gradual ascent in films, first in small roles, then in juvenile parts. When Fox Films merged with 20th Century in 1935 and Darryl F. Zanuck was named production chief, Beck felt his career derailed.

He was kept busy the next two years playing an occasional male lead, but most often had featured roles, typically as the love interest or a best friend. Although he was the leading man-type (handsome, cultured and well-mannered), the studio's plum roles always seemed to go to contractees like Tyrone Power, Don Ameche and Henry Fonda.

Stiff competition among the male contract players and his unfavorable opinion of Zanuck cast a dark cloud over Beck's film career. After the studio

Thomas Beck in ***White Fang*** **(1936). (Courtesy of Thomas Beck.)**

refused to raise his salary a third time, Beck wanted to be released from his contact. His request was granted.

He freelanced in Hollywood another year, then returned to New York, where he intended to continue on the stage. He joined the Army instead and served for several years in World War II.

After a brief return to Broadway, Beck worked for an advertising firm, then opened a real estate office with his long-time companion. He retired from the business in the late 1970s.

Beck was eager to discuss his film and stage career with me in November 1992, but the onslaught of Alzheimer's Disease had begun its erosion of his memory. He had trouble remembering details that had been so familiar not long before. He recognized the slow progression of his condition and apologized for his "absent-mindedness."

His death on September 23, 1995, was attributed to Alzheimer's Disease and heart problems.

Although his film career ended amid frustration, Beck said that films were never of any real interest to him and that he was not enthusiastic about a lasting career on the big screen. The motivation for his work in the studios came from two sources. "First, I was just pleased to be busy," he said. "Second, I was interested in the unusual, and the people I found in Hollywood were just that!"

He was born Thomas McAdam Beck on December 28, 1909, in New York City. His father, John Lane Beck, and mother, Dorothy Reynolds, an English stage actress, were married in England. They returned to New York as Dorothy was preparing to give birth to her only son (Tom had two sisters). They eventually returned to Baltimore (his father's home), where the boy lived until he graduated from college.

Tom's father supervised the Maryland Workshop for the Blind. At one time, he had been an explorer, making an expedition to the upper Amazon River at the turn of the century.

After graduating from Forest Park High School in 1928, young Beck enrolled at Johns Hopkins University. He studied science and had intentions of becoming an engineer. Gifted in the arts, he studied piano at Peabody Conservatory of Music and painting at the Maryland Institute of Fine Arts. He also appeared in many plays, joining the Vagabonds (a Baltimore theater group) and, while a senior at Johns Hopkins, the University Players.*

During this time he appeared on the stage with Henry Fonda, but never knew the man, then or when they were both under contract to 20th Century–Fox. "We never got along with each other," Beck said. "He was a peculiar man."

After graduating from college in 1932, Beck decided there was little demand for engineers during the height of the Depression. He went to New York to see a buddy who had encouraged him to come up and try for the stage.

"My mother thought it was a grand idea because she had been in show business. She gave me some good advice on the theater," said Beck. "My father had the idea that if a man wanted to do something, he should be permitted to do it. He didn't hold me back."

When Beck got to New York, another friend told him his timing was perfect. His friend was leaving immediately for Magnolia, Massachusetts, where he was opening a summer stock company. "He said for me to come along, that he would keep me busy. I called my father and asked him to pack a trunk for me, as I was going to Massachusetts for the summer."

During the summer of 1932, Beck appeared in *Our Wife, Gangway*, and *The Mad Hopes*. It was during the summer that he was introduced to the Brady family, who cast him that October in his first Broadway play, *Mademoiselle*, as Alice Brady's son and Grace George's† grandson. The play ran for 103 performances.

His next play, *Raw Meat*, was not as successful. As the son of two famous explorers, he captures an escaped circus lion. The play opened in Greenwich Village in March 1933 and closed about a week later.

That summer, he returned to Magnolia, Massachusetts, where he worked in stock in *The Gioconda Smile, Oliver, Oliver* and *Love in a Black Hat.*

It was his role as Pauline Frederick's son in the play *Her Majesty the Widow*, which ran on Broadway in June 1934, that led Beck to Hollywood. He had been approached several times before about making screen tests. He declined all offers, as he was more interested in the stage. It was after his doctor recommended Beck take some time to recuperate from health problems that he decided to head west.

"His words were to take it easy, not get involved in anything and just go

**The University Players theater group was formed in 1928 by Henry Fonda, Joshua Logan and Myron McCormick. Margaret Sullavan, Mildred Natwick and James Stewart were later members.*

†Grace George was the wife of legendary stage producer William A. Brady and the stepmother of Alice Brady.

out on the beach and rest," Beck said. "I thought, how could I do that in New York when there was such a big beach in California."

Beck's decision to go west came about the same time an agent saw him in *Her Majesty the Widow* and urged him to make a series of tests. This time, Beck, curious about the movies and seeking a warmer climate, consented. After some tests, Fox Films signed him to a five-year contract. He left for California in the fall of 1934. He lived first at the Hollywood Athletic Club, then moved to Malibu, where he lived in a house on the beach for the next five years.

In his first films, *Hell in the Heavens* and *Lottery Lover*, made in the fall of 1934, Beck's roles were small and insignificant. However, he soon made two films in the Charlie Chan series that he considered among his favorites.

In *Charlie Chan in Egypt* (1935), Beck was cast as the assistant to an archaeologist (George Irving) and as the boyfriend of Pat Paterson; in *Charlie Chan in Paris* (1935), he was a bank clerk and Mary Brian's fiancé.

"I especially liked Warner Oland* as Charlie Chan," Beck said. "He was so delightful. I asked him how he could portray an Oriental man when he was Swedish. It was simple, he said. He had always been able to raise his eyebrows and squint his eyes without making wrinkles on the forehead. He was given a great deal of respect from the studio because of the success of the Charlie Chan films." Beck later made two more Charlie Chan films, *Charlie Chan at the Race Track* (1936) and *Charlie Chan at the Opera* (1936).

In *Life Begins at 40*, Beck appeared with Will Rogers in a story of small-town life and its complications. "Rogers was such a funny man. He was always philosophizing, and he had a daily column in a newspaper that meant a lot to him. He used to concentrate so much on it and get so involved in it that no one could make him work. The whole set would sit and wait."

Music Is Magic was filmed in mid–1935 during the merger of 20th Century Pictures and Fox Films. It was a Hollywood story centering on Bebe Daniels, a star who struggles to come to grips with her waning stardom. Alice Faye, who rises from chorus girl status to replace Daniels, is an instant hit. Beck was cast as the wealthy playboy who pursues Daniels.

"Alice Faye was a darling," said Beck. "I also liked Bebe. She was a typical star, very dignified and preoccupied, but very nice to me."

In Beck's final film in 1935, *My Marriage*, he appeared as Pauline Frederick's son, the black sheep of the family, who is mixed up in the murder of Claire Trevor's brother. Tom had been friendly with Frederick† since appearing as

**Warner Oland (1880–1938) appeared as Charlie Chan 16 times from 1931 to 1938. He often played Oriental villains on the silent screen. He also appeared in such films as* Sin *(1915),* The Jazz Singer *(1927),* Dishonored *(1931) and* Shanghai Express *(1932). His death was attributed to bronchial pneumonia.*

†Pauline Frederick (1883–1938) had been a major stage actress during the 1910s. She entered films in 1915 and worked steadily (often as overbearing mothers) throughout the silent era. Her film work slowed with the coming of sound. She died following an asthma attack, an illness that had plagued her for a decade.

Thomas Beck and Claire Trevor in *My Marriage* (1936). (Courtesy of Thomas Beck.)

her brother in *Her Majesty the Widow* several years before, but he didn't know she was back in Hollywood making films until they were cast in *My Marriage*.

As production chief of the newly formed 20th Century–Fox, Darryl Zanuck began building his stable of contract players. His two aces were Shirley Temple and Will Rogers. Beck felt he became lost in the shuffle. Because he was never a favorite of Zanuck's and he never played the games of studio politics, the best parts went to other people, leaving him in juvenile lead parts in studio programmers. Roles in big-budget, impressive films like *Suez, In Old Chicago* and *Ramona* went to others.

Beck, however disillusioned, was busy and worked hard in 1936 and 1937, turning out 15 pictures in the two-year period.

Studio politics, Beck said, ruined his death scene in *Under Two Flags* (1936). Claudette Colbert's fights with director Frank Lloyd resulted in much of the scene ending up on the cutting room floor.

In the scene, Ronald Colman rushes to the aid of a Legionnaire (Beck) who has been mortally wounded by an Arab attacker. "I was very serious about the scene," Beck said. "I had gone to a hospital to talk with doctors about what happens to people in those situations. Frank Lloyd was very strict about set noises, because he wanted to capture my praying in a very weak voice.

"When I went to the premiere, I was in shock. What Colman actually did in the final version, much different from the scene we shot, was to lift me off the ground, drop me and walk away. My whole scene was stolen by Claudette Colbert, who died in the picture in the arms of Colman. She did exactly as I had done in the scene."

Beck appeared with Peter Lorre in *Crack-Up* (1938) and in two films in the low-budget Mr. Moto series, *Think Fast, Mr. Moto* and *Thank You, Mr. Moto* (both 1937).

"Lorre* was typically a menacing character in films, but he was amusing, a joker off the set," Beck said. "One of the things he liked to do was to pretend he was determined to get some pretty girl to sleep with him. He was a funny man, a comedian."

In *White Fang*, Beck was cast as the weakling brother of Jean Muir and inherited a mine in the Klondike. When Beck's character commits suicide, a guide (Michael Whalen) is accused of murder. Whalen and another member of the cast, John Carradine, became two of Beck's closest Hollywood friends. He appeared again with Whalen at 20th Century–Fox in *Woman-Wise* (1937) and *Walking Down Broadway* (1938).

One of the best roles of Beck's career was as Pastor Schultz in *Heidi* (1937), a Shirley Temple classic. "She was a lovely child, always letter perfect in front of the cameras," Beck said. "She was a little spoiled, but she worked very hard and didn't have a lot of time to be charming. She started growing up, and the studio changed her clothing so her upper body looked smaller. Zanuck, insisting she have star treatment, wanted her to be picked up every time we went to a new camera setup.

"I got to where I hated carrying her. While I was walking with her, she would suddenly, without warning, kick me in the groin. I didn't know what to do about it. I went to Michael [Whalen], and he said she did it to him all the time.† When she does it again, he said, just let her go, drop her. That's exactly what I did, and I never had any more trouble with her."

In 1937, the studio loaned Beck out for the first and only time to appear in MGM's *The Thirteenth Chair*. In it he played a role similar to the others at his home studio: He was a supporting player in love with Madge Evans in this mystery about clairvoyance and seances.

Back at his home studio, his disillusionment over the poor progression of his career, coupled with his feelings for Zanuck, caused Beck to yearn for the stage. "I had known Katharine Hepburn for a few years, and we like each other very much. She wanted me for a role in *The Philadelphia Story,* so I went to the studio and

**Peter Lorre (1904–1964) gained popularity after his sinister performance as a child murderer in Fritz Lang's* M *(1931). In 1935, he left Germany for Hollywood where he appeared as Raskolnikov in* Crime and Punishment *(1935). After the Mr. Moto film series, he did some of his best work at Warner Brothers in such films as* The Maltese Falcon, Casablanca, Three Strangers, The Verdict *and others.*

†Michael Whalen (1902–1974) appeared with Shirley Temple in Poor Little Rich Girl *(1936) and* Wee Willie Winkie *(1937).*

Thomas Beck sings to Astrid Allwyn in *Woman-Wise* (1937). (Courtesy of Thomas Beck.)

asked if they would let me do the play. They said I was needed on the lot in Hollywood, where I sat for another six months waiting for something to come along."

Twice, Beck asked for a salary increase, and twice, because of the studio's poor financial state, he was turned down. "The third time, I went on vacation to Carmel. I told my agent I was going to be away when my contract came up for renewal, that he was to let them know I would sign my contract at the salary it called for plus a raise. Otherwise, let me go." The studio refused a third time, and Beck was dropped.*

"I never liked Zanuck, so I was glad to have that experience behind me. I felt I never knew him," Beck said. "In all my other careers, I knew who I was working for. It was the only time I didn't know my boss."

Freelancing in 1939, he made *I Stand Accused* for Republic and *The Family Next Door* and *They Asked for It* for Universal. Still, his heart was not in movies, but the theater. He left for New York on Labor Day 1939.

"That was so much fun," he recalled. "I packed a sleeping bag and took off across the United States in my Ford convertible. I followed the old exploratory roads. At night I slept in the fields. I met some nice farm people that way. On my way to New York, I stopped off to see my family in Baltimore."

**Beck's final film for 20th Century–Fox was* Road Demon *(1938).*

Joan Valerie and Thomas Beck in *Road Demon* (1938), Beck's final film for 20th Century–Fox. (Courtesy of Thomas Beck.)

In 1940, after appearing on stage in *Delicate Story* (pre–Broadway), Beck enlisted in the Army and was stationed in New York, San Francisco, Hawaii and Japan throughout World War II. He was discharged as a major in 1945. Beck returned briefly to the stage in 1946 when he appeared on Broadway with Blanche Yurka in *Temper the Wind.*

After the play closed in January 1947, Beck joined an advertising firm, where he worked for 17 years. He then retired to Connecticut, where he opened his own real estate office with his companion (he had been a partner in the advertising business). They operated the business for 12 years. In 1977, they moved to Florida, first to Key West, then to Miami Shores. His partner of more than 35 years died in 1986.

Beck collected art over the years and painted in oil and watercolor. He penned a book of poetry, *Astride the Wind*, in 1990. "I found myself getting older and duller. I said, 'This is not the way I want to leave a message to the world. I've got to do something.' So I published a book of my poetry I had been working on since the 1940s."

He said he enjoyed his work on the stage more than in films, and that his only regret was not having worked in his chosen profession, as an engineer. "If I had," he said, "I would have been a busy person in a private way."

His summation of his film career was that it was a good way to make a living during the Depression. "I was making about $700 a week and that wasn't bad. My career didn't advance like I thought it should. I had as much opportunity in films as I might have had. If I had some different contacts, things might have been different."

Overall, those were good times for Thomas Beck, but calling them the Golden Age of Hollywood was off-track.

"Not for me they weren't," Beck said. "I was in a different caste. The golden days in filmmaking were for people like Henry Fonda and Tyrone Power, not for Thomas Beck."

Filmography

1934: ***Hell in the Heavens.*** Fox. Director: John Blystone. Cast: Warner Baxter, Conchita Montenegro, Russell Hardie, Herbert Mundin, Andy Devine, William Stelling, Ralph Morgan, Vince Barnett, William Stack, J. Carrol Naish, Johnny Arthur, Vincent Carato, Louis Mercier, Thomas Beck, Patrick Cunning, Fred Wallace, Gene Renault. ***Lottery Lover.*** Fox. Director: William Thiele. Cast: Lew Ayres, Pat Paterson, Peggy Fears, Sterling Holloway, Walter King, Alan Dinehart, Reginald Denny, Eddie Nugent, Nick Foran, Rafaela Ottiano, Gaston Glass, Fred Wallace, Thomas Beck, Richard Brodus, William Stelling, Patrick Cunning, Harry Shumway. **1935:** ***Charlie Chan in Paris.*** Fox. Director: Lewis Seiler. Cast: Warner Oland, Mary Brian, Thomas Beck, Erik Rhodes, John Miljan, Murray Kinnell, Minor Watson, John Qualen, Keye Luke, Henry Kolker, Dorothy Appleby, Ruth Peterson, Perry Ivins, Gino Corrado, Gloria Roy. ***Charlie Chan in Egypt.*** Fox. Director: Louis (Luis on film) King. Cast: Warner Oland, Pat Paterson, Thomas Beck, Rita Cansino, Stepin Fetchit, Jameson Thomas, Frank Conroy, Nigel de Brulier, James Eagles, Paul Porcasi, Arthur Stone, George Irving, Anita Brown, John Davidson, Gloria Roy. ***Life Begins at 40.*** Fox. Director: George Marshall. Cast: Will Rogers, Richard Cromwell, George Barbier, Rochelle Hudson, Jane Darwell, Slim Summerville, Sterling Holloway, Thomas Beck, Roger Imhof, Charles Sellon, John Bradford, Ruth Gillette, Jed Prouty, T. Roy Barnes, Claire Du Brey, John Ince, Creighton Hale, Barbara Barondess, Gloria Roy. ***Music Is Magic.*** Twentieth Century–Fox. Director: George Marshall. Cast: Alice Faye, Ray Walker, Bebe Daniels, Frank Mitchell, Jack Durant, Rosina Lawrence, Thomas Beck, Andrew Tombes, Luis Alberni, Hattie McDaniel, Niles Welch, Gene Morgan. **1936:** ***My Marriage.*** Twentieth Century–Fox. Director: George Archainbaud. Cast: Claire Trevor, Kent Taylor, Pauline Frederick, Paul Kelly, Helen Wood, Thomas Beck, Beryl Mercer, Henry Kolker, Colin Tapley, Noel Madison, Ralf Harolde, Charles Richman, Lynn Bari, Arthur Hoyt, Sam Flint. ***Champagne Charlie.*** Twentieth Century–Fox. Director: James Tinling. Cast: Paul Cavanagh, Helen Wood,

Thomas Beck, Minna Gombell, Herbert Mundin, Noel Madison, Montagu Love, Delma Byron, Madge Bellamy, Jed Prouty. ***Every Saturday Night.*** Twentieth Century–Fox. Director: James Tinling. Cast: June Lang, Thomas Beck, Jed Prouty, Spring Byington, Paul Stanton, Paxton Sisters, Florence Roberts, Kenneth Howell, George Ernest, June Carlson, William Mahan, Kay Hughes, Phyllis Fraser, Oscar Apfel. ***White Fang.*** Twentieth Century–Fox. Director: David Butler. Cast: Michael Whalen, Jean Muir, Slim Summerville, Charles Winninger, John Carradine, Jane Darwell, Thomas Beck, Joseph Herrick, George Ducount, Marie Chorre, Ward Bond. ***Charlie Chan at the Race Track.*** Twentieth Century–Fox. Director: H. Bruce Humberstone. Cast: Warner Oland, Keye Luke, Helen Wood, Thomas Beck, Alan Dinehart, Gavin Muir, Gloria Roy, Jonathan Hale, G. P. Huntley Jr., George Irving, Frank Coghlan, Jr., Frankie Darro, John Rogers, John H. Allen, Harry Jans, Robert Warwick, Sidney Bracy, Jack Mulhall, Holmes Herbert, Pat O'Malley. ***Can This Be Dixie?*** Twentieth Century–Fox. Director: George Marshall. Cast: Jane Withers, Slim Summerville, Helen Wood, Thomas Beck, Sara Haden, Claude Gillingwater, Donald Cook, James Burke, Jed Prouty, Hattie McDaniel, Troy Brown, Robert Warwick, Billy Bletcher, Otis Harlan, William Benedict. ***Charlie Chan at the Opera.*** Twentieth Century–Fox. Director: H. Bruce Humberstone. Cast: Warner Oland, Boris Karloff, Key Luke, Charlotte Henry, Thomas Beck, Margaret Irving, Gregory Gaye, Nedda Harrigan, Frank Conroy, Guy Usher, William Demarest, Maurice Cass, Tom McGuire. ***Under Two Flags.*** Twentieth Century–Fox. Director: Frank Lloyd. Cast: Ronald Colman, Claudette Colbert, Victor McLaglen, Rosalind Russell, Gregory Ratoff, Nigel Bruce, C. Henry Gordon, Herbert Mundin, John Carradine, Lumsden Hare, J. Edward Bromberg, Onslow Stevens, Fritz Leiber, Thomas Beck, William Ricciardi, Frank Reicher, Francis McDonald, Nicholas Soussanin, Frank Lackteen, Marc Lawrence, Rolfe Sedan. ***Crack-Up.*** Twentieth Century–Fox. Director: Malcolm St. Clair. Cast: Peter Lorre, Brian Donlevy, Helen Wood, Ralph Morgan, Thomas Beck, Kay Linaker, Lester Matthews, Earle Foxe, J. Carrol Naish, Gloria Roy, Oscar Apfel, Lynn Bari, Madge Bellamy, William Benedict. **1937: *Woman-Wise.*** Twentieth Century–Fox. Director: Allan Dwan. Cast: Rochelle Hudson, Michael Whalen, Thomas Beck, Alan Dinehart, Douglas Fowley, George Hassell, Astrid Allwyn, Chick Chandler, Pat Flaherty, Lynn Bari, Bradley Page, Francis McDonald, Babe Hunt, George Turner, Ward Bond, Gino Corrado. ***Seventh Heaven.*** Twentieth Century–Fox. Director: Henry King. Cast: Simone Simon, James Stewart, Jean Hersholt, Gregory Ratoff, Gale Sondergaard, J. Edward Bromberg, John Qualen, Victor Kilian, Thomas Beck, Sig Rumann, Mady Christians, Rollo Lloyd, Rafaela Ottiano. ***Think Fast, Mr. Moto.*** Twentieth Century–Fox. Director: Norman Foster. Cast: Peter Lorre, Virginia Field, Thomas Beck, Sig Rumann, Murray Kinnell, John Rogers, Lotus Long, George Cooper, J. Carrol Naish, Virginia Sale, Frank Mayo, Bert Roach. ***The Thirteenth Chair.*** MGM. Director: George B. Seitz.

Cast: Dame May Whitty, Madge Evans, Lewis Stone, Elissa Landi, Thomas Beck, Henry Daniell, Janet Beecher, Ralph Forbes, Holmes Herbert, Heather Thatcher. ***The Great Hospital Mystery.*** Twentieth Century–Fox. Director: James Tinling. Cast: Jane Darwell, Sig Rumann, Sally Blane, Thomas Beck, Joan Davis, William Demarest, George Walcott, Wade Boteler, Howard Phillips, Gloria Roy, Lona Andre. ***Heidi.*** Twentieth Century–Fox. Director: Allan Dwan. Cast: Shirley Temple, Jean Hersholt, Arthur Treacher, Helen Westley, Pauline Moore, Thomas Beck, Mary Nash, Sidney Blackmer, Mady Christians, Marcia Mae Jones, Delmar Watson, Egon Brecher, George Humbert, Sig Rumann. ***45 Fathers.*** Twentieth Century–Fox. Director: James Tinling. Cast: Jane Withers, Thomas Beck, Louise Henry, The Hartmans, Richard Carle, Nella Walker, Andrew Tombes, Leon Ames, Sammy Cohen, George Givot, Ruth Warren, Hattie McDaniel. ***Thank You, Mr. Moto.*** Twentieth Century–Fox. Director: Norman Foster. Cast: Peter Lorre, Thomas Beck, Pauline Frederick, Jayne Regan, Sidney Blackmer, Sig Rumann, John Carradine, William Von Brincken, Nedda Harrigan. **1938: *Walking Down Broadway.*** Twentieth Century–Fox. Director: Norman Foster. Cast: Claire Trevor, Phyllis Brooks, Leah Ray, Dixie Dunbar, Lynn Bari, Thomas Beck, Jayne Regan, Michael Whalen, Douglas Fowley, Jed Prouty, Leon Ames, William Benedict, Robert Graves, Claire Du Brey, Paul Fix, Lon Chaney, Jr. ***Road Demon.*** Twentieth Century–Fox. Director: Otto Brower. Cast: Henry Arthur, Joan Valerie, Henry Armetta, Thomas Beck, Bill Robinson, Jonathan Hale, Murray Alper, Edward Marr, Lon Chaney, Jr., Inez Palange. **1939: *The Family Next Door.*** Universal. Director: Joseph Santley. Cast: Hugh Herbert, Joy Hodges, Eddie Quillan, Ruth Donnelly, Bennie Bartlett, Juanita Quigley, Thomas Beck, Cecil Cunningham, James Bush, Frances Robinson, Dorothy Granger. ***They Asked for It.*** Universal. Director: Frank McDonald. Cast: William Lundigan, Joy Hodges, Michael Whalen, Isabel Jewell, Lyle Talbot, Thomas Beck, Spencer Charters, James Bush, Charles Halton, James Flavin, Betty Compson. ***I Stand Accused.*** Republic. Director: John H. Auer. Cast: Robert Cummings, Helen Mack, Lyle Talbot, Thomas Beck, Gordon Jones, Robert Paige, Leona Roberts, Robert Middlemass, Thomas E. Jackson, John Hamilton, Howard Hickman, Harry Stubbs.

4

Mary Brian

It was 2:15 on a Friday afternoon in October 1994, and we were 15 minutes early for our appointment with Mary Brian, known as far back as the 1920s as the Sweetest Girl in Pictures. She had invited the actress Jean Porter and me over for the afternoon. She promised there would be time for an interview.

Brian, who enjoyed a successful film career of over 75 films from the mid–1920s to the 1940s, admitted she didn't enjoy interviews and she seldom gave them. She was doing this one as a favor to Porter, the wife of director Edward Dmytryk. Porter had tried on another occasion (March 1994) to get the two of us together. At first, Porter considered gathering several of the old-timers together for lunch, after which Brian and I would find a corner and talk. That idea was scratched, and Porter then approached her with the idea of the three of us getting together. Brian agreed.

The day and time were set, but at the last minute, a visit to her optometrist canceled our appointment. *Next* time, Brian promised.

Rather than arrive early, Porter and I pulled away from the house (located just blocks from the Hollywood Freeway and Ventura Boulevard), and drove around her Studio City neighborhood. Porter pointed out the home of Arthur Dreifuss, one of her directors, and said we should stop in, but there wasn't time.

Old friends of Brian's, neighbors for years, had either died or moved away, she later told us. Giant, palatial homes were going up around her and bringing in strangers. It was a neighborhood in transition. Her ranch-style house, surrounded by lush vegetation, stood on a one-acre tract as a fortress against the modern, multi-million dollar monstrosities that were invading her quiet world.

Fifteen minutes later, we were back, right on time. Brian met us at the door with a firm handshake and a genuine smile. She retained the beauty that charmed millions of moviegoers decade ago. Her skin was flawless, and her eyes, the color of the sky, were large and expressive, giving an occasional glance that I took as a hint of mischievousness — and shyness — in her personality.

Her timidness, coupled with her loyalty to "her" Hollywood and her fierce desire for privacy, made this a difficult interview, the most challenging one for this book.

"You don't really give many interviews, do you, Mary?" I asked as she was slicing a piece of cake she prepared for the visit. The mention of the word prompted her to grimace and she paused with the knife in her hand.

"The reason I feel this way is there are many unpleasant things written about Hollywood," she said. "So many things written that are untrue."

Mary Brian in the late 1920s.

There would be time for questions later; first she wanted to show us around her home. From a formal living room, we stepped down into a cozy den, an intimate room lined with bookcases and seasoned with a modest representation of her film-related memorabilia. She had earmarked a copy of Douglas Fairbanks, Jr.'s, autobiography that mentioned their work together in *The Air Mail* (1925), her second film. She and Fairbanks had recently appeared together at a function.

Her paintings were everywhere, including a portrait (hanging in her bedroom) of her best friend, the late Esther Ralston. We ventured into her bright, sunny studio where she painted, and then into the kitchen, in which hung what must have been her finest work.

She told the story of the painting. Many years after playing Wendy in her first film, *Peter Pan* (1924), Brian was asked by the film's director, Herbert Brenon, to paint a scene of how she envisioned the fictional "never-never land." The work would be reproduced in Brenon's autobiography. She painted herself as Wendy and actress Betty Bronson as Peter Pan in a mystical setting. Brenon, however, died before the book could be finished, thereby limiting the exposure the fine piece of art deserved.

We decided it was time to get down to business. We settled in her den, I on the sofa and she across from me in a lounge chair. Jean Porter found a chair within earshot, no doubt to intervene and change the line of questioning if the topic became too personal. I retrieved my notes and tape recorder from my bag. Brian stiffened at the sight of the recorder.

"Okay, let's talk about that," she warned. "If we use the tape recorder, I will give you a performance and we'll be finished in half an hour. Or you can put it away, and I'll give you an interview."

I put it away and stayed the whole afternoon.

Mary Brian was born Louise Byrdie Dantzler in Corsicana, Texas, on February 17. The accepted year of her birth is generally recorded in film references as 1908; however, the 1910 and 1920 U.S. censuses indicates 1906. Mary and her brother Lawrence were raised in Dallas by their mother Louise. Their father died when Mary was a month old.

"My father, who was from a family of doctors, had been a jeweler," Brian said. "He and a partner had bought some diamonds on consignment. He was thrown from a carriage in which he was riding and died the next day. The partner absconded, and my mother had to pay the consignees off.

"My mother was a bright woman, especially good in mathematics. She worked at a jewelry store, where she wrote ads and designed displays."

Mrs. Dantzler was a working mother and Mary's brother was several years older than she. Consequently Mary spent a lot of time alone growing up. "Mine was a very lonely childhood, with my mother working. Through that, I think I developed a very independent spirit. I was responsible at a very early age. That was good, because when I got into pictures, I was thrown in with a bunch of grown-up people while I was still a teenager."

With her mother working, Brian passed a lot of time at the movies and talking with her friends about her ambitions of becoming an actress. Unlike many who aspired to the acting profession, she shunned school plays. "Oh, no, I could have never done those. I was too shy, too timid for that. I did go to the movies, however. My favorites were Mary Pickford, Jackie Coogan and Lillian Gish. I have never forgotten the thrill of being invited to Pickfair later when I was in Hollywood. Most girls back then wanted to be in the movies. It was something to aspire to, but none of us thought it would happen. Some people say it was destined—not I. I had no idea what was in store for me."

It started in the early 1920s when Brian's mother, thinking a brighter future might be found, decided to move the family to Los Angeles to be near a sister.

Not long after the move, Brian entered and won second place (as "Miss Personality") in a beauty contest in Ocean Park, California. Esther Ralston, one of the contest judges, wrote about the contest in her autobiography.* Several days later, Ralston and Brian met officially on the set of *Peter Pan* (Esther portrayed Mrs. Darling, Wendy's mother) and began what became a life-long friendship†.

Although it has been written the contest led Brian to Paramount's attention, she insisted it had nothing to do with the start of her career.

*Some Day We'll Laugh, *by Esther Ralston (The Scarecrow Press, Inc., 1985).*

†Ralston named her first child (born 1931) for Mary Brian.

Mary Brian (kneeling) as Wendy in her first film, *Peter Pan* (1924). Pictured here with Betty Bronson.

The attention, Brian said, came on one of the days she was visiting the studios. On this occasion, she went to Paramount, where she met casting director Al Kaufman, the brother-in-law of Jesse Lasky, Paramount's production executive. Kaufman was scouting for young unknowns for *Peter Pan.* He instructed Brian to return for an interview and screen test.

"I went back thinking I might be cast as one of the fairies whose faces are never seen," Brian said. On her return to the studio, she was introduced to director Herbert Brenon.* "I will never forget the day I met him. My mother went back to the studio with me, but she did not go in to meet Mr. Brenon. I was taken to a dark room in a studio bungalow. Mr. Brenon had recently had some

**Herbert Brenon (1880–1958) was one of the silent era's most prestigious directors. Born in Ireland, he emigrated to the U.S. in 1906 and began his career in motion pictures as a screenwriter in 1909. He enjoyed success through the silent era, directing some of the era's most popular stars (Alla Nazimova, Theda Bara, Ronald Colman, Lon Chaney and others). His career waned with the coming of sound. He later directed films in England.*

eye surgery and needed as little light as possible for his sensitive eyes. He turned a spotlight on me. I had long curls at that time, and he asked me if they were real. I told him they were and that he could pull them if he wanted."

Brian was called back to the studio a second time and was tested with Betty Bronson, who had been cast as Peter Pan. It was after this session that Brian was given the role of Wendy in her first film. "The reason he selected me was that I was an unknown. It seemed more like a fairy tale if Wendy and the lost boys were not known to movie audiences."

Not surprisingly, Brian was ecstatic. "I had read the story of Peter Pan long before I made the film. It's still one of my favorite stories. You outgrow some of them, but *Peter Pan* was different."

While some found Brenon a demanding director, Brian enjoyed working with him. "He was known as a tough director, but he was always nice to me. I was his choice; he selected me."

Brian slept in the nursery set at night while tracks above were changed for each character. She would be awakened when it was time to fly. "They had boards running across the top out of sight of the camera. A guy would run across the planks with the cables attached to us. That's how we flew."

After working into the night, Brian and her mother would go home for some rest before they met the crew at San Pedro at daybreak to film the scenes on the pirate ship. "I remember thinking it was a lot of work and that this must be the way they make motion pictures. I can tell you, I never worked this hard again."

After the picture was released, the cast made some personal appearances to promote the movie. "The kids would come to see us, which was wonderful," she said. "They were so hyped-up over the movie. They would ask me to fly for them, and I would tell them I hadn't brought my fairy dust. I had to think up a lot of answers in a hurry."

The studio, impressed with Brian's potential as an actress, signed her to a long-term contract. "It was a seven-year contract with options — all on their side, of course. It's true I didn't have to wait long for success, but I went through my long period later with some forgettable films I made."

Molding her into a studio commodity, Paramount gave a good, hard look at her name. "They were looking for something short and sweet, something that would fit nicely on a marquee. Mary sounded sweet, and I had some Brians in my family back in England. After mulling it over, they came up with Mary Brian. I like it."

After Brian signed with Paramount, life at home changed very little for the Dantzlers. Because she was so busy, however, Brian had little time for school. She attended classes on the Paramount lot. "Everything for me has been on-the-job training. My mother was such a bright woman and had wanted me to get a good education. Because of my working, however, there were lapses in my education. On the lot, I was memorizing my schoolwork. It went in one ear and out the other.

"Some resented this, especially later on. Most people who start this young in films say they had a miserable childhood, but I had a wonderful one."

After *Peter Pan*, Brian went to work instantly and almost never slowed down. Brenon boosted her popularity by using her in three more pictures: *The Little French Girl* (1925), *The Street of Forgotten Men* (1925) and *Beau Geste* (1926). "Needless to say, Mr. Brenon was indeed very influential in the early part of my career," said Brian.

The cast of *The Little French Girl*, which included Alice Joyce, Esther Ralston and Neil Hamilton, went on location to Bermuda to shoot the picture. "Alice Joyce was a charming woman, just like her roles on screen. Bermuda was quite a place to go on location. I can tell you that all of them weren't as nice as that."

Like, for instance, the smoldering Arizona deserts, the location for *Beau Geste*,* in which Mary played Isobel, Ronald Colman's love interest. It was the studio's biggest epic of the year, with production exceeding $1 million.

"That was a good role for me, but it was basically a man's picture," Brian said. "I liked Ronald Colman. To this day, he is my idea of a gentleman. Later, he and Benita [Hume, his wife] would ask me up to their house for gatherings with their English friends. I thought a lot of him."

Her status was heightened when the studio began loaning her out, first to MGM for *Brown at Harvard* (1926) with Jack Pickford, and then to Producers Distributing Corporation for *Paris at Midnight* (1926), in which she appeared with Jetta Goudal† and Lionel Barrymore.

"I was so in awe of Lionel Barrymore, but there was not much communication between us," Brian said. "Goudal was the *grande dame* to the fullest. We didn't find a lot of things to say to each other. I used to see her much later on in Santa Monica when she was Mrs. Harold Grieve. She was in a wheelchair and I would talk briefly with her, but on the set, we didn't communicate."

In 1926, Brian was named one of the 13 Wampas Baby Stars of that year, joining Joan Crawford, Dolores Del Rio, Mary Astor, Janet Gaynor, Fay Wray, Joyce Compton, Dolores Costello, Marceline Day, Sally Long, Edna Marion, Sally O'Neil and Vera Reynolds. It was a good indication of her budding popularity and her potential for stardom in motion pictures.

Through her work, Brian developed a screen reputation of sweet virginity and girlish innocence, the epitome of purity. The studio, cashing in on her persona, labeled her "The Sweetest Girl in Pictures."

Throughout the 1920s, Brian worked constantly, often without a break between pictures. She made eight films in 1926 and seven in 1927 and in 1928. Brian enjoyed the work and was constantly with people who had become friends:

**The 1926* Beau Geste *was the first of three film versions of Percival Christopher Wren's classic story of three devoted brothers serving in the Foreign Legion. It was remade in 1939 and 1966.*

†Goudal (1891–1985), who specialized in exotic siren roles in the silent era, retired in the early 1930s to marry Harold Grieve, a motion picture art director.

Mary Brian and Ralph Forbes in *Beau Geste* (1926).

Charles "Buddy" Rogers, Douglas Fairbanks, Jr., Esther Ralston, Richard Arlen, Gary Cooper, Arthur Lake, Jack Oakie and others.

"The work never seemed that unusual to me. We worked six days a week, and I just went from one film to another. I never had a day that I didn't have to go to the studio," she said. "We worked together day in and day out. We got to know the people we worked with, especially when we went on location. If you liked them, you like them a lot. There were a lot of practical jokes on the set. Nowadays, with these big-budget pictures, there's not time for playing around. If we had taken ourselves too seriously, I could see we might have been miserable, and if I hadn't been friends with those I was working with, it might have been a lonely experience for me."

Another actor she befriended was W. C. Fields. She was cast as his daughter in the three films they made together. In 1927, they made *Running Wild* and *Two Flaming Youths.* Then eight years later, Fields, fighting with Paramount over casting selections, insisted that Brian recreate the role of his daughter in the *Running Wild* remake, *The Man on the Flying Trapeze* (1935).

"Fields was a wonderful guy. He liked to try to throw me off during our scenes," she said. "We'd go into a scene, and, for example, I would go over to get my overcoat. It wouldn't be there, and I'd have to look for it. Or, I'd get on the phone and would hear something funny on the other end. He wanted to get my reaction without spoiling the scene. He tried, but he was never able to throw me off.

"We were neighbors when he lived in Toluca Lake. We had ducks and three swans on the lake. He would come out and bang on his door, and all the ducks would go over to him. We soon found out he was putting bread crumbs, soaked in wine, in the duck pan."

Brian said Fields' drinking on the set of *Trapeze* never got out of hand. While his liquor was always present, usually in a glass from which he sipped, it never interfered with his work.

Paramount soon joined the industry in the change from silent to talking pictures. Although she made several part-silent, part-sound films, Brian's, first all-talking film was *The Man I Love* (1929) with Richard Arlen.

"To me, those early films, where they had half-sound and half-silent, sounded funny to me, but audiences accepted them. After all, sound was just breaking in, and it was breaking us in too. I had no doubt sound would last. It was a new innovation. Everyone at Paramount was concerned about it—I was, too!"

In another early sound film, Marshall Neilan* directed the actress in his first sound film, *Black Waters* (1929). A British film company produced the film in Hollywood after it was unable to find suitable sound equipment and technicians in England.

"Mickey Neilan was one of those charming Irishmen," she said. "He had gone through a whole lifetime by the time I met him. He was charming and nice to me, but he was tired by then. He did the best he could with the picture, but a lot of the juice was gone from him by that time."

At the dawn of sound, Brian found herself playing opposite Gary Cooper in three films: *The Virginian* (1929), Cooper's first sound film; *Only the Brave* (1930); and *Paramount on Parade* (1930).

"The studio took a chance with *The Virginian,* in which I played a schoolteacher. We went to Sonora, in the High Sierras, for several weeks of shooting.

**Marshall "Mickey" Neilan (1891–1958) was one of Hollywood's busiest directors (and playboys) of the silent era. He starred with and later directed Mary Pickford in some of her finest films. Excessive drinking, coupled with erratic behavior, led to the decline of his career. At one time, he was married to actress Blanche Sweet.*

The innovation, as far as sound was concerned, was using microphones outside, instead of on sound stages. It was quite a challenge."

Paramount gathered its top stars, directors and composers for its talkie extravaganza *Paramount on Parade.* Brian and Cooper appeared with Richard Arlen, Jean Arthur, Virginia Bruce, James Hall, Phillips Holmes and Fay Wray in the "Let Us Drink to the Girl of My Dreams" sketch.

After her contract with Paramount expired in 1931, Brian freelanced. The first film on her own was one of her best roles, that of Peggy Grant, Pat O'Brien's fiancée in *The Front Page* (1931), now considered one of the screen's best "newspaper" stories. It was the first screen adaptation of the successful play that ran on Broadway in 1928.

Not only was it one of Brian's plum roles, it was among her most enjoyable film experiences. "*The Front Page* was a fun picture to make, because of all the comedians — Pat O'Brien had a wonderful wit. We would start at noon and work through dinner. They had a long table where we'd sit for dinner. We could, but didn't want to, go off the set to eat. Then, we'd work until midnight. It turned out better because we didn't have to eat from a lunch box, nor did we have to get up so early. A couple of times, the director, Lewis Milestone,* would call for me when he knew they weren't filming my scenes. He just wanted to talk. He was a fine man and a wonderful director."

Brian played a similar role (and gave one of her finest film performances) in *Blessed Event* (1932), a newspaper comedy based on columnist Walter Winchell. Dick Powell also appeared (one of his first noticeable parts). Brian and Ken Murray, who at the time were an item, were first introduced to Powell in the early 1930s while on a vaudeville tour. Once Powell was in Hollywood, he and Brian were linked in the gossip columns for almost two years.

By the mid–1930s, the quality of Brian's roles was eroding; she did her best in some low-budget programmers for Majestic, Allied and Monogram. In England in 1936, she appeared in three pictures: *Romance and Riches* with Cary Grant, *Two's Company* and *Weekend Millionaire* with long-time friend Buddy Rogers.

While in England, Brian and Cary Grant developed a close relationship — Mary consoled him over the death of his father.† Back in the States, Grant hinted at marriage, but Brian hesitated long enough for him to change his mind, due in part to his developing fascination with actress Phyllis Brooks.

Although she came close to breaking her screen persona of virginal sweetness in *The Royal Family of Broadway* (1931), it was her part in *Spendthrift* (1936), in which she played a conniving gold digger opposite Henry Fonda, that Mary cracked the mold.

*The Front Page *was Lewis Milestone's second hit in a row. He had just won a Best Director Oscar for* All Quiet on the Western Front *(1930).*

†*The relationship is covered in more detail in* Cary Grant: The Lonely Heart, *by Charles Higham and Roy Moseley (Harcourt, Brace and Jovanovich, 1989).*

Adolphe Menjou, Mary Brian and Pat O'Brien in *The Front Page* (1931).

"It was my first role as a bitch," Brian said. "It was about time. I loved the film and had fun with the part. Hank Fonda had so much going on. He would bicycle over to another stage to see whomever he was going with at the time. I never got acquainted with him. I'd see him at William Randolph Hearst's parties, but I think he sort of lost interest in the film."

Breaking free from years of being stereotyped, however, came a little too late for Brian. By then, she said, it didn't matter. With fewer film offers, she turned her attention to the stage. She appeared in vaudeville shows in 1938 and worked for a season at the Cape Playhouse in Massachusetts.

In 1939, she appeared with long-time friend Esther Ralston in *Yes, My Darling* on the straw-hat circuit and signed for the Broadway-bound *Three After Three*, appearing with Simone Simon. The play closed in Chicago, however, and Brian and Simon were replaced; the play opened as *Walk with Music* on Broadway. *Off the Record,* another Broadway-bound show in which she appeared, also closed before the troupe made it to New York.

During World War II, Brian lent her talent to the war effort, entertaining troops, often on the front lines, in Europe and North Africa. "We didn't have a very big troupe. I went with Jack Haley. He did 'Red, Hot and Blue,' and I did a couple of numbers. It was interesting, because we never knew what kind of a stage we would have. We lived right with the Army in the tents. We made about three stops a day, and by that time we'd be a long way from the base and wouldn't get back until about midnight. We were there during the invasion of south France.

Then, I went back with Frank McHugh and June Clyde to England on a troop show."

Brian made four low-budget, highly forgettable films in 1943 and bid a farewell to the screen after making *The Dragnet* (1947) for Screen Guild.

After appearing as Janet Archer for almost 40 weeks in the *Meet Corliss Archer* CBS series in 1955, Brian retired from show business.

Although she had been linked in Hollywood with such actors as Rudy Vallee, Jack Oakie, Buddy Rogers, Cary Grant and Dick Powell (her most serious Hollywood romance), Brian waited until 1941 to wed. Her marriage to artist Jon Whitcomb lasted three months. In 1947, she married film editor George Tomasini.* Their union ended with his death in 1964. Brian did not remarry.

Brian remained active over the years, devoting herself to her life-long hobby, painting. She was also known for her loyalty to friends. At the time of this interview, she had taken in a cocker spaniel that belonged to Letitia Fairbanks (Douglas, Jr.'s, cousin), who died the year before.

Although she had solid careers in both silent and talking films, Brian said she never considered herself a silent film actress.

"I liked sound pictures better," she said. "There is something in favor of silent films, but not much. They [the directors] could talk to you when you needed to be doing something else [in silent films]. It was distracting. At the beginning that was okay, but it wasn't good to hear it all the time, especially when I had some ideas of my own."

One of the factors that might have limited her career was the ever-present tag, "The Sweetest Girl in Pictures." "When I was working, I didn't want to keep playing the same role. I would like to have done many different things, but it's hard to break away in people's minds. I was never really able to do it."

Still, she considered her career as an actress the right choice for her. "My mother had hoped I would go to college, but I think being an actress is a wonderful role for a woman who wants to have her own life, and it opens a lot of different things if you only realize it. I found when going away from Hollywood [to New York and London] that there was a whole other world out there. Being an entertainer opens the world for you to see other opportunities. If it's your whole life, however, I believe it would be too confining.

"I had fun with my career, but I discovered very early that I didn't have the kind of ambition that Joan Crawford had, the sort of ambition that drives you and everyone around you crazy."

To her, the Hollywood in which she worked, was the golden era of filmmaking.

"Sure it was," she said. "When you look back and contrast it with today, it was the golden age. People think it was the lap of luxury in those days, but it

**(Tomasini was a favorite of director Alfred Hitchcock and worked with "Hitch" on* To Catch a Thief *[1955],* The Wrong Man *[1957],* Vertigo *[1958],* North by Northwest *[1959] and* Psycho *[1960].)*

wasn't that at all. It was hard work. The golden age to me simply means we made some really good films. I'm glad I was there. I wouldn't have missed it!"

Filmography

1924: *Peter Pan.* Paramount. Director: Herbert Brenon. Cast: Betty Bronson, Ernest Torrence, Cyril Chadwick, Virginia Brown Faire, Anna May Wong, Esther Ralston, George Ali, Mary Brian, Philippe De Lacy, Jack Murphy. **1925: *The Air Mail.*** Paramount. Director: Irvin Willat. Cast: Warner Baxter, Billie Dove, Mary Brian, Douglas Fairbanks, Jr., George Irving, Richard Tucker, Guy Oliver, Lee Shumway, John Webb Dillon. ***The Little French Girl.*** Paramount. Director: Herbert Brenon. Cast: Alice Joyce, Mary Brian, Neil Hamilton, Esther Ralston, Anthony Jowitt, Jane Jennings, Mildred Ryan, Eleanor Shelton, Maurice Cannon, Maude Turner Gordon, Paul Doucet, Julia Hurley, Mario Majeroni. ***The Street of Forgotten Men.*** Paramount. Director: Herbert Brenon. Cast: Percy Marmont, Mary Brian, Neil Hamilton, John Harrington, Juliet Brenon, Josephine Deffry, Riley Hatch, Agostino Borgato, Albert Roccardi, Dorothy Walters. ***The Regular Fellow.*** Paramount. Director: Edward Sutherland. Cast: Mary Brian, Raymond Griffith, Tyrone Power, Edgar Norton, Nigel De Brulier, Gustav von Seyffertitz, Kathleen Kirkham, Carl Stockdale, Michael Dark, Lincoln Plummer, Jacqueline Gadsden, Jerry Austin. **1926: *The Enchanted Hill.*** Paramount. Director: Irvin Willat. Cast: Jack Holt, Florence Vidor, Noah Beery, Mary Brian, Richard Arlen, George Bancroft, Ray Thompson, Brandon Hurst, Henry Hebert, George Kuwa, Mathilde Comont, Willard Cooley, George Magrill. ***Behind the Front.*** Paramount. Director: Edward Sutherland. Cast: Wallace Beery, Raymond Hatton, Mary Brian, Richard Arlen, Hayden Stevenson, Chester Conklin, Tom Kennedy, Frances Raymond, Melbourne MacDowell. ***Brown of Harvard.*** MGM. Director: Jack Conway. Cast: William Haines, Jack Pickford, Mary Brian, Francis X. Bushman, Jr., Mary Alden, David Torrence, Edward Connelly, Guinn Williams, Ernest Gillen. ***Paris at Midnight.*** Producers Distributing Corp. Director: E. Mason Hopper. Cast: Jetta Goudal, Lionel Barrymore, Mary Brian, Edmund Burns, Emile Chautard, Brandon Hurst, Jocelyn Lee, Mathilde Comont, Carrie Daumery, Fannie Yantis, Jean De Briac, Charles Requa. ***More Pay—Less Work.*** Fox. Director: Albert Ray. Cast: Albert Gran, Mary Brian, E. J. Ratcliffe, Charles Rogers, Otto Hoffman, Charles Conklin. ***Beau Geste.*** Paramount. Director: Herbert Brenon. Cast: Ronald Colman, Neil Hamilton, Ralph Forbes, Alice Joyce, Mary Brian, Noah Beery, Norman Trevor, William Powell, George Rigas, Bernard Siegel, Victor McLaglen, Donald Stuart, Paul McAllister, Redmond Finlay, Ram Singh, Maurice Murphy, Philippe De Lacy, Mickey McBan. ***The Price of Tempters.*** First National. Director: Lothar Mendes. Cast: Lois Moran, Ben Lyon, Lya De Putti, Ian Keith, Mary Brian, Olive Tell, Sam Hardy, Henry Vibart, Judith Vosselli, Frazer Coulter, J. Barney Sherry. ***Stepping Along.***

First National. Director: Charles Hines. Cast: Johnny Hines, Mary Brian, William Gaxton, Ruth Dwyer, Edmund Breese, Dan Mason, Lee Beggs. **1927:** ***Her Father Said No.*** Film Booking Offices (FBO). Director: Jack McKeown. Cast: Mary Brian, Danny O'Shea, Al Cooke, Kit Guard, John Steppling, Frankie Darro, Gene Stone, Betty Caldwell. ***High Hat.*** First National. Director: James Ashmore. Cast: Ben Lyon, Mary Brian, Lucien Prival, Osgood Perkins, Jack Ackroyd, Iris Gray, Ione Holmes. ***Knockout Reilly.*** Paramount. Director: Malcolm St. Clair. Cast: Richard Dix, Mary Brian, Jack Renault, Harry Gribbon, Osgood Perkins, Lucia Backus Seger, Larry McGrath, Myrtland La Varre. ***Running Wild.*** Paramount. Director: Gregory La Cava. Cast: W. C. Fields, Mary Brian, Claud Buchanan, Marie Shotwell, Barney Raskle, Frederick Burton, J. Moy Bennett, Frankie Evans, Ed Roseman, Tom Madden, Rex (dog). ***Man Power.*** Paramount. Director: Clarence Badger. Cast: Richard Dix, Mary Brian, Philip Strange, Charles Hill Mailes, Oscar Smith, George Irving, Charles Clary, Charles Schaeffer. ***Shanghai Bound.*** Paramount. Director: Luther Reed. Cast: Richard Dix, Mary Brian, Charles Byer, George Irving, Jocelyn Lee, Tom Maguire, Frank Chew, Tom Gubbins, Arthur Hoyt, Tetsu Komai. ***Two Flaming Youths.*** Paramount. Director: John Waters. Cast: W. C. Fields, Mary Brian, Chester Conklin, Jack Luden, George Irving, Cissy Fitzgerald, Jimmy Guinn. **1928:** ***Under the Tonto Rim.*** Paramount. Director: Herman C. Raymaker. Cast: Richard Arlen, Mary Brian, Alfred Allen, Jack Luden, Harry T. Morey, William Franey, Harry Todd, Bruce Gordon, Jack Byron. ***Partners in Crime.*** Paramount. Director: Frank Strayer. Cast: Wallace Beery, Raymond Hatton, Mary Brian, William Powell, Jack Luden, Arthur Housman, Albert Roccardi, Joseph W. Girard, George Irving, Bruce Gordon, Jack Richardson. ***Harold Teen.*** First National. Director: Mervyn LeRoy. Cast: Arthur Lake, Mary Brian, Lucien Littlefield, Jack Duffy, Alice White, Jack Egan, Hedda Hopper, Ben Hall, William Bakewell, Lincoln Stedman, Fred Kelsey, Jane Keckley, Ed Brady, Virginia Sale. ***The Big Killing.*** Paramount. Director: F. Richard Jones, Cast: Wallace Beery, Raymond Hatton, Anders Randolf, Mary Brian, Gardner James, Lane Chandler, Paul McAllister, James Mason, Ralph Yearsley, Ethan Laidlaw, Leo Willis, Buck Moulton, Robert Kortman, Walter James, Roscoe Ward. ***Forgotten Faces.*** Paramount. Director: Victor Schertzinger. Cast: Clive Brook, Mary Brian, Baclanova, William Powell, Fred Kohler, Jack Luden. ***Varsity.*** Paramount. Director: Frank Tuttle. Cast: Charles (Buddy) Rogers, Mary Brian, Chester Conklin, Phillips R. Holmes, Robert Ellis, John Westwood. ***Someone to Love.*** Paramount. Director: F. Richard Jones. Cast: Charles (Buddy) Rogers, Mary Brian, William Austin, Jack Oakie, James Kirkwood, Mary Alden, Frank Reicher. **1929:** ***Black Waters.*** World Wide Pictures. Director: Marshall Neilan. Cast: James Kirkwood, Mary Brian, John Loder, Robert Ames, Frank Reicher, Hallam Cooley, Lloyd Hamilton, Noble Johnson, Ben Hendricks. ***The Man I Love.*** Paramount. Director: William Wellman. Cast: Richard Arlen, Mary Brian, Baclanova, Harry Green, Jack Oakie, Pat O'Malley, Leslie Fenton, Charles Sullivan, Sailor Vincent, Robert

Perry. ***River of Romance.*** Paramount. Director: Richard Wallace. Cast: Charles (Buddy) Rogers, Mary Brian, June Collyer, Henry B. Walthall, Wallace Beery, Fred Kohler, Natalie Kingston, Walter McGrail, Anderson Lawler, Mrs. George Fawcett, George Reed. ***The Virginian.*** Paramount. Director: Victor Fleming. Cast: Gary Cooper, Walter Huston, Richard Arlen, Mary Brian, Chester Conklin, Eugene Pallette, E. H. Calvert, Helen Ware, Victor Potel, Tex Young, Charles Stevens. ***The Marriage Playground.*** Paramount. Director: Lothar Mendes. Cast: Mary Brian, Fredric March, Lilyan Tashman, Huntly Gordon, Kay Francis, William Austin, Seena Owen, Philippe De Lacy, Anita Louise, Little Mitzi, Billy Seay, Ruby Parsley, Donald Smith, Jocelyn Lee, Maude Turner Gordon, David Newell, Armand Kaliz, Joan Standing, Gordon De Main. **1930:** ***The Kibitzer.*** Paramount. Director: Edward Sloman. Cast: Harry Green, Mary Brian, Neil Hamilton, Albert Gran, David Newell, Guy Oliver, Tenen Holtz, Henry Fink, Lee Kohlmar, E. H. Calvert, Thomas Curran, Eddie Kane, Henry Barrows, Paddy O'Flynn, Dick Rush, Eugene Pallette. ***Burning Up.*** Paramount. Director: Edward Sutherland. Cast: Richard Arlen, Mary Brian, Francis McDonald, Sam Hardy, Charles Sellon, Tully Marshall. ***Only the Brave.*** Paramount. Director: Frank Tuttle. Cast: Gary Cooper, Mary Brian, Phillips Holmes, James Neill, Morgan Farley, Guy Oliver, John Elliott, E. H. Calvert, Virginia Bruce, Elda Voelkel, William Le Maire, Freeman Wood, Lalo Encinas. ***The Light of Western Stars.*** Paramount. Director: Otto Brower, Edwin H. Knopf. Cast: Richard Arlen, Mary Brian, Harry Green, Regis Toomey, Fred Kohler, William Le Maire, George Chandler, Sid Taylor, Guy Oliver, Gus Saville. ***Paramount on Parade.*** Paramount. Director: Edward Sutherland. Cast: Iris Adrian, Richard Arlen, Jean Arthur, Mischa Auer, William Austin, George Bancroft, Clara Bow, Evelyn Brent, Mary Brian, Clive Brook, Virginia Bruce, Nancy Carroll, Ruth Chatterton, Maurice Chevalier, Gary Cooper, Cecil Cunningham, Leon Errol, Stuart Erwin, Henry Fink, Kay Francis, Skeets Gallagher, Edmund Goulding, Harry Green, Mitzi Green, Robert Greig, James Hall, Phillips Holmes, Helen Kane, Dennis King, Abe Lyman and His Band, Fredric March, Nino Martini, Mitzi Mayfair, Marion Morgan Dancers, David Newell, Jack Oakie, Warner Oland, Zelma O'Neal, Eugene Pallette, Joan Peers, Jack Pennick, William Powell, Charles (Buddy) Rogers, Lillian Roth, Rolfe Sedan, Stanley Smith, Fay Wray. ***The Social Lion.*** Paramount. Director: Edward Sutherland. Cast: Jack Oakie, Mary Brian, Skeets Gallagher, Olive Borden, Charles Sellon, Cyril Ring, E. H. Calvert, James Gibson, Henry Roquemore, William Bechtel, Richard Cummings, Jack Byron. ***Only Saps Work.*** Paramount. Director: Cyril Gardner. Cast: Leon Errol, Richard Arlen, Mary Brian, Stuart Erwin, Anderson Lawler, Charles Grapewin, George Irving, Nora Cecil, Charles Giblyn, Fred Kelsey, G. Pat Collins, George Chandler, Jack Richardson, Clarence Burton, Clifford Dempsey. **1931:** ***The Royal Family of Broadway.*** Paramount. Director: George Cukor, Cyril Gardner. Cast: Ina Claire, Fredric March, Mary Brian, Henrietta Crosman, Arnold Korff, Frank Conroy, Charles Starrett, Royal C. Stout, Elsie Edmonde, Murray Alper, Wesley

Stark, Herchel Mayall. ***Captain Applejack.*** Warner Brothers. Director: Hobart Henley. Cast: Mary Brian, John Halliday, Louise Closser Hale, Kay Strozzi, Alec B. Francis, Claud Allister, Julia Swayne Gordon, Arthur Edmund Carew, Otto Hoffman, William Davidson. ***The Front Page.*** United Artists. Director: Lewis Milestone. Cast: Adolphe Menjou, Pat O'Brien, Mary Brian, Edward Everett Horton, Walter L. Catlett, George E. Stone, Mae Clarke, Slim Summerville, Matt Moore, Frank McHugh, Clarence H. Wilson, Freddy Howard, Phil Tead, George Strong, Spencer Charters, Maurice Black, Effie Ellsler, Dorothea Wolbert, James Gordon, Dick Alexander. ***Gun Smoke.*** Paramount. Director: Edward Sloman. Cast: Richard Arlen, Mary Brian, Eugene Pallette, Louise Fazenda, Charles Winninger, Guy Oliver, James Durkin, Brooks Benedict, William Boyd, J. Carrol Naish, William Arnold, Stanley Mack, William V. Mong, Jack Richard, Willie Fung, Dawn O'Day. ***The Runaround.*** RKO. Director: William J. Craft. Cast: Mary Brian, Marie Prevost, Geoffrey Kerr, Johnny Hines, Joseph Cawthorn, George Irving. ***The Homicide Squad.*** Universal. Director: George Melford. Cast: Leo Carrillo, Mary Brian, Noah Beery, Russell Gleason, George Brent, J. Carrol Naish, Walter Percival, Pat O'Malley. **1932: *It's Tough to Be Famous.*** Warner Brothers. Director: Alfred E. Green. Cast: Douglas Fairbanks, Jr., Mary Brian, Harold Minjir, Emma Dunn, Walter Catlett, David Landau, Oscar Apfel, Terrance Ray, J. Carrol Naish, Claire McDowell, Louise Beavers, Lilian Bond, Ivan Linow, Clarence Nordstrom. ***Blessed Event.*** Warner Brothers. Director: Roy Del Ruth. Cast: Mary Brian, Lee Tracy, Allen Jenkins, Ruth Donnelly, Ned Sparks, Dick Powell, Milton Wallace, Edwin Maxwell, Emma Dunn, Isabel Jewell, George Chandler, Frank McHugh, Tom Dugan, Walter Miller, William Halligan, George Meeker, Walter Walker, Ruth Hall, Jesse DeVorska, Jack La Rue. ***The Unwritten Law.*** Majestic. Director: Christy Cabanne. Cast: Greta Nissen, Skeets Gallagher, Mary Brian, Louise Fazenda, Lew Cody, Hedda Hopper, Purnell Pratt, Theodore Von Eltz, Mischa Auer, Arthur Rankin, Wilfred Lucas, Ernie Adams, Harold Foshay, Betty Tyree. ***Manhattan Tower.*** Remington Pictures. Director: Frank Strayer. Cast: Mary Brian, Irene Rich, James Hall, Hale Hamilton, Noel Francis, Nydia Westman, Clay Clement, Billy Dooley, Jed Prouty, Wade Boteler. **1933: *Hard to Handle.*** Warner Brothers. Director: Mervyn LeRoy. Cast: James Cagney, Mary Brian, Ruth Donnelly, Allen Jenkins, Claire Dodd, Robert McWade, Gavin Gordon, Emma Dunn, John Sheehan, Matt McHugh, Louise Mackintosh, Sterling Holloway, Berton Churchill, Harry Holman, Douglass Dumbrille, Walter Walker. ***The World Gone Mad.*** Majestic. Director: Christy Cabanne. Cast: Pat O'Brien, Evelyn Brent, Neil Hamilton, Mary Brian, Louis Calhern, J. Carrol Naish, Buster Phelps, Richard Mitchell, Wallis Clark, Huntly Gordon, Max Davidson, Joe Girard, Lloyd Ingraham, Inez Courtney. ***Girl Missing.*** Warner Brothers. Director: Robert Florey. Cast: Ben Lyon, Mary Brian, Glenda Farrell, Peggy Shannon, Lyle Talbot, Guy Kibbee, Harold Huber, George Pat Collins, Edward Ellis, Helen Ware, Louise Beavers. ***Song of the Eagle.*** Paramount. Director: Ralph Murphy. Cast: Charles

Bickford, Richard Arlen, Mary Brian, Jean Hersholt, Louise Dresser, Andy Devine, George E. Stone, Gene Morgan, Bert Sprotte, George Meeker, Julie Haydon, Harry Walker. ***Moonlight and Pretzels.*** Universal. Director: Karl Freund. Cast: Leo Carrillo, Mary Brian, Roger Pryor, Lillian Miles, Herbert Rawlinson, Bobby Watson, William Frawley, Alexander Gray, Bernice Claire, Mary Lange, Max Stamm, James Carson, John Hundley, Richard Keene, Doris Carson. ***One Year Later.*** Allied. Director: E. Mason Hopper. Cast: Mary Brian, Russell Hopton, Donald Dillaway, George Irving, Will Ahern, Gladys Ahern, DeWitt Jennings, Jackie Searl, Pauline Garon, Marjorie Beebe, Edward Keene, Harry Holman, Lloyd Whitlock, William Humphrey, Nina Guilbert, John Ince, Pat O'Malley, James Mack, Walter Brennan, Herbert Evans, Myrtle Stedman, Virginia True Boardman. ***Fog.*** Columbia. Director: Albert Rogell. Cast: Donald Cook, Mary Brian, Reginald Denny, Robert McWade, Helen Freeman, Samuel S. Hinds, G. Pat Collins, Edwin Maxwell, Maude Eburne, Marjorie Gateson, Montague Shaw. ***Shadows of Sing Sing.*** Columbia. Director: Phil Rosen. Cast: Mary Brian, Bruce Cabot, Grant Mitchell, Harry Woods, Claire Du Brey, Bradley Page, Irving Bacon, Dewey Robinson, Fred Kelsey, Charles Wilson, Hooper Atchley, Pat Hartigan. **1934: *Ever Since Eve.*** Fox. Director: George Marshall. Cast: George O'Brien, Mary Brian, Herbert Mundin, Betty Blythe, Roger Imhof, Russell Simpson, George Meeker. ***Private Scandal.*** Paramount. Director: Ralph Murphy. Cast: ZaSu Pitts, Phillips Holmes, Mary Brian, Ned Sparks, Lew Cody, June Brewster, Harold Waldridge, Jed Prouty, Charles Sellon, Rollo Lloyd, Olive Tell, Olin Howland, Charles B. Middleton, John M. Qualen. ***Monte Carlo Nights.*** Monogram. Director: William High. Cast: Mary Brian, John Darrow, Yola D'Avril, Astrid Allwyn, George Hayes, Kate Campbell, Robert Frazer, Carl Stockdale, George Cleveland, Henry De Silva. ***College Rhythm.*** Paramount. Director: Norman Taurog. Cast: Joe Penner, Jack Oakie, Lanny Ross, Lyda Roberti, Helen Mack, George Barbier, Mary Brian, Franklin Pangborn, Robert McWade, Harold Minjir, Dean Jagger, Mary Wallace. ***Charlie Chan in Paris.*** Fox. Director: Lewis Seiler. Cast: Warner Oland, Mary Brian, Thomas Beck, Erik Rhodes, John Miljan, Murray Kinnell, Minor Watson, John Qualen, Keye Luke, Henry Kolker, Dorothy Appleby, Ruth Peterson, Perry Ivins, Gino Corrado, Gloria Roy. ***The Man on the Flying Trapeze.*** Paramount. Director: Clyde Bruckman. Cast: W. C. Fields, Mary Brian, Kathleen Howard, Grady Sutton, Vera Lewis, Lucien Littlefield, Oscar Apfel, Lew Kelly, Arthur Aylesworth, Tammany Young, Walter Brennan, Tor Johnson, Rosemary Theby. **1936: *Spendthrift.*** Paramount. Director: Raoul Walsh. Cast: Henry Fonda, Mary Brian, Pat Paterson, George Barbier, Edward Brophy, Richard Carle, J. M. Kerrigan, Spencer Charters, June Brewster, Halliwell Hobbes, Jerry Mandy, Miki Morita, Greta Meyer, Robert Strange. ***Weekend Millionaire.*** Gaumont British Picture Corp. Director: Arthur Woods. Cast: Mary Brian, Charles (Buddy) Rogers, W. H. Berry, Billy Milton, Haver and Lee, Charles Carson, Norah Gale, Nadine March, Iris Hoey, Veronica Rose. ***Three Married Men.*** Paramount. Director: Eddie

Buzzell. Cast: Roscoe Karns, William Frawley, Lynne Overman, Mary Brian, George Barbier, Marjorie Gateson, Betty Ross Clark, Mabel Colcord, Bennie Bartlett, Gail Sheridan, Cora Sue Collins, Donald Meek, Charles Wilson, Harrison Greene, Henry Sylvester, Neil Craig. ***Killer at Large.*** Columbia. Director: David Selman. Cast: Mary Brian, Russell Hardie, George McKay, Thurston Hall, Henry Brandon, Betty Compson, Harry Hayden, Boyd Irwin, Charles R. Moore, Harry Bernard, Lee Shumway, Lon Chaney, Jr. ***Two's Company.*** British & Dominions — United Artists. Director: Tim Whelan. Cast: Ned Sparks, Gordon Harker, Mary Brian, Patric Knowles, Harry Holman, Olive Blakeney, Morton Selten, Robb Wilton, Gibb McLaughlin. **1936: *Romance and Riches.*** Garrett Clement — United Artists (British). Director: Alfred Zeisler. Cast: Cary Grant, Mary Brian, Henry Kendall, Leon M. Lion, Garry Marsh, John Turnbull, Iris Ashley, Arthur Hardy. **1937: *Navy Blues.*** Republic. Director: Ralph Staub. Cast: Dick Purcell, Mary Brian, Warren Hymer, Joseph Sawyer, Edward Woods, Horace MacMahon, Chester Clute, Lucille Gleason, Ruth Fallows, Alonzo Price, Mel Ruick, Carleton Young. ***Affairs of Cappy Ricks.*** Republic. Director: Ralph Staub. Cast: Walter Brennan, Mary Brian, Lyle Talbot, Frank Shields, Frank Melton, Georgia Caine, Phyllis Barry, William B. Davidson, Frank Shannon, Howard Brooks, Anthony Pawley. **1943: *Calaboose.*** United Artists. Director: Hal Roach, Jr. Cast: Jimmy Rogers, Noah Beery, Jr., Mary Brian, Bill Henry, Paul Hurst, Marc Lawrence, William Davidson, Jean Porter, Iris Adrian, Sarah Edwards. ***I Escaped from the Gestapo.*** Monogram. Director: Harold Young. Cast: Dean Jagger, John Carradine, Mary Brian, Bill Henry, Sidney Blackmer, Ian Keith, Anthony Warde, Edward Keane, Norman Willis, Peter Dunne, Spanky McFarland, Billy Marshall, Greta Granstedt. ***Danger! Women at Work.*** Producers Releasing Corp. Director: Sam Newfield. Cast: Patsy Kelly, Mary Brian, Isabel Jewell, Wanda McKay, Betty Compson, Cobina Wright, Jr., Allan Byron, Warren Hymer, Vince Barnett, Michael Kirk, Charles King, Jack Ingram. ***The Dragnet.*** Screen Guild. Director: Leslie Goodwins. Cast: Henry Wilcoxon, Mary Brian, Douglass Dumbrille, Virginia Dale, Douglas Blackley, Tom Fadden, Don Harvey, Maxine Seman, Ralph Dunn, Bert Conway, Douglas Evans, Paul Newlan, Allan Nixon.

5

Pauline Curley

Near the dawn of motion pictures, director Allan Dwan knelt down for an eye-to-eye look at the fledgling child actress standing before him. He sensed something special in her, a certain potential. Thinking her prime material for the movies, he bestowed upon her his blessings and his influence.

Eighty years later, in her first interview since she retired from the screen in the late 1920s, Pauline Curley spoke almost with reverence of the man she credited with discovering her for the movies.

"I was sitting in a car on location and Mr. Dwan walked up with this little round rock in his hand. He said, 'See this, Pauline? I just found it and it's a lucky rock. I'm going to give it to you and it's going to give you a lot of luck.'"

While it's true that a certain amount of luck was involved, Pauline Curley also had talent. During her almost 20-year career in motion pictures, which extended from 1911 to 1929, is there anything she didn't have a chance to do?

From the stage (she played on Broadway), she went into the movies as a child actress in the early 1910s. Appearing older than her age, she graduated to ingenues mid-decade, playing opposite the likes of Douglas Fairbanks, Harold Lockwood, John Gilbert and Lloyd Hughes.

In the early 1920s, she was a Vitagraph serial heroine in two cliffhangers starring Antonio Moreno. She finished her career in two-reel comedies and riding the range with Western greats Tom Mix and Jack Perrin. With the talkie revolution claiming the silents, she left the screen in 1929 at the advent of sound.

Curley had a lot going for her: Dwan's belief in her ability; her innate talent; and a bit of good luck. Then again, it didn't hurt that she had a mother determined to see her daughter excel in the movies.

Rose Curley was an ambitious lady. By the time Pauline was four years old (she was born Dec. 19, 1903,* in Holyoke, Massachusetts), her mother had her enrolled in dancing school. Pauline was performing on stage in talent shows when her mother decided to take a big leap in the game of chance.

"My mother decided that if I could do those talent shows, why couldn't I be in pictures," Pauline said. Rose talked over the possibilities with Pauline's father, John. He gave the two his blessings, but added that he would not leave his business and accompany his wife in her search for stardom.

"He thought my mother would try it out for a while and then come home," Pauline said. "However, she made up her mind that she wanted me to be an actress and she just stuck to it."

And so, in 1911, when Pauline was only seven years old, she and her mother, leaving behind their family (Pauline had an older brother and sister), left for New York City.

Once they were settled, Rose had no trouble getting Pauline small roles in one- and two-reelers. She worked in most of the studios in New York City and New Jersey: Biograph, Majestic, Reliance, Ramo and others. She garnered stage experience in about 1912 when she was hired by the Jack Packard Stock Company. With Rose coaching her, Pauline appeared in the weekly performances of *Uncle Tom's Cabin* and *Little Lord Fauntleroy.*

Eighty years later, Pauline vividly remembered how humiliated she was as Little Eva in *Uncle Tom's Cabin* during her "going to Heaven" scene one evening, when some clouds (part of the scenery) fell, exposing the ladder on which she was climbing to "Heaven."

When Pauline was 10, she and her mother (who was by now working as an actress in films) joined the B. P. Keith Vaudeville Circuit and toured the U. S. and Canada for about a year in *A Daddy by Express.* Hans Roberts was the star.

Since coming to New York, Pauline had appeared in child roles in some of Allan Dwan's† films. *The Straight Road* (1914), Dwan's next picture, called for something a little different: a boy.

"My mother took me in to see him about a role in the picture. He said he had to have a boy for the part. My mother said I could play a boy. She borrowed boys' clothes, rented a wig and took me back in there all dressed up. He took one look at me and said, 'Pauline has the part.'"

After *The Straight Road*, Pauline's career began advancing. In the mid–1910s, she appeared for a year on Broadway in *Polygamy* and in such films as *The Dancing Doll* and *The Unbroken Road*, both in 1915.

**At least one reference gives 1896 as the year of birth. "I wouldn't be here talking with you if I had been born that far back," Curley said.*

†Allan Dwan (1885–1981), one of Hollywood's most prolific directors— he directed over 400 films, began his career in 1911. Such stars as Lon Chaney, Mary Pickford, Douglas Fairbanks, Lillian and Dorothy Gish, and Gloria Swanson worked under his direction. He made an easy transition to sound and continued working into the late 1950s.

By the time *Polygamy* closed, Pauline was 12 and outgrowing children roles. Her mother dressed her in long dresses and announced that her daughter was now available for more mature parts.

Life Without Soul (1915), the first feature-length version of the Frankenstein saga, marked Curley's emergence as an ingenue. The film, the first to be released by Ocean Film Corporation, was shot on location in Jacksonville and St. Augustine, Florida, and in Dahlonega, Georgia.

Pauline Curley in the late 1910s. (Courtesy of Pauline Curley.)

Herbert Brenon (a perfectionist) directed her in *The Fall of the Romanoffs* (1917), a story about the Russian Revolution, and Arthur Rosson directed her at Triangle in *A Case at Law* and in *Cassidy,* in which she played the daughter of a district attorney (Frank Currier) who is saved from white slavery by Dick Rosson.

Working at Triangle that fall was particularly trying for Curley. The huge skylights used to light the sets made working conditions smoldering and suffocating. She remembered workers bringing in buckets of ice water in which the actors could cool their arms.

Curley had always appeared older than her age. About a month before she turned 14, she and her mother went to director Fred Balshofer about an upcoming role opposite Harold Lockwood in *The Square Deceiver* (1917).

"My mother told Mr. Balshofer that I was 16," said Curley. "I looked 16; I acted 16; and I had been working as an ingenue since I was 12 years old. He must have believed it because I got the role."

In the picture, Lockwood, a millionaire, takes the job of a chauffeur to be near Beatrice (Curley), a penniless pauper, who works for a society woman set on marrying her daughter to Lockwood. By the end of the last reel, Lockwood and Curley seal their love in marriage.

Off camera, Lockwood* was convinced Pauline was older than her 14 years

**Harold Lockwood (1887–1918), a former vaudevillian, entered films in 1911, gaining popularity in the 1910s as a romantic star opposite Dorothy Davenport, Kathlyn Williams, Marguerite Clark and Mary Pickford. He achieved his greatest fame in 1916–17 when he was teamed with May Allison. They formed one of the earliest romantic couples in films, rivaling the popularity of Francis X. Bushman and his screen and real-life partner, Beverly Bayne.*

Harold Lockwood points an accusing finger at Pauline Curley in a scene from *The Square Deceiver* (1917). Director Fred J. Balshofer is holding the megaphone at left. (Courtesy of Pauline Curley.)

and began taking a special interest in her. After *The Square Deceiver,* he took Curley (and her mother) to Florida, to appear opposite him in *The Landloper* (1918). Then, they were off to Hollywood, where she worked with him in *Lend Me Your Name* (1918).

With Lockwood's attentions on her, especially on the set of *Lend Me Your Name,* "I thought I was really in," said Pauline. "Harold had a limousine that he went on location with every morning. He'd always bring his girlfriend with him and at lunch time, they would go to a hotel or a restaurant for lunch. This one particular morning, he didn't bring his girlfriend. Instead, he asked me if I would like to go with him in his limousine. Of course, I was thrilled, because I thought he was really something. I must say it was flirtation, and I knew how to flirt.

"We went on location, then to a hotel where we had lunch. That went on for a few days. Then the girlfriend came back with him again and I wondered what was going on. So finally I told my mother that I didn't understand. 'I can tell you why,' Rose Curley replied. 'I showed him your birth certificate.' That was the end of that."

It rained for an entire week when Curley and her mother arrived in Hollywood. Curley, expecting the Southern California sunshine, was disappointed.

After staying for a short time in a hotel on Hollywood Boulevard, the two decided to remain in Hollywood. They rented a bungalow on Lexington Avenue.

John Curley, who had remained behind in New York, later joined his wife and daughter in California, where he eventually got a job in Paramount's paint department.

For Pauline, Rose Curley was the head of the house. She was at the helm of her daughter's career and she controlled her finances. Several former child players, after having grown into adulthood, have told of being forced to work beyond their strengths while their parents lavishly spent their money. Pauline insisted her situation was different, because she was not the sole breadwinner for the family. John Curley still had his own business, and Ma Curley, as she was becoming known in the business, worked in films every chance she got.*

"My mother definitely ran everything and she was boss. I would endorse my checks and turn them over to her. I'm not saying that my mother wouldn't buy me everything I wanted. If I ever wanted anything, she never denied me." When her mother agreed to a $5-a-week allowance, Pauline saved her money for two weeks and rushed around the corner from the studio to a drugstore where she bought a bottle of Coty's perfume.

Thanks to Allan Dwan, Curley was cast with Douglas Fairbanks in *Bound in Morocco* (1919). "Now there was a wonderful man," the actress said of Fairbanks. "He was so nice to work with." Working with Fairbanks and Dwan made up for the distaste she had for her role. "I had to wear this veil and it was supposed to be a harem thing. I just didn't care too much for it."

P. T. Tally, the owner of the Broadway Theater in Los Angeles, recommended Curley to director King Vidor for his next film, *The Turn in the Road* (1919). Filmed in late 1918, the picture was Vidor's first full-length feature, as well as the first production of the Brentwood Film Corporation.

The film, in which Curley, the wife of Lloyd Hughes, dies during childbirth, was an immediate success. It played in Los Angeles to sell-out crowds for eight weeks beginning in December 1918, before the Robertson-Cole Company purchased the film for national distribution. It established Vidor as a first-class director.

"Vidor was one of our finest directors," said Curley. "He wanted perfection. If he didn't like the way you were doing something, he'd criticize and say you should do the scene this way. His suggestions were always a whisper, never a shout."

Of Lloyd Hughes, her husband in the film, Curley said simply, "He was absolutely gorgeous."

In the summer of 1919, Curley worked with Sessue Hayakawa, John Gilbert and Helen Jerome Eddy in *The Man Beneath*, produced by Hayakawa's company,

**Many of Rose "Ma" Curley's roles were unbilled. She can be seen briefly in* King Kong *(1933) and in* Of Human Bondage *(1934). She continued working until her death in 1942.*

Pauline Curley about the time she appeared with Douglas Fairbanks in *Bound in Morocco* (1919). (Courtesy of Pauline Curley.)

Hayworth. Curley played John Gilbert's* fiancée in the film. In real life, she developed a crush on the actor. Gilbert asked her for a date and she couldn't resist, even though she knew her mother would never allow it. She devised a scheme. Back in New York, Curley had been friendly with Jack Sherrill, the son of a producer with whom she had worked. Knowing they were visiting California, Curley went to her mother and told her that Jack—she dare not give the last name—wanted to take her out. Knowing Sherrill's background, her mother agreed.

"When Jack Gilbert arrived, my mother was horrified, but it was too late to do anything about it," Curley said. "We got to go out on one date, but that was it."

Vitagraph placed Curley under contract in 1919 and cast her in two 15-chapter serials starring Antonio Moreno,† *The Invisible Hand* and *The Veiled Mystery.* The studio gave Curley her own dressing room.

Each serial, said Curley, took about a year to film. She spent a lot of time with Moreno and considered him a close friend and her favorite of the actors with whom she worked.

While they were filming *The Invisible Hand,* Rose Curley, as she had always done, accompanied her daughter to the studio. She would remain in Pauline's dressing room while she (Pauline) was on the set. Members of the cast and employees of the studio were amused that Pauline, now 16, never came to work without her mother.

**John Gilbert (1899–1936), when he appeared in* The Man Beneath, *was still six years from becoming one of the silent screen's greatest romantic idols. He achieved success in such films as* He Who Gets Slapped *(1924),* The Merry Widow *(1925),* The Big Parade *(1925) and* La Bohème *(1926), but it was with Greta Garbo in* Flesh and the Devil *(1927),* Love *(1927) and* A Woman of Affairs *(1928) that he peaked as one of the most popular screen lovers of the silent era.*

†Antonio Moreno (1886–1967), one of the silent screen's most popular Latin lovers, made on-screen love to the industry's top female stars: Greta Garbo, Pola Negri, Gloria Swanson, Mary Miles Minter, Alice Terry, Billie Dove, Lillian Gish and others. He turned to character parts in the early 1930s. His other Vitagraph serials were: The House of Hate *(1918),* The Iron Test *(1918) and* Perils of Thunder Mountain *(1919).*

Top: Helen Jerome Eddy, Pauline Curley, Sessue Hayakawa and John Gilbert in ***The Man Beneath*** (1919). (Courtesy of Pauline Curley.) ***Bottom:*** Antonio Moreno and Pauline Curley in ***The Veiled Mystery*** (1920). (Courtesy of Pauline Curley.)

"So, when we made *The Veiled Mystery*, I told my mother not to come with me again. I said I was too old, and that from now on, I would be going to the studio alone. I was not going to have people making fun of me."

Not only did Curley begin going to the studio alone when she was 16, she also began dating. She was often seen on the arm of race car driver Harry Hart. Once, she remembered going with him to a party at the home of Wallace Reid. On Saturday nights, she went to dances at the Hollywood Hotel, a haven for motion picture people. The Green Mill was another nightclub she frequented. She was also a member of the Regulars, composed of the most popular actresses of the day.* Curley often hosted meetings of the group in her apartment.

By the spring of 1922, Curley had been seeing Kenneth Peach, a cameraman, for some time and the relationship appeared to be getting serious. So intense, in fact, that her mother and father forbade the two to see one another again. Seeing no alternative, the couple eloped (on May 2, 1922) to Santa Ana, California.

The newlyweds returned to Hollywood to face Pauline's enraged parents, who were determined to have the marriage annulled. Pauline was just as determined she would not only keep her husband, but her career as well. She kept both.

Through her friendship with director Eugene Forde, the brother-in-law of Tom Mix, Curley was cast as Mix's leading lady in *Hands Off* (1921). Mix, she said, was "just one of the cowboys" and like by everyone. *Hands Off* marked the beginning of Curley's long stint in Westerns, and, from indications, the decline of her film career.

In 1923, she worked in the Range Rider series of two-reelers with Leo Maloney.† "Leo was a drinker. He was drinking one day and he wanted me to do a flying mount onto a horse. I told him I couldn't do it. He said I was going to do it if we had to stay on location all day. I tried and tried. Finally, I did it."

In 1924 and 1925, she worked almost exclusively with Kit Carson§ in almost ten features. She worked with Jack Perrin in *West of Rainbow's End* (1926), *The Laffin' Fool* (1927), *Thunderbolts Tracks* (1927) and *Code of the Range* (1927).

Curley found the work demanding and not very glamorous as fans believed it to be. She had to supply her own wardrobe, apply her own makeup and style her own hair.

"It was hard work," the actress said of her work in Westerns. "We did one feature a week and we worked six days a week in those days, five days on locations and Saturdays on interiors."

**Some of the actresses who belonged to the Regulars were: Mary Astor, Dorothy Devore, Mary Brian, Jobyna Ralston, Priscilla and Marjorie Bonner, Mary Philbin and others.*

†Leon (Leo) Daniel Maloney (1888–1929), a popular and talented star of Pathé Westerns in the 1920s, often wrote, directed, produced and starred in his own films. His Mascot serial The Vanishing West *(1928) brought him his greatest success. His death was attributed to acute and chronic alcoholism.*

§Kit Carson (1899–1979) also appeared in films as Boris Bullock and William Barrymore.

In addition to the hard work involved, there were also the dangers associated with filming on location. Curley had a particularly close call along the Columbia River in Oregon during the filming of *Shackles of Fear* (1924). The cameraman was shooting some scenes along the rapids and he wanted to take some close-ups of Curley in the canoe. The prop men had the canoe secured with cables. Once Curley was out along the rapids, however, the wire snapped and she was thrown into the water. The canoe was smashed to pieces, while Curley tore her fingernails trying to cling to a rock until help arrived. She was taken to the hospital with leg injuries, and after several days of rest she was eager to finish the picture.

While lying in bed recuperating from her ordeal, Curley must have questioned why her career had made a drastic change after *Hands Off* with Tom Mix. Why had she gone from playing opposite Douglas Fairbanks, Lloyd Hughes, Harold Lockwood and Antonio Moreno at major studios to appearing in low-budget Westerns at independent studios (and, later two-reel Rayart comedy series).

"I have no idea," she said. "The main thing was that I worked full-time. I didn't look down on them. It didn't make any difference what I did. I enjoyed everything."

Curley appeared as one of the "dames"—the other two were Carole Lombard and Joan Bennett—in *Power* (1928) with William Boyd and Alan Hale. After an unbilled bit in the early talkie *The Locked Door* (1929), Curley retired from the screen.

"Not only was I pregnant, I thought I had worked long enough," she said of her decision to quit films. "I had worked from the time I was seven and that was it."

By this time, her husband was head of special effects at Tiffany-Stahl. "His career was going on, and I was more interested in what he was doing," she said.

A son, Kenneth, Jr., was born in June 1930; a daughter, Pauline, was born in 1935; and another son, Marty, in July 1949, when Pauline was 45.

Kenneth Peach's career continued to advance. He worked on some of the special effects in *King Kong* and later got into production. In television, he worked on such series as *Lassie, The Cisco Kid,* and *Topper*. When he died in 1988, he and Pauline had been married over 65 years.

Pauline Curley's oldest son continued the family tradition. He has worked on television series such as *Remington Steele, Falcon Crest, The Jackie Thomas Show* and *Roc.*

When I visited Pauline Curley in her Calabasas, California, home in March 1993, she was recovering from physical and psychological injuries she suffered at home that previous December when she surprised an intruder, who knocked her unconscious and left her for dead.

Giving up did not factor into her plans for the future. She continued to drive and refused to allow the experience deter her from living alone in the home she loved. As we sat going through her show business scrapbooks, her face brightened as she recalled details from a satisfying Hollywood career.

It might seem so at first thought, but it's not really surprising that her attitude was so positive. Consider that while most kids her age were just learning to read, Pauline was already entertaining in vaudeville houses far from home and emoting before the camera on smoldering movie sets. No matter how impossible the situation seemed, she understood that the show must go on.

FILMOGRAPHY

1913: ***The Better Way.*** Ramo Pictures. Director: Wray Physioc. Cast: Mary Alden, Jack Hopkins, James F. Ayres. Pauline Curley. ***The Call of the Road.*** Ramo Pictures. Cast: Mr. Logan, Mr. Rising, Pauline Curley. **1914:** ***The Straight Road.*** Famous Players Film Co. Director: Allan Dwan. Cast: Gladys Hanson, William Russell, Iva Shepard, Arthur Hoops, Lorraine Huling, Pauline Curley. **1915:** ***The Dancing Doll.*** Kalem. Director: George Sargent. Cast: Vivian Wessell, Wayne Nunn, E. T. Roseman, George Moss, Harland B. Moore, Pauline Curley. ***The Unbroken Road.*** Life Photo Film Corp. Cast: Mary Nash, William H. Tooker, Alexander Gadan, Thomas O'Keefe, Arthur Morrison, Joseph Baker, Charles Graham, Sue Balfour, Walter James, Edna Spence, Frank Dufrane, Nellie Dent, James F. Ayres, Pauline Curley. ***Life Without Soul.*** Ocean Film Corp. Director: Joseph W. Smiley. Cast: William W. Cohill, Percy Darrell Standing, George De Carlton, Jack Hopkins, Lucy Cotton, Pauline Curley, David McCauley, Violet De Biccari. **1917:** ***A Case at Law.*** Triangle Film Corp. Director: Arthur Rosson. Cast: Riley Hatch, Pauline Curley, Dick Rosson, Jack Dillon, Ed Sturgis. ***Cassidy.*** Triangle Film Corp. Director: Arthur Rosson. Cast: Dick Rosson, Pauline Curley, Frank Currier, Mac Alexander, Eddie Sturgis, John O'Connor, Jack Snyder. ***The Square Deceiver.*** Yorke-Metro. Director: Fred J. Balshofer. Cast: Harold Lockwood, Pauline Curley, William Clifford, Dora Mills Adams, Kathryn Hutchison, Betty Marvin, Dick L'Estrange. ***Intrigue.*** Vitagraph. Director: John Robertson. Cast: Peggy Hyland, Marc MacDermott, Bobby Connelly, Mrs. Remley, Templer Saxe, Brinsley Shaw, Harry Southwell, Miss Curley (Pauline), Nellie Spitzer. ***The Girl Philippa.*** Vitagraph. Director: S. Rankin Drew. Cast: Anita Stewart, S. Rankin Drew, Frank Morgan, Miss Curley (Pauline), Billie Billings, Captain Eyerman, Ned Hay, Stanley Dunn, Anders Randolf. **1918:** ***The Fall of the Romanoffs.*** Iliodor Pictures Corp. Director: Herbert Brenon. Cast: Edward Connelly, Iliodor, Alfred Hickman, Conway Tearle, Charles Craig, George Deneuburg, R. Paton Gibbs, William E. Shay, Lawrence Johnson, W. Francis Chapin, Peter Barbierre, Ketty Galanta, Pauline Curley, Sonia Marcelle, Nance O'Neil, Charles Edward Russell. ***Her Boy.*** Metro. Director: George Irving. Cast: Effie Shannon, Niles Welch, Pauline Curley, James T. Galloway, Pat O'Malley, William A. Bechtel,

Charles W. Sutton, Charles Riegel, Violet Axzell, Robert Chandler, Ferike Boros. ***His Daughter Pays.*** Piedmont Pictures Corp. Director: Paul Trinchera. Cast: Gertrude McCoy, Pauline Curley, Charles Graham, Johnny Walker. ***The Landloper.*** Yorke-Metro. Director: George Irving. Cast: Harold Lockwood, Pauline Curley, William Clifford, Stanton Heck, Gertrude Maloney, Bert Starkey. ***Lend Me Your Name.*** Yorke-Metro. Director: Fred J. Balshofer. Cast: Harold Lockwood, Pauline Curley, Bessie Eyton, Bert Starkey, Stanton Heck, Peggy Prevost, Harry De Roy. ***Bound in Morocco.*** Famous Players-Lasky. Director: Allan Dwan. Cast: Douglas Fairbanks, Pauline Curley, Edythe Chapman, Tully Marshall, Frank Campeau, Jay Dwiggins, Fred Burns, Albert McQuarrie. **1919: *The Man Beneath.*** Haworth Pictures Corp. Director: William Worthington. Cast: Sessue Hayakawa, Helen Jerome Eddy, Pauline Curley, John Gilbert, Fontaine La Rue, Wedgewood Nowell, Fanny Ridgley. ***The Solitary Sin.*** New Art Film Company. Director: Frederick Sullivan. Cast: Jack Mulhall, Helene Chadwick, Pauline Curley, Anne Schaefer, Edward Cecil, Gordon Griffith, Irene Aldwyn, Kate Lester. ***The Turn in the Road.*** Brentwood Film Corp./Robertson-Cole. Director: King Vidor. Cast: George Nichols, Lloyd Hughes, Winter Hall, Pauline Curley, Helen Jerome Eddy, Ben Alexander, Charles Arling. **1920: *The Invisible Hand.*** Vitagraph (15-chapter serial). Director: William J. Bowman. Cast: Antonio Moreno, Pauline Curley, Brinsley Shaw, Jay Morley, Sam Polo, Gordon Sackville. ***The Veiled Mystery.*** Vitagraph (15-chapter serial). Directors: F. J. Grandon, Webster Cullison, William J. Bowman. Cast: Antonio Moreno, Pauline Curley, H. A. Barrows, Nenette de Courcy, W. L. Rogers, George Cooper. ***The Valley of Tomorrow.*** American Film Corp. Director: Emmett J. Flynn. Cast: William Russell, Mary Thurman, Frank Brownlee, Pauline Curley, Harvey Clark, Jeffrey Sloan. **1920: *Hands Off.*** Fox. Director: George E. Marshall. Cast: Tom Mix, Pauline Curley, Charles K. French, Lloyd Bacon, Frank Clark, Sid Jordan, William McCormick, Virginia Warwick. ***Judge Her Not.*** Harmony/Sunset. Director: George E. Hall. Cast: Jack Livingston, Pauline Curley. **1922: *The Prairie Mystery.*** Bud Osborne Feature Films/Truart Film Corp. Director: George E. Hall. Cast: Bud Osborne, Pauline Curley, Pearl May Norton, Ben Hall, Hazel Evans. ***Border Law.*** Pathé. Directors: Leo Maloney, Ford Beebe. Cast: Leo Maloney, Pauline Curley, Bud Osborne. **1923: *Smoked Out.*** Pathé. Directors: Leo Maloney, Ford Beebe. Cast: Leo Maloney, Pauline Curley. ***Double Cinched.*** Pathé. Directors: Leo Maloney, Ford Beebe. Cast: Leo Maloney, Pauline Curley, Bud Osborne. ***Lost, Strayed or Stolen.*** Pathé. Directors: Leo Maloney, Ford Beebe. Cast: Leo Maloney, Pauline Curley, Tommy Grimes, Bud Osborne. **1924: *The Desert Secret.*** H & B Film Company. Director: Frederick Reel, Jr. Cast: Bill Patton, Pauline Curley. ***Midnight Secrets.*** Robert J. Horner Productions/Rayart. Director: Jack Nelson. Cast: George Larkin, Ollie Kirby, Pauline Curley, Jack Richardson. ***Shackles of Fear.*** J. J. Fleming Productions/Davis Distributing. Director: Al Ferguson. Cast: Al Ferguson, Pauline Curley, Fred Dayton, Les Bates,

Frank Clark, Bert De Vore, Paul Emery. ***The Trail of Vengeance.*** J. J. Fleming Productions/Davis Distributing. Director: Al Ferguson. Cast: Al Ferguson, Pauline Curley. **1925: *His Greatest Battle.*** Aywon. Director: Robert J. Horner. Cast: Jack Randall, Kit Carson, Pauline Curley, Jack Richardson, John Pringle, Gladys Moore. ***Ridin' Wild.*** Aywon. Director: Leon De La Mothe. Cast: Kit Carson, Pauline Curley, Jack Richardson, Walter Maley. ***Cowboy Courage.*** Aywon. Director: Robert J. Horner. Cast: Kit Carson, Pauline Curley, Gordon Sackville. **1926: *Walloping Kid.*** Aywon. Director: Robert J. Horner. Cast: Kit Carson, Jack Richardson, Dorothy Ward, Frank Whitson, Al Kaufman, Jack Herrick, Pauline Curley. ***The Channel Swim.*** Rayart. ***Twin Six O'Brien.*** Aywon. Director: Robert J. Horner. Cast: Kit Carson, Pauline Curley. ***Pony Express Rider.*** Aywon. Director: Robert J. Horner. Cast: Kit Carson, Pauline Curley. ***The Millionaire Orphan.*** Fred Balshofer Productions. Director: Robert J. Horner. Cast: William Barrymore, Jack Richardson, Hal Ferner, Pauline Curley, Rex McIllvaine. ***West of the Rainbow's End.*** Rayart. Director: Bennett Cohn. Cast: Jack Perrin, Pauline Curley, Billy Lamar, Tom London, James Welch, Milburn Morante. ***Prince of the Saddle.*** Fred Balshofer Productions. Cast: Fred Church, Boris Bullock, Pauline Curley. ***Two Fisted Buckaroo.*** Fred Balshofer Productions. Cast: Fred Church, Pauline Curley. **1927: *The Laffin' Fool.*** Rayart. Director: Bennett Cohn. Cast: Jack Perrin, Pauline Curley. ***Thunderbolt's Tracks.*** Rayart. Directors: J. P. McGowan, Bennett Cohn. Cast: Jack Perrin, Pauline Curley, Jack Henderson, Billy Lamar, Harry Tenbrook, Ethan Laidlaw, Ruth Royce. ***Code of the Range.*** Rayart. Directors: Bennett Cohn, Morris R. Schlank. Cast: Jack Perrin, Pauline Curley, Nelson McDowell, Lew Meehan, Chic Olsen. ***Baby Eyes.*** Rayart. **1928: *Devil Dogs.*** Anchor Film Distributors, Crescent Pictures. Director: Fred Windermere. Cast: Alexander Alt, Pauline Curley, Stuart Holmes, Ernest Hilliard, J. P. McGowan. ***Power.*** Pathé. Director: Howard Higgin. Cast: William Boyd, Alan Hale, Jacqueline Logan, Jerry Drew, Joan Bennett, Carole Lombard, Pauline Curley. ***Baby Faces.*** Rayart-Radiant. **1929: *From Now On.*** Rayart-Radiant. ***The Locked Door.*** United Artists. Director: George Fitzmaurice. Cast: Rod La Rocque, Barbara Stanwyck, William Boyd, Betty Bronson, Harry Stubbs, Harry Mestayer, Mack Swain, ZaSu Pitts, George Bunny, Purnell Pratt, Fred Warren, Charles Sullivan, Edgar Dearing, Mary Ashcraft, Violet Bird, Pauline Curley.

6

Billie Dove

A Hollywood columnist, writing in the 1950s, dubbed Billie Dove the Elizabeth Taylor of the 1920s. It didn't matter that she had been out of the business for over 20 years; her reputation was solid. She was undeniably one of the most dazzling personalities of her generation.

Her contemporaries, those who knew her in her heyday, said it best: "She really takes your breath away," columnist Adela Rogers St. Johns; "I have to say Billie Dove was the prettiest woman I have ever seen," Mary Brian; "She was the most beautiful woman in Hollywood," Louis B. Mayer; "The loveliest of all was Billie Dove," screenwriter Anita Loos.

Combine her extraordinary features with the adulation the movie camera had for her — it was said she could be photographed from any angle at equal advantage — and it's easy to understand why movie audiences in the 1920s adored Billie Dove.

In those days, her public lifted her up as "The All-American Beauty" or simply "The Dove." She insisted hers was just another face.

She was a reluctant interview. Just as she had spent most of her career in the silents, she had been equally quiet on her Hollywood career since its abrupt ending over 60 years ago, after *Blondie of the Follies* (1932).

She had been unattainable for an in-depth look into her past. Even during her heyday, she was publicity-shy and avoided interviews and talking about her life to strangers. Over the years, she gave random quotes now and then, but had not sat for anything extensive. The reason she gave me was that she intended to write her own book and was saving her memories for herself.

I telephoned her in early August 1993 with the question: Are you or are you not writing your memoirs? "I'm not writing anything," was her short answer. She offered no more.

"How would you feel about answering some questions" — I avoided that

A 1928 studio portrait of Billie Dove.

sometimes threatening word, "interview"—"about your career?" There again was silence. I continued. "I'd like to know how Florenz Ziegfeld discovered you for his Follies in 1919; your ambitions as a child; your parents' reaction to your being in show business."

"Yes," she answered, encouraging me to continue.

"I'd like to know some of the things you've never talked about. What were some of your experiences as a showgirl? How was it that you left New York for Hollywood in 1922, and how did Ziegfeld react to losing you to the screen?

"I'd like to know how you met your first husband, director Irvin Willat; your first impressions of Hollywood; how you were selected as Douglas Fairbanks' leading lady in *The Black Pirate* [1925] and how you became a star at First National."

I avoided the question interviewers tended to ask first: Did Howard Hughes really pay your husband hundreds of thousands of dollars to divorce you? In fact, I assured her in the beginning that I would refrain from prying into her personal life, particularly the delicate subject of her relationship with Hughes, which I believe contributed to her caution about speaking of her contribution to motion pictures.

She listened patiently, but offered very little during that first phone conversation. "Would you please call back another time? I'm ill with laryngitis."

I waited a couple of weeks and called again in early September. Her voice was raspy, and it obviously strained her to speak. "I'm still sick and couldn't possibly be interviewed now. Would you please call back some other time."

A month later, in early October, I tried a third time. "I'm not well," she replied. "I still have laryngitis and this is not my normal voice, but I'll do the best I can."

What followed was a two-hour conversation and the most complete interview Billie Dove had ever given. (That initial interview, Dove told me later, was done from her kitchen, where she had to stand propped against a kitchen counter, because the phone cord would only reach that far, and there was no place to sit.)

After several more conversations over the next six months, she was no longer the reluctant subject, but freely and often candidly shared parts of her life that had previously been off limits. Every so often she would pause, surprising herself over her revelations. Amused, she would say, "I'm giving you things I've never told anyone."

A year and a half later, in December 1994, I spent the day with Billie Dove at her Rancho Mirage home.* It was during this session, fact-to-face, that she opened up about her relationship with Hughes. Dove, nearing her mid–90s, was in good health and had retained her radiance and stately manner.

We sat together during the early part of the afternoon on the sofa Hughes gave her decades ago and she discussed, often teary-eyed, the bashful billionaire.

We toured her studio, still filled with many of her paintings, and her "memorabilia room" packed with dusty stills and scripts from over half a century ago. She ran two of her pictures on video, *The Marriage Clause* and *Cock of the Air*, giving running commentaries on the production and remembrances of each. Before dinner that evening, she insisted on lighting the candelabra. The ambiance reminded her of the parties and good times at William Randolph Hearst's ranch in San Simeon.

Those were good days, her salad days, and ones to which she continued to cling with the passage of time. "All my life has been interesting, but back in my picture days, I was happy all the time. I was on the screen."

Although Billie Dove was forthcoming about most issues in her life, there were two subjects strictly off limits: the circumstances surrounding her breakup with Hughes and her age. She was particularly vague about dates and years. They were irrelevant, beside the point. She once commented that even her husbands never knew how old she was.

"I simply don't believe that the number of years a person has lived is how old they are. Two people, exactly the same age, can be entirely different. It's what you have absorbed that counts."

Her year of birth, recorded in film encyclopedias over the years, varies from 1900 to 1904. The U. S. Census (the 1920 listing) indicated 1903. A longtime friend insisted it was 1900.

Whatever the date, Billie Dove was born Lillian Bohny on May 14 in New York City. Her parents, Charles and Bertha, were Swiss, and immigrated to the United States during the end of the last century.

Billie and her brother Charles† were raised in what she called a normal household in Washington Heights, far from the theater district and movie studios. "It could have been a million miles away," she said of the show business atmosphere. "We knew nothing about it at all."

**Former president Gerald Ford, Alice Faye and Arthur Lake were her neighbors.*

†Charles Bohny became a cameraman in Hollywood. In 1931, he was employed by Howard Hughes Productions.

The girls in the adjoining apartment buildings gathered in the courtyard on each other's stoops to talk about the films they had seen at the local theaters.* Their aspirations were to get into films. Dove was different from the other girls who shared their dreams; she said nothing to her playmates about her ambitions. It was more than a dream to her; she felt it was destined.

"I knew I was going to be in pictures," she revealed. "There was no doubt about it. I didn't know where or how or when. I didn't want the stage, I wanted motion pictures. It was just taken for granted that I would be an actress. I knew for sure what I would be doing, and I'm not the least bit psychic."

As a child, she appeared in church plays and concentrated on her studies (she was an "A" student). History—not her favorite subject—was enhanced by several European vacations she made with her family as a child.

Word got around the apartment building that she was serious about becoming an actress. A neighbor who worked in movies and was a model for illustrators instructed her mother where to take her to register for work. Soon, she was posing for such magazine illustrators as James Montgomery Flagg, Charles Dana Gibson, Howard Chandler Christy and others, and working as an extra in films.†

"I remember one time I was posing for a cover for the Christmas issue," Dove said of her modeling days. "It was in the middle of summer, and I was dressed in a fur that came up around my neck. I got two dollars for three hours' work. I would save money by walking instead of taking the subway."

There was plenty of time for her to contemplate the future on those walks to the various artists' studios around Washington Square. If she was working, she thought she needed a professional name. She liked "Lillian Swan." Her mother didn't.

Why not combine her childhood nickname, Billie, and the name James Montgomery Flagg gave her, "The Dove." Why not Billie Dove? She agreed with her mother.

"I was so glad for the name because one counters the other," she said. "Dove takes the boyishness out of Billie, and Billie takes the sweetness from Dove. It was a short name, and when you put it on the marquee, you had Billie Dove there and still had room for the title of the picture. It wasn't like Helen Twelvetrees."

When she graduated from grammar school (the eight grade), Dove intended to finish her education at Washington Irving High School. Her father, who didn't approve of show business or anyone revolving in those circles and who felt his daughter might be leaning in that direction, wanted to steer his daughter into a "useful" profession. He intervened and enrolled her in the Eastman-Gaines Business School.

**Billie remembered that the first film she saw was the 1915 serial* The Black Box, *starring Herbert Rawlinson.*

†Billie remembered little of her extra work in the 1910s, but said she appeared frequently in Westerns and in a Mabel Normand film.

Dove, who was taught to obey her parents, agreed, but continued to work, without her father's knowledge, as a model and extra. She was studying at the school when a call came through one day. The man on the phone identified himself as an assistant for Broadway producer Florenz Ziegfeld. He instructed Dove to come to Ziegfeld's office at three P.M. the next afternoon.

Ziegfeld, it seemed, had been struck by a *Saturday Evening Post* advertisement for which she had posed. He ordered his assistant to find the model.

"I'm not sure I had even heard of Florenz Ziegfeld,* Dove said. "When my boyfriend would make some money, we would go down on the subway and get balcony seats for plays. We saw Helen Hayes and Katharine Cornell, but we never saw any musicals."

Dove thought there was no reason to make the appointment when her ultimate goal was to be in the movies. She did not like the idea of being a showgirl. She made every excuse to put Ziegfeld off. Then, before she could think of another reason not to go, it occurred to her that maybe Ziegfeld could help her break into films "the right way."

It was mid–1919, and the theatrical district was stricken with an actors' strike. The "Ziegfeld Follies of 1919" had opened in June, but closed in August when members of the principal cast (Eddie Cantor, Gus Van, John Steele, Johnny and Ray Dooley and Eddie Dowling) failed to appear for the night's performance. The plans were for Dove to be among the replacements for the striking chorus girls not being rehired.

Dove had no idea Ziegfeld's "office" was the New Amsterdam Theater when she arrived that afternoon. She didn't wait long before being summoned to meet the producer. "The next day I went there wearing a very plain dress my mother had made me," she said. "I was with some other girls who were really made up — furs, full makeup, everything. I remember when I was called in, Mr. Ziegfeld stood, took one look at me and sat down again."

Taking it for granted she wanted to be a Follies girl, Ziegfeld talked with her, then sent her two doors down the hall to the office of Ned Wayburn, Ziegfeld's stage director and dance choreographer. Dove followed Ziegfeld's instructions and joined the other young recruits. Wayburn taught the group the "Ziegfeld Walk." Dove remembered him giving instructions: "Stick your head up a little more. Make your hands look like dancer's hands. Your feet are too far apart. Push back your shoulders."

After only three days of classes, Dove realized she was in the wrong place. "I was pretty sick of it. I thought, 'This is really ridiculous.'" She wrote a letter of resignation to Ziegfeld, who immediately summoned her to his office.

"What's the matter?" he asked. "I told him, 'Mr. Ziegfeld, I don't want to

**Florenz Ziegfeld (1867–1932) was one of Broadway's greatest producers of musical comedies and the mastermind behind the long-running "Ziegfeld Follies" review series. Ziegfeld produced such shows as* Sally, Kid Boots, Whoopee *and* Showboat. *He was married to actresses Anna Held and Billie Burke.*

be a chorus girl.'" He was completely understanding, Dove said, and assured her being a showgirl was not his plan for her.

The "Follies of 1919" reopened, and Billie Dove appeared, dressed in a dazzling Ziegfeld costume, sitting midair in a giant hoop. "I smiled just like Vanna White does on *Wheel of Fortune*. They pulled me to the top of the ceiling, while I was being serenaded."

Dove thought, after that night's performance, that she had been introduced to the glamorous world of show business.

"After the show, the girls were coming out in their furs — simply gorgeous — to their chauffeured-driven limousines, where their beaus waited inside. I came down, and I had someone to meet me — my mother. Can you imagine a mother coming down to pick up her daughter from the Ziegfeld Follies? I wanted to go through the floor as fast as possible.

She was young and very naive about life. "I didn't drink nor smoke, and I had made up my mind I would be a virgin when I married — I was," she said.

The other girls in the show knew of her naiveté and protected her from the wolves of the Great White Way. "In the dressing room, I'd listen to them talk about their guys, and some of them were married men. I took no clothes or furs or jewels from any of them myself — I only accepted one gift. I wasn't sleeping with anyone."

Still, Dove said she wasn't a "deadbeat." "I used to go to all their parties. I'd be up all night. It didn't make any difference. I had a good time."

Ziegfeld made Dove one of his "special girls." She wasn't a showgirl, but she did wear the Ziegfeld costumes and she did do the Ziegfeld walk. Whenever there were lines to be delivered in response to Eddie Cantor or other principals, the special girls answered.

Dove was frustrated, however, and kept her resignation letters to Ziegfeld steady. She found the monotony of the shows boring, and she wanted to be in the movies. One complaint was her salary. "You're paying me $50 a week, Mr. Ziegfeld. If that's all I'm worth to you, then I'm not worth anything at all," she said she told him. He raised her salary to $75 and forbade her to disclose the increase to the other girls.

Sensing her restlessness, Ziegfeld placed her in the "Midnight Frolic" of 1919 — that meant more money. The show, held on the roof of the New Amsterdam from midnight to two A.M., had a more intimate appeal than the spectacular Follies productions.

Dove's mother had been a supporter of her daughter's theatrical endeavors. By the time Dove joined the Follies, her parents had separated amiably, and her father wasn't aware of his daughter's work on the stage. "My father always told me that if I ever came upon theatrical people, to get as far away from them as I could. They're bad."

The day came when Dove decided to break the news to her "papa." She told him there was something she wanted to show him, and the two went down to the lobby of the New Amsterdam. They approached the line of photos of Follies players displayed on easels. She pointed them out: Eddie Cantor, Marilyn Miller, W. C. Fields and so on. They came to the last one, a picture of Billie Dove. Her father stared, waiting for an explanation. It was definitely his daughter's picture, with the name Billie Dove underneath.

"Who's Billie Dove and why is your picture there?" he asked her. She explained it was her professional name and that she was pursuing her dream. They left the theater and went to discuss the issue. "He could see I hadn't changed and that I had very definite ideas of my own. Very, very definite."

For the next three years, Dove worked in the Frolics and danced for a brief time in *Sally* which starred Marilyn Miller—"a darling person." She also continued to secretly go to the movie studios during the day for extra work.*

In 1920, Billie did a test for a part in Lillian Gish's upcoming film, *World Shadows.*† She lost to someone else, went home and cried herself to sleep. "That was my big chance, to get to work with Gish," she said.

She appeared in a scene with Elaine Hammerstein and Conway Tearle in *One Week of Love* (1922). One day, as she went to the office to collect a check for some extra work, she met Johnny Hines.§ He asked her if she would make a test for his next picture. She played the female lead—her first big role—in the one-reeler.

Dove appeared as Norman Kerry's girlfriend in *Get-Rich-Quick-Wallingford* (1921) with Sam Hardy and Doris Kenyon. In two Robertson-Cole productions, *At The Stage Door* (1921) and *Beyond the Rainbow* (1922), she earned $50 a week and was required to supply her own clothes. Clara Bow made her film debut in the latter picture. "Clara came in dressed like a kid from the streets," Dove said. "You would have never dreamed she would become the 'It Girl.' She was a great gal."

Dove was in Boston on a personal appearance for Ziegfeld in 1922 when she was approached by a man who told her they were playing *Beyond the Rainbow* across town. He asked her if she would make a personal appearance at the theater the next week. She agreed, but then it was back to New York with little thought of her promise.

The promoter followed up, and Dove went to press agent Nils Granlund with her dilemma. "I said, 'Nils, I couldn't do it. I'd be scared to death.' He told me, 'Now, wait a minute. Do you want to get along in pictures or don't you?' 'All right,' I said, 'you've got me.'"

**Dove was reluctant to disclose her desire to work in the movies because Ziegfeld disliked that side of the business. They were not only competition, but he had lost some of his greatest talents to Hollywood: Mae Murray, W. C. Fields, Marion Davies, Eddie Cantor, Will Rogers, Nita Naldi, Lilyan Tashman and Ina Claire.*

†The producing company folded, and the picture was never made.

§Johnny Hines (1895–1970) was a star comedian in Hollywood silents. His career virtually ended with the coming of sound.

Granlund assisted Dove with her speech and accompanied her and her mother to Boston for the appearance. When they arrived, the party was told that Dove would not have time to go to the hotel to freshen up as planned, that *Beyond the Rainbow* was running at that moment. She was expected to go on stage when the film ended. At the theater, Dove found a mirror hanging from the wall. She removed her hat, combed her hair and redid her face just before the film ended, and she was pushed on stage.

She walked out to meet blinding spotlights that made it impossible to see the front row. She composed herself and began her speech. It went something like this: "You've just seen me on the screen and that was acting. There are no directors here and here is something from my innermost soul." With that, she threw the audience a kiss. "That's not acting."

With their applause, her adoring public spoke, and Dove said it was then that she knew her career in pictures was soon to come.

The personal appearances continued, and Dove soon felt at home on the stage. She was invited to speak to organizations and at luncheons. A northeastern tour of the U. S. was planned for her; however, it was canceled shortly before she was to leave.

Before she could question what was going on, she was told the tour would not take her to the northeast, but to the Deep South and then west to Hollywood, where a year's contract with Metro Pictures Corporation waited for her.

She broke the news to Ziegfeld. She told him she was quitting the Follies to pursue the screen. He was understanding. "There wasn't anything he could say," Dove remembered. "He knew I had something good. He was the kindest man I have ever known."

Throughout the years, Dove's relationship with the famed producer has been the subject of speculation. It has been written that after Ziegfeld's breakup with Marilyn Miller, he continued his extramarital affairs with Dove and actress Jessie Reed. Moreover, it has been written that Ziegfeld's wife, actress Billie Burke, assisted in Dove's abrupt departure to Hollywood in 1922 in order to get her out of town and away from her husband.*

"I read that too," Dove said. "I was so mad ... and surprised. We didn't have any sort of a relationship. I knew nothing about his private life at all. To me, he was Mr. Ziegfeld, the man who ran the show. He never, ever put his hands on me."

The only suggestive remark she remembered Ziegfeld ever making toward her was over some photographs for which he wanted her to pose. Alfred Cheney Johnston, Ziegfeld's photographer, had made some photos of Dove draped only in a thin piece of silk. "I didn't have to wear a bra and you could see exactly how I was built through the silk. One day, Mr. Ziegfeld called me into his office

**This accusation appears in* The Ziegfeld Touch: The Life and Times of Florenz Ziegfeld Jr. *by Richard and Paulette Ziegfeld. (Harry N. Abrams, Inc., Publishers, 1993).*

and told me he wanted me to do another set of photos for him. He wanted me to do Lady Godiva. I said, 'Mr. Ziegfeld, I'm sorry, I will not do it.' I turned around and walked out of his office. Nothing else was ever said about Lady Godiva."

Still, she conceded that Burke might have harbored some resentment, however unwarranted, toward her. "After Mr. Ziegfeld died, Billie Burke came up to me at a party and said, 'You are the only girl in this world I have ever been jealous of.'"

Her contract with Metro, which awaited her on the West Coast, had actually been arranged by an admirer, Joseph Engel, then the manager of Metro Pictures Corporation. "Joe Engel would be on the Roof (where the Frolics were held) all the time — he had his own table. He would send notes back to me and we'd go out after the show to those little places that used to stay open very late into the morning."

Dove claimed she had no knowledge, before leaving New York for Hollywood, of Engel's position at Metro nor that it was he who arranged the career move for her. "I still didn't get the whole gist of it," she said. "I didn't realize he had done it all."

In the spring of 1922, Dove and her mother (brother Charles was enrolled in a military school) sold their belongings and left New York for warm and sunny California.

On a three-day public appearance in Atlanta for *Beyond the Rainbow* (she made subsequent appearances in Birmingham, Memphis and New Orleans), one columnist wrote in a 1922 *Weekly Film Review*, "Atlanta has entertained many stars — some great, some near-great — but not one radiated more genuine charm than this lovely girl who is a star in the making. She has the poise that is the heritage of our metropolitans, she has a grace and ease of manner that is the gift of the gods, but next to her beauty, her joyous, effervescent youth is her richest asset."

Not only did Engel meet Dove and her mother at the California train station, he also made arrangements for them to stay at his home and instructed his assistant to show them around Hollywood and Beverly Hills.

Dove reported to work on *Youth to Youth* (1922), playing a country girl who makes a hit on Broadway. It was during this picture, that Dove claimed to have learned Engel's true feelings for her. "We were sitting one evening in front of the fireplace — Mother was tired and had gone up to bed. He never touched me at all, but he had his arm on my back. We were talking and finally he said to me, 'Billie, I can't ask you to marry me, because I promised my mother, while she was alive, I would only marry a Jewish girl.'"

"Well, I almost went through the floor. Imagine! He had been in love with me all this time and I hadn't known it. I was stunned." It helped Dove to get over her shock and to distance herself from the odd situation when she and a female companion from New York were sent to San Francisco on location for *All the Brothers Were Valiant* (1923), a film about whaling on the high seas.

"The action was to have taken place in the middle of the ocean, so we'd have to get on a real whaling ship," she reminisced. "We'd meet the rest of the crew in the lobby at four o'clock in the morning and someone would take us down to the boat. That ship had the worst odor in the world. We didn't have to catch whales, the other boat did, thank God!"

In the film, Billie played the wife of Malcolm McGregor, who is made captain of the ship after his brother, Lon Chaney, is lost at sea. Director Irvin Willat* was captivated by Dove.

"All the way out there and all the way back and between scenes, all he would say was, 'Marry me, marry me, marry me, marry me, marry me.' That's all I heard, and we were gone for an entire month. Finally, I said yes, just to get him to shut up."

Dove and Willat exchanged vows on October 27, 1923, in Santa Monica, California. Engel was devastated. "It was a tragedy as far as he was concerned," said Dove, "because he was in love with me." Billie didn't work at Metro again for years.†

Willat directed his wife in three films for Paramount: *Wanderer of the Wasteland* (1924), the first major commercial feature to be filmed in Technicolor; *The Air Mail* (1925), a story of mail theft in the skies; and *The Ancient Highway* (1925). Willat was a tough director known for his hot temper, but Dove said he was a great professional and, like John Ford, a man's director.

A far step from her days on the Ziegfeld stage, Dove found herself in Hollywood, riding the range as the leading lady with such stars as Tom Mix, Hoot Gibson, Richard Talmadge, George O'Brien and Jack Holt. In one of the two films she made with Mix, she remembered hanging by one arm from "Tony," Mix's horse, while she tried to catch a train. She was the classic heroine, and it mattered little to her that the work was sometimes dusty, hot and tiresome.

"I didn't think I looked too Western, but I loved making them. My lunch times were spent trying on clothes for the next picture I was going to make. I'd finish a picture one day, and they'd say, 'Where's Billie Dove?' Then, I'd be working on the next picture. It was very hard work, but I loved it."

It was on the location for *Wild Horse Mesa* that she met and became friendly with Zane Grey, the writer on whose story the film was based. Grey gave her a silver ring he had bought from the finger of an Indian woman. During the filming of the picture, Dove placed the ring in a pocket. In the filming of a scene, she lost the treasured piece. "I never forgave myself," she said. "I was so fond of Zane Grey. He told me I was very much like his favorite character. When I wasn't filming a scene, we would go horseback riding together. He was darling."

**Before becoming a director, Willat (1892–1976) had been an actor with Independent Motion Picture Company (IMP) and had appeared in several Mary Pickford films. His career in films spanned from 1910 to the coming of sound. His films tended to emphasize action and adventure.*

†Not counting her appearance in MGM's Blondie of the Follies *(1932), made eight years following the merger of Metro, the Goldwyn Picture Corporation and Louis B. Mayer Pictures.*

It was while on location in Washington with her husband and Jack Holt for *The Ancient Highway* (1925) that Dove received a call from Douglas Fairbanks. "When are you finishing your picture?" he asked. She didn't know. "When you do," he continued, "let me know. I want you to be my next leading lady."

Fairbanks had been testing relatively unknown actresses in Hollywood for the part of his leading lady in his next picture, *The Black Pirate* (1926). He had seen how her magnificent looks were enhanced by Technicolor in *Wanderer of the Wasteland.*

Dove concluded Fairbanks had approached her for two reasons. First, he was planning on Technicolor for *The Black Pirate.* Second, his popularity exceeded hers.

"I certainly wondered, but I didn't ask him why he chose me," Dove said. "I was just thrilled that he did. When I returned from location, they had my clothes and wigs all ready."

Once the production started, Dove discovered Mary Pickford was never far from the action. Then, it might have made her nervous; later, she found it humorous. Pickford, it seemed, was extremely jealous and wouldn't allow Fairbanks to kiss his leading ladies.

"As a matter of fact, I saw the picture recently on my VCR, and in the distance, at the end of the picture, there are two people kissing. It's supposed to be me and Douglas Fairbanks, but it wasn't. It was Mary with my wig on, but you couldn't tell it from that far away."

The role of the princess didn't require much in the way of acting—"I just stood around and looked scared," she said. If it accomplished nothing else for Dove, *The Black Pirate* opened Hollywood's eyes to her potential.

Universal and director Lois Weber took notice and cast her in *The Marriage Clause* (1926). In the film, Dove plays a Broadway star who falls in love with her producer, but is prohibited from marrying him because of a contract clause. It was one of the few good female roles in Hollywood at the time, and Dove was given the opportunity to shine. It proved she not only had the looks, but the talent as well.

Offers came from seemingly every studio in town. Without the assistance of a manager or agent, the actress considered her choices.

"MGM was the one you signed with, because they had all the big stars; however, Norma Shearer was married to Irving Thalberg, and we played the same type of roles. Naturally, she would get the best ones. Joan Crawford was there, and we played the same roles. There were too many girls there, so I skipped them completely." She considered First National and looked at its roster of contract players. "Dick Barthelmess* was fine; Colleen [Moore] and I were friends, and she was a comedienne; so I signed with them."

**It was reported in the press in 1928 that Dove and Barthelmess, at work on separate First National sound stages when a fire broke out in one of the studio's warehouses, raced into the burning buildings in an attempt to save valuable negatives. Asked about the item, Dove said it never happened, that it was only publicity.*

First National assigned her first as a Follies girl who returns to the stage after her husband (Lloyd Hughes) loses his job in *An Affair of the Follies* (1927). She appeared again with Hughes in *The Stolen Bride* and *American Beauty* (both 1927). In *American Beauty*, Dove must choose between a chemist (Hughes) or a wealthy socialite (Walter McGrail)—she chooses Hughes. The title of the film suited its star, and soon the studio was using the name to describe her in its publicity.

Dove was thrilled to be assigned once again with Lois Weber in *Sensation Seekers* (1927), a story—another great woman's role—about a Jazz baby (Billie) who is arrested during a roadhouse raid. Dove was determined to do anything Weber asked, even if it meant learning to smoke for the role of "Egypt" Hagen. "Are you kidding? I didn't even know how to light a cigarette, much less smoke.

"Lois Weber* was so wonderful," Dove exclaimed. "If I had my say in those days the way they do today, I would have had it in my contract that she would direct all my pictures. I thought that much of her. There was an understanding there, and she was so simple to work with."

Dove was a leading contender for the role of Helen of Troy in Alexander Korda's *The Private Life of Helen of Troy* (1928), but Korda insisted his wife Maria Corda play the part. "Everyone thought I was supposed to play the role, and there was a little controversy by other people because I didn't play it. I just shrugged. My philosophy at that time was that, if I wasn't selected for the part, the role wasn't meant for me. It was that simple. It didn't make any difference."

Korda kept Dove in mind, however, and showcased her in four of his films: *The Stolen Bride* (1927), *The Yellow Lily* (1928), *The Night Watch* (1928) (the first film she made after First National's merge with Warner Brothers) and *Her Private Life* (1929). "Korda was, in my opinion, an excellent director," she said.

Because of her good looks and statue in films, Dove played opposite some of Hollywood's most dashing leading men: Douglas Fairbanks, Lloyd Hughes, Gilbert Roland, Rod LaRocque, Antonio Moreno, George O'Brien, Edmund Lowe and others. How did her husband feel about constantly seeing his wife in the arms of another man?

"He was not jealous of anyone; he had no reason to be," she said emphatically. "He believed me when I told him I could never fall in love with my leading men. I liked all of my leading men—all of them. However, the moment they would come over to the mirror and powder their noses, that was it. I could never fall for that."

While the merger of the two studios was taking place, Hollywood was in the midst of a revolution: talkies. Many stars cringed in fear at the thought of making the transition. Not Billie Dove. "I never had fear of anything. It didn't matter to me if films were silents or talkies. We just didn't think talkies would last—I didn't."

**Lois Weber (1881–1939) was a former concert pianist when she entered films, first as an actress in the early 1910s. She co-starred with her husband Phillips Smalley in many early films. She turned to directing in 1913 and later became the world's highest-paid female director. Her themes frequently dealt with women's issues. Her success ended with the silent era.*

Top: Armand Kaliz, Billie Dove and Gilbert Roland in ***The Love Mart*** (1927). (Courtesy of Roi Uselton.) ***Bottom:*** A ***New York Times*** reviewer wrote that Billie Dove (***left***) and Lilyan Tashman appeared to be vying for the low-cut gown prize in ***The Stolen Bride*** (1927).

Talkies, they learned, were more than just a fad. One day, Warner Brothers called Dove in for a voice test, to see how her voice registered for sound. It was a "very, very long an grueling test," she said. When the test was finished, studio executives tore up her contract (she had one year remaining) and signed her for two additional years. She had passed the test for sound.

If there was any doubt of her potential in talking pictures, they were dashed by her appearance in the part-talkie *Careers* (1929). The scene during which Dove pleads with Noah Beery for the sake of her husband (Antonio Moreno) was the talk of the lot for days, she said.

"We started shooting, and I cried throughout the scene. Beery was leering at me, and I was trying to save my husband. I was begging and pleading with him, and I was trying so hard." The director (J. Francis Dillon) allowed the scene to continue for ten minutes. When it was over, everyone applauded her performance. "Print it," a satisfied Dillon said as he left the set.

The critics were less impressed with her performance. "Miss Dove talks and screams, moving the Strand audience to a derisive laughter at a moment when she's using an intense barrage of histrionics," wrote a *New York Times* reviewer.

Dove went into talkies with ease, although many of her early talking films were programmers, and far below the standards of her silent films. Her looks compensated for the often poorly written scripts and technical deficiencies in early talkies.

Not only was 1929 a rather disappointing year professionally, but her personal life was also in turmoil. She had married Irvin Willat in 1923, but said she had not been prepared for a "sit-down" marriage.

"I didn't love Irvin in the real sense of the word," she admitted. "I didn't know what true love was. I didn't realize it until a few years after we were married. I realized then it wasn't the kind of love you have in a family with the person you live with.

"He'd go on location and I would pack his things for him and I'd put in a little note that said, 'I love you,' but I didn't mean that kind of love."

Because of her feelings (or lack thereof) for Willat, as well as the momentum of her career, Dove made the decision not to have children during the marriage. "If you were in motion pictures," she said, "you could be married; but if you had a baby, you were no longer considered romantic. Therefore, a baby was out of the question for me."

Dove and Willat separated permanently in September 1929. She went to live with her mother and clung to the support of friends, fellow actresses who comprised the "Our Girls" group.* Ruth Roland and Marion Davies were two of her closest friends.

**Some of the actresses who comprised the "Our Girls" club (and who were some of Billie's closest friends) were Virginia Valli, Laura La Plante, Gloria Hope, Virginia Fox, May McAvoy, Claire Windsor, Patsy Ruth Miller, Lois Wilson and Carmel Myers.*

Dove gave an engagement party for Roland* and Ben Bard in 1929 and was a bridesmaid at the wedding. She also spent a lot of time with Davies and her companion, William Randolph Hearst, the newspaper magnate, at her beach house in Santa Monica and at the Hearst Castle in San Simeon.

Dove never called Hearst's "Enchanted Hill" a castle. To her, it was always "The Ranch." "I spent a lot of time there, and it's funny, but Mr. Hearst — that's what I always called him — always treated me as though I was doing him a favor by coming. For a time, it was my second home. The ranch was a wonderful place."

Hearst was a kind and gentle man, said Dove, but he had strict rules for those enjoying the comforts of his estate. His guests were required to attend lunch and dinner, to give the right of way to his menagerie of animals, to respect the masterpiece he had built† and to refrain from excess alcohol.

"You'd drive up the road leading to the main house at 15 miles per hour, because there were animals all around," Dove said. "If there was a buffalo in the road, you'd wait until it decided to get up and move. If we went horseback riding, you'd have to really watch out for the ostriches, because they didn't like the horses."

Hearst particularly enjoyed horseback riding. Dove once accompanied a group of about 16 on an overnight riding expedition over the mountains and through the valleys of his vast estate. "We got on our horses and rode a certain distance with only a toothbrush, comb and the clothes on our backs. We got to a place where his men had built a tremendous fire and had prepared a feast for us. We slept in tents and bathed the best we could the next morning. There was no path back to the ranch, but he seemed to know the way. It took us five hours to get back. Hearst led the way, then Marion and the rest of us."

Marion Davies, said Dove, was petrified of the horses and found such excursions grueling. "Marion would get along as best she could. Pretty soon, she'd get terrified and would slowly back up the horse. She'd get out of line and let herself go back to Harry Crocker,§ who always carried a flask. When she came back, he knew to give her some whiskey or liquor until she got herself

**Billie was shocked in 1934 when Roland (1892–1937) filed a lawsuit against her (for over $25,000) after Dove's police dog bit Roland on the arm. The veteran actress and serial queen told the press her arm was so severely mangled, she would be unable to keep her screen and concert engagements. "Ruth wanted to give me a baby shower. That's the reason she had come over to the house. My husband had bought me a dog for protection. When she got there, he was sitting by the door and Ruth was afraid to get out of the car. Finally, she got up her nerve and got out. That made him suspicious. He jumped her and bit her on the arm. He wasn't serious about attacking her, or he would have gone for the neck." Roland who had invested wisely, was a multi-millionaire. "That's what I don't understand," said Dove. "She didn't need the money. It sounded terrible when it came out in the papers, but Ruth asked me first if we were insured before she sued. She was one, I think, who really liked money."*

†Hearst found little humor in a practical joke several guests played by dressing some of the statuary in women's lingerie. Dove, who witnessed the incident, said the two jokers were never invited back.

§Harry Crocker (1893–1958) was an actor and Hearst crony, often working as his (Hearst's) personal assistant.

together and could make it. When she couldn't stand it again, she'd go back. When we got back to the house, Hearst told Marion he understood and that he would never ask her to go riding again."

Hearst discouraged excessive drinking — those who became intoxicated were not invited back — but knew of his Marion's addiction. "There was nothing that escaped him. Of course he knew it," said Dove. "We had wine or champagne with dinner and some type of liquor afterwards. That was it. However, the girls had to go to the johnnie quite a lot, because Marion had a special butler who always stocked it with champagne. Hearst never said a word about it, but he knew."

Dove also knew of Davies' problem with the bottle, but said she never saw her intoxicated at the ranch. "I did later, however, after Hearst had died. She was coming out of a hotel and two men were holding her up. I wanted so badly to go over and say, 'Marion, stop it!' But, it was none of my business. She was too far along with it and died not long after."*

In addition to being a friend, Marion Davies played another role in Dove's life late in 1929: that of a matchmaker. It was she who introduced Dove to Howard Hughes during a Mayfair Ball at the Biltmore Hotel.

"Marion came over with Howard and said, 'Billie, Howard Hughes asked to meet you.' I smiled, but he never smiled at all. He just glared. He was shy, but there was something on his mind. At that time, he was making *Hell's Angels.*†"

Dove was at first unimpressed by the billionaire film producer. They didn't seem to have anything to talk about, nothing in common. "He would just glare at me. He didn't talk or anything. I thought of him as a zombie."

It became more than a coincidence when Howard began showing up wherever Dove went. "Knowing him later, I have an idea he had me cased. Every time I would be at a place where there was dancing, pretty soon the door would open and there would stand Howard. He'd look around, spot the table I was at, make a bee-line for me and pull up a chair and stay the whole evening. As I got to know him, I realized what a brilliant man he was, how perfectly sweet he was."

The two soon became inseparable, and it wasn't long before Hollywood was buzzing with the romance. Dove and Hughes offered no public statements. Both being rather shy, increasingly so under public scrutiny, they remained discreet, preferring to spend their evenings alone in the privacy of their own homes, which were about a mile apart. After all, both were still legally married.

One place they could be totally isolated from the public was the open sea.

**Marion Davies died of cancer in 1961.*

†Howard Hughes (1905–1976) began investing some of the profits of Hughes Tool Company in motion pictures in the mid–1920s. Among the early pictures he produced were Two Arabian Nights *(1927),* The Front Page *(1931) and* Scarface *(1932). He made a name for himself as director-producer of* Hell's Angels *(1930). At the time he met Billie, Howard was married to Ella Rice.*

When neither was working, they chartered a yacht and traveled to Santa Catalina Island for the weekend. Usually, they would anchor near the island, take a dinghy to Avalon and ride two horses, kept for them on the island, deep into the surrounding mountains. "We just wanted to be alone together," Dove said.

On one weekend excursion, Hughes suggested that, instead of going ashore, they meet some of his friends on their yacht. Dove said she felt the idea peculiar, as Hughes usually liked to be alone. The 200-foot boat, with a crew of 60, was named "Hilda." "It was an absolutely beautiful boat," she said. "It even had a baby grand piano. Howard asked me what I thought about it. I told him it was beautiful. He said, 'Okay, it's yours.' That's the way he was."

Rather than officially rename the boat, which was considered bad luck, they simply called it "Rodeo," after the role Dove was currently playing in the film *The Painted Angel* (1929).

By late 1929, the relationship, said Dove, had grown into "deep love and affection." Had they been free, she was sure they would have wed immediately. "Howard wanted to get married right away. We were very much in love, but he was only halfway through his divorce, and I was still Mrs. Irvin Willat."

Still, they planned their lives together. In February 1930, First National denied rumors Dove was leaving the studio. They insisted she would fulfill her remaining two years and would begin filming *Devil's Playground* within three weeks. By the end of April, however, the studio issued a statement confirming the industry's suspicions: Billie Dove bought her contract from the studio and announced she was taking an extended vacation before signing with another company.

In truth, it was Hughes, wanting exclusive rights to his new love, who purchased the contract for $250,000. He quickly signed her to a personal contract (five films at $85,000 each) to his production company, the Caddo Company, Inc.

So far, the stubborn Willat had not budged from his refusal to grant his wife a divorce. Knowing, however, of Hughes' wealth and his apparent willingness to stop at nothing to possess his wife, Willat finally agreed to grant the divorce, in exchange for $325,000.

In her suit, Dove charged Willat with "extreme cruelty." Her complaint mentioned his ungovernable temper, and she testified he had twice knocked her down in the presence of guests. When questioned about the matter by this author, Dove vehemently denied any physical abuse.

"I was very much against the idea of paying the money to Irvin," said Dove. "I begged Howard not to do it, but he did. After that, I lost all the respect I had for Irvin Willat."

While the divorce was expensive for Hughes, it also cost Dove. She never told about the money (it accumulated to about $40,000) she gave Willat in 1928, when he needed money to close a deal to purchase an apartment house. "So, it cost me 'that' much," she said.

Billie Dove and Kenneth Thomson embrace in *The Other Tomorrow* (1930). (Courtesy of Roi Uselton.)

Hell's Angels opened at Grauman's Chinese Theater with much fanfare in June 1930. Dove and Hughes arrived arm-in-arm for the premiere. "We sneaked in a side door early in order to avoid the crowds. We sat on the back row, so no one would recognize us, and then we slipped out before the picture was finished." From there, they went a couple of blocks down Hollywood Boulevard to the Montmartre Cafe, where Dove hosted a post-premiere party.

Several days later, in early July, the two boarded a train and were off to New York City for the East Coast premiere. From there, they traveled to Europe for an extended vacation, as well as to confer with a renowned physician in Czechoslovakia over Hughes' worsening loss of hearing.

"We had a lot of hope that the doctor, who was one of the best, could do something for him, but it was hopeless. His Uncle Rupert wore a hearing aid, but Howard wouldn't. He could hear well on an airplane and telephone. But, when we'd go to a party, I'd have to tell him what was happening. He could understand me, because I knew how to regulate my voice for him."

While traveling with Hughes over Europe that summer, Dove became aware of his obsessive compulsion over germs and cleanliness. Before he decided on a hotel, Hughes insisted on inspecting the bathrooms. "If they were slightly dirty, he would say, 'No, we're nothing staying here,'" she recounted. "I remember there was this one hotel in Paris that was just opening. That one he liked; it hadn't been used."

Dove returned to Hollywood to work on two films for Caddo: *The Age for*

Love (1931) and *Cock of the Air* (1932). The latter cast her as a French temptress in love with an American aviator (Chester Morris). The film was considered risqué for 1932.

"Will Hays* cut about 800 feet from the film, so it was hard to tell where we were and what was happening. It made no sense the way they released it. I don't know if my dresses were cut too low or not — that's what they wrote, but Chester Morris' character in the film chased me around throughout the picture."

While Hollywood was sure wedding bells were in store for Billie Dove and Howard Hughes, by the time *Cock of the Air* was released in January 1932, all hopes were squelched. Their relationship had unraveled and the two couldn't see each other face-to-face; instead, Hughes wired Dove of his enthusiasm over the film's final outcome. After two films for Caddo, Dove's contract was settled for $100,000.

The specifics surrounding their breakup remained a mystery. "That's something I don't tell anyone," Dove said. "It wasn't another man or woman. We were not quarreling when we separated. It was trivial, over the most infinitesimal thing imaginable."

Hughes' possessiveness and infidelity were certainly enough to strain the relationship. "At the time I knew him, Howard was not the womanizer he later became.† He was the jealous type and was possessive of me." It had been rumored that Hughes had a brief romance with Jean Harlow while working on *Hell's Angels* and that Dove put an end to the fling. Also, George Raft told his biographer§ years later that Hughes almost discovered him in an uncompromising position with Dove at the Ambassador Hotel while he was filming Hughes' *Scarface*. Dove herself brought up the accusation during the course of conversation and said simply, "Someone told a terrible lie about me in their book, and I was so mad when I read it."

For whatever reason, the breakup was painful for both, said Dove. "We both carried torches for a long, long time."

Dove and Hughes saw each other several times over the years, once in San Simeon and again in New York. "At the ranch, he asked me if he could fly me home. I told him it wasn't a good idea, that I should go back on the train with those I had come. Then, in New York, he asked if we could have lunch. Instead of going out where the press would have been on us again, we had lunch in my hotel suite. We talked about a lot of things, but we never discussed us."

During my visit with Dove, the question was asked if she had ever thought

**The Hays Office, named for Will H. Hays (1879–1954), created in 1930 the Motion Picture Production Code, self-regulatory laws governing the contents of motion pictures.*

†After Billie, Howard Hughes dated scores of Hollywood actresses: Ginger Rogers, Rita Hayworth, Katharine Hepburn, Yvonne De Carlo and a host of others. He was married to actress Jean Peters (b. 1926) from 1957–1971. The starlet Terry Moore also insists she and Hughes were married secretly in 1949 and were never divorced.

§George Raft *by Lewis Yablonsky, McGraw Hill, 1974.*

of how her life might have been different had she married Howard Hughes. She brushed it off with an, "I don't know" response, but by the evening she had given the idea some thought. "I've often wondered over the years. We might have had children together, but only after I got out of pictures. It might have worked. Of course, I have no way of knowing."

After her split from Howard Hughes, Dove was a frequent date of New York Mayor Jimmy Walker. Although the press gave much coverage to their relationship, Dove insisted they were only friends. "We weren't steady dates, we just went out once in a while. Monday nights were the big nights at the Palace, and he would pick me up in his limousine. We would sit in the back and hold hands, but we were just good friends. He had a police escort to the theater. When we'd walk down the aisle, everyone would applaud us as we were seated. The people just loved him. He had a wonderful sense of humor and loved practical jokes."

One of the gags Dove played on Walker centered around a date he had with Pola Negri. "Pola was just a little bit older than me and I liked her, but when I found out about his date with her, I sent him a pair of crutches. He howled over that."

Getting herself back into the social scene was just part of her plan to ease the pain of leaving perhaps the greatest love of her life behind her. She also went back to work.

Dove accepted an offer to appear with long-time pal Marion Davies in *Blondie of the Follies* (1932). It should have been a pleasant experience for her to work with Davies and Hearst (who oversaw Marion's films), but she was so disappointed over the experience that she originally declined to discuss the film.

Later, she decided to set the record straight, but was still so ashamed of the film's outcome that she implored me to never see the film. "It was truly a heartbreaking experience," she said.

Dove's association with *Blondie of the Follies* began at a 1932 birthday party (in May) columnist Louella Parsons threw for her. During the festivities, director Edmund Goulding approached her with an offer to appear in a film with Davies and Robert Montgomery.

"I told him I thought it was silly, that all of us were stars in our own right — they didn't have all-star casts in those days — and why should we all work together?" She declined the offer.

Irving Thalberg, MGM's head of production, intervened. In fact, Dove said, he twisted her arm, asking, "Billie, will you do me a favor and read this script?" Dove agreed, went home and realized the part of Lottie Callahan had been written for her. "I couldn't get to the phone fast enough. 'You've got your gal,' I told him. It was the most wonderful part I have ever read."

The picture, centering around the Follies rivalry between Dove and Marion Davies, was filmed from mid–June to mid–July 1932. Before the last scene,

Hearst ordered a halt to the production. The cast and crew gathered in the projection room, and the film was run.

"After it was over, there was dead silence," said Dove. "We didn't dare say anything. We just sat there. Finally, from this big man with a small voice came, 'Well, it's a good Billie Dove picture.' I knew it was. I had given a damned good performance."

Hearst, financing Davies pictures at MGM, demanded her films showcase her in the best light. He stopped the *Blondie* production for ten days, ordered scenes rewritten to favor Davies and brought the cast back for entire retakes of scenes.

As the production continued, it became apparent to Dove that Hearst, in his attempt to favor his mistress, was making Dove the villain. "I had never played a heavy in my life," she said. In one scene, Davies is supposed to miss Dove's grip in a dance routine and tumble into the orchestra pit. In the final cut, Dove said a close-up shot of two hands (supposedly hers) was edited into the reel, making it appear as though Dove pushed Davies off the stage.

"It broke my heart," said Dove. "If you put the two films together, they were entirely two different stories. I realized too late that I should not have done the picture. I should have known better. After all, it was Hearst's money. It was my own fault."

If it had been anyone else, Dove said, she would have sued over the drastic script changes that completely altered her part. "I couldn't sue Marion and Mr. Hearst; they were friends of mine."

Dove went with an escort to a screening of the final version of *Blondie of the Follies*. Midway through the film, she turned to her beau. "Let's go. I've had it," she said she told him. "I never saw the end of it. I couldn't bear it."

Despite her hurt over the film, Dove said it had no effect on her friendship with Davies. The subject was never discussed.

Dove insisted her abrupt retirement from films after *Blondie of the Follies* had nothing to do with her disappointment over the picture. In fact, she said that at the time she had no idea this would be her last film. It just seemed that no other projects materialized for her. "Also, I thought I had attained everything I wanted to attain. I was still in my 20s (or early 30s), and I wanted to do like other people. I wanted a family."

Dove explained her retirement to a reporter in 1962: "I had seen some of the other girls try to hang on to their careers after they had started to slide. I vowed that would never happen to me."

With her career behind her, Dove married millionaire Robert Kenaston in May 1933. They had met on a ship while returning from New York. A son, Robert Jr., was born in April, 1934, and they adopted a girl, Gail, in 1937. As Mrs. Kenaston, the former film star took college courses over the years, painted and played golf. She was also busy raising her family and maintaining a household.

Billie Dove signed this photo to her fan club president, Lenore Heidorn, in the early 1930s. The inscription reads, "To you, Lenore, from me." (Courtesy of Lenore H. Foote.)

In the late 1950s, her son Bob considered becoming an actor; however, after small parts in several films, he decided the profession wasn't for him.*

Dove made headlines in 1962 when she entered and won a contest in which she supplied the missing line for a jingle exploiting Columbia's *Gidget Goes Hawaiian* (1962). She won a trip to Hawaii and a chance to appear in *Diamond Head* (1962), being filmed on the islands. She refused to play the role, but agreed to a token appearance in a luau scene, just to keep the winning honest.

Dove was widowed in 1973, and in that year, she married (and divorced) John Miller, an architect.

She lived quietly in her sprawling Rancho Mirage, California, home until 1996, when she went to live in an area retirement home in Rancho Mirage. In 1997, she relocated to the Motion Picture Country House in Woodland Hills. She died there on December 31, 1997, of pneumonia. Her obits gave her age as 97.

The details of her personal and professional life were private to her, and it was never easy for "outsiders" to persuade her to speak. She had good intentions of writing her memoirs over the years, but as she said, "there's not enough time now." This conclusion figured greatly into her decision to give this interview.

Of her films, she said her best work was done in *The Marriage Clause*, and that its director, Lois Weber, was her favorite.

In addition to her work in films, one must consider her legendary beauty. It is the conclusion of some film historians that it is for her beauty, not her talent, that she will be remembered. It was Dove's opinion that her looks were never a hindrance.

"Why should they have been? I think many people have proven otherwise," she said. "Don't you agree that other people who are absolutely beautiful have made successes by their wonderful acting? I do. One doesn't necessarily have to be beautiful."

**Bob Kenaston, Jr., died of cancer in 1995.*

Still, the story has persisted for generations that, in those days, if you stopped any man on the street and asked him who the most beautiful woman in the world was, he would give the name Billie Dove.

"I don't like to repeat that," Dove said. "It sounds like I'm bragging, but that's what they said. I did have that reputation. To be honest with you, I never thought I was particularly pretty, no prettier than any one else. I just thought of myself as one of the girls."

FILMOGRAPHY

1921: ***Get-Rich-Quick Wallingford.*** Paramount/Cosmopolitan. Director: Frank Borzage. Cast: Sam Hardy, Norman Kerry, Doris Kenyon, Diana Allen, Edgar Nelson, Billie Dove. ***At the Stage Door.*** Robertson-Cole. Director: Christy Cabanne. Cast: Frances Hess, Elizabeth North, Miriam Battista, Billie Dove, Margaret Foster, William Collier, Jr., C. Elliott Griffin, Myrtle Maughan, Charles Craig, Viva Ogden, Billy Quirk, Huntly Gordon, Doris Eaton. **1922:** ***Polly of the Follies.*** First National. Director: John Emerson. Cast: Constance Talmadge, Horace Knight, Thomas Carr, Harry Fisher, Kenneth Harlan, James Gleason, George Fawcett, Ina Rorke, Theresa Maxwell Conover, Billie Dove, John Daly Murphy. ***One Week of Love.*** Selznick. Director: George Archainbaud. Cast: Elaine Hammerstein, Conway Tearle, Billie Dove, Kate Lester, Hallam Cooley. ***Beyond the Rainbow.*** Robertson-Cole. Director: Christy Cabanne. Cast: Harry Morey, Billie Dove, Virginia Lee, Diana Allen, James Harrison, Macey Harlam, Rose Coghlan, George Fawcett, Walter Miller, Clara Bow, Huntly Gordon. ***Youth to Youth.*** Metro. Director: Emile Chautard. Cast: Billie Dove, Edythe Chapman, Hardee Kirkland, Sylvia Ashton, Jack Gardner, Cullen Landis, ZaSu Pitts, Lincoln Stedman, Noah Beery. **1923:** ***All the Brothers Were Valiant.*** Metro. Director: Irvin Willat. Cast: Malcolm McGregor, Billie Dove, Lon Chaney, William H. Orlamond, Robert McKim, Robert Kortman, Otto Brower, Curt Rehfeld, William V. Mong, Leo Willis, Shannon Day. ***Madness of Youth.*** Fox. Director: Jerome Storm. Cast: John Gilbert, Billie Dove, Donald Hatswell, George K. Arthur, Ruth Boyd, Julanne Johnston. ***Soft Boiled.*** Fox. Director: John G. Blystone. Cast: Tom Mix, Joseph Girard, Billie Dove, L. C. Shumway, Tom Wilson. ***The Lone Star Ranger.*** Fox. Director: Lambert Hillyer. Cast: Tom Mix, Billie Dove, L. C. Shumway, Stanton Heck. ***The Thrill Chaser.*** Universal. Director: Edward Sedgwick. Cast: Hoot Gibson, Billie Dove, James Neill, William E. Lawrence. **1924:** ***On Time.*** Truart Film Co. Director: Henry Lehrman. Cast: Richard Talmadge, Billie Dove, Stuart Holmes, George Siegmann, Tom Wilson. ***Try and Get It.*** PDC. Director: Cullen Tate. Cast: Bryant Washburn, Billie Dove, Edward Everett Horton, Joseph Kilgour, Lionel Belmore. ***Yankee Madness.*** FBO. Director: George Plympton. Cast: Billie Dove, George Larkin, Walter Long, Earl Schenck, Ollie Kirby, Arthur Millett. ***Wanderer of the Wasteland.*** Paramount. Director:

Irvin Willat. Cast: Jack Holt, Billie Dove, Noah Beery, George Irving, Kathlyn Williams, James Mason, Richard R. Neill, James Gordon. ***The Roughneck.*** Fox. Director: John Conway. Cast: George O'Brien, Billie Dove, Harry T. Morey, Cleo Madison, Charles A. Sellon, Anne Cornwall, Harvey Clark, Maryon Aye. ***The Folly of Vanity.*** Fox. Director: Henry Otto. Cast: Jack Mulhall, Billie Dove, Betty Blythe, John Sainpolis, Fred Becker, Otto Matiesen, Edna Mae Cooper. **1925: *The Air Mail.*** Paramount. Director: Irvin Willat. Cast: Warner Baxter, Billie Dove, Mary Brian, Douglas Fairbanks, Jr., George Irving, Richard Tucker, Guy Oliver, Lee Shumway, John Webb Dillon. ***Light of the Western Stars.*** Paramount. Director: William K. Howard. Cast: Jack Holt, Billie Dove, Noah Beery, Alma Bennett, William Scott, George Nichols, Mark Hamilton, Robert Perry, Eugene Pallette. ***The Lucky Horseshoe.*** Fox. Director: John G. Blystone. Cast: Tom Mix, Billie Dove, Malcolm Waite, J. Farrell MacDonald, Clarissa Selwynne, Ann Pennington. ***Wild Horse Mesa.*** Paramount. Director: George B. Seitz. Cast: Jack Holt, Billie Dove, Noah Beery, Douglas Fairbanks, Jr., George Magrill, George Irving, Edith Yorke, Margaret Morris. ***The Fighting Heart.*** Fox. Director: John Ford. Cast: George O'Brien, Billie Dove, J. Farrell MacDonald, Victor McLaglen, Diana Miller, Bert Woodruff, Francis Ford. ***The Ancient Highway.*** Paramount. Director: Irvin Willat. Cast: Jack Holt, Billie Dove, Montagu Love, Stanley Taylor, Lloyd Whitlock, William A. Carroll, Marjorie Bonner. **1926: *The Black Pirate.*** United Artists. Director: Albert Parker. Cast: Douglas Fairbanks, Billie Dove, Donald Crisp, Sam de Grasse, Tempe Piggott, Anders Randolph, Charles Stevens, John Wallace. ***The Lone Wolf Returns.*** Columbia. Director: Ralph Ince. Cast: Bert Lytell, Billie Dove, Freeman Wood, Gustav von Seyffertitz, Gwen Lee, Alphonse Ethier. ***The Marriage Clause.*** Universal. Director: Lois Weber. Cast: Billie Dove, Francis X. Bushman, Warner Oland, Henry La Garde, Grace Darmond, Carolynne Snowden, Oscar Smith. ***Kid Boots.*** Paramount. Director: Frank Tuttle. Cast: Eddie Cantor, Clara Bow, Billie Dove, Lawrence Gray, Natalie Kingston, Malcolm Waite, William Worthington, Harry von Meter, Fred Esmelton. **1927: *An Affair of the Follies.*** First National. Director: Millard Webb. Cast: Billie Dove, Lewis Stone, Lloyd Hughes, Arthur Stone, Arthur Hoyt, Bertram Marburgh. ***The Tender Hour.*** First National. Director: George Fitzmaurice. Cast: Ben Lyon, Billie Dove, Montagu Love, Alec B. Francis, Constantine Romanoff, Laska Winter, T. Roy Barnes, Charles A. Post, Anders Randolph, Frank Elliott, Lionel Belmore, Lon Poff, Yola d'Avril. ***The Stolen Bride.*** First National. Director: Alexander Korda. Cast: Billie Dove, Lloyd Hughes, Armand Kaliz, Frank Beal, Lilyan Tashman, Cleve Moore. ***American Beauty.*** First National. Director: Richard Wallace. Cast: Billie Dove, Lloyd Hughes, Walter McGrail, Margaret Livingston, Lucien Prival, Al St. John, Edythe Chapman, Alice White, Yola d'Avril. ***The Love Mart.*** First National. Director: George Fitzmaurice. Cast: Billie Dove, Gilbert Roland, Raymond Turner, Noah Beery, Armand Kaliz, Emile Chautard, Boris Karloff. ***Sensation Seekers.*** Universal. Director: Lois Weber. Cast: Billie Dove, Huntly Gordon, Raymond Bloomer, Peggy Montgomery, Will Gregory,

Helen Gilmore, Edith Yorke, Phillips Smalley, Nora Cecil. **1928: *Heart of a Follies Girl.*** First National. Director: J. Francis Dillon. Cast: Billie Dove, Larry Kent, Lowell Sherman, Clarissa Selwynne, Mildred Harris. ***The Yellow Lily.*** First National. Director: Alexander Korda. Cast: Billie Dove, Clive Brook, Gustav von Seyffertitz, Marc MacDermott, Nicholas Soussanin, Eugenie Besserer, Jane Winton, Charles Puffy. ***The Night Watch.*** First National. Director: Alexander Korda. Cast: Billie Dove, Paul Lukas, Donald Reed, Nicholas Soussanin, Nicholas Bela, George Periolat, William Tooker, Anita Garvin. ***Adoration.*** First National. Director: Frank Lloyd. Cast: Antonio Moreno, Billie Dove, Emile Chautard, Lucy Dorraine, Nicholas Bela, Nicholas Soussanin, Winifred Bryson, Lucien Prival. **1929: *Careers.*** First National. Director: J. Francis Dillon. Cast: Billie Dove, Antonio Moreno, Thelma Todd, Noah Beery, Holmes Herbert, Carmel Myers, Robert Frazer, Andre de Segurola, Robert Schable, Robert T. Haines, Crauford Kent. ***The Man and the Moment.*** First National. Director: George Fitzmaurice. Cast: Billie Dove, Rod La Rocque, Gwen Lee, Robert Schable, Charles Sellon, George Bunny. ***Her Private Life.*** First National. Director: Alexander Korda. Cast: Billie Dove, Walter Pidgeon, Holmes Herbert, Montagu Love, Thelma Todd, Roland Young, Mary Forbes, Brandon Hurst, ZaSu Pitts. ***The Painted Angel.*** First National. Director: Millard Webb. Cast: Billie Dove, Edmund Lowe, George MacFarlane, Cissy Fitzgerald, J. Farrell MacDonald, Norman Selby, Nellie Bly Baker. **1930: *The Other Tomorrow.*** First National. Director: Lloyd Bacon. Cast: Billie Dove, Kenneth Thomson, Grant Withers, Frank Sheridan, William Granger, Otto Hoffman, Scott Seaton. ***A Notorious Affair.*** First National. Director: Lloyd Bacon. Cast: Billie Dove, Basil Rathbone, Kay Francis, Montagu Love, Kenneth Thomson, Philip Strange, Gino Corrado, Elinor Vandivere. ***The Lady Who Dared.*** First National. Director: William Beaudine. Cast: Billie Dove, Sidney Blackmer, Conway Tearle, Judith Vosselli, Cosmo Kyrle Bellew, Ivan Simpson, Lloyd Ingraham. ***Sweethearts and Wives.*** First National. Director: Clarence Badger. Cast: Billie Dove, Clive Brook, Sidney Blackmer, Crauford Kent, Leila Hyams, John Loder, Fletcher Norton, Albert Gran, Alphonse Martell, Rolfe Sedan. ***One Night at Susie's.*** First National. Director: J. Francis Dillon. Cast: Douglas Fairbanks, Jr., Billie Dove, Helen Ware, Tully Marshall, James Crane, John Loder, Claude Fleming. **1931: *The Age For Love.*** Howard Hughes/Caddo/United Artists. Director: Frank Lloyd. Cast: Billie Dove, Edward Everett Horton, Mary Duncan, Charles Starrett, Betty Ross Clarke, Adrian Morris, Lois Wilson. **1932: *Cock of the Air.*** Howard Hughes/Caddo/United Artists. Director: Tom Buckingham. Cast: Billie Dove, Chester Morris, Matt Moore, Walter Catlett, Katya Sergevia, Yola d'Avril, Vivien Oakland, Emile Chautard. **1933: *Blondie of the Follies.*** MGM. Director: Edmund Goulding. Cast: Marion Davies, Robert Montgomery, Billie Dove, Jimmy Durante, James Gleason, ZaSu Pitts, Sidney Toler, Douglass Dumbrille, Sarah Padden, Louise Carter, Clyde Cook, Rocky Twins, Charles Williams.

7

Edith Fellows

Edith Fellows suffered many setbacks and disappointments in her Hollywood experiences, first as a child star in the 1930s, and later as a teenager and adult. Her first heartbreak came the day she left her small Southern hometown for the prospects of a career in movies. She remembered nothing about the long and tiring train ride over the vast United States, only that one agonizing moment the train pulled from the station.

"It was a big day in my hometown, and all the kids and their mothers came down to see my grandmother and me off. All I could look for or care about was my daddy—he wasn't there. The train started pulling out of the station, and I started crying. My heart was broken. We got a little ways out and the train was beginning to pick up speed. All of a sudden, I looked into the distance and I see this speck coming towards us and it was getting bigger and bigger. It was my daddy on a white horse. He rode up alongside the train and that made it all okay. That was the way we said goodbye."

The year was 1927, and Edith Fellows was at the beginning of a film career that would extend to the early 1940s. Under the strict guidance of her grandmother, who accompanied her to Hollywood, she played small roles in films for several dark years. Her grandmother took housekeeping jobs to keep the two fed and clothed. Their luck changed when little Edith caught the attention of Columbia Studios after her appearance in *She Married Her Boss* (1935). The studio signed the 12-year-old to a long-term contract.

She was an immensely talented youngster in singing and dancing, and as an actress, Fellows was considered a natural, totally believable in her film roles as mischievous brats, orphans and outcasts.

Portraying naughty children on the screen, Fellows said, allowed her to exorcise many of the demons trapped inside her as a result of the pressures associated

Edith Fellows in *The Little Adventuress* (1938).

with being a working actress during her childhood and being raised by a domineering grandmother.

By the time we sat down for an interview in Raleigh, North Carolina, in 1989, Fellows had overcome a life's worth of hardships. After her screen career, she worked for years in Broadway musicals and on the straw hat circuit. A severe case of stage fright in the 1950s led to a fear of performing. Her anxieties, dulled by drug and alcohol abuse, continued for years.

Beaten by her fear and addictions, Fellows didn't perform on stage for over 20 years. Working, she found, replaced her addictions. She faced her problems, conquered her fear and resumed her stage and television career.

"Getting the courage to work again was a long time coming. It was something I had wondered about for years. Could I still work? I had to prove to not only those around me, but to myself that I still had it in me."

She was born Edith Fellows on May 20, 1923, in Boston. When she was only two months old, her mother abandoned the family. Her father put her grandmother Elizabeth in charge of rearing his daughter. When Fellows was two, the family went South, settling in Charlotte, North Carolina.

As Fellows grew, she became so pigeon-toed it was difficult for her to walk. Rather than put her legs in casts, a doctor suggested her grandmother put the little girl in dancing classes to help correct the problem. Her grandmother, who had wanted a show business career for herself years before in England, saw a second chance for stardom. Fellows was immediately enrolled at the Henderson School of the Dance.

When the school gave a recital one evening, the four-year-old was a featured dancer. A Hollywood talent scout came backstage after her performance.

"The man told my grandmother he thought I belonged in Hollywood. He said Hal Roach will absolutely love me. He gave my grandmother the whole line, and she fell for it, hook, line and sinker."

For his services, the scout told Elizabeth he needed $50 up front and that he would make arrangements for their trip to Hollywood and would help represent Fellows on their arrival. Elizabeth gave him the money, and he handed her his business card. Little Edith and Elizabeth went home and planned their future.

The community rallied behind the two. It was the first time one of their own had left their hometown for a chance at a career in the movies. The dance school, knowing the family's dismal financial state, took up a collection to purchase their train fare to California.

When the two arrived in Hollywood, they checked into a hotel and began searching for the address printed on the business card. They had no luck in locating it on their own. Elizabeth, realizing Hollywood was spread out for blocks, asked a local policeman to help in her search. He had little trouble finding the address: a vacant lot.

The bogus talent scout had swindled Elizabeth out of $50 (a lot of money to them), but not out of her dreams of seeing Fellows succeed on the big screen. There was never a question of them returning to North Carolina.

"Oh no, not my grandmother," Fellows said. "She was a determined soul. We were out there and, by God, she was going to fulfill this career for me. When she was a young girl in England, she wanted to become a stage actress. In the 1800s that was a no-no. She was told she was evil if she thought of going on the stage."

Mrs. Fellows suppressed her own ambitions, and after she came to the United States, tried to steer her own three children into show business. They resisted.

"When I came along, I was the perfect target. My mother had left us, and my grandmother was free to raise me and do as she wished," Fellows said.

Once the shock of the cruel prank wore off, Fellows' grandmother supported them by doing housework. Most of the time, Fellows accompanied her grandmother on the various jobs. On the occasion that a customer didn't like children in their home, she stayed with a neighbor.

It was while staying with a neighbor (while her grandmother worked) that she got her first break in films. The neighbor had a son, about Fellows' age, who occasionally did extra work. While staying with the neighbor one afternoon, Hal Roach's studio called and asked the mother to bring her son down for an interview.

The neighbor had no choice but to take Fellows along for the appointment. The little boy was cast in a small role in *Movie Night* (1927), a two-reeler with comedian Charley Chase, and was to report at the beginning of the next week. During the weekend, however, he developed chicken pox. When his mother called the studio to inform them of her son's illness, she was told to bring the boy's "sister" (Edith) instead. They could easily change the character to a girl.

"I got a copy of the film recently and was amazed that, although I was just a child, I could do all that. What interested me was that I had such discipline," said Fellows. "My grandmother, of course, was very proud. She was finally on her way."

Her grandmother thought the two were headed in the right direction, but success was slow in coming. "The next four or five years were rough ones for us," Edith said. "Work came very slowly, and we went hungry a lot. I remember there were times when my grandmother would turn off the lights and we'd sit and meditate by the phone, hoping it to ring. After a while, it did."

For the next five years, Fellows' bits and extra parts often went unbilled. She appeared in several of the *Little Rascals* two-reelers and worked briefly in *Madame X* (1929) with Ruth Chatterton and *Huckleberry Finn* (1931) with Jackie Coogan and Mitzi Green. She had fond memories of playing Myrna Loy as a child in *Emma* (1932), a Marie Dressler vehicle.

"I remember Marie Dressler as well today as if this film had happened yesterday," said Fellows. "She was the dearest lady." Fellows also associated Dressler with a publicity stunt her grandmother concocted for her at the film's premiere. Fellows' grandmother had planned to drop her off near the theater, and Fellows was to wander through the crowd crying as if she were lost. She was instructed to find Dressler in the confusion of the premiere and to create a scene for the press.

"I didn't like that because it was a lie," said Fellows. "It went against my grain so much that I told her I wouldn't do it. She told me that I was going to. On the night of the premiere, I got the worst earache I had ever had in my life. That's when I realized that psychosomatic illnesses were real. There was no way I could have said no to my grandmother. Getting sick was the only way out of her plan."

Fellows had a more important role, one of the many orphans she played, in a Tom Mix Western, *Rider of Death Valley* (1932). In the film, her father (Willard Robertson)dies and she (Edith) is taken in by her aunt (Lois Wilson).

She was an extra in *Cimarron* (1931), but she made such an impression on star Richard Dix that he requested she play his daughter three years later in *His Greatest Gamble* (1934). The role, in which she played Dorothy Wilson as a child, was her first big part.

"Richard Dix was the man to end all men," she said. "He was gorgeous to look at and was one of the most unselfish men I have ever known. I have never forgotten his kindness to me."

Her next big role came several months later when she was cast in *Mrs. Wiggs of the Cabbage Patch* (1934). As the daughter of Pauline Lord, Fellows is raised, with her siblings, in a shantytown after their father leaves to strike it rich in the Klondike. Romance enters the poverty-stricken town when W. C. Fields, a new arrival, begins to court a local matron (ZaSu Pitts).

The shantytown was created in Calabasas, then a remote section of the San Fernando Valley. The temperatures were scorching during the shoot, and barbed-wire fencing had to be erected to remind the crew not to wander off because of rattlesnakes in the area. Tents were used as dressing rooms and for the makeshift school Fellows attended while on location.

Although Fields had a reputation for disliking children, Fellows said she got along well with the actor, with the exception of one episode. "I was walking down the road on my way to school one morning when I heard this voice say, 'Little girl, come here.' I went into this tent, and there was Fields with what looked to me to be a bottle of water. He said, 'Little girl, I like you better than any of them and I'd hate to see you get bitten by the snakes.' He said he had some medicine that would help me in case a snake bit me, and he poured me a shot of his liquor.

"I took a swig, and it burned my mouth. I ran screaming to the teacher and told her what happened. She came back and raised hell with him and threatened to take him to the board. It was quite a scene."

For the rest of 1934 and 1935, Fellows played small roles in such films as *The Life of Vergie Winters* with Ann Harding and John Boles; *Black Fury* with Paul Muni; and *Dinky* with Jackie Cooper. She played an orphan trained in beekeeping in *The Keeper of the Bees* (1935) at Monogram.

She gained considerable attention at Columbia in 1935 when she played Melvyn Douglas' conniving daughter who refuses to accept his new love interest (Claudette Colbert) in *She Married Her Boss.* She was such a perfect menacing brat that the studio signed her to a seven-year contract.

She played a similar naughty role in *And So They Were Married* (1936) as the daughter of Mary Astor who tries to keep Astor and her new boyfriend (Melvyn Douglas) apart.

With Fellows on the payroll, the money started coming in regularly. She and her grandmother finally began climbing out of the near poverty-stricken conditions they had known since their arrival in Hollywood eight years before. The grandmother had never seen so much money and understood little about financial management. Harry Cohn, Columbia's boss, called Mrs. Fellows into his office one morning and told her it was time for Edith, now that she was under contract, to start looking like a star. He instructed Mrs. Fellows to take some of the salary and purchase a nice wardrobe for the girl and get her out of the tattered clothing she was wearing.

In 1935, her grandmother answered the door one afternoon to Edith's mother and maternal grandmother. A vicious custody battle ensued over the child star and her earnings, her mother contending she had been kidnapped and brought to Hollywood without her consent.

When the dust settled, Mrs. Fellows retained custody, and Edith's earnings were placed in a trust. Edith, who had substantial emotional scars over the court battles, had mixed feelings about the settlement. Although her grandmother could be cruel to her, she was the only mother she had ever known.

The young actress enjoyed her greatest popularity at Columbia. The studio cast her most often as either a brat or an orphan. She was billed third, below Bing Crosby and Madge Evans, in *Pennies from Heaven* (1936). She considered the role her best film performance. "I was a brat and an orphan in that one," she said. "I was sweet, feisty and funny. It kind of rolled them all into one."

During the filming of the picture, Fellows said a teenage crush she developed on Crosby made some scenes difficult to film. "There was a scene where I run and hide in Bing Crosby's trunk because Madge Evans, a child welfare worker, is coming to take me away to an orphanage. After Madge leaves, I begin crying because Bing is going overseas. I must tell him I don't want him to go away because I am in love with him.

"I thought by saying that, the whole set would know I really loved Bing. That was the hardest line I have ever had to say. Every time I see the film, I smile and think, 'Oh, Edith.' It's funny what you remember that no one else knows about."

Fellows appeared as orphans at her home studio in *Tugboat Princess* (1936), *Life Begins with Love* (1937), *City Streets* (1938), *The Little Adventuress* (1938) and *Nobody's Children* (1940).

Throughout her teenage years, the motivating force behind Fellows continued to be her grandmother. It didn't seem to be enough for her to be busy at the studio. She attended school at Hollywood Professional Children's School and later finished high school on the Columbia lot with a private tutor. Her grandmother also insisted on voice and violin lessons.

"The reins were very tight on me," said Fellows. "I told her I couldn't do all this, that she was spreading me too thin. I was allowed to quit violin and harp and to concentrate on my voice. Looking back, that was great because it allowed me to make a nice living later back East on the stage."

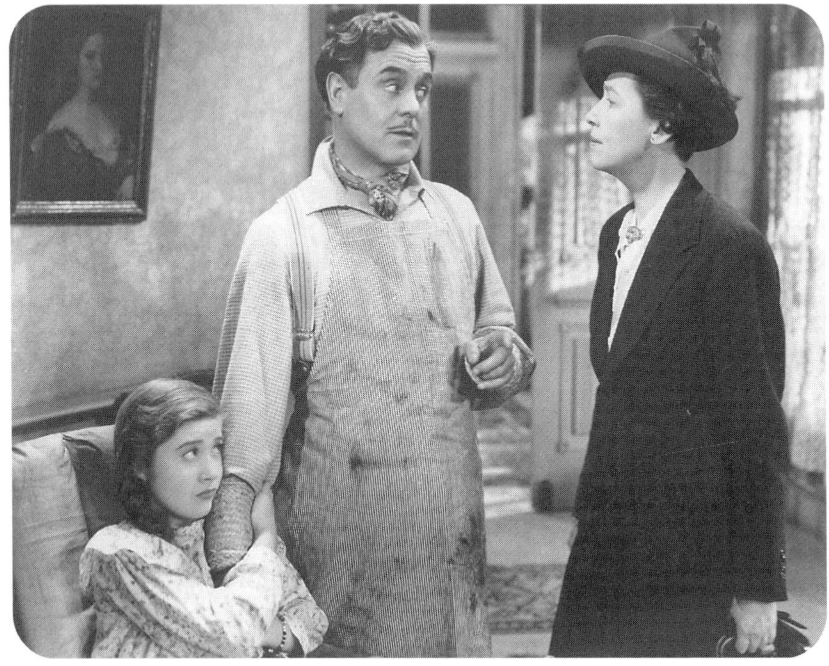

Edith Fellows, Leo Carrillo and Helen Jerome Eddy in *City Streets* (1938).

Fellows enjoyed being part of a studio family. It gave her freedom from the sometimes boring life she had at home with her grandmother and enabled her to cultivate friends her own age. When she wasn't working, Fellows and other studio kids would wander out to Columbia's ranch (where many of the locations were filmed) and play make-believe on the sets.

"We liked to go over to the *Lost Horizon* [1937] set—they kept it up for seven or eight years—and pretend we were in Shangri-La. We'd go from one make-believe to another.

"At the studio, we were protected. We were living in a fairy tale, because we weren't dealing with reality. The day I found out what the real world was like was quite a shock."

In the late 1930s, Fellows was featured in the *Five Little Peppers* series of four family-oriented programmers: *Five Little Peppers and How They Grew, Five Little Peppers at Home, Out West with the Peppers* and *Five Little Peppers in Trouble.*

Columbia dropped Fellows after *Music in My Heart* (1940), a musical with Rita Hayworth and Tony Martin, and *Her First Beau* (1941), a Jane Withers vehicle in which Fellows appeared briefly. She appeared in several coming-of-age films and in two 1942 Gene Autry Westerns, *Heart of the Rio Grande* and *Stardust on the Sage.*

One of Fellows' last films, *Girls Town* (1942), an independent feature, cast

Edith Fellows as she appeared in *Five Little Peppers and How They Grew* (1939).

her and June Storey as two sisters who go to Hollywood with hopes of becoming movie stars.

Portraying a hopeful movie actress could not have been farther from Fellows' own ambitions. She had taken the Hollywood route, spent her childhood on a sound stage, and was ready for a change. Her grandmother died in 1941, and Fellows was free to pursue her own interests.

"They didn't know what to do with me any more," she said. "I was no longer a child. Amazingly, I wasn't hurt by it at all, as were some former child stars. It was hard to leave my friends, but in the back of my mind, I always knew I wanted to go on the stage. I thought it was time to split."

About her years as a child actress in Hollywood, Fellows said there was an unexplainable element in her talent that no director was ever to pull from her. "I always had a feeling there was something that only a director like Frank Capra could pull out. I was sad that I never got a chance to work with him. Most of my directors were wonderful men, but they let me do it on my own. They never helped me dig in and find out who I was playing. By leaving me on my own, they weren't helping me. I withheld a lot."

Holding back in performances, she said, was probably best, for it might have reflected "a part of me I didn't want to see. That's why I hated those crying scenes. I always wanted to do comedy, because I didn't want anyone to see me cry. I didn't want people to see that vulnerable side of me. I wanted to be the tough little girl."

She preferred playing the hardened child, the brat. "In those roles, I could let off a lot of steam that I couldn't let off at home," she said. "I could throw things, and believe me, I threw."

With her picture career behind her, Fellows went to New York to make her living on the stage. She appeared in such plays as *Marinka* (1945), *Louisiana Lady* (1947) and *Uncle Willie* (1956), her last Broadway play. In television in the early 1950s, she appeared in four episodes of *Tales of Tomorrow.* She also made appearances on *Musical Comedy Time* (1950), *Summer Theater* (1952), *Armstrong Circle Theater* (1952) and *Medallion Theater* (1954).

In June 1946, she married agent Freddie Fields. A daughter, Kathy Lynn, Fellows' only child, was born in January 1947. The union lasted nine years.

Fellows was performing in a benefit show in New York in 1958 when she froze on stage. "All of a sudden, a wave came over me, and I started to cripple up. I could hardly get through it." She wrote it off as a bad night, but she stiffened again during an audition two weeks later and broke down after receiving a call about doing a live television show.

Her doctor told her she had been stricken with incurable stage fright. Her psychiatrist told her there was nothing he could do. "I listened to him. In those days, you thought psychiatrists were gods," she said. "My mistake was that I didn't get a second opinion. He said he had a new medication [Librium] that would help me through the trauma."

For years, Fellows was hooked on tranquilizers (she later switched to Valium) and alcohol. She was married in the 1960s to businessman Hal Lee. He eventually told her she should get back into show business* and he agreed to be her manager. The idea horrified her. The marriage eventually ended in divorce in 1970.

In the late 1970s, Fellows analyzed her fear and began to face her addictions.

**Edith appeared in Columbia's* Lilith *(1964), which starred Warren Beatty and Jean Seberg.*

"I just went cold-turkey," she said. "I said to myself, 'You're afraid of what? What do you mean? You've been in the business all your life. Let's go back and try.'"

In 1979, she appeared in the stage play *Dreams Deferred* and by the early 1980s was appearing regularly on television in such series as *The Brady Brides, Father Murphy, Scarecrow and Mrs. King, Cagney & Lacey, St. Elsewhere,* and *Simon and Simon.* She also appeared in the made-for-television movies *Between Two Brothers* (1982), *Grace Kelly* (1983) and *Happy Endings* (1983). She was Talia Balsam's mother in *In the Mood* (1987).

"The only reason I came back was to make sure I had conquered my fears. If I never worked again, I didn't care. I would hate to think I had to get out of the business because I couldn't do it. That would have been hard. That's over with, and life is very peaceful.

"It was great to be working again after so long. I guess you could call those dark years my intermission."

Filmography

1929: ***Madame X.*** MGM. Director: Lionel Barrymore. Cast: Lewis Stone, Ruth Chatterton, Raymond Hackett, Holmes Herbert, Eugenie Besserer, John P. Edington, Mitchell Lewis, Ullrich Haupt, Sidney Toler, Richard Carle, Carroll Nye, Claude King, Chappel Dossett, Edith Fellows. **1931:** ***Daddy Long Legs.*** Fox. Director: Alfred Santell. Cast: Janet Gaynor, Warner Baxter, Una Merkel, John Arledge, Claude Gillingwater, Effie Ellsler, Kendall McComas, Kathlyn Williams, Elizabeth Patterson, Louise Closser Hale, Sheila Mannors, Edwin Maxwell, Martha Lee Sparks, Edith Fellows. ***Huckleberry Finn.*** Paramount. Director: Norman Taurog. Cast: Jackie Coogan, Junior Durkin, Mitzi Green, Jackie Searl, Eugene Pallette, Clarence Muse, Clara Blandick, Jane Darwell, Oscar Apfel, Warner Richmond, Charlotte V. Henry, Lillian Harmer, Guy Oliver, Doris Short, Cecil Weston, Aileen Manning, Frank McGlynn, Edith Fellows. ***Cimarron.*** RKO. Director: Wesley Ruggles. Cast: Richard Dix, Irene Dunne, Estelle Taylor, Nance O'Neil, William Collier, Jr., Roscoe Ates, George E. Stone, Stanley Fields, Robert McWade, Edna May Oliver, Nancy Dover, Eugene Jackson, Otto Hoffman, William Orlamond, Frank Beal, Helen Parrish, Donald Dillaway, Junior Johnson, William Janney, Edith Fellows. **1932:** ***Emma.*** MGM. Director: Clarence Brown. Cast: Marie Dressler, Richard Cromwell, Jean Hersholt, Myrna Loy, John Miljan, Purnell B. Pratt, Leila Bennett, Barbara Kent, Kathryn Crawford, George Meeker, Dale Fuller, Wilfred Noy, Andre Cheron, Dorothy Peterson, Edith Fellows. ***Rider of Death Valley.*** Universal. Director: Albert Rogell. Cast: Tom Mix, Lois Wilson, Fred Kohler, Forrest Stanley, Edith Fellows, Willard Robertson, Mae Busch, Otis Harlan, Francis Ford, Max Asher, Pete Morrison, Edmund Cobb. ***Law and Lawless.*** Majestic. Director: Armand Schaefer. Cast: Jack Hoxie, Hilda Moreno,

Julian Rivero, Yakima Canutt, Jack Mower, Wally Wales, J. Frank Glendon, Edith Fellows, Bob Burns, Helen Gibson, Fred Burns, Alma Rayford, Joe de la Cruz, Elvira Sanchez, William Quilan, Al Taylor. **1933: *The Devil's Brother.*** MGM. Director: Hal Roach. Cast: Dennis King, Thelma Todd, James Finlayson, Lucille Browne, Arthur Pierson, Henry Armetta, Matt McHugh, Lane Chandler, Nena Quartaro, Wilfred Lucas, James C. Morton, Stan Laurel, Oliver Hardy. ***Girl Without a Room.*** Paramount. Director: Ralph Murphy. Cast: Charles Farrell, Charlie Ruggles, Marguerite Churchill, Gregory Ratoff, Grace Bradley, Walter Woolf, Sam Ash, Leonid Snegoff, Leonid Kinsky, Mischa Auer, Alexander Mellish, Spec O'Donnell, Edith Fellows, Harry Stubbs. **1934: *His Greatest Gamble.*** RKO. Director: John Robertson. Cast: Richard Dix, Dorothy Wilson, Bruce Cabot, Erin O'Brien-Moore, Edith Fellows, Shirley Grey, Leonard Carey, Eily Malyon. ***Cross Streets.*** Chesterfield. Director: Frank R. Strayer. Cast: Claire Windsor, Johnny Mack Brown, Anita Louise, Kenneth Thomson, Matty Kemp, Josef Swickard, Niles Welch, Edith Fellows. ***Kid Millions.*** United Artists. Director: Roy Del Ruth. Cast: Eddie Cantor, Ann Sothern, Ethel Merman, George Murphy, Berton Churchill, Warren Hymer, Paul Harvey, Jesse Block, Eve Sully, Otto Hoffman, Stanley Fields, Edgar Kennedy, Jack Kennedy, John Kelly, Doris Davenport, The Nicholas Brothers, Henry Kolker, Lucille Ball, Tommy Bond, William Arnold, Edith Fellows. ***Jane Eyre.*** Monogram. Director: Christy Cabanne. Cast: Virginia Bruce, Colin Clive, Beryl Mercer, David Torrence, Aileen Pringle, Edith Fellows, John Rogers, Jean Darling, Lionel Belmore, Jameson Thomas, Ethel Griffies, Claire Du Brey, William Burress, Joan Standing, Richard Quine. ***Mrs. Wiggs of the Cabbage Patch.*** Paramount. Director: Norman Taurog. Cast: Pauline Lord, W. C. Fields, ZaSu Pitts, Evelyn Venable, Kent Taylor, Donald Meek, Jimmy Butler, George Breakston, Virginia Weidler, Carmencita Johnson, Edith Fellows, Charles Middleton, George Reed, Mildred Gover, Arthur Housman. **1935: *The Keeper of the Bees.*** Monogram. Director: Christy Cabanne. Cast: Neil Hamilton, Betty Furness, Emma Dunn, Edith Fellows, Hobart Bosworth, Helen Jerome Eddy, Marion Shilling, Barbara Bedford, Lafe McKee. ***Dinky.*** Warner Brothers. Directors: D. Ross Lederman, Howard Bretherton. Cast: Jackie Cooper, Mary Astor, Roger Pryor, Henry Armetta, Betty Jane Haney, Henry O' Neill, Jimmy Butler, George Ernest, Edith Fellows, Sidney Miller, Richard Quine, Addison Richards, Florence Fair. ***Black Fury.*** Warner Brothers. Director: Michael Curtiz. Cast: Paul Muni, Karen Morley, William Gargan, Barton MacLane, John Qualen, J. Carrol Naish, Vince Barnett, Tully Marshall, Henry O'Neill, Joe Crehan, Mae Marsh, Sarah Haden, Willard Robertson, Effie Ellsler, Wade Boteler, Egon Brecher, George Pat Collins, Ward Bond, Akim Tamiroff, Purnell Pratt, Eddie Shubert, Samuel S. Hinds, Claire McDowell, Addison Richards, Edith Fellows, Wally Albright, Jr. ***She Married Her Boss.*** Columbia. Director: Gregory La Cava. Cast: Claudette Colbert, Melvyn Douglas, Michael Bartlett, Raymond Walburn, Jean Dixon, Katherine Alexander, Edith

Fellows, Clara Kimball Young, Grace Hale, Charles E. Arnt, Buddy Roosevelt, Selmer Jackson, John Hyams, Georgia Caine, Lillian Rich, Ruth Clifford, Bess Flowers. ***One Way Ticket.*** Columbia. Director: Herbert Biberman. Cast: Lloyd Nolan, Peggy Conklin, Walter Connolly, Edith Fellows, Gloria Shea, Nana Bryant, Thurston Hall, George McKay, Robert Middlemass, Willie Fung, Jack Clifford, James Flavin. **1936:** ***And So They Were Married.*** Columbia. Director: Elliott Nugent. Cast: Melvyn Douglas, Mary Astor, Edith Fellows, Jackie Moran, Donald Meek, Dorothy Stickney, Romaine Callender, Douglas Scott, Margaret Armstrong, George McKay, Phyllis Godfrey, Olaf Hytten, Hooper Atchley, Wade Boteler. ***Pennies from Heaven.*** Columbia. Director: Norman Z. McLeod. Cast: Bing Crosby, Madge Evans, Edith Fellows, Louis Armstrong, Donald Meek, John Gallaudet, William Stack, Nana Bryant, Tommy Dugan, Nydia Westman, Tom Ricketts, Morgan Wallace, Arthur Hoyt, Sid Saylor, George Chandler. ***Tugboat Princess.*** Columbia. Director: David Selman. Cast: Walter C. Kelly, Valerie Hobson, Edith Fellows, Clyde Cook, Lester Matthews, Reginald Hincks. **1937:** ***Life Begins with Love.*** Columbia. Director: Raymond B. McCarey. Cast: Jean Parker, Douglass Montgomery, Edith Fellows, Leona Maricle, Lumsden Hare, Aubrey Mather, James Burke, Minerva Urecal, Scotty Beckett, Joel Davis, Joyce Kay. **1938:** ***Little Miss Roughneck.*** Columbia. Director: Aubrey Scotto. Cast: Edith Fellows, Leo Carrillo, Scott Colton, Jacqueline Wells, [Julie Bishop], Margaret Irving, Inez Palange, George McKay, Thurston Hall, Frank C. Wilson, John Gallaudet, Walter O. Stahl, Wade Boteler, Iris Meredith, Ann Doran. ***The Little Adventuress.*** Columbia. Director: D. Ross Lederman. Cast: Edith Fellows, Richard Fiske, Jacqueline Wells [Julie Bishop], Cliff Edwards, Virginia Howell, Harry C. Bradley, Charles Waldron, Kenneth Harlan, Helen Brown, Anthony Hughes, Jack Clifford, Kane Richmond, Wade Boteler, George Pearce, Edmund Cobb, Brooks Benedict, Bess Flowers. ***City Streets.*** Columbia. Director: Albert S. Rogell. Cast: Edith Fellows, Leo Carrillo, Tommy Bond, Mary Gordon, Helen Jerome Eddy, Joseph King, Frank Sheridan, Arthur Loft, George Humbert, Frank Reicher, Grace Goodall, Margaret Fielding, Bess Flowers, Ann Doran, Lee Shumway. **1939:** ***Pride of the Blue Grass.*** Warner Brothers. Director: William McGann. Cast: Edith Fellows, James McCallion, Gantry (horse), Granville Bates, Aldrich Bowker, Arthur Loft, DeWolf [William] Hopper, Frankie Burke, Fred Tozere, Edgar Edwards, John Butler, Creighton Hale, Crauford Kent. ***Five Little Peppers and How They Grew.*** Columbia. Director: Charles Lamont. Cast: Edith Fellows, Clarence Kolb, Dorothy Peterson, Ronald Sinclair, Charles Peck, Tommy Bond, Jimmy Leake, Dorothy Ann Seese, Bruce Bennett, Maurice Costello. **1940:** ***Music in My Heart.*** Columbia. Director: Joseph Santley. Cast: Tony Martin, Rita Hayworth, Edith Fellows, Alan Mowbray, Eric Blore, George Tobias, Joseph Crehan, George Humbert, Joey Ray, Don Brodie, Julietta Novis, Eddie Kane. ***Five Little Peppers at Home.*** Columbia. Director: Charles Barton. Cast: Edith Fellows, Dorothy Ann Seese, Clarence Kolb, Dorothy Peterson,

Ronald Sinclair, Charles Peck, Tommy Bond, Bobby Larson, Rex Evans, Herbert Rawlinson, Spencer Charters, Bruce Bennett, Ann Doran. ***Five Little Peppers in Trouble.*** Columbia. Director: Charles Barton. Cast: Edith Fellows, Dorothy Ann Seese, Dorothy Peterson, Pierre Watkin, Ronald Sinclair, Charles Peck, Tommy Bond, Bobby Larson, Rex Evans, Kathleen Howard, Mary Currier, Helen Brown, Rita Quigley, Bess Flowers. ***Out West with the Peppers.*** Columbia. Director: Charles Barton. Cast: Edith Fellows, Dorothy Ann Seese, Dorothy Peterson, Charles Peck, Tommy Bond, Bobby Larson, Victor Kilian, Helen Brown, Hal Price, Pierre Watkin. ***Her First Romance.*** Monogram. Director: Edward Dmytryk. Cast: Edith Fellows, Wilbur Evans, Jacqueline Wells [Julie Bishop], Alan Ladd, Judith Linden, Roger Daniel, Marion Kerby, Marlo Dwyer. **1941:** ***Her First Beau.*** Columbia. Director: Theodore Reed. Cast: Jane Withers, Jackie Cooper, Edith Fellows, Josephine Hutchinson, William Travy, Martha O'Driscoll, Edgar Buchanan, Jonathan Hale, Kenneth Howell, Addison Richards. **1942:** ***Girls Town.*** Producers Releasing Corp. Director: Victor Halperin. Cast: Edith Fellows, June Storey, Kenneth Howell, Anna Q. Nilsson, Warren Hymer, Alice White, Vince Barnett, Paul Dubov, Peggy Ryan, Bernice Kay, Helen McCloud, Charlie Williams. ***Heart of the Rio Grande.*** Republic. Director: William Morgan. Cast: Gene Autry, Smiley Burnette, Fay McKenzie, Edith Fellows, Pierre Watkin, Joseph Strauch, Jr., William Haade, Sarah Padden, Jean Porter, Milton Kibbee, Edmund Cobb, Nora Lane. ***Stardust on the Sage.*** Republic. Director: William Morgan. Cast: Gene Autry, Smiley Burnette, William Henry, Edith Fellows, Louise Currie, Emmett Vogan, George Ernest, Roy Barcroft, Rex Lease, Franklyn Farnum, Edmund Cobb, Frank O'Connor, Lee Shumway. ***Criminal Investigator.*** Monogram. Director: Jean Yarbrough. Cast: Robert Lowery, Edith Fellows, John Miljan, Jan Wiley, Charles Jordan, Gloria Faye, Paul Bryar, George O'Hanlon, Vivian Wilcox, Charles Hall, Mauritz Hugo. **1964:** ***Lilith.*** Columbia. Director: Robert Rossen. Cast: Warren Beatty, Jean Seberg, Peter Fonda, Kim Hunter, Anne Meacham, Jessica Walter, Gene Hackman, James Patterson, Robert Reilly, Olympia Dukakis, Edith Fellows, Walter Arnold, Ron Cunningham, Page Jones, Jeno Mate, Dina Paisner, Gunnar Peters. **1987:** ***In the Mood.*** Lorimar. Director: Phil Alden Robinson. Cast: Patrick Dempsey, Talia Balsam, Beverly D'Angelo, Michael Constantine, Betty Jinnette, Kathleen Freeman, Peter Hobbs, Tony Longo, Douglas Rowe, Ernie Brown, Kim Myers, Brian McNamara, Dana Short, Josh Cadman, Nan Woods, Gillian Grant, Lisanne Falk, Edith Fellows.

8

Rose Hobart

Rose Hobart could always count on change, on her life suddenly altering directions without much notice. To be uprooted never stunted her growth as a person. Rather, she said, it only reinforced her spirit. Rose Hobart flourished under the uncertainty of change.

"I have always thrived on change," she said. "When everything got nice and comfortable, I got bored and nervous. It was time for something different. That's the way it has always been with me."

She was a well-established stage actress in the late 1920s, having worked with such greats as Eva Le Gallienne, Jane Cowl and Helen Hayes when Hollywood called her West at the coming of sound. After several years under contract to Universal, however, Hobart, disillusioned over weak ingenue parts, strenuous working conditions and loanouts to other studios, begged Carl Laemmle, Jr., to release her from her contract. She returned to the New York stage.

Hobart entertained live audiences for the next seven years. When she felt the theater wasn't giving her the roles she deserved, she returned to films. Free-lancing, she enjoyed a second Hollywood career as a character actress, often playing the villainess.

Suspected of being a Communist, Rose was blacklisted in the late 1940s. Although she appeared on the stage and later in television, she never worked in films again.

When I met this outspoken and highly intelligent actress in her cottage on the grounds of the Motion Picture Country House in early 1989, there was no evidence of bitterness at being forced from the business she loved. After all, the Communist witch-hunts were a long time ago, and she insisted she didn't dwell on her disappointments. It was one of many experiences, the many pieces of the puzzle that, when put together, made Rose Hobart the wise and contented person she was in later years.

"All the changes I've gone through in my life have made me very adaptable," she said. "Whatever happens doesn't bother me, because that has been my life for as long as I can remember."

She was born Rose Kefer on May 1, 1906, in New York City. Her father Paul was a cellist for the New York Symphony; her mother Marguerite was an opera singer.

One of the reasons Rose became so adaptable to change, she said, was because of the diversity of her childhood experiences. When she was seven, her parents divorced, and Rose and her sister Polly went to live in France with their paternal grandmother.

"We were supposed to stay with her for three years, but my sister and I hated her. We were very happy when Mother came over and got us at the outbreak of World War I. We returned to the United States and were put in boarding schools."

Hobart knew by age six she wanted to be an actress. "We used to spend our summers in Woodstock. One summer, they decided to have a summer feast day and put on a play that night. This was the first live stage performance I ever saw.

"The play they chose was by Edna St. Vincent Millay, a well-known poetess of the day. She came up for the play, and I talked with her during the rehearsals in a daisy field between our two houses. She was a great influence. I decided then what I wanted to do with my life."

Hobart made her professional debut in *Cappy Ricks* on the Chautauqua Circuit in the early 1920s. The play opened in Louisiana and closed 18 weeks later in Montana. Rose was 15 and went on tour unchaperoned.

"I lied and told them I was 18. They didn't find out until my birthday. I turned 16 that year, and they couldn't afford to bring somebody else out to replace me. They allowed me to finish the tour."

Hobart toured with Eva Le Gallienne in *Liliom* (which opened in Atlantic City, New Jersey, in October 1922) throughout the East and Midwest. Le Gallienne, who later founded the Civic Repertory Theater in 1926, became Rose's mentor and friend.

It was on opening night in Atlantic City that Edna St. Vincent Millay, who was in the audience, came backstage after Hobart's performance and said, "You made it!" "I have never forgotten the thrill of that night," Hobart said.

Hobart's Broadway debut came in 1923 in *Lullaby* with Florence Reed. The play ran through the winter of 1924. That spring, she married writer and theatrical producer Ben Winter in New York.

Her work on the stage during the 1920s was impressive. She was trained by some of the theater's greatest talents. She appeared (as Charmian) with Helen Hayes in *Caesar and Cleopatra* in 1925 and in *What Every Woman Knows* in 1926. She appeared again with Le Gallienne in 1926 in *Saturday Night* and

An early Rose Hobart portrait.

The Three Sisters. She enjoyed a long Midwestern tour in Noël Coward's play *The Vortex* in 1925 and was directed by Jane Cowl in *Diversion* (1928).

While in Europe in the summer of 1928, Hobart made her London debut in *The Comic Artist.* The play ran one performance. Hobart and her husband had gone overseas to salvage their troubled marriage. Their efforts failed and they were divorced that year.

Hobart replaced Katharine Hepburn as Grazia in *Death Takes a Holiday*, which opened at the Ethel Barrymore Theater in December 1929. After a long string of theatrical disappointments, Hobart was relieved this play was a hit.

Although deeply involved in the theater, Hobart was aware of the revolution sweeping the motion picture industry: the coming of sound. Hollywood producers and talent scouts scrambled to discover New York talent for the screen.

While appearing in *Death Takes a Holiday*, Hobart was approached with film offers from both Universal and Fox. She wanted to postpone any decision until the play closed in the summer. The actress signed with Universal after they agreed with her terms.

A week after Hobart signed with the studio, Fox offered her a contract and was prepared to cast her immediately in *Liliom* (1930), based on the stageplay she appeared in eight years before. Hobart explained to Fox that she could not sign a long-term contract, but would come to Hollywood ahead of her Universal contract to make the picture.*

Liliom was a big-budget picture for Fox and should have been a hit. Hobart said the miscasting of male lead Charles Farrell and the technical problems during the infancy of sound films contributed to the film's failure at the box office. "When I first saw the picture in New York," she said, "I walked into the lobby and thought, 'Charlie doesn't sound too bad,' because he had a very high, squeaky voice. When I got inside, the low voice was mine and the high voice was his."

After *Liliom*, Hobart remained in Hollywood to fulfill her Universal contract. The first of the three films she did for her home studio was *A Lady Surrenders* (1930), as Conrad Nagel's wife.

She was on the lot only a short time before the studio began loaning her out to other companies. "I was furious about it because they were making lots of money on me," she said. Always headstrong and opinionated, Hobart clashed early on with Universal production executive Carl Laemmle, Jr., over the issue. "We fought the whole time I was there, but he couldn't have cared less about me or my feelings."

At First National in 1931, Hobart appeared with Douglas Fairbanks, Jr., in *Chances* and with Ben Lyon in *Compromised*. On loan to Paramount that same year, she made one of the films for which she is best remembered: *Dr. Jekyll and Mr. Hyde* (as Muriel Carew). Although she liked working with star Fredric March (he was her fiancé in the picture) and considered March and his wife Florence Eldridge true professionals, she found her part "the dullest role I ever played." She kept her distance from the "difficult" Miriam Hopkins (luckily she had no scenes with her) and found director Rouben Mamoulian to be stern and devoid of a sense of humor.

*Liliom *had been purchased as a vehicle for Fox's love team Charles Farrell and Janet Gaynor. However, Gaynor was fighting with the studio over being cast in musicals—*High Society Blues, *(1930) was the final straw for her. She was off the payroll for seven months, and while waiting for the matter to be settled, lost the plum role in* Liliom *to Hobart.*

In her final films for Universal, Hobart appeared as the wife of Charles Bickford in *Scandal for Sale* (1932) and *East of Borneo* (1931). In the latter, her character goes to Borneo in search of her doctor/husband. Once there, she is pursued by a prince who shoots her husband and forces himself on her. She escapes the wilds of the jungle as a volcano is erupting in the distance.

Rose Hobart about the time she made *Dr. Jekyll and Mr. Hyde (1932).*

Hobart chuckled at the mention of the picture. "*East of Borneo* is the worst picture ever made," she said. "We shot for three weeks, from six o'clock at night to five o'clock in the morning. It was a rough shoot. We had to work outdoors when it was dark, and by 3 A.M. it was freezing."

Everything associated with the picture was "outrageously fake," Hobart recalled. "For instance, they sent a unit to Borneo because they wanted actual footage of monkeys, jaguars and other animal life. The guys got there and found it was like the flats of New Jersey. There was no jungle within 75 miles of any river and there were no monkeys in Borneo."

Not only did Hobart bristle at the long work hours and poor working conditions during the filming of *East of Borneo*, she also rebelled over a scene she was to play with a 24-foot python.

"The snake was down on me, and they had about ten guys on his tail. The man handling the snake came up to me just before we were ready to shoot and said, 'I wish you'd tell them not to shoot this scene. If the snake is close enough to attack, ten men on his tail isn't going to be enough.'"

Hobart refused to do the scene. "They tried everything. They attempted to put glass between the snake and me. They tried using a fake snake. When it was over, they decided not to use the python, because they don't move that much unless they're hungry, and if that had been the case, it would have been dangerous as hell."

After *East of Borneo*, Hobart asked Laemmle for her release. "I had had enough of him and the studio," she said. "I made it very difficult for them. There were no unions then, and they could do what they wanted. I used to stamp around and say, 'You can't do this and that.' But, they did. They were loaning me out all the time because they didn't want me, and every time I did a film at Universal, it was something like *East of Borneo*."

As she was preparing to sign what she thought were her release papers,

Hobart noticed in the fine print that she was actually signing a suspension, prohibiting her from working at any studio or theatrical company. She threw the document (unsigned) on Laemmle's desk and stormed from the office. Realizing the business relationship was impossible, however, Laemmle agreed to release her from the studio.

In April 1932, Hobart appeared with Ralph Forbes at San Francisco's Geary Theater in *Let Us Divorce*, a play directed by Ruth Chatterton (Forbes' wife). The actress returned to New York later that year and in October married William Grosvenor, Jr., a chemist.

Hobart was happy to be back in New York, which she had always considered her home. She was at the beginning of a new marriage, was eager to resume work on the stage, and renew old acquaintances — Osgood and Jane Perkins* were two of her closest friends.

She appeared with Humphrey Bogart in two plays, *I Loved You Wednesday* (1932) and *Our Wife* (1933), and continued working steadily on the stage throughout the mid–1930s. She also made two independent films, *The Shadow Laughs* (1933) and *Convention Girl* (1935), on the East Coast.

By the late 1930s, Hobart was disillusioned, "restless," she said, over the dwindling stage offers. "People like Margaret Sullavan, who were big in pictures then, were coming back to New York and getting all the good parts. I thought I'd better come back out and be a movie star again. I knew a lot about motion pictures by this time, what to expect and what could and couldn't be done. When I first came out in 1929, I thought films were like the theater. Of course, films have no relation to the theater."

Her second career in Hollywood was much more fulfilling than her first. She gladly left ingenue and gentle heroine parts back in the early 1930s, opting in the 1940s for character roles, often as evil, vindictive women.

"When I came back to Hollywood, I was freelancing. I wasn't under contract. I didn't have the backing I had under contract, but I did the films I wanted to do. If I saw I was getting into a real stinker, I could say, "Sorry, kids, I don't want to do that one.'"

Ironically, her first picture back in Hollywood, *Tower of London* (1939), was for Universal. In the film, set in the 1400s, she appeared with Boris Karloff, Basil Rathbone, Barbara O'Neil and Ian Hunter.

"I only agreed to do the film after I learned Junior Laemmle was no longer the head of the studio. Otherwise, I would have never done the film. They treated me fine that time."

Hobart was greatly impressed by Boris Karloff, whom she had known from her early Hollywood years. "He was a doll. Far from being the monster he always played, he was an English gentleman. He was the gentlest man I have ever known."

She played socialite Irene Burroughs in *Susan and God* (1940), which

**The parents of actor Anthony Perkins.*

Rose Hobart, Fredric March and Nigel Bruce in *Susan and God* (1940).

starred Joan Crawford and Fredric March. "It was great to be working with Freddie again. Joan was a tough gal. When she was on the set, she was a complete professional to work with, which was nice."

In California in 1941, she appeared in two plays, *No Time for Comedy* and *The Man Who Came to Dinner*. She also directed the play *Don Juan in Hell*. In 1942, Hobart and her second husband divorced.

She was particularly effective as the heavy in such films as *Singapore Woman* (1941), *The Soul of a Monster* (1944), *The Cat Creeps* (1946) and *Bride of Vengeance* (1949). She was also an evil Nazi agent in the Universal 12-chapter serial *The Adventures of Smilin' Jack* (1943). "I loved playing those parts. They were much more interesting characters than the sweet ingenues."

Hobart worked for the third time with Humphrey Bogart in the film noir classic *Conflict* (1945). This time, she played the wife he wants to dispose of so he can marry her younger sister (Alexis Smith). He strangles Hobart, pushes her car from a cliff and plans his future. A series of bizarre incidents, however, causes him to wonder if she's really dead.

"Bogey was very interesting. He was an absolute bastard when he was not a success," said Hobart. "The minute he came back out to Hollywood and fell in love with Betty Bacall, he turned into one of the nicest guys you could possibly want. He was the only person I know who improved with success. Everybody else got worse."

Sydney Greenstreet and Rose Hobart in *Conflict* (1945).

Hobart had supporting parts, sometimes small roles in such films as *Ziegfeld Girl* (1941) with Jimmy Stewart, Hedy Lamarr, Judy Garland and Lana Turner, *Nothing but the Truth* (1941) with Bob Hope and Paulette Goddard, *Claudia and David* (1946) with Robert Young, Dorothy McGuire and Mary Astor, *The Farmer's Daughter* (1947) with Loretta Young and Joseph Cotten and *Cass Timberlane* (1947) with Spencer Tracy, Lana Turner and Zachary Scott. She had top billing in *I'll Sell My Life* (1941) with Roscoe Ates and Stanley Fields and *Prison Girls* (1942) with Sidney Blackmer.

Hobart's career ended without notice in 1949 when she was investigated by the House Committee on Un-American Activities for her early union activity and her participation in the Actor's Laboratory Theater, which had taken her on tour (in *Male and Female* [1944–45]) throughout the Aleutian Islands.

During her testimony before the HUAC, Hobart revealed nothing about her friends in the Actor's Lab, some of whom she knew to be Communists. "We all had to say the same things to protect everybody," she said. "Everybody knew there were Communists working in the Lab. I thought that people were people and what they believe in had nothing to do with me. At the testimony, I took the First Amendment, because I didn't want the few that we knew to get nailed."

Hobart soon found herself being investigated. "The guy who put the finger on me was one I would never have dreamt would do it. He told them he had been to an open Communist meeting at my house. It turned out that when I was in the Aleutians, I had rented the bottom half of my house to somebody I didn't know. That was where the party had been. I tried to tell the Committee this, but they wouldn't believe it."

Hobart's career disintegrated. "My life changed completely and totally at that point," she said. "The sad thing was that acting had been what I had wanted to do since I could remember. One day I was working. The next day, nobody was speaking to me."

It was during this dark period that Hobart discovered she was pregnant.* "This was the best thing that could have happened to me at this point, because I had been told all my life I couldn't have children. I was 42 at that point, which is a little late to be having your first child. I got absolutely fascinated about having a child and completely engrossed in being a mother. It was a new experience in life."

It was after the birth of her son Judson that she decided to go back to work. When she met with a casting director, she was told she was blacklisted from the business. "I really had no idea. I just knew I wasn't working."

Hobart went through a second hearing "to try and get it straightened out. They knew every place I had lived from the time I was born," she said. "I asked them for a transcript and when I proved something in my favor, it was cut out. They had their minds made up, and there was nothing I could do."

Throughout the 1950s, Hobart worked on stage in such plays as *Years Ago* (1950), *The Cocktail Party* (1952), *Quadrille* (1958) and *Clerembard* (1958). On television, she appeared on *The Danny Thomas Show, Gunsmoke, Cannon, The FBI* and *Dan August.* She played the maid on *Peyton Place* (1966–68).

Hobart harbors little bitterness about being blacklisted from her chosen profession. "The lesson I learned is that you can survive anything if you are flexible enough and if you recognize that not everything is as it seems. If you can really find out what the truth of something is, you can pretty well cope with it."

Along the way, Hobart earned a degree in psychology and became involved in metaphysics. She entered the Motion Picture Country House in 1982, and for a while she edited their in-house publication, *The Haven News.* Her autobiography was published in 1994.†

By the time we met, Hobart felt she had fulfilled her life's ambitions. "I don't have any more goals in life except to die as quickly as possible," she said. "I have been very fortunate in that I was in the picture business at its peak, but I'm very happy I'm not in it today. I have had the best life I could possibly have.

"My philosophy is simple. I believe that everything that happens to you,

**Rose had married architect Barton H. Bosworth on October 10, 1948.*

†A Steady Digression to a Fixed Point: The Autobiography of Rose Hobart. *The Scarecrow Press, Inc., 1994.*

whether good or bad, you do yourself, whether you know it or not. It's not so much what happens to you, but it's your reaction to things that makes your life what it is."

FILMOGRAPHY

1930: ***Liliom.*** Fox. Director: Frank Borzage. Cast: Charles Farrell, Rose Hobart, Estelle Taylor, Lee Tracy, James Marcus, Walter Abel, Mildred Van Dorn, Quinn Williams, Lillian Elliott, Bert Roach, H. B. Warner, Dawn O'Day. ***A Lady Surrenders.*** Universal. Director: John M. Stahl. Cast: Genevieve Tobin, Rose Hobart, Conrad Nagel, Basil Rathbone, Edgar Norton, Carmel Myers, Franklin Pangborn, Vivian Oakland, Grace Cunard. **1931:** ***Chances.*** First National. Director: Allan Dwan. Cast: Douglas Fairbanks, Jr., Rose Hobart, Anthony Bushell, Holmes Herbert, Mary Forbes, Edmond Breon, Harry Allen, Florence Britton, Edward Morgan, Tyrrel Davis, Mae Madison, William Austin, Jean Fenwick. ***East of Borneo.*** Universal. Director: George Melford. Cast: Rose Hobart, Charles Bickford, Georges Renavent, Lupita Tovar, Noble Johnson. ***Compromised.*** First National. Director: John G. Adolfi. Cast: Rose Hobart, Ben Lyon, Florence Britton, Claude Gillingwater, Emma Dunn, Bert Roach, Delmar Watson, Louise MacIntosh, Juliette Compton, Edgar Norton, Adele Watson, Virginia Sale. ***Dr. Jekyll and Mr. Hyde.*** Paramount. Director: Rouben Mamoulian. Cast: Fredric March, Miriam Hopkins, Rose Hobart, Holmes Herbert, Halliwell Hobbes, Edgar Norton, Tempe Pigott, Arnold Lucy. **1932:** ***Scandal for Sale.*** Universal. Director: Russell Mack. Cast: Charles Bickford, Rose Hobart, Pat O'Brien, Claudia Dell, J. Farrell MacDonald, Harry Beresford, Berton Churchill, Glenda Farrell, Tully Marshall, Mitchell Harris, Hans von Twardowski, Lew Kelly, Mary Jane Graham, Buster Phelps, Paul Nicholson, James Farley, Jack Richardson, Angie Norton. **1933:** ***The Shadow Laughs.*** Trojan. Director: Arthur Hoerl. Cast: Hal Skelly, Rose Hobart, Harry T. Morey, Walter Fenner, Geoffrey Bryant, Robert Keith, John Morrissey, Hal Short, Bran Nossem. **1935:** ***Convention Girl.*** Falcon Pictures Corp. Director: Luther Reed. Cast: Rose Hobart, Weldon Heyburn, Sally O'Neil, Herbert Rawlinson, Shemp Howard, Lucile Mendez, James Spottswood, Nancy Kelly, Alan Brooks, Nell O'Day, Toni Reed, Ruth Gillette, William H. White. **1939:** ***Tower of London.*** Universal. Director: Rowland V. Lee. Cast: Basil Rathbone, Boris Karloff, Barbara O'Neil, Ian Hunter, Vincent Price, Nan Grey, Ernest Cossart, John Sutton, Leo G. Carroll, Miles Mander, Lionel Belmore, Rose Hobart, Ronald Sinclair, John Herbert-Bond, Ralph Forbes, Frances Robinson, G. P. Huntley, Jr., John Rodion, Walter Tetley. **1940:** ***Wolf of New York.*** Republic. Director: William McGann. Cast: Edmund Lowe, Rose Hobart, James Stephenson, Jerome Cowan, William Demarest, Maurice Murphy, Charles D. Brown, Edward Gargan, Andrew Tombes, Ben Welden, Ann Baldwin, Roy Gordon.

Susan and God. MGM. Director: George Cukor. Cast: Joan Crawford, Fredric March, Ruth Hussey, John Carroll, Rita Hayworth, Nigel Bruce, Bruce Cabot, Rose Hobart, Constance Collier, Rita Quigley, Gloria DeHaven, Richard O. Crane, Norma Mitchell, Marjorie Main, Aldrich Bowker. ***A Night at Earl Carroll's.*** Paramount. Director: Kurt Neumann. Cast: Ken Murray, Rose Hobart, Blanche Stewart, Elvia Allman, J. Carrol Naish, Russell Hicks, Jack Norton, John Laird, Ruth Rogers, Betty McLaughlin, Beryl Wallace, John Harmon, Ray Walker, William Davidson, Ralph Emerson, George Meeker, Vera Lewis, Earl Carroll. **1941: *Ziegfeld Girl.*** MGM. Director: Robert Z. Leonard. Cast: James Stewart, Judy Garland, Hedy Lamarr, Lana Turner, Tony Martin, Jackie Cooper, Ian Hunter, Charles Winninger, Edward Everett Horton, Philip Dorn, Paul Kelly, Eve Arden, Dan Dailey, Al Shean, Fay Holden, Felix Bressart, Rose Hobart, Bernard Nedell, Ed McNamara, Mae Busch, Renie Riano, Josephine Whittell, Sergio Orta. ***Singapore Woman.*** Warner Brothers. Director: Jean Negulesco. Cast: Brenda Marshall, David Bruce, Virginia Field, Jerome Cowan, Rose Hobart, Heather Angel, Richard Ainley, Dorothy Tree, Bruce Lester, Connie Leon, Douglas Walton, Gilbert Emery, Stanley Logan, Abner Biberman, Eva Puig. ***Lady Be Good.*** MGM. Director: Norman Z. McLeod. Cast: Eleanor Powell, Ann Sothern, Robert Young, Lionel Barrymore, John Carroll, Red Skelton, Virginia O'Brien, Tom Conway, Dan Dailey, Reginald Owen, Rose Hobart, Phil Silvers. ***Nothing but the Truth.*** Paramount. Director: Elliott Nugent. Cast: Bob Hope, Paulette Goddard, Edward Arnold, Leif Erickson, Helen Vinson, Willie Best, Glenn Anders, Grant Mitchell, Catherine Doucet, Rose Hobart, Mary Forbes. ***I'll Sell My Life.*** Select Attractions. Director: Elmer Clifton. Cast: Rose Hobart, Michael Whalen, Stanley Fields, Joan Woodbury, Roscoe Ates, Richard Bond, Ben Taggart, Paul Maxey. ***No Hand on the Clock.*** Paramount. Director: Frank McDonald. Cast: Chester Morris, Jean Parker, Rose Hobart, Dick Purcell, Astrid Allwyn, Rod Cameron, James Kirkwood, Billie Seward, Grant Withers, George Lewis. ***Mr. and Mrs. North.*** MGM. Director: Robert B. Sinclair. Cast: Gracie Allen, Stanley Andrews, Fortunio Bonanova, Felix Bressart, Tom Conway, Inez Cooper, Jerome Cowan, Stuart Crawford, Virginia Grey, Porter Hall, Rose Hobart, Paul Kelly, Keye Luke, Lucien Littlefield. **1942: *A Gentleman at Heart.*** Twentieth Century–Fox. Director: Ray McCarey. Cast: Cesar Romero, Carole Landis, Milton Berle, J. Carrol Naish, Richard Derr, Rose Hobart, Jerome Cowan, Elisha Cook, Jr., Chick Chandler, Kane Richmond. ***Who Is Hope Schuyler?*** Twentieth Century–Fox. Director: Thomas V. Loring. Cast: Joseph Allen, Janis Carter, Cliff Clark, Jeff Corey, Ricardo Cortez, Pat Flaherty, Byron Foulger, Paul Guilfoyle, Rose Hobart, Sheila Ryan, Joan Valerie. ***Prison Girls*** (aka ***Gallant Lady***). Producers Releasing Corp. Director: William Beaudine. Cast: Rose Hobart, Sidney Blackmer, Claire Rochelle, Lynn Starr, Jane Novak, Vince Barnett, Jack Baxley, Crane Whitley, John Ince, Frank Brownley, Richard Clarke, Spec O'Donnell, Pat McKee, Henry Hastings. ***Dr. Gillespie's New Assistant.***

MGM. Director: Willis Goldbeck. Cast: Lionel Barrymore, Van Johnson, Susan Peters, Richard Quine, Keye Luke, Alma Kruger, Nat Pendleton, Stephan McNally, Frank Orth, Walter Kingsford, Nell Craig, Rose Hobart, Eddie Acuff. **1943: *Salute to the Marines.*** MGM. Director: S. Sylvan Simon. Cast: Wallace Beery, Fay Bainter, Reginald Owen, Keye Luke, Ray Collins, Marilyn Maxwell, William Lundigan, Donald Curtis, Noah Beery, Dick Curtis, Russell Gleason, Rose Hobart. ***Swing Shift Maisie.*** MGM. Director: Norman Z. McLeod. Cast: Ann Sothern, James Craig, Jean Rogers, Connie Gilchrist, John Qualen, Kay Melford, Marta Linden, George Chandler, Jim Davis, Myron Healey, Rose Hobart. ***Adventures of Smilin' Jack.*** Universal (12-chapter serial). Directors: Ray Taylor and Lewis D. Collins. Cast: Tom Brown, Marjorie Lord, Philip Ahn, Jay Novello, Nigel de Brulier, Edgar Barrier, Turhan Bey, Rose Hobart, Keye Luke, Sidney Toler, Cyril Delevanti. ***The Mad Ghoul.*** Universal. Director: James Hogan. Cast: David Bruce, Evelyn Ankers, George Zucco, Turhan Bey, Milburn Stone, Robert Armstrong, Rose Hobart, Charles McGraw, Addison Richards. ***Crime Doctor's Strangest Case.*** Columbia. Director: Eugene J. Forde. Cast: Warner Baxter, Lynn Merrick, Barton MacLane, Virginia Brissac, Rose Hobart, Jerome Cowan, Reginald Denny, Gloria Dickson, George Lynn, Lloyd Bridges, Constance Worth, Sam Flint. **1944: *Song of the Open Road.*** United Artists. Director: S. Sylvan Simon. Cast: Edgar Bergen, Jane Powell, W. C. Fields, Bill Christy, Reginald Denny, Bonita Granville, Rose Hobart, Jackie Moran. ***The Soul of a Monster.*** Columbia. Director: Will Jason. Cast: Rose Hobart, George Macready, Jim Bannon, Jeanne Bates, Ernest Hilliard, Erik Rolf. **1945: *The Brighton Strangler.*** RKO. Director: Max Nosseck. Cast: John Loder, June Duprez, Michael St. Angel, Gilbert Emery, Rose Hobart, Miles Mander, Ian Wolfe, Rex Evans, Lydia Bilbrook. ***Conflict.*** Warner Brothers. Director: Curtis Bernhardt. Cast: Humphrey Bogart, Alexis Smith, Sydney Greenstreet, Rose Hobart, Charles Drake, Grant Mitchell, Patrick O'Moore, Edwin Stanley, Ann Shoemaker, James Flavin, Frank Wilcox, Mary Servoss. **1946: *The Cat Creeps.*** Universal. Director: Erle C. Kenton. Cast: Noah Berry, Jr., Lois Collier, Paul Kelly, Douglass Dumbrille, Fred Brady, Rose Hobart, Jonathan Hale, Vera Lewis, Iris Clive, Arthur Loft, William B. Davidson. ***Canyon Passage.*** Universal. Director: Jacques Tourneur. Cast: Dana Andrews, Brian Donlevy, Susan Hayward, Patricia Roc, Ward Bond, Hoagy Carmichael, Fay Holden, Stanley Ridges, Lloyd Bridges, Andy Devine, Rose Hobart, Halliwell Hobbes, Onslow Stevens, Dorothy Peterson. ***Claudia and David.*** Twentieth Century–Fox. Director: Walter Lang. Cast: Dorothy McGuire, Robert Young, Mary Astor, John Sutton, Gail Patrick, Rose Hobart, Harry Davenport, Florence Bates, Jerome Cowan, Else Janssen, Henry Mowbray, Clara Blandick, Betty Compson. **1947: *The Farmer's Daughter.*** RKO. Director: H. C. Potter. Cast: Loretta Young, Joseph Cotten, Ethel Barrymore, Charles Bickford, Rose Hobart, Rhys Williams, Harry Davenport, Lex Barker, Keith Andes, Don Beddoe, James Arness, Anna Q. Nilsson, William B. Davidson, William

Bakewell, Thurston Hall. ***The Trouble with Women.*** Paramount. Director: Sidney Lanfield. Cast: Ray Milland, Teresa Wright, Brian Donlevy, Rose Hobart, Charles Smith, Lewis Russell, Iris Adrian, Frank Faylan, Rhys Williams, Lloyd Bridges, Norma Varden, Matt McHugh, John Hamilton. ***Cass Timberlane.*** MGM. Director: George Sidney. Cast: Spencer Tracy, Lana Turner, Zachary Scott, Tom Drake, Mary Astor, Albert Dekker, Margaret Lindsay, Rose Hobart, John Litel, Mona Barrie, Josephine Hutchinson, Selena Royle, Richard Gaines, Cameron Mitchell, Milburn Stone, Walter Pidgeon. **1948:** ***Mickey.*** Eagle-Lion. Director: Ralph Murphy. Cast: Lois Butler, Bill Goodwin, Irene Hervey, John Sutton, Rose Hobart, Hattie McDaniel, Skippy Homeier, Beverly Wills, Leon Tyler. **1949:** ***Bride of Vengeance.*** Paramount. Director: Mitchell Leisen. Cast: Paulette Goddard, John Lund, Macdonald Carey, Albert Dekker, John Sutton, Raymond Burr, Charles Dayton, Donald Randolph, Rose Hobart, Nicholas Joy, Fritz Leiber, William Farnum, Anthony Caruso, Billy Gilbert, Frank Puglia, Morgan Farley.

9

William Janney

Actor Edward Arnold thought he was seeing a ghost the night he bumped into his old pal William (Bill) Janney at a party in the early 1940s. "My God, I thought you were dead," Arnold, who was pale with disbelief, said as he thought back to an obituary that appeared in *Variety* several years before.

Janney reassured Arnold, explaining it was the "other" actor of the same name who had died and whose obit he had read.

The juvenile lead who went from the New York stage in the 1920s to Hollywood sound stages in the 1930s spent the last 50 years of his life persuading people he was still alive. Film historians reported the suspected death over the years and even many of his friends spoke of him in the past.

Janney enjoyed reminiscing about his years as an actor, but getting together for an interview presented a challenge. First, he agreed to do an interview by mail, where he would answer a list of questions. When he saw the list, "I was overwhelmed," he said, and decided against the idea. Because of his hearing deficiency, a telephone interview was out. When it looked as though a William Janney interview was impossible, he suggested another idea.

It had been some time since the 83-year-old actor had ventured from the small town in Idaho where he lived with his son. He was bored with his current situation; he missed Los Angeles and the diversity the city offered. He suggested a trip to Atlanta to meet with me and film historian Roi Uselton.

The idea materialized, and he arrived in October 1991. Over the course of his week-long stay, Janney gave his first in-depth interview.

The former actor saw life as an adventure, and even though his health and mind were beginning to fail, he didn't want to disappoint anyone interested in his contribution to film. While his short-term memory was poor, one would

William Janney with Mary Nolan in ***Young Desire*** (1930). (Courtesy of William Janney.)

only say, "Bill, I have a question about this or that film" to see his face light up and his eyes twinkle with enthusiasm. He was instantly back in the era of his youth.

During the week, Janney was questioned extensively about his films, his opinion of Hollywood in the late 1920s and 1930s and his professional and personal dealings with fellow film players. He was often critical of himself, his co-workers and his profession, but also gave credit where it was due. His willingness to tackle any question asked and answer with honesty was a refreshing change from those who tend to glamorize the past.

A decision he made in 1930 brought fresh tears of frustration and lost opportunity as he discussed turning down the role (offered by Columbia mogul Harry Cohn) that might have made him a star.

It troubled him that he never made it into starring roles, never quite graduated from juvenile leads, but he felt fortunate to have had some quality roles and to have worked alongside some of Hollywood's brightest luminaries (Clara Bow, Mary Pickford, George Arliss, Barbara Stanwyck and Lionel Barrymore) and with a roster of some of Hollywood's finest directors (John Ford, Frank Tuttle, Howard Hawks and G. W. Pabst).

He was born Russell Dixon Janney, Jr., on February 15, 1908, in New York City. His father, a successful theatrical producer, and his mother, a chorus girl, met while he (the father) was a student at Yale University.

As far back as Janney could remember, he loved movies, especially Westerns — William S. Hart was his favorite cowboy. He could not remember a time when being an actor was not on his mind. In 1918, at the age of ten, he was cast as the lead in *A Bone of Contention*, a film written and produced by Rosalee Ashton, a friend of his mother. The film was shot on the banks of the Hudson River.

After his parents separated, Janney and his mother moved to Long Beach, California, and lived with his Grandma Cramer, who was a wardrobe mistress in the theater. Here, Janney started going to school. It was a miserable experience, except for the school play in which he appeared.

"They would call me a sissy, and the principal said I was causing a disturbance and that I should be whipped for shooting paper wads," Janney said. His mother pulled him from the school after four years and moved the two of them back to New York.

Soon after Janney and his mother arrived in the East, theatrical producer George C. Tyler, a friend of Janney's grandfather, decided to help the young hopeful. "He said maybe I could cut it, so he let me read a line or two for him," he said.

Tyler saw potential in the 14-year-old and cast him in *Merton of the Movies*. The play, which opened in 1922 and starred Glenn Hunter, was the story of backstage life in the theater.

Hunter* became a close friend and mentor. He took Janney under his wing and introduced him to his young male friends who often came backstage to gab after the show. It was during this time that Janney met tennis pro Bill Tilden and Ramon Novarro, fresh from his appearance in *The Prisoner of Zenda* (1922).

"They all liked young boys," said Janney, "but I wasn't interested in that sort of thing. It wasn't my cup of tea."

Nevertheless, Janney looked up to Hunter, considered him a role model. "Glenn would wear shirts with button-down collars and I would buy the same things. I was at that age where I liked to imitate famous people," he said.

Because he had no time for public school, Janney enrolled in the Professional Children's School in New York City. Ruby Keeler, a classmate, became his first girlfriend. Others in the class were Helen Mack, Marguerite Churchill, Gaylord (Steve) Pendleton and Ashley Buck, a writer who became a lifelong friend.

During the run of the play, Janney organized a special junior performance version of *Merton of the Movies* featuring some of his classmates. Janney, who played Glenn Hunter's role, received a glowing review for his performance by Alexander Woollcott in his book *Enchanted Aisles. Merton of the Movies* ran on Broadway for almost a year before going on tour.

Hunter secured Janney the role of his kid brother in *Grit* (1924), a film directed by Frank Tuttle, a "very nice guy and a good director, but sort of a quiet person."

At 14, Janney was at the right age to take particular notice of a young actress in the cast, Clara Bow. "Part of our scenes were filmed around some old boats, and we would climb around on them. I'd get all excited because she wore an old dress and would pull up her skirt for me. My goodness, she was wild. She had me aroused practically every time I was around her, because she was so sexy."

Working in *Grit* instilled in Janney the desire to become a movie actor. He was all for it, but his next role would not come until the beginning of talkies, some five years later.

In 1927, Janney created the title role in *Tommy*, a successful play (produced by George C. Tyler) that ran on Broadway for almost a year. Following its New York run, *Tommy* took Janney on a tour across the country. It was an eye-opening, unforgettable experience for a 20-year-old.

"On the road, we were treated as second-class citizens, a step above robbers and thieves. They would put us in places where we had no heat," he said. "We were only actors to them and it didn't make any difference if we dropped dead."

By the time the company arrived in Los Angeles, Janney was determined

**Glenn Hunter (1894–1945) did most of his work on the stage in the 1920s and 1930s, but he enjoyed a brief screen career in the 1920s. He appeared with such silent screen stars as Dorothy Gish [*The Country Flapper *(1922)]; Norma Talmadge [*Smilin' Through *(1922]; May McAvoy, [*West of the Water Tower *(1924)]; Constance Bennett [*The Pinch Hitter *(1925)]; and, Alyce Mills [*A Romance of a Million Dollars *(1926)]. Among his plays were* Waterloo Bridge *(1929) and* The Petrified Forest *(1935).*

to break into the movies. He had everything going for him: stage experience, a fine speaking voice, good looks and youthful enthusiasm.

He learned through the grapevine that United Artists had purchased the rights to bring *Coquette,* a successful play, to the screen. It was announced that Mary Pickford, in her first talkie, would play the title role,* that of a spoiled Southern belle. Auditions were conducted for the remaining roles, including that of Pickford's brother, the part that appealed to Janney.

He went to United Artists, met with Pickford and made a screen test. That should have been enough, he thought, but Pickford had trouble deciding. "She had me come back and come back," Janney said. "I was determined to get into the movies, however, so I kept going for more tests."

His quest for the coveted role went on for almost ten weeks. Finally, Pickford saw Janney in a performance of *Tommy* and decided to give him a chance.

Coquette went into production just after Christmas in 1928 and was released the following spring. It was a critical success for Pickford and won her a Best Actress Academy Award.

Janney found Pickford to be an "awfully nice person." He had lunch with her in her bungalow several times during the production and he was later invited to Pickfair on several occasions.

After the run of *Tommy,* Janney decided to stay in Hollywood and in the movies. He brought his mother to California and got an agent to help him secure roles. He was soon introduced to the permissive lifestyle Hollywood offered. For a summer, he shared a beach house with his friend Gaylord Pendleton. "He would bring in girls all the time from the street," he said.

His mother gave him a membership to the Hollywood Athletic Club, to which many film actors belonged. After several trips to the club, certain members began to take notice of him. Being propositioned was nothing new for Janney. Once, back in New York, he said he had to discourage the advances of Bill Tilden in the back seat of a car.

"I remember Randolph Scott came to me at the club and said Nils Asther† was interested in meeting me for that reason," Janney said. "Nils would follow me around and pat me on the arm and shoulder. I didn't do anything with him; it just made me nervous."

Two of Janney's early Hollywood friends were Anderson Lawler§ and Gary Cooper, then deep into his relationship with Lupe Velez, the Mexican Spitfire.

**Helen Hayes had the leading role on Broadway in 1927.*

†Nils Asther (1897–1981) entered films in Europe under the guidance of director Mauritz Stiller. He arrived in Hollywood in 1927 and was a popular romantic star during the last years of the silent era. He was married to actress Vivian Duncan.

§Virginia-born Anderson Lawler (1904–1959) came to Hollywood in the late 1920s from New York, where he appeared on the stage in Her First Affair *and* Caste. *He secured contracts at Paramount and RKO, and worked steadily in films (and sometimes on the stage) throughout the 1930s. When his film career dried up, he returned to Broadway as a producer of plays. His relationship with Cooper is covered in* Cooper's Women *by Jane Ellen Wayne (Prentice Hall Press, 1988).*

"I remember a big party once where there was a lot of drinking going on," Janney said. "After much to drink, we all went to some place to spend the night. There were two beds in the room. I slept in one, and Andy, Gary and Lupe in the other. All during the night, all I heard was giggling and all sorts of carrying on.

"I asked Andy the next morning what was going on over there. He said they were having a threesome, a *ménage à trois.* They were a wild bunch."

Director John Ford liked Janney's performance in *Coquette* and cast him in his next picture, *Salute* (1929), a Fox production centering around the rivalry between West Point and Annapolis. Filmed on location in Annapolis, Maryland, the picture starred George O'Brien and featured Helen Chandler, Johnny Mack Brown and Joyce Compton. John Wayne, then Duke Morrison, had a small role.

"John Ford had Duke carry around my football boots and stuff for me," Janney said. "I liked everybody in the film, with the exception of Ford. I didn't think he was such a wonderful director. It was only my second picture in Hollywood, and I kept asking him if I was doing all right in the part. 'If you're not all right, I'll tell you,' he said to me. 'Don't ask me again.' Frankly, I thought he was a bully."

Ford, said Janney, frequently held up production while he (Ford) recovered from nights of drinking.

Back in Hollywood, Janney signed to play Barbara Stanwyck's young husband in *Mexicali Rose* (1930). He was hardly prepared for her temperament.

When director Erle C. Kenton introduced the two, Janney said Stanwyck turned to her director and barked, "My God, he makes me look like his mother. I don't like him."

Their feelings for each other did not warm as the production continued. "We did this one scene where Stanwyck was rubbing herself all over me. It did not excite me at all. It did nothing for me. She would say something like, 'All right, let's get on with the scene,' just bored to death with the whole damned thing."

Careers in Hollywood could be made or destroyed on the basis of one picture. Janney felt he was at the brink of stardom when Columbia boss Harry Cohn offered him the lead in *Tol'able David (1930).* His mother had other ideas. She asked her son to turn down the part.

The words his mother told him still wrenched his soul 60 years later. "She told me there was this old woman friend of hers whose son had always wanted to play the part.* She said I didn't want to play it anyway. To this day, I don't understand her."

Janney said he made a test for the picture, and that Cohn offered him the role. "Cohn would call me and beg me to come over to talk about the part. I

**Richard Cromwell (1910–1960) had only done a few days of extra work when he was selected to play the leading role in* Tol'able David. *His career lasted into the 1940s. He was married briefly to actress Angela Lansbury.*

turned it down all because this neighbor wanted her son to play the part. When I talk about it, it depresses the hell out of me.

"This really spoiled the whole thing for me, because I might have been offered a contract with Columbia. As it turned out, I never did get a contract, and Harry Cohn never offered me anything else."

Bad luck, Janney felt, was his destiny. He found himself being cast in small roles, well below his potential. He was so distraught over his menial role in *The Girl Said No* (1930) that he went to director Sam Wood to complain.

"I think this picture is awful, Mr. Wood," Janney said. "I played Barbara Stanwyck's husband in the picture before this one and now I'm doing this." Not surprisingly, Janney never again worked for Wood.

The one good thing that came out of *Shooting Straight* (1930)—Janney didn't care for the picture or his role—was his friendship with Richard Dix, who appeared in the film. Dix liked Janney from the start and later wanted him for a fairly important role in *Cimarron* (1931). "I tested for the part, but I photographed too young. They said, 'You can't age this man.' So, I lost out on that,"* said Bill. As it turned out, Janney was an extra in the film and received no screen credit.

In *Young Desire* (1930), Janney was cast as the leading man, but the picture was "a mess." In the film, he falls for a carnival performer (Mary Nolan) and tries to help her plot a better course in life. He wants marriage, but she hesitates, feeling her reputation will alienate him from his parents (George Irving and Claire McDowell) and jeopardize his future. She solves the dilemma by jumping to her death.

What to do with Mary Nolan† both in the film's plot and on the set were causes of concern for Janney. "Mary Nolan took dope and practically everything else," he said. "She was supposed to have had all of these venereal diseases and it scared me to death. She would rub herself all over me, and I didn't like it when she played with my toes, sticking her fingers all between them. Then we'd do these love scenes in which she would stick her tongue down my throat. After the director yelled cut, I would go to the dressing room and gargle with Listerine, because I was afraid she would give me something."

A number of years later, Janney was walking down Broadway when he passed a nightclub where Nolan was working. "She was so happy to see me," he said. "She told the audience in a drunken slur, 'This is my leading man.' I felt so sorry for her."

**Donald Dilloway played the part.*

†Mary Nolan (1905–1948) started on the stage in the early 1920s as Imogene "Bubbles" Wilson. She worked in the Ziegfeld Follies until a scandal surrounding her affair with a married man drove her out of the country to Germany, where she appeared in foreign productions as Mary Imogene Robertson. At 22, she went to Hollywood as Mary Nolan and appeared in 20 films before her retirement from the screen in 1932. Known as the "Hard Luck Girl," she died in 1948 of a liver ailment. In her last years, she had twice attempted suicide and had been hospitalized for malnutrition.

Helen Chandler, William Janney, Joyce Compton and (standing in front) George O'Brien in *Salute* (1929). (Courtesy of William Janney.)

William Janney and Barbara Stanwyck display affection for the benefit of the cameras in ***Mexicali Rose*** (1929). (Courtesy of William Janney.)

Douglas Fairbanks, Jr., William Janney and Richard Barthelmess in *The Dawn Patrol* (1930). (Courtesy of William Janney.)

In *The Dawn Patrol* (1930), Janney joined Douglas Fairbanks, Jr. (he played his brother in the picture), Richard Barthelmess and Neil Hamilton as doomed British World War I aviators. The picture was director Howard Hawks' first talkie.

"I really liked Hawks as a director and as a person," said Janney. "I remember his brother had been killed in a plane accident* and he wouldn't allow us to do any of our own stunts.

Still, according to Janney, the picture was strenuous to make. Long hours and the stifling conditions of an air-tight sound stage took its toll on the cast.

"I did this one scene and it was hot as hell. I got up in a plane [hanging in the studio] and puked all over everything. It was terrible."

Two good roles came Janney's way when George Arliss cast him in two of his pictures, *The Man Who Played God* and *A Successful Calamity*, both released in 1932. In *The Man Who Played God*, Arliss is a concert pianist who goes deaf and learns to read lips. From his window overlooking the park, he reads the

**Kenneth Hawks was killed in January 1930 when two planes collided during the filming of an aerial scene for* Such Men Are Dangerous *(1930). At the time, he was married to actress Mary Astor.*

lips of Janney and Grace Durkin as they discuss some financial need. He immediately sends a check down to relieve their burden.

Janney never had scenes with Bette Davis, also in the cast; however, he did run into her at the studio from time to time. "One time during the filming of *The Man Who Played God*, she came into the studio commissary and sat down next to me and snapped, 'Get up, I've got some friends coming and I don't want you around. You're going to spoil my party.' It turns out she had a magazine writer coming to interview her."

In *A Successful Calamity*, Janney appeared as the son of Arliss and Mary Astor. "Mary was a great beauty and I liked working with her," said Janney, "but what language. Here was this beautiful face with all this profanity coming out."

On the merits of the Arliss films, Warner Brothers cast Janney in several other pictures that year: *Two Seconds* with Edward G. Robinson; *Crooner* with David Manners and Ann Dvorak; and *The Mouthpiece* with Warren William, who became a good friend.

He played a sheriff's son in *I Am a Fugitive from a Chain Gang* (1932); however, the scene in which Janney picks up Paul Muni in a Model T Ford, was cut from the final print. The next year, he appeared with Muni again, this time as his grandson in *The World Changes* (1933).

"Muni's wife Bella was right there on the set," Janney recalled. "She was never far from him, always watching him. As far as she was concerned, it was to hell with the rest of us."

His role as Mary Carlisle's boyfriend in *Should Ladies Behave?* was one of his best. The film was based on the play *The Vinegar Tree*, in which Janney and Billie Burke appeared. MGM cast him in the film version, but selected Alice Brady to play the role Burke created on stage.

Burke, a friend of Janney's, felt he didn't do enough to help her secure the part. "I told Billie I wanted her to have the part, but there was really nothing I could do. I didn't get jobs all the time—none this good, and I had to take what came along."

In the picture, Janney had a number of scenes with Lionel Barrymore. "They told me he wouldn't bother to read the script with me, so I would have to learn his part as well as my own. They were right. I did the best I could. Barrymore and I got along fine."

Another role of substance was that of Richard Barthelmess' son in *A Modern Hero* (1934). The film, which featured Jean Muir and Marjorie Rambeau, was director G. W. Pabst's* only American film. "He was very nice to me, but the problem was, we couldn't understand what the hell he was talking about. He hardly spoke any English at all. I had a terrible time with the picture."

**G. W. Pabst (1885–1967) had been a European film director since the early 1920s. He directed Greta Garbo in* The Street of Sorrow *(1925) and Louise Brooks in* Pandora's Box *(1929) and* The Diary of a Lost Girl *(1929).*

Without Children, *Sweepstake Annie* and *Born to Gamble*, all made in 1935 for Liberty, were quickies and "just as well forgotten," said Janney. "These were the films I'd take when I would get broke and was not getting any calls. Let's please forget them." His memories of Fox's *The Great Hotel Murder* (1935) were just as bad. Madge Bellamy, a beauty from the silent screen, was back on her old lot and hoping for a comeback with her small role as Tessie. "One morning, poor Madge came riding up in this old, beat-up limousine. Her father, wearing a tattered chauffeur's uniform, was her driver. It just made me sick. I wanted to go over and say hello, but she didn't look like she wanted to talk, so I just let it go."

Bonnie Scotland, a Laurel and Hardy comedy, was Janney's best film of 1935 and one of the last good roles of his career. He played the love interest of June Lang.

"Oliver Hardy was the nice one," said Janney. "Stan Laurel was okay. One time I said something that was kind of a joke and Laurel said, 'Look, I'm the comedian around here.' I told him I was sorry, that I didn't mean anything by it."

Sutter's Gold (1936), the story of California gold pioneer John Sutter, should have done better at the box office, said Janney. "I was disappointed that it didn't turn out to be a big deal. I liked James Cruze, the director, but no one seemed to take him seriously."

Janney put his screen career on hold in 1937 to appear on the New York stage in *Never Trouble Trouble*. The following year, he was back in Hollywood and appeared in his final film, *Clipped Wings* (1938), an independent aviation drama. "Some people in Texas had put up the money to make the film, but it was just awful," he said. "They asked me to come back to do a scene over for free, because they had run out of money. I told them I had had enough of it."

He didn't know, while filming *Clipped Wings*, it would be his last film. "I knew I was getting into a rut and that I just wasn't doing well in pictures. I just let it go—I quit."

He moved to New York and got into radio, but said the work never appealed to him. It was just a job that paid well. For almost two years, he had his own children's radio show, *Howie-Wing*. He did other shows and appeared in commercials.

It was through radio that he met his first wife, scriptwriter Madlin Hobbs. They were married in 1940. A son, Russell, was born in 1950.

Before the U. S. Army could draft Janney into service, he joined the U. S. Coast Guard. He worked in the entertainment aspect of the service for two-and-a-half years and was discharged after World War II.

After his release, Janney and his wife followed one of his service buddies to Arkansas where, under the G. I. Bill, he enrolled at the University of Arkansas. After earning a degree, he taught one semester of English at a local high school.

Realizing the teaching profession wasn't for him, Janney moved the family to California. In 1961, he went to work for the *Los Angeles Times* as a security guard. His wife died in 1968.

Janney remained in California, and through a friend met real estate broker Venice Daniels. The two were married in 1970. He retired from his job in 1973.

After losing his second wife to diabetes in 1989, Janney sold their home in Tujunga and moved to Idaho, where he lived with his son and family until his death on December 27, 1992.

Although sometimes critical of his career, he relished recalling his show business past. He said he liked working in the theater better than in movies, and that he should have concentrated his efforts more toward the stage.

"The theater was more interesting to me," he said, "because you felt like you had an audience. Movies were kind of cold and impersonal. I didn't care for them too much."

Also, he regretted never being able to "grow up" on the screen. "I got so tired of being somebody's little kid brother all the time," he said.

While some of his closest friends, i.e. Lionel Atwill and Warren William, were in show business, Janney never cared for actors as a whole. "They were out for themselves, and I found them to be selfish, self-centered and egotistical. There was an awful lot of phoniness [in 1930s Hollywood]. I didn't think it was such a wonderful place to be."

When pressed to give his best films, he hesitated, but finally came up with two: *Coquette* and *Should Ladies Behave?* "They were all right, but I don't think any of them were very good," he said. "I don't think there was anything I did that set the world on fire."

FILMOGRAPHY

1917: *A Bone of Contention.* Director: Rosalee Ashton. Cast: William Janney. **1924: *Grit.*** Film Guild-Hodkinson. Director: Frank Tuttle. Cast: Glenn Hunter, Helenka Adamowska, Roland Young, Osgood Perkins, Clara Bow, William Janney. **1929: *Coquette.*** United Artists. Director: Sam Taylor. Cast: Mary Pickford, John Mack Brown, Matt Moore, John Sainpolis, William Janney, Henry Kolker, George Irving, Louise Beavers. **1930: *Salute.*** Fox. Director: John Ford. Cast: George O'Brien, Frank Albertson, William Janney, Helen Chandler, Joyce Compton, Rex Bell, David Butler, Stepin Fetchit, John Wayne. ***Mexicali Rose.*** Columbia. Director: Erle C. Kenton. Cast: Barbara Stanwyck, Sam Hardy, William Janney, Louis Natheaux, Arthur Rankin. ***The Girl Said No.*** MGM. Director: Sam Wood. Cast: William Haines, Leila Hyams, Polly Moran, Marie Dressler, William Janney, Francis X. Bushman, Clara Blandick, Junior Coghlan. ***Those Who Dance.*** Warner Brothers. Director: William Beaudine. Cast: Betty Compson, William Boyd, William Janney, Lila Lee, Monte Blue, Wilfred Lucas, Cornelius Keefe, DeWitt Jennings. ***Shooting***

Straight. RKO. Director: George Archainbaud. Cast: Richard Dix, Mary Lawlor, James Neill, Matthew Betz, George Cooper, William Janney, Robert E. O'Connor. ***Young Desire.*** Universal. Director: Lewis D. Collins. Cast: Mary Nolan, William Janney, Mae Busch, Ralf Harolde, George Irving, Claire McDowell, Alice Lake. ***The Dawn Patrol.*** First National. Director: Howard Hawks. Cast: Richard Barthelmess, Douglas Fairbanks, Jr., Neil Hamilton, William Janney, Gardner James, James Finlayson, Clyde Cook. ***The Pay Off.*** RKO. Director: Lowell Sherman, Marian Nixon, Hugh Trevor, William Janney, Helene Millard, George F. Marion, Walter McGrail, Lita Chevret. **1931:** ***The Right of Way.*** First National. Director: Frank Lloyd. Cast: Conrad Nagel, Loretta Young, Fred Kohler, William Janney, Snitz Edwards, George Pearce, Halliwell Hobbes, Olive Tell, Brandon Hurst, Yola D'Avril. ***Girls Demand Excitement.*** Fox. Director: Seymour Felix. Cast: Virginia Cherrill, John Wayne, Marguerite Churchill, Edward Nugent, Helen Jerome Eddy, Terrance Ray, Martha Sleeper, William Janney, David Rollins. ***Cimarron.*** RKO. Director: Wesley Ruggles. Cast: Richard Dix, Irene Dunne, Estelle Taylor, Nance O'Neil, William Collier, Jr., Roscoe Ates, George E. Stone, Stanley Fields, Robert McWade, Edna May Oliver, Nancy Dover, Eugene Jackson, Otto Hoffman, William Orlamond, Frank Beal, Helen Parrish, Donald Dillaway, Junior Johnson, William Janney, Edith Fellows. ***Meet the Wife.*** Columbia. Director: A. Leslie Pierce. Cast: Lew Cody, Laura LaPlante, Joan Marsh, Harry Myers, Claud Allister, William Janney, Aileen Carlyle, Edgar Norton. **1932:** ***The Man Who Played God.*** Warner Brothers. Director: John G. Adolfi. Cast: George Arliss, Violet Heming, Bette Davis, Andre Luget, Louise Closser Hale, Donald Cook, Ivan Simpson, Oscar Apfel, Charles Evans, Hedda Hopper, William Janney, Fred Howard, Murray Kinnell, Paul Porcasi, Raymond [Ray] Milland, Dorothy LeBaire, Grace Durkin. ***Two Seconds.*** First National. Director: Mervyn LeRoy. Cast: Edward G. Robinson, Vivienne Osborne, Guy Kibbee, Preston Foster, J. Carrol Naish, Frederick Burton, Harry Beresford, Dorothea Wolbert, Berton Churchill, William Janney, Edward McWade, Adrienne Dore, Otto Hoffman. ***The Mouthpiece.*** Warner Brothers. Directors: James Flood, Elliott Nugent. Cast: Warren William, Sidney Fox, Aline MacMahon, John Wray, Mae Madison, Ralph Ince, Morgan Wallace, Guy Kibbee, J. Carrol Naish, Walter Walker, Stanley Fields, Murray Kinnell, Noel Francis, William Janney, Polly Walters, Jack La Rue. ***A Successful Calamity.*** Warner Brothers. Director: John G. Adolfi. Cast: George Arliss, Mary Astor, Evalyn Knapp, Grant Mitchell, Hardie Albright, William Janney, David Torrence, Randolph Scott, Hale Hamilton. ***Crooner.*** Warner Brothers. Director: Lloyd Bacon. Cast: David Manners, Ann Dvorak, Ken Murray, J. Carrol Naish, Guy Kibbee, Claire Dodd, Allen Vincent, Edward J. Nugent, William Janney, Teddy Joyce, Sheila Terry. ***The Iron Master.*** Allied. Director: Chester M. Franklin. Cast: J. Farrell MacDonald, Reginald Denny, Lila Lee, Esther Howard, William Janney, Virginia Sale, Tom London, Nola Luxford, Astrid Allwyn, Otto Hoffman. ***Under-Cover Man.***

Paramount. Director: James Flood. Cast: George Raft, Nancy Carroll, Roscoe Karns, Lew Cody, Gregory Ratoff, Noel Francis, David Landau, Paul Porcasi, William Janney. ***I Am a Fugitive from a Chain Gang.*** Warner Brothers. Director: Mervyn LeRoy. Cast: Paul Muni, Glenda Farrell, Helen Vinson, Noel Francis, Preston Foster, Allen Jenkins, Berton Churchill, Edward Ellis, David Landau, Hale Hamilton, Sally Blane, Louise Carter, Willard Robertson, Robert McWade, Robert Warwick, William Le Maire, Edward J. McNamara, Sheila Terry, Edward Arnold, Oscar Apfel, William Janney, C. Henry Gordon, Spencer Charters, Roscoe Karns, Charles Middleton, Jack La Rue. **1933:** ***The Crime of the Century.*** Paramount. Director: William Beaudine. Cast: Jean Hersholt, Wynne Gibson, Stuart Erwin, Frances Dee, Gordon Westcott, Robert Elliott, David Landau, William Janney, Bodil Rosing, Samuel S. Hinds. ***Terror Aboard.*** Paramount. Director: Paul Sloane. Cast: John Halliday, Charlie Ruggles, Shirley Grey, Neil Hamilton, Jack La Rue, Verree Teasdale, Stanley Fields, Leila Bennett, Morgan Wallace, Thomas Jackson, William Janney, Paul Hurst, Frank Hagney, Paul Porcasi, Bobby Dunn. ***Secret of the Blue Room.*** Universal. Director: Kurt Neumann. Cast: Lionel Atwill, Gloria Stuart, Paul Lukas, Edward Arnold, Onslow Stevens, William Janney, Elizabeth Patterson, Muriel Kirkland, Robert Barrat, Russell Hopton. ***King of the Wild Horses.*** Columbia. Director: Earl Haley. Cast: Rex, Lady, Marquis, William Janney, Dorothy Appleby, Wallace MacDonald, Harry Semels, Ford West, Art Mix. ***Should Ladies Behave?*** MGM. Director: Harry Beaumont. Cast: Lionel Barrymore, Alice Brady, Conway Tearle, Katherine Alexander, Mary Carlisle, William Janney, Halliwell Hobbes. ***The World Changes.*** First National. Director: Mervyn LeRoy. Cast: Paul Muni, Aline MacMahon, Mary Astor, Donald Cook, Jean Muir, Guy Kibbee, Patricia Ellis, Theodore Newton, Margaret Lindsay, Gordon Westcott, Alan Dinehart, Henry O'Neill, Anna Q. Nilsson, Arthur Hohl, William Janney, Mickey Rooney, Douglas Dumbrille, Marjorie Gateson, Oscar Apfel, Alan Mowbray. ***A Modern Hero.*** Warner Brothers. Director: G. W. Pabst. Cast: Richard Barthelmess, Jean Muir, Marjorie Rambeau, Verree Teasdale, Florence Eldridge, Dorothy Burgess, Hobart Cavanaugh, William Janney, Arthur Hohl, Theodore Newton. ***As the Earth Turns.*** Warner Brothers. Director: Alfred E. Green. Cast: Jean Muir, Donald Woods, Russell Hardie, Emily Lowry, Arthur Hohl, Dorothy Peterson, David Landau, Clara Blandick, William Janney, Dorothy Appleby, Sarah Padden, Egon Brecher. ***A Successful Failure.*** Monogram. Director: Arthur Lubin. Cast: William Collier, Sr., Lucille Gleason, Russell Hopton, George Breakston, William Janney, Gloria Shea, Clarence Wilson, Jameson Thomas. **1935:** ***Without Children*** (a.k.a. ***Penthouse Party***). Liberty. Director: William Nigh. Cast: Bruce Cabot, Marguerite Churchill, Evelyn Brent, Reginald Denny, Dorothy Lee, William Janney, Dickie Moore, Cora Sue Collins, Lillian Harmer. ***Sweepstake Annie.*** Liberty. Director: William Nigh. Cast: Tom Brown, Marian Nixon, Wera Engels, Inez Courtney, Ivan Lebedeff, Lucien Littlefield, Dorothy Peterson, William

Janney, Carol Tevis. ***The Great Hotel Murder.*** Fox. Director: Eugene Forde. Cast: Edmund Lowe, Victor McLaglen, Rosemary Ames, Mary Carlisle, Henry O'Neill, C. Henry Gordon, William Janney, Charles C. Wilson, John Wray, John Qualen, Herman Bing, Madge Bellamy, Mary Alden, Otto Hoffman. ***Born to Gamble.*** Liberty. Director: Phil Rosen. Cast: Onslow Stevens, H. B. Warner, Maxine Doyle, Eric Linden, Lois Wilson, William Janney, Ben Alexander, Lucien Prival, Crauford Kent. ***Bonnie Scotland.*** MGM. Director: James W. Horne. Cast: Stan Laurel, Oliver Hardy, June Lang, William Janney, Anne Grey, Vernon Steel, James Finlayson, David Torrence, Maurice Black, Daphne Pollard. **1936:** ***Sutter's Gold.*** Universal. Director: James Cruze. Cast: Edward Arnold, Lee Tracy, Binnie Barnes, Katherine Alexander, Montagu Love, Addison Richards, John Miljan, Harry Carey, William Janney, Nan Grey, Robert Warwick, Morgan Wallace, Allen Vincent. ***Sitting on the Moon.*** Republic. Director: Ralph Staub. Cast: Roger Pryor, Grace Bradley, William Newell, Pert Kelton, Henry Kolker, Henry Wadsworth, Joyce Compton, Pierre Watkin, William Janney, June Martel. ***Hopalong Cassidy Returns.*** Paramount. Director: Nate Watt. Cast: William Boyd, George Hayes, Gail Sheridan, Evelyn Brent, Stephen Morris [Morris Ankrum], William Janney, Irving Bacon, Grant Richards. **1938:** ***Clipped Wings.*** Ace Pictures. Director: Stuart Paton. Cast: Lloyd Hughes, Delmar Watson, Rosalind Keith, William Janney, Glen Boles, Henry Otho, Russell Hicks, Joseph Girard, Jason Robards.

10

Marcia Mae Jones

"When I was sitting in the classroom, I wanted to be on the set. When I was on the set, I wanted to be back at school. I never really wanted to be where I was. Does that make sense?"

This conflict was only part of the agony going on in the mind of one of the Golden Age's most talented child stars: Marcia Mae Jones.

One only needs to view her work to see the talent she had. Jones began her career, under the guidance of her sometimes overbearing mother, in the early 1930s, playing bits and extras until director William Wyler, sure of her abilities, cast her in the finest role of her long career: *These Three* (1936).

Wyler was perfect in his casting, for Jones brilliantly portrayed the qualities called for in Rosalie: shyness, insecurity and fear. It's true she pulled the performance from her own talent as an actress; however, she also brought those qualities of extreme insecurity to the role from her real-life situation. She identified with Rosalie.

From childhood and throughout much of her adult life, Jones tried to cope with the expectations that came with being a child performer. Like her mother, she battled insecurity and agonized over the feeling of never belonging in her surroundings.

"When I was a kid, I was told to act like an adult," she said. "Then, I was told to act like a child. I never knew which way I was supposed to act."

It took a mental breakdown in the 1960s to bring Jones face-to-face with her problems, which also included alcoholism. Getting to know the real person inside her through years of therapy led her to the understanding of the trauma she experienced in her childhood.

A week before Halloween in 1993, Marcia Mae Jones and I met at her Sherman Oaks apartment where she lived quietly with several cats. Before we sat down for an interview, we had first made plans to have dinner. She left the choice of restaurant up to me—I picked Chinese. We found a tiny restaurant on Ventura Boulevard in Sherman Oaks.

Over dinner she wanted to clarify several points before we got to questioning later. First, she had forgotten certain portions of her childhood, a film here and there, because of certain traumas she blocked from memory. Second, she and her mother (in later years) worked through their strained relationship, and Jones forgave her for the often unbearable pressures and sometimes extreme behavior.

With dinner over, the waiter brought the check and two fortune cookies. While we broke open our cookies, I made the remark, "I hope my fortune is not a bad one."

"Not to worry," she said. "If it *is* bad, we'll just trade. How about that?"

An early publicity portrait of Marcia Mae Jones. (Courtesy of Marcia Mae Jones.)

She offered no more then, but I knew there was more left unsaid. Later, back at her place, she said she had finally grown accustomed to the misfortunes that had plagued her. Unfortunate turns in her life were almost expected.

"Some people have luck and some people don't," she said. "I am one of those people who has never really had good luck."

If she had luck at all, she said, it was that she survived to tell the story of her life. "Many of the kids I grew up with are dead because of alcohol and drugs. I'm lucky to be sitting here talking with you."

Marcia Mae Jones' mother and father, William and Freda, met in Seattle, Washington, and married out of loneliness. Freda had spent time in a Catholic orphanage before being sent to live with some aunts in Canada, and William ran away from home in North Carolina after accidentally (while smoking a corncob pipe) setting the farm on fire.

They eventually settled in Los Angeles, where he became a telegraph operator for the *Los Angeles Times*, a position he held for the rest of his career.*

**Marcia made a point of explaining that she was never the sole breadwinner for the family, as is the case with many child performers. Her father always worked.*

Marcia, born August 1, 1924, was the youngest of five children (a sister died in infancy from an enlarged heart). Jones' mother had a love for the motion picture industry and may have had early ambitions of being an actress, but it was her children whom she first led into the business. The family lived rather modestly, and she wanted her children to have nice clothes and for the family to find better living arrangements than their duplex on Kingsley Avenue, a short walk from Paramount Studios.

In the mid–1920s, while their father was traveling with his job, their mother was busy courting the studios in search of work for her children. Marcia's siblings, Marvin, Macon and Margaret, started to work first. One day, when the Jones' baby sitter failed to show, Mrs. Jones took Marcia with her to Paramount, where Margaret was working.

During the day, director James Cruze walked by and, seeing Marcia, said, "That's the baby." He cast her in *Mannequin* (1926)—she played Dolores Costello as an infant.

While it's true that life as a child actress was not a particularly happy one for Marcia, and that she blocked out certain parts from her memory, she was also too young (at five or six years old) to remember the details of her early films. For instance, she said she had unbilled extra and bit parts in many films during the early 1930s. There was a film with Jean Harlow and Franchot Tone and some *Our Gang* comedies of which she has no recollection.

One of the first parts she remembered was as a dying child in *Night Nurse* (1931) with Barbara Stanwyck and Clark Gable. Not much about the film itself did she remember, only one scene. "I'm sitting in this tub—they had put me in a milk bath—with my head leaning over, and I'm supposed to be dying. I kept getting up, and they kept sitting me back down. They had the fire too hot underneath, and finally the prop man said, 'My God, no wonder she can't sit still. We've got the fire too hot.' After the picture was completed, Clark Gable gave me an autographed photo on which he wrote, 'To the lady in the milk bath.'"

It was during the making of *The Champ* (1931), in a scene with Jackie Cooper, that Marcia learned to spit—or at least tried. "Jackie has always kidded me about the scene in which he's trying to teach me to spit. The camera was rolling and I'm trying to spit, but all I can do is drool. The director, King Vidor, was getting annoyed with me. I did finally get it."

The routine of playing bits and extras changed suddenly when Marcia was cast as Rosalie in *These Three*. She was on the 20th Century–Fox lot filming *Gentle Julia* (1936) with Jane Withers when her mother insisted she come immediately with her to an interview. It didn't matter that Marcia was hot, tired and dirty from her current picture; they could waste no time in getting to United Artists.

"My hands were dirty, and I was filthy all over. I was so embarrassed," Marcia said. "I walked into this office and there was William Wyler sitting at a desk. I started to apologize for my hands and dress being so dirty. He said,

'That's Rosalie.' I turned around to see who Rosalie was. He was talking about me. He selected me right then and there for the part."

These Three, an adaptation of Lillian Hellman's Broadway play *The Children's Hour*, told the story of two women (Miriam Hopkins and Merle Oberon) operating a girls' school and the way they are ruined by the malicious lies of one of the students, Mary Tilford (Bonita Granville). Marcia was praised for her touching performance, bringing to life the shy, inhibited Rosalie, whom Mary cruelly manipulates and bullies into lying.

Wrote one *New York Times* critic, "The honors really belong to Bonita Granville as Mary Tilford and to Marcia Mae Jones as Rosalie, her 'vassal' among the schoolgirls. Both youngsters are splendid, and if our personal vote goes to little Miss Jones, then it may be because Florence McGee has branded the role of Mary (in the stage performance) indelibly in our memory of hers."

Although 12-year-old Marcia brought her own inhibitions to the role, she also credited Wyler for pulling out the performance of her career. "He was very tough to work for, but what a marvelous director. He would make us shoot scenes over and over again. He would just sit there and look at us, and we knew we were not doing something right.

"We had to redo the sound in the scene where Bonita confesses to lying, because they were getting ready to tear down the set for another film. I had cried so much during that scene I had no tears left. Wyler didn't know what to do. Finally, he said, 'You're faking it,' which I was. Then he turned to me and said, 'You know, I interviewed over 300 little girls and chose you. I guess I made a mistake.' That was it—I cried." Wyler later apologized for the remark.*

Marcia marveled at the cast of *These Three,* the sheer talent and beauty before her. "I couldn't keep my eyes off of Merle Oberon, and while Miriam Hopkins wasn't a terribly warm person, she was always very lovely to me. Margaret Hamilton was also a nice woman."

Because of her intense love of children, Hamilton had a difficult time with a scene in which she had to discipline Bonita's character. "She was very upset, because she was pregnant and didn't believe in slapping." So difficult was the scene that Hamilton called Bonita by her real name instead of her character name, Mary. "The line read something like, 'Come here, Mary,' but Margaret said, 'Come here, Bonita.' You never hear it because you're wrapped up in the action, but it's there—I caught it."

Bonita Granville,† who appeared with Marcia in several other films and

**Marcia kept in touch with Wyler over the years and said she would have liked to work with him as an adult.* These Three *was later remade (by Wyler) as* The Children's Hour *(1962). "I saw Wyler later and he asked if I had seen the second version. He said, 'Our version was the best.' He was right."*

†Bonita Granville (1923–1988) started her career on the stage and was acting in films by 1932. She played the fictional Nancy Drew character in a series of films in the late 1930s. After her marriage to millionaire Jack Wrather, she retired from the screen, but returned later to supervise the Lassie *television series, to which her husband had bought the rights.*

Bonita Granville, William Wyler and Marcia Mae Jones on the set of *These Three* (1936). (Courtesy of Marcia Mae Jones.)

became a childhood friend, also came from a strict background and entered films under the force of a strong stage mother. "Her mother wouldn't allow Bonita to ride a bicycle. Our house on Curson Avenue, where we lived at the time, wasn't far from Goldwyn Studios, and we'd go home for lunch. Bonita would come over, get on my bike and, unknown to her mother, learned to ride."

Granville's performance as the lying, malicious schoolgirl garnered her a nomination for Best Supporting Actress and attracted attention from moviegoers. "After *These Three* was released, someone in England sent Bonita a Bible and told her that if she read a chapter a day, she would become a good girl. It made her feel really terrible."

These Three also elevated Marcia's status in the business.* Her performance demonstrated her true talent as an actress. It did little, however, for her low self-esteem.

"One minute I was praised, the next minute I was downed. These were the very unfair things that took me years to understand. I constantly heard, 'You've got to be quiet, Marcia Mae has to learn her lines.' It was Marcia Mae this and Marcia Mae that. That's where the jealousy from my siblings came from. They blamed me for it, when it was my mother who was doing it."

**Marcia recreated her role as Rosalie in the* Lux Radio Theatre *version of* These Three *in 1937. Cecil B. DeMille hosted and directed the program in which Barbara Stanwyck, Mary Astor and Errol Flynn also appeared.*

There was no escaping the attention she received at school, where matters grew worse. "Especially after *These Three*, the kids at school began to call me the little star. I developed an I-don't-care attitude that made me seem snobbish, but I wasn't. I just didn't know how to deal with the attention."

If there was comfort to be found, it was in the work, which she always enjoyed. After *These Three*, Goldwyn signed both Jones and Granville to a year's contract and loaned them to David Selznick to appear together in *The Garden of Allah* (1936).

Jones then played an invalid in *Heidi* (1937) with Shirley Temple. "We were on location at Lake Arrowhead for that one. Shirley and I would play miniature golf, and there would be about eight or nine bodyguards around us. It didn't bother Shirley, but it sure annoyed me."

The industry buzz was that Jones' performance in *Heidi* was so impressive that Shirley's mother would see to it Marcia would never again appear with her daughter. It was strictly publicity, because Mrs. Temple requested Jones for *The Little Princess* (1939), another of her best films. "I liked both Shirley and her mother a lot," Jones said. "Mrs. Temple, who was always dressed in a hat and gloves, used to sit next to the camera on a stool. At four in the afternoon, she would give Shirley and me a piece of chocolate. She would say, 'Now, sparkle, Shirley. Sparkle, Marcia Mae.'

"Shirley had a bounce about her. There was nothing insecure about Shirley Temple, let me tell you. I used to love to go into her dressing room. It was all white and full of dolls."

Jones worked with Paul Muni in the highly acclaimed *The Life of Emile Zola* (1937). She was made to fear the great actor before she met him. "When I went to the set, the dialogue director asked if I knew my line, explaining that Paul Muni wouldn't work with anyone who didn't know their lines. I got the same from my mother and the director, William Dieterle. I was drilled and drilled, until I was scared to death of the man.

"In the scene, I am walking down this hall carrying a tray of dishes and food to him, because he's a sick man. I'm so frightened by Muni, you can actually hear every one of those dishes rattling. I've seen the film several times on television, and every time I see it, I die laughing. I was so nervous. Guess who blew their lines? Paul Muni did! At the minute he goofed, he apologized to me for blowing his lines while I was having to carry that tray of dishes. I thought he was terrific."

Jones worked again with Margaret Hamilton in *Mountain Justice* (1937) and struggled under the direction of the demanding Michael Curtiz. "That was a wild film. Curtiz was so emotional. In one scene, I'm on the witness stand defending my sister. Curtiz would yell, 'Tears, Garcia, tears, Garcia'—he had a lot of trouble with English and couldn't say Marcia. It was about 104 [degrees] in the Valley that day, and my face was dripping wet, not from tears, but from perspiration."

Marcia Mae Jones (left) and Shirley Temple in *Heidi* (1937). (Courtesy of Marcia Mae Jones.)

It was during the film that Jones fell in love with the attorney (George Brent). "He had that charm and was so real. What a wonderful sense of humor he had. We'd be in the middle of an emotional scene, and he would come up with some joke. Curtiz got so mad at him, he ordered him off the set, because everything to him [Curtiz] was a big deal."

In *Two Wise Maids* (1937), the maids being Alison Skipworth and Polly Moran, Jones is sent to jail for stealing a pair of skates. "Poor Alison had a drinking problem," said Jones. "I remember every time she'd pull me over to her, the odor would knock me down."

In 1938, David Selznick signed Jones to play Becky in *The Adventures of Tom Sawyer.* After an extensive search for Tom Sawyer, Tommy Kelly, an unknown juvenile, was cast. Because Jones was taller than Kelly, she said she was replaced by Ann Gillis and was given the role of Mary, Tom's sister.

In *Lady Behave!* (1938), Jones had the role of Neil Hamilton's teenage daughter. She liked working with Hamilton, but was not so impressed with Sally Eilers and Joseph Schildkraut. "I don't want to imply that Sally was a bad person, but she was carried away with herself. She wanted very much to be the star. Schildkraut got his kicks out of talking about sex. It frightened me then, but later, he came into Greg Bautzer's office when I was working there and tried to pull that again. I told him I was not the little girl I was, that I was a woman, and for him to get the hell out of that office."

By the early 1940s, Jones had grown from child roles to playing ingenues (she was teamed with Jackie Moran in six films at Monogram). Her career, like those of many child performers, began a decline with advancing adolescence. Part of the blame fell on her mother's lack of security, Jones said. She put the pressure on Jones, not on the industry.

"My mother never fought for raises or for better billing for me. She was fearful of the business. She just wanted me to get the job, didn't want to do anything that might hurt my chances. She never got the right agent for me. I always got the agent who was the little guy instead of the big one."

Getting a solid education was another aspect of Jones' life that was neglected because of work. She attended public schools (high school with Peter Lawford, Judy Garland, Mickey Rooney, Ricardo Montalban and others) until she transferred to Long's Professional School as a teenager.

"I paid $10 for a velvet blue diploma, and I graduated knowing absolutely nothing," Jones said. "They should not have let me graduate. My mother didn't mean to hurt me, but getting a good education was not a top priority for her. Of course, the day came when I had to get a job, and I didn't know how to do anything."

Jones married Lieutenant Robert Chic in February 1943, she said, to escape from her mother. Ironically, she never left home. "On the way to San Francisco to get married, I decided I really didn't want to go through with it, but my mother said I had to. She was all for it, because she knew I was marrying a weak man, therefore she could still control me — she did!"

It was her mother who insisted that Jones report to the studio to continue work on *Nine Girls* (1944), despite being ill with scarlet fever. "I was so sick during that film, I didn't care whether I lived or died," she said. "They put me in a dressing room by myself, and I only came out to do my scenes."

The next year (1945), a son, Robert Dennis, was born. A second son, Tim, came in 1947. "My two sons were the only good that came from that marriage.* My husband wasn't a bad man. He drank and could not assume responsibility for the children. He wanted me to leave them and travel with him. I wouldn't do it."

She was appearing in *Caught* (1949) when she gave Chic the ultimatum. "I packed our things and went to a hotel. I told him he would either get us a house or that was it." Their marriage disintegrated and their divorce was final in 1951.

Jones hoped her role in *The Daughter of Rosie O'Grady* (1950) would breathe new life into her foundering career. She even got a new name during the picture. Director David Butler suggested a shorter and simpler Marsha Jones. "He thought this new name and my part, a good one, would help my career. I should have zoomed, but the only person who zoomed was Debbie Reynolds. And, I have to tell you, that new name didn't do me a bit of good."

**Robert "Bob" Chic is a stage manager for* The Price Is Right *game show, and Tim is an actor.*

In the early 1950s, Jones went to work as Hollywood lawyer Greg Bautzer's receptionist. "I thought I knew about the motion picture industry until I went to work for him. I found out I didn't know anything. He was a real SOB, but he liked me because I stood up to him. After that, I could do no wrong."

A Marcia Mae Jones portrait from *First Love* (1939). (Courtesy of Marcia Mae Jones.)

Bautzer allowed Jones to work in television and make an occasional film. She appeared on *I Married Joan, The George Burns and Gracie Allen Show, The Adventures of Wild Bill Hickok* and others.

During the time she worked with Bautzer, he and Joan Crawford were ending their much-publicized romance, due in part, Jones said, to Crawford's treatment of her children. Jones witnessed Crawford's cruel handling of her children firsthand while on vacation for two weeks at a resort north of Los Angeles. "Joan was there with the children. She'd snap her fingers and they would jump. They'd dash over to light her cigarette. Let me tell you, that girl [Christina] didn't tell [in her book, *Mommie Dearest*] half of what she went through."

To win back Bautzer's affections, Crawford would often send son Christopher into the office to see the lawyer, as they had an almost father/son relationship. "Then, one day, she came in to see him herself," Jones recalled. "He had always told me what to do if she came in. I was to tell her he was in a deposition and that she was to walk up and down the street in front [the offices were at Hollywood and Vine] and that he would be watching her. I thought he was kidding, but he said to do it.

"She came in, and I told her to go out and walk up and down the sidewalk. After just having spent two weeks with her at the resort, I thought she would tell me to go to hell, but she did it! Do you know where Greg was? He was in the men's room. There was no deposition."

The list of Hollywood luminaries she encountered while working for Bautzer was endless. She almost showed Howard Hughes the door after mistaking him for a solicitor. She remembered the flawless complexion of a "loaded" Marion Davies the day she shuffled in with the help of two nurses.

Jones retired from the screen when she married TV writer DeWitt (Bill) Davenport in 1955. "My desire had always been to have a home and kids, and to have a nice, normal life. It sounds like I had a horrible life up to then — I didn't. It just wasn't normal."

Their marriage was a stable and happy one for about five years. She continued to work in television (*Mr. Ed* and *Peyton Place*) and raise her two boys. After struggling privately with her husband's worsening mental illness, Jones had him institutionalized. "He met a patient there who happened to be a member of the Folger [coffee] family. They flew to Mexico and got married. Of course, he was still married to me, and she to someone else. You live with that sort of stuff and it will make you nuts. When you live with insanity, it makes you sick, not the insane person."

After divorcing Davenport in the mid–1960s, Jones' life unraveled. Her stressful and emotional marriage, coupled with the frustration of having been a child actress, resulted in a nervous breakdown. For two years, she plunged into a personal hell of alcoholism.

"After the breakdown, we lost everything," she admitted. "I just didn't want to feel anything, so I used alcohol to help me sleep and it soon got a hold on me. I was blaming my mother for my drinking, but my mother never poured me a drink in her life. I blamed the wrong people."

Finally, Jones began a process to gain control of herself. She entered therapy to help her sort out her troubled life, to help her deal with her drinking, her insecurity and her family relationships.

Along the way, she earned a degree in religious science and went back to work. She made appearances in *A Great American Tragedy* (1972), a television movie, and on such shows as *My Three Sons, Family Affair* and *Barnaby Jones.* She appeared as Peggy Vanderbilt in *The Way We Were* (1973) with Barbra Streisand and Robert Redford.

"Streisand was very cold. You practically had to show them your birthmark to get on the stage," she said. "I had to stop and look at her. She's terribly insecure and is jealous of other women. All that money and she still can't get rid of her insecurities."

The mention of Redford left Jones speechless. Finally, she sighed, then hesitated. "What is it? Is there a story there?" I asked. "I wish there was, but no. He was terrific, a very nice man."

After *The Way We Were*, Jones continued working in television; she had a recurring role on *General Hospital* in the early 1980s. For ten years, she was a counselor for drunken drivers. She moved around Los Angeles over the years, from Venice, to Hollywood, and finally, to the San Fernando Valley, where she was living at the time of this interview.

Still available for acting when we met, Jones said she found casting directors hesitant when they learned of her experience in the business. "Being an old-timer is the worst thing that can happen to you," she said. "The minute they say, 'Oh, you're the child actress,' I want to scream, because I know it's going to hurt me."

Jones was very proud of the strides she made in dealing with the past. "My mother did some wrong things, there's no question about it. I've done some wrong things, but that's the way we learn. There are many things I will never get over, but will learn to live with, and they will become less and less as time goes on."

Dealing with her self-esteem, her insecurities, was ongoing. "I'm not ashamed to admit there are many times when I don't want to leave this apartment," she confessed.

Through all the trauma in her life, Jones said she finally came to a place in the last decade where she accepted herself as an adult, comfortable with making her own decisions and living life for herself. She finally freed herself from the shackles that kept her chained to the past. She finally became her own person.

"I've had a very difficult time becoming mature, becoming an adult, but I think I finally grew up. I did it, but let me tell you, it has been one of the hardest things I've ever had to do in my life."

FILMOGRAPHY

1926: *Mannequin.* Paramount. Director: James Cruze. Cast: Alice Joyce, Warner Baxter, Dolores Costello, ZaSu Pitts, Walter Pidgeon, Freeman Wood, Charlot Bird, Marcia Mae Jones. **1927: *Smile, Brother, Smile.*** First National. Director: John Francis Dillon. Cast: Jack Mulhall, Dorothy Mackaill, Philo McCullough, E. J. Ratcliffe, Harry Dunkinson, Ernest Hilliard, Charles Clary, Jack Dillon, Yola D'Avril, Hank Mann, T. Roy Barnes, Jed Prouty, Sam Blum, Marcia Mae Jones. **1930: *Bride of the Regiment.*** First National. Director: John Francis Dillon. Cast: Vivienne Segal, Allan Prior, Walter Pidgeon, Louise Fazenda, Myrna Loy, Lupino Lane, Ford Sterling, Harry Cording, Claude Fleming, Herbert Clark, Marcia Mae Jones. ***The King of Jazz.*** Universal. Director: John Murray Anderson. Cast: Paul Whiteman and His Orchestra, John Boles, Laura La Plante, Glenn Tryon, Jeanette Loff, Merna Kennedy, Stanley Smith, Slim Summerville, Otis Harlan, William Kent, Bing Crosby and the Rhythm Boys, The Sisters G, The Brox Sisters, George Chiles, Jacques Cartier, Frank Leslie, Charles Irwin, Al Norman, Grace Hayes, Paul Howard, Marion Stattler, Don Rose, Nell O'Day, Walter Brennan, George Sidney, Marcia Mae Jones. **1931: *The Champ.*** MGM. Director: King Vidor. Cast: Wallace Beery, Jackie Cooper, Irene Rich, Rosco Ates, Edward Brophy, Hale Hamilton, Jesse Scott, Marcia Mae Jones, Andy Shuford. ***Street Scene.*** United Artists. Director: King Vidor. Cast: Sylvia Sidney, William Collier, Jr., Estelle Taylor, Beulah Bondi, David Landau, Matt McHugh, Russell Hopton, Greta Granstedt, Eleanor Wesselhoeft, Allan Fox, Nora Cecil, Margaret Robertson, Walter James, Max Montor, Walter Miller, T. H. Manning, Conway Washburne, John M.

Qualen, Anna Konstant, Adele Watson, Lambert Rogers, George Humbert, Helen Lovett, Richard Powell, Jane Mercer, Marcia Mae Jones. ***Night Nurse.*** Warner Brothers. Director: William Wellman. Cast: Barbara Stanwyck, Ben Lyon, Joan Blondell, Clark Gable, Charlotte Merriam, Vera Lewis, Blanche Friderici, Charles Winninger, Edward Nugent, Ralf Harolde, Allan Lane, Walter McGrail, Marcia Mae Jones, Betty Jane Graham, Betty May. **1934: *Imitation of Life.*** Universal. Director: John M. Stahl. Cast: Claudette Colbert, Warren William, Rochelle Hudson, Ned Sparks, Louise Beavers, Fredi Washington, Baby Jane, Alan Hale, Henry Armetta, Wyndham Standing, Marilyn Knowlden, Sebie Hendricks, Dorothy Black, Clarence Hummel Wilson, Henry Kolker, G. P. Huntley, Jr., Paul Porcasi, Paullyn Garner, Alice Ardell, Walter Walker, Noel Francis, William Austin, Joyce Compton, Barry Norton, Marcia Mae Jones. ***Kid Millions.*** United Artists. Director: Roy Del Ruth. Cast: Eddie Cantor, Ann Sothern, Ethel Merman, George Murphy, Berton Churchill, Warren Hymer, Paul Harvey, Jesse Block, Eve Sully, Otto Hoffman, Stanley Fields, Edgar Kennedy, Jack Kennedy, John Kelly, Doris Davenport, The Nicholas Brothers, Henry Kolker, Lucille Ball, Tommy Bond, Marcia Mae Jones. ***Madame Du Barry.*** Warner Brothers. Director: William Dieterle. Cast: Dolores Del Rio, Reginald Owen, Victor Jory, Osgood Perkins, Verree Teasdale, Ferdinand Gottschalk, Anita Louise, Maynard Holmes, Henry O'Neill, Hobart Cavanaugh, Dorothy Tree, Virginia Sale, Halliwell Hobbes, Arthur Treacher, Marcia Mae Jones. **1935: *The Good Fairy.*** Universal. Director: William Wyler. Cast: Margaret Sullavan, Herbert Marshall, Frank Morgan, Reginald Owen, Eric Blore, Beulah Bondi, Alan Hale, Cesar Romero, Luis Alberni, June Clayworth, Al Bridge, George Davis, Hugh O'Connell, Torben Meyer, Matt McHugh, Frank Moran, Lillian Lawrence, Edith Kingdon, Marcia Mae Jones. **1936: *Strike Me Pink.*** United Artists. Director: Norman Taurog. Cast: Eddie Cantor, Ethel Merman, Sally Eilers, Parkyakarkus, William Frawley, Helen Lowell, Gordon Jones, Brian Donlevy, Jack LaRue, Sunnie O'Dea, Rita Rio, Edward Brophy, Sidney H. Fields, Don Brodie, Charles McAvoy, Stanley Blystone, Duke York, Charles Wilson, Marcia Mae Jones. ***The Garden of Allah.*** United Artists. Director: Richard Boleslawski. Cast: Marlene Dietrich, Charles Boyer, Basil Rathbone, C. Aubrey Smith, Joseph Schildkraut, John Carradine, Alan Marshal, Lucile Watson, Henry Brandon, Tilly Losch, Helen Jerome Eddy, Marcia Mae Jones, Ann Gillis, Nigel de Brulier, Pedro de Cordoba, Bonita Granville, Leonid Kinsky. ***Gentle Julia.*** Twentieth Century–Fox. Director: John Blystone. Cast: Jane Withers, Tom Brown, Marsha Hunt, Jackie Searl, Frances Ford, George Meeker, Maurice Murphy, Harry Holman, Myra Marsh, Eddie Buzard, Frank Sully, Wiles Welsh, Frederick Lee, Florence Wix, Tom Ricketts, Mary Carr, Marcia Mae Jones, Hilda Vaughn, Arthur Hoyt. ***These Three.*** United Artists. Director: William Wyler. Cast: Joel McCrea, Miriam Hopkins, Merle Oberon, Alma Kruger, Bonita Granville, Marcia Mae Jones, Catherine Doucet, Carmencita Johnson, Margaret Hamilton, Marie Louise Cooper, Walter Brennan. **1937: *Heidi.*** Twentieth Century–Fox. Director: Allan Dwan. Cast:

Shirley Temple, Jean Hersholt, Arthur Treacher, Helen Westley, Pauline Moore, Thomas Beck, Mary Nash, Sidney Blackmer, Mady Christians, Marcia Mae Jones, Delmar Watson, Egon Brecher, George Humbert, Sid Rumann. ***The Life of Emile Zola.*** Warner Brothers. Director: William Dieterle. Cast: Paul Muni, Joseph Schildkraut, Gale Sondergaard, Donald Crisp, Gloria Holden, Erin O'Brien Moore, Henry O'Neill, Morris Carnovsky, Louis Calhern, John Litel, Ralph Morgan, Robert Barrat, Vladimir Sokoloff, Grant Mitchell, Harry Davenport, Robert Warwick, Marcia Mae Jones, Dickie Moore, Frank Mayo, Montagu Love, Bonita Granville, Irving Pichel. ***Mountain Justice.*** Warner Brothers. Director: Michael Curtiz. Cast: Josephine Hutchinson, George Brent, Guy Kibbee, Mona Barrie, Robert Barrat, Margaret Hamilton, Robert McWade, Fuzzy Knight, Edward Pawley, Elisabeth Risdon, Granville Bates, Russell Simpson, Sybil Harris, Guy Wilkerson, Marcia Mae Jones. ***Two Wise Maids.*** Republic. Director: Phil Rosen. Cast: Alison Skipworth, Polly Moran, Hope Manning, Donald Cook, Jackie Searl, Lila Lee, Luis Alberni, Maxie Rosenbloom, Marcia Mae Jones, Harry Burns, Clarence Wilson, Selmer Jackson, John Hamilton, Theresa Conover, Raymond Brown, James C. Morton, Stanley Blystone, Bob McClung. **1938: *The Adventures of Tom Sawyer.*** United Artists. Director: Norman Taurog. Cast: Tommy Kelly, Jackie Moran, Ann Gillis, May Robson, Walter Brennan, Victor Jory, David Holt, Nana Bryant, Victor Kilian, Olin Howland, Donald Meek, Charles Richman, Margaret Hamilton, Marcia Mae Jones, Mickey Rentschler, Cora Sue Collins, Philip Hurlic, Spring Byington, George Billings, Byron Armstrong, Roland Drew, Frank O'Connor. ***Barefoot Boy.*** Monogram. Director: Karl Brown. Cast: Jackie Moran, Marcia Mae Jones, Bradley Metcalfe, Johnnie Morris, Marilyn Knowlden, Ralph Morgan, Claire Windsor, Helen MacKellar, Matty Fain, Frank Puglia, J. Farrell MacDonald, Charles D. Brown, Roger Gray, Earl Hodgins, Henry Roquemore, Hal Cooke. ***Lady Behave.*** Republic. Director: Lloyd Corrigan. Cast: Sally Eilers, Neil Hamilton, Joseph Schildkraut, Grant Mitchell, Patricia Farr, Marcia Mae Jones, George Ernest, Warren Hymer, Robert Greig, Charles Richman, Spencer Charters, Mary Gordon. ***Mad About Music.*** Universal. Director: Norman Taurog. Cast: Deanna Durbin, Herbert Marshall, Gail Patrick, Arthur Treacher, William Frawley, Marcia Mae Jones, Jackie Moran, Elisabeth Risdon, Helen Parrish, Nana Bryant, Charles Peck, Sid Grauman. **1939: *First Love.*** Universal. Director: Henry Koster. Cast: Deanna Durbin, Robert Stack, Eugene Pallette, Helen Parrish, Lewis Howard, Leatrice Joy, June Storey, Frank Jenks, Kathleen Howard, Thurston Hall, Marcia Mae Jones, Samuel S. Hinds, Doris Lloyd, Charles Coleman, Jack Mulhall, Mary Treen, Dorothy Vaughan, Lucille Ward. ***The Little Princess.*** Twentieth Century–Fox. Director: Walter Lang. Cast: Shirley Temple, Anita Louise, Richard Greene, Ian Hunter, Cesar Romero, Arthur Treacher, Mary Nash, Sybil Jason, Miles Mander, Marcia Mae Jones, Beryl Mercer, Deidre Gale, Ira Stevens, E. E. Clive, Eily Malyon, Clyde Cook, Holmes Herbert. ***Meet Dr. Christian.*** RKO. Director: Bernard Vorhaus. Cast: Jean Hersholt, Enid Bennett, Robert Baldwin, Dorothy

Lovett, Jackie Moran, Maude Eburne, Paul Harvey, Marcia Mae Jones, Frank Coghlan, Patsy Lee Parsons, Sarah Edwards, John Kelly, Eddie Acuff. **1940: *Anne of Windy Poplars.*** RKO. Director: Jack Hively. Cast: Anne Shirley, James Ellison, Henry Travers, Patric Knowles, Slim Summerville, Elizabeth Patterson, Louise Campbell, Joan Carroll, Katharine Alexander, Minnie Dupree, Alma Kruger, Marcia Mae Jones, Ethel Griffies, Clara Blandick, Gilbert Emery, Wright Kramer, Jackie Moran, Kathryn Sheldon, Leona Roberts, Grady Sutton. ***Dr. Kildare's Strange Case.*** MGM. Director: Harold S. Bucquet. Cast: Lew Ayres, Lionel Barrymore, Laraine Day, Shepperd Strudwick, Samuel S. Hinds, Emma Dunn, Nat Pendleton, Walter Kingsford, Alma Kruger, John Eldredge, Neil Craig, Marie Blake, Charles Waldron, George Lessey, Tom Collins, George H. Reed, Paul Porcasi, Horace MacMahon, Frank Orth, Margaret Seddon, Fay Helm, Marcia Mae Jones. ***Haunted House.*** Monogram. Director: Robert McGowan. Cast: Marcia Mae Jones, Jackie Moran, George Cleveland, Christian Rub, Henry Hall, John St. Polis, Clarence Wilson, Mary Carr, Jessie Arnold, Hooper Atchley, Marcelle Ray, Buddy Swann. ***The Old Swimmin' Hole.*** Monogram. Director: Robert McGowan. Cast: Marcia Mae Jones, Jackie Moran, Leatrice Joy, Charles Brown, Theodor Von Eltz, George Cleveland, Dix Davis, Dorothy Vaughan, Sonny Boy Williams, Si Jenks. ***Tomboy.*** Monogram. Director: Robert McGowan. Cast: Marcia Mae Jones, Jackie Moran, Grant Withers, George Cleveland, Clara Blandick, Marvin Stephens, Charlotte Wynters, Gene Morgan. **1941: *Nice Girl?*** Universal. Director: William A. Seiter. Cast: Deanna Durbin, Franchot Tone, Robert Stack, Walter Brennan, Robert Benchley, Ann Gillis, Anne Gwynne, Marcia Mae Jones, Elisabeth Risdon, Nana Bryant, Helen Broderick, Tommy Kelly. ***Let's Go Collegiate.*** Monogram. Director: Jean Yarbrough. Cast: Frankie Darro, Jackie Moran, Marcia Mae Jones, Mantan Moreland, Gale Storm, Keye Luke, Frank Sully, Billy Griffin, Gene O'Donnell. ***The Gang's All Here.*** Monogram. Director: Jean Yarbrough. Cast: Frankie Darro, Marcia Mae Jones, Jackie Moran, Mantan Moreland, Keye Luke, Robert Homans, Irving Mitchell, Edward Cassidy, Pat Gleason, Jack Kenney, Laurence Criner, Paul Bryar, Jack Ingram. **1943: *The Youngest Profession.*** MGM. Director: Edward Buzzell. Cast: Virginia Weidler, Edward Arnold, John Carroll, Jean Porter, Marta Linden, Dick Simmons, Ann Ayars, Agnes Moorehead, Marcia Mae Jones, Raymond Roe, Scotty Beckett, Walter Pidgeon, Lana Turner, William Powell, Greer Garson, Robert Taylor, Marjorie Gateson, Thurston Hall, Aileen Pringle, Nora Lane, Dorothy Christy, Mary Vallee, Gloria Tucker, Hazel Dawn, Edward Buzzell, Sara Haden. ***Top Man.*** Universal. Director: Charles Lamont. Cast: Richard Dix, Susanna Foster, Lillian Gish, Anne Gwynne, Peggy Ryan, Noah Beery, Jr., Marcia Mae Jones, David Holt, Count Basie, Louise Beavers, Martha Vickers, Donald O'Connor, Samuel S. Hinds. ***Nobody's Darling.*** Republic. Director: Anthony Mann. Cast: Mary Lee, Jackie Moran, Louis Calhern, Gladys George, Lee Patrick, Bennie Bartlett, Roberta Smith, Marcia Mae Jones, Jonathan Hale, Billy Benedict. **1944: *Nine Girls.*** Columbia. Director: Leigh Jason. Cast: Ann Harding, Evelyn Keyes, Anita

Louise, Jinx Falkenberg, Leslie Brooks, Lynn Merrick, Jeff Donnell, Nina Foch, Shirley Mills, Marcia Mae Jones, William Demarest, Grady Sutton. **1945: *Snafu.*** Columbia. Director: Jack Moss. Cast: Robert Benchley, Vera Vague, Conrad Janis, Marcia Mae Jones, Nanette Parks, Janis Wilson, Jimmy Lloyd, Enid Markey. **1948: *Trouble Preferred.*** Twentieth Century–Fox. Director: James Tinling. Cast: Peggy Knudsen, Lynne Roberts, Charles Russell, Mary Bear, Paul Langton, James Cardwell, June Storey, Paul Guilfoyle, Marcia Mae Jones. ***Street Corner.*** Viro Pictures. Director: Albert Kelley. Cast: Joseph Crehan, Marcia Mae Jones, John Treul, Billie Jean Eberhart, John Duncan, Jean Fenwick, Don Brodie, Jan Sutton, Milton Ross, Jean Andren, Stuart Holmes, Eddie Gribbon. **1949: *Caught.*** MGM-Enterprise. Director: Max Ophuls. Cast: James Mason, Barbara Bel Geddes, Robert Ryan, Ruth Brady, Curt Bois, Frank Ferguson, Natalie Schafer, Art Smith, Sonia Darrin, Bernadene Hayes, Ann Morrison, Wilton Graff, Jim Hawkins, Vicki Raw Stiener, Marcia Mae Jones. ***Tucson.*** Twentieth Century–Fox. Director: William Claxton. Cast: Jimmy Lydon, Penny Edwards, Deanna Wayne, Charles Russell, Joe Sawyer, Walter Sande, Lyn Wilde, Marcia Mae Jones, John Ridgely, Grandon Rhodes, Gil Stratton, Harry Lauter. **1950: *Hi-Jacked.*** Lippert. Director: Sam Newfield. Cast: Jim Davis, Marcia Mae Jones, Sid Melton, David Bruce, Paul Cavanagh, Ralph Sanford, House Peters, Jr., Iris Adrian, George Eldredge, William E. Green, Margia Dean, Kit Guard, Myron Healey. ***The Daughter of Rosie O'Grady.*** Warner Brothers. Director: David Butler. Cast: June Haver, Gordon MacRae, Debbie Reynolds, Jane Darwell, Marcia Mae Jones, James Barton, S. Z. Sakall, Gene Nelson, Sean McClory, Virginia Lee. ***Chicago Calling.*** United Artists. Director: John Reinhardt. Cast: Dan Duryea, Mary Anderson, Gordon Gebert, Judy Brubaker, Ross Elliott, Marcia Mae Jones, Melinda Plowman. **1968: *Live a Little, Love a Little.*** MGM. Director: Norman Taurog. Cat: Elvis Presley, Rudy Vallee, Michele Carey, Don Porter, Dick Sargent, Sterling Holloway, Celeste Yarnall, Eddie Hodges, Joan Shawlee, Mary Grover, Emily Banks, Michael Keller, Merri Ashley, Phyllis Davis, Ursula Menzel, Susan Shute, Edie Baskin, Marcia Mae Jones. ***Rogue's Gallery.*** Paramount. Director: Leonard Horn. Cast: Roger Smith, Farley Granger, Brian Donlevy, Edgar Bergen, Dennis Morgan, Greta Baldwin, Marcia Mae Jones. **1969: *The Gypsy Moths.*** MGM. Director: John Frankenheimer. Cast: Burt Lancaster, Deborah Kerr, Gene Hackman, Sheree North, William Windom, Bonnie Bedelia, Dick Donford, John Napier, Ford Rainey, Scott Wilson, Marcia Mae Jones. **1973: *The Way We Were.*** Columbia. Director: Sydney Pollock. Cast: Barbra Streisand, Robert Redford, Bradford Dillman, Lois Chiles, Patrick O'Neal, Viveca Lindfors, Allyn Ann McLerie, Murray Hamilton, Herb Edelman, Diana Ewing, Sally Kirkland, Marcia Mae Jones, Don Keefer, Eric Boles, Barbara Peterson, Roy Jensen, James Woods. **1974: *The Spectre of Edgar Allan Poe.*** Director: Mohy Quandour. Cast: Cesar Romero, Tom Drake, Robert Walker, Jr., Mary Grover, Frank Packard, Carol Ohmart, Mario Milano, Marcia Mae Jones, Dennis Fimple, Paul Bryar.

11

Barbara Kent

When asked to discuss the past, especially those years she was a film actress during the 1920s and the 1930s, Barbara Kent had little time or patience for a barrage of questions. First, life was busy at the moment; second, she lived in the present and considered her "picture days" ancient history.

"Do you ever think about Hollywood?" was among my first questions.

"Never!" she answered politely, but firmly.

Kent not only blocked those years from her thoughts, she also kept them hidden at times from even her closest friends, some of whom never knew she was once an actress. It was either not important for them to know, or it never came up.

I warned Kent in a letter I would be phoning her to discuss her career. When I called one afternoon in February 1997, she was not sitting by the phone ready to conjure up an anecdote. She was out on the golf course participating in a women's golf tournament. Golfing, not her scrapbooks, was her favorite pastime.

Kent returned the call later in the evening and confirmed what her husband told me earlier: She was an avid golfer and her sentiments didn't lie with the movies. Her ambivalence can be credited to the fact that she was never impressed with the movies or with show people and that she did not take her career very seriously.

Approaching her 90th birthday, remembering those bygone years was not easy, she said. It was a long time ago, and the people she knew and the 35 films she made between 1926 and 1941 tended to blend together. The details were difficult, the highlights easy.

First, she was a beauty contest winner and graduate of Hollywood High School. Then she caught the eye of Universal Studios, who first tested the youngster and signed her to a studio contract. She made a Western before being loaned to MGM to appear with Greta Garbo and John Gilbert in *Flesh and the Devil* (1927). The role, the best of her career, she said, gave her momentum, and she spent the rest of the decade playing opposite such stars as Richard Barthelmess, Douglas Fairbanks, Jr., Reginald Denny and Harold Lloyd.

Her roles during the silent era, typically as a shy, innocent ingenue, mirrored her own rather sheltered life at the time, she said. In her early films, Kent often suffered over the loss of her beau to a woman of the world, only to win him back by the final reel. Reviewers often noted her sincerity and charm in their critiques.

Kent made an easy transition to sound as leading lady to Harold Lloyd, but after her contract ended, her career drifted. Like other silent film players, she found herself on Poverty Row in independent productions.

Her 1932 marriage to Hollywood agent Harry Edington gave her the perfect opportunity to bow out. She made eight more films, then retired from the screen with no regrets. At 35, Barbara Kent had a lot of living ahead of her.

Barbara Cloutman was born December 16, 1907* in the small Canadian town of Gadsby. When she was 13, the family (Barbara had two brothers and two half brothers) moved to California. The family settled in Hollywood.

Although there seemed to be a studio on every corner and a movie star in every car, she had no ambition to be an actress. "I really didn't know what I wanted to do with my life, but being an actress was not it." Only after her move to Los Angeles did Kent go regularly to films. Her favorite stars were glamour queens Barbara La Marr and Gloria Swanson.

After graduating from Hollywood High School in 1924, Kent still had little understanding of the direction in which she wanted her life to go. That is, until she won the title of "Miss Hollywood, 1925."

"My folks sent my picture in to the newspaper holding the contest without telling me. They feared, I think, I would not approve and go through with it. I won the contest and that's what led me into films."

As "Miss Hollywood," Kent was asked one afternoon to model a piece of jewelry for a Hollywood Boulevard jewelry store. During the session, a man approached her and introduced himself as Paul Kohner,† a film producer for Universal Studios. He invited her to the studio and arranged a screen test which impressed studio executives. Kent was signed in November 1925 to a five-year contract. Her mother's maiden name, Kent, replaced Barbara's own last name, Cloutman. She became professionally known as Barbara Kent.

Ernst Laemmle directed her in her first film, *Prowlers of the Night* (1926).§

**Although 1906 and 1909 have been given as her year of birth, the correct year is 1907.*

†Paul Kohner later became an agent and the husband of actress Lupita Tovar, one of the subjects interviewed for this book.

§Although she is credited in The American Film Institute Catalog, Feature Films, 1921–1930 *as having written the scenarios for* Moonlight and Honeysuckle *(1921) and* Damaged Hearts *(1924), Kent said the credits are not hers and that her first work in motion pictures was as an actress in* Prowlers of the Night.

She is the heroine, the daughter of a bandit leader who helps nurse Fred Humes back to health after he is wounded in a shootout.

One Western hardly prepared Kent for her next assignment. She was selected in the fall of 1926 by director Clarence Brown to play the ingenue, Hertha, in MGM's *Flesh and the Devil* (1927) with John Gilbert, Hollywood's top romantic idol, and Greta Garbo, rapidly rising to stardom in her third American film.

A Universal Studios portrait of Barbara Kent, late 1920s. (Courtesy of Barbara Kent.)

In the movie, Kent clings to a teenage crush on the dashing Gilbert and, in the end, has her finest scene as she pleads with Garbo to stop a duel between Gilbert and Lars Hanson over her(Garbo's) affections.

Barbara called the experience of working with the enormously popular and talented Gilbert and Garbo almost "overwhelming. I was timid, there is no question about it. I was still very young, and, I'm sorry to say, not very sophisticated when I made *Flesh and the Devil.* The picture business, especially this film, amazed me."

She credited her fine performance to Clarence Brown's patient direction of not only herself, but the entire cast. "Mr. Brown had a style that allowed us to rehearse and to find our own characters," she reminisced. "He was a very quiet man and would talk to us in the softest voice. He was especially careful with Garbo and would almost whisper his instructions to her."*

Kent knew Garbo better during her (Barbara's) marriage to Harry Edington, Garbo's agent and business manager, who was credited with developing her strict code of silence and mysterious allure.†

"More than being aloof, as we've all heard about her, Garbo was very shy.

**Clarence Brown (1890–1987) became Garbo's favorite director. He came to the attention of MGM after directing Rudolph Valentino and Vilma Banky in* The Eagle *(1925) and signed with the studio in 1926. He directed Garbo again in* A Woman of Affairs *(1928);* Anna Christie *(1930);* Romance *(1930);* Inspiration *(1931);* Anna Karenina *(1935); and* Conquest *(1937).*

†In Garbo: Her Story, *author Antoni Gronowicz, writing in Garbo's words and voice, said the actress had deep friendships in Hollywood with actresses Marie Dressler, Dorothy Sebastian, Barbara Kent, Paulette Duval and Florence Lake. Kent denied having a relationship with the actress and said they were not what one would even consider friends. "My husband [Edington] knew her quite well and she depended on him a great deal," she said.*

Barbara Kent, John Gilbert, Greta Garbo and Lars Hanson in *Flesh and the Devil* (1927). (Courtesy of Barbara Kent.)

She was a very quiet person and one of the most beautiful women who ever lived. She was absolutely gorgeous."

On the basis of her solid performance in *Flesh and the Devil*, Kent was named a 1927 Wampas Baby Star* and was loaned to First National to appear opposite Richard Barthelmess in *The Drop Kick* (1927). In the film, she plays Barthelmess' wholesome sweetheart who waits patiently while he, a college football star, unravels his romantic entanglement with his coach's wife (Dorothy Revier). "Barbara Kent is winsome and earnest," the *New York Times* wrote about her performance in *The Drop Kick*.

At her home studio that year (1927), Kent appeared in the World War I melodrama *The Lone Eagle* as a French girl who meets and marries Raymond Keane, an American aviator. In the comedy *The Small Bachelor*, her mother (Vera Lewis) plots to prevent her marriage to an artist (Andre Beranger), preferring a wealthy socialite (William Austin) instead.

The next year at Universal in *That's My Daddy* (1928), she discovers true

**The 1927 Wampas Baby Stars were: Kent, Patricia Avery, Rita Carewe, Helene Costello, Natalie Kingston, Gwen Lee, Mary McAllister, Gladys McConnell, Sally Phipps, Sally Rand, Martha Sleeper, Iris Stuart and Adamae Vaughn.*

love with Reginald Denny after an orphan (Jane La Verne) saves him from marrying a society girl (Lillian Rich). On loan to Columbia for *Modern Mothers* (1928), she plays the daughter of Helene Chadwick who, on a visit, attracts the attention of Kent's boyfriend, an aspiring playwright (Douglas Fairbanks, Jr.). In the film, Kent is once again left at home while the one she loves sorts out his romantic feelings.

Kent garnered favorable reviews for her touching performance in Universal's *Lonesome* (1928) with Glenn Tryon. The film follows the events of a single day in which she and Tryon, both lonely young people, meet by chance on Coney Island, are instantly attracted to one another and enjoy the park together before becoming separated. Giving each other up for lost, they return home to their drab apartment building only to find they were neighbors all along. The next year at Universal, William Wyler directed her in *The Shakedown* (1929), in which she appears as a waitress in love with a prizefighter (James Murray).

Both *Lonesome* and *The Shakedown* were originally shot as silents, but with the emerging talking picture revolution, the actors were called back to the studio to add talking sequences. While some established silent films personalities panicked at the looming microphone and the threat of sound, Kent said she was not fazed. "I knew talking pictures were to stay and I accepted it. The atmosphere at Universal during the transition was not as bad as it was at some of the other studios where they had the bigger stars. MGM was quite concerned about people like Garbo and Jack Gilbert, who had a high-pitched voice for a man."

Kent remembered being given a voice test with other Universal contract players. She passed and made an easy transition to sound.

"I never worried about whether I would continue in talking films. I just did what the studio told me. I knew I didn't have a high voice and that I would be okay in it."

It was at a party after Christmas 1928 that Kent met comedian Harold Lloyd. His current film *Welcome Danger* (1929), a silent, was three months into production with no leading lady.

"I remember Harold Lloyd standing beside me and I didn't know why. Afterward, I realized he was sizing me up to see how tall I was, because he wasn't a very tall man."

The next day, John L. Murphy, Lloyd's personal production manager and general advisor, called Kent to Metropolitan Studios, where she was tested and selected as Lloyd's leading lady.

Welcome Danger was to be released as a silent film at a time when most films were all talkies. Lloyd, feeling the picture was doomed at the box office as a silent, had the actors dub dialogue straight into the film.

"It sounds like a very difficult project, but it really wasn't," Kent revealed. "As an independent producer, if something went wrong, Mr. Lloyd had us do it over and over until we got it right. Lloyd made the strenuous work fun. He

Barbara Kent and Harold Lloyd in *Welcome Danger* (1929), the first of two films they made together. (Courtesy of Barbara Kent.)

was so easygoing, and his was a very easy, casual group to be with." The famed comedian had the same professional feelings for Kent.

She next appeared in the Universal crime drama, *Night Ride* (1930), with Joseph Schildkraut and Edward G. Robinson, and in *What Men Want,* a society drama in which she, a naive youngster, and her beguiling sister Pauline Starke vie for Ben Lyon's affections. Then, in the summer of 1930, Harold Lloyd hired her as the feminine lead in his next film, *Feet First* (1930).

After her universal contract ended, Kent freelanced. "I preferred being under contract to freelancing. Under contract, I didn't have to worry about getting a picture job. They were just assigned to me. Plus, I liked working for the Laemmles. Carl Laemmle* was a very nice man, very respectful of me."

With no contractual obligation, Kent's future looked secure. In *Indiscreet* (1931), Gloria Swanson plays a society girl trying to steer her younger sister (Barbara) clear of a romantic relationship she knows will spell disaster. "Gloria was very different from the other people I had appeared with. She was very, very ... what do I want to say? She was not exactly unfriendly, but was very, very much the star. That's putting it perfectly. She was not my favorite person to work with."†

**Movie mogul and Universal's production chief.*

†Swanson's dissatisfaction with Indiscreet *might have accounted for her temperament on the set. She wrote in her 1980 autobiography* Swanson On Swanson, *"In synopsis the story didn't seem too bad, but the final script was dismal; and although the songs were by Tin Pan Alley's famous trio of De Sylva, Brown and Henderson, they were undistinguished as well as quite wrong for my kind of voice."*

Barbara Kent in *Guard That Girl* (1935).

Kent made a Tom Keene Western, *Freighters of Destiny* (1931), for RKO, then appeared at MGM in *Emma* (1932) as one of Jean Hersholt's disgruntled children who refuses to accept his marriage to their housekeeper (Marie Dressler). "Clarence Brown directed the film, and it was nice working with him again. He handled the cast very similar to the way he did on *Flesh and the Devil*, with his very quiet manner. Marie Dressler was a lovely, lovely person and so easy to know."

Without the guidance of a studio contract, Kent's career took a downward turn in the early 1930s. Freelancing, she found herself working in low-budget films at such Poverty Row companies as Action, Chesterfield, Allied, Eagle, Mascot, Mayfair, Monarch and Monogram.

Working in these quickies, she found herself working with players who had once been popular in silent films: Carmel Myers and Rex Lease in *Chinatown After Dark* (1931); Conway Tearle in *Vanity Fair* (1932); Dorothy Revier in *Beauty Parlor* (1932); Pauline Frederick and Claire Windsor in *Self-Defense* (1932); and Gilbert Roland and Noah Beery in *No Living Witness* (1932).

On her birthday in 1932, Kent surprised even her closest friends when she married agent Harry Edington* in Yuma, Arizona. Her mother and two brothers attended the ceremony. The two met at a dinner party given by mutual friends about a year before their wedding.

In January 1933, Kent went to work at Monogram on *Oliver Twist* with Dickie Moore. She made two other films that year. In 1934, she and her husband accompanied actress Ann Harding, a client, to England, where she (Harding) was working on a film.

Marriage diverted Kent's attention from her career. She appeared at RKO in *Old Man Rhythm* (1935) and at Columbia in *Guard That Girl* (1935) and *Blondie Meets the Boss* (1939). She turned in her last performance in Columbia's *Under Age* (1941).

The Edingtons led a normal, but busy life, Kent said "We had a regular

**Harry Edington's work in the entertainment industry began as an executive at MGM in the mid–1920s, but he left the studio to open his own agency. Some of his clients were Garbo, John Gilbert, Ann Harding, Marlene Dietrich, Cary Grant, Claudette Colbert, Ruth Chatterton and Charles Boyer.*

life together. We went to dinners and shows, and traveled back and forth to New York frequently."

For the most part her friends were not in the entertainment profession. "Mr. Edington had many friends in the business, but I was never terribly friendly with picture people. I was much younger than the people he represented."

After Edington's death in 1949, Kent lost touch with Hollywood and the motion picture industry. She married her second husband, a Lockheed engineer, in the mid–1950s. He built the P-38 planes during World War II, then opened and operated a restaurant in Burbank.

Said her husband, "I was a flyer, and Barbara said that if we were going to be married, she was going to learn to fly. I gave her a few lessons, and before I knew it, she was flying."

During their years together, Kent and her husband lived in Idaho, then in Washington. They divide their time between their home on Washington's Olympic Peninsula and Southern California.

"We've had a wonderful life together," said her husband. "We play golf three times a week, and when we are in Washington, she goes crabbing and fishing with me. She's the most agile girl you ever saw. She's amazing."

With her active lifestyle, Barbara Kent had little time to talk about the past. During our second conversation, a week after our first, she had just returned from a luncheon at her country club and soon had to have her hair styled for that evening's dinner with friends.

"I really don't talk about those years I was in films, I really don't," she insisted. "I was never crazy about the picture business and was not enthusiastic at all about being an actress. When I started working, I was very unsophisticated and immature for my age. Maybe that's part of it.

"Also, being terribly shy, I didn't have the right personality to be an actress. I've always thought one had to be an exhibitionist to be in pictures. That wasn't me."

FILMOGRAPHY

1926: ***Prowlers of the Night.*** Universal. Director: Ernst Laemmle. Cast: Fred Humes, Barbara Kent, Slim Cole. John T. Prince, Joseph Belmont, Walter Maly. ***Flesh and the Devil.*** MGM. Director: Clarence Brown. Cast: John Gilbert, Greta Garbo, Lars Hanson, Barbara Kent, William Orlamond, George Fawcett, Eugenie Besserer, Marc MacDermott, Marcelle Corday. **1927:** ***No Man's Law.*** Pathé. Director: Fred Jackman. Cast: Rex (horse), Barbara Kent, Jimmy Finlayson, Theodore Von Eltz, Oliver Hardy. ***The Drop Kick.*** First National. Director: Millard Webb. Cast: Richard Barthelmess, Barbara Kent, Dorothy Revier, Eugene Strong, Alberta Vaughn, James Bradbury, Jr., Brooks Benedict, Hedda Hopper, Mayme Kelso, George Pearce. ***The Lone Eagle.*** Universal. Director: Emory

Johnson. Cast: Raymond Keane, Barbara Kent, Nigel Barrie, Jack Pennick, Donald Stuart, Cuyler Supplee, Frank Camphill, Marcella Daly, Eugene Pouyet, Wilson Benge, Brent Overstreet. ***The Small Bachelor.*** Universal. Director: William A. Seiter. Cast: Barbara Kent, Andre Beranger, William Austin, Lucien Littlefield, Carmelita Geraghty, Gertrude Astor, George Davis, Tom Dugan, Vera Lewis, Ned Sparks. **1928: *That's My Daddy.*** Universal. Director: Fred Newmeyer. Cast: Reginald Denny, Barbara Kent, Lillian Rich, Tom O'Brien, Armand Kaliz, Jane La Verne, Mathilde Brundage, Wilson Benge, Rosa Gore, Charles Coleman, Arthur Currier. ***Stop That Man.*** Universal. Director: Nat Ross. Cast: Arthur Lake, Barbara Kent, Eddie Gribbon, Warner Richmond, Walter McGrail, George Siegmann, Joseph W. Girard. ***Modern Mothers.*** Columbia. Director: Philip Rosen. Cast: Helene Chadwick, Douglas Fairbanks, Jr., Ethel Grey Terry, Barbara Kent, Alan Roscoe, Gene Stone, George Irving. ***Lonesome.*** Universal. Director: Paul Fejos. Cast: Barbara Kent, Glenn Tryon, Fay Holderness, Gustav Partos, Eddie Phillips. ***The Shakedown.*** Universal. Director: William Wyler. Cast: James Murray, Barbara Kent, George Kotsonaros, Wheeler Oakman, Jack Hanlon, Harry Gribbon. ***Welcome Danger.*** Paramount. Director: Clyde Bruckman. Cast: Harold Lloyd, Barbara Kent, Noah Young, Charles Middleton, William Walling, James Wang, Douglas Haig. **1930: *Night Ride.*** Universal. Director: John S. Robertson. Cast: Joseph Schildkraut, Barbara Kent, Edward G. Robinson, Harry Stubbs, De Witt Jennings, Ralph Welles, Hal Price, George Ovey. ***Dumbbells in Ermine.*** Warner Brothers. Director: John G. Adolfi. Cast: Robert Armstrong, Barbara Kent, Beryl Mercer, James Gleason, Claude Gillingwater, Julia Swayne Gordon, Arthur Hoyt, Mary Foy, Charlotte Merriam. ***What Men Want.*** Universal. Director: Ernst Laemmle. Cast: Pauline Starke, Ben Lyon, Robert Ellis, Barbara Kent, Hallam Cooley, Carmelita Geraghty. ***Feet First.*** Paramount. Director: Clyde Bruckman. Cast: Harold Lloyd, Robert McWade, Lillian Leighton, Barbara Kent, Alec B. Francis, Arthur Housman. **1931: *Indiscreet.*** United Artists. Director: Leo McCarey. Cast: Gloria Swanson, Ben Lyon, Arthur Lake, Barbara Kent, Monroe Owsley, Maude Eburne, Henry Kolker, Nella Walker. ***Chinatown After Dark.*** Action Pictures. Director: Stuart Paton. Cast: Carmel Myers, Rex Lease, Barbara Kent, Edmund Breese, Frank Mayo, Billy Gilbert, Lloyd Whitlock, Laska Winter, Michael Visaroff. ***Freighters of Destiny.*** RKO. Director: Fred Allan. Cast: Tom Keene, Barbara Kent, Mitchell Harris, Frederick Burton, Frank Rice, Billy Franey, William Welsh, Fred Burns, Charles Whittaker, Tom Bay. ***Grief Street.*** Chesterfield. Director: Richard Thorpe. Cast: Barbara Kent, John Holland, Dorothy Christy, Crauford Kent, Lillian Rich, Lloyd Whitlock, Lafe McKee, Creighton Hale, Ray Largay, Arthur Brennan. **1932: *Emma.*** MGM. Director: Clarence Brown. Cast: Marie Dressler, Richard Cromwell, Jean Hersholt, Myrna Loy, John Miljan, Purnell B. Pratt, Leila Bennett, Barbara Kent, Dale Fuller, Kathryn Crawford, George Meeker, Wilfred Noy, Andre Cheron, Dorothy Peterson, Edith Fellows. ***Vanity Fair.*** Allied Pictures. Director: Chester M. Franklin. Cast: Myrna Loy, Conway Tearle, Barbara Kent, Walter Byron, Anthony Bushell, Herbert Bunston, Montagu

Love, Mary Forbes, Billy Bevan, Lionel Belmore, Lilyan Irene. ***Beauty Parlor.*** Chesterfield. Director: Richard Thorpe. Cast: Barbara Kent, Joyce Compton, John Harron, Dorothy Revier, Albert Gran, Wheeler Oakman, Mischa Auer, Betty Mack, Harry Bradley. ***Exposed.*** State Rights (Eagle Pictures). Director: Albert Herman. Cast: William Collier, Jr., Barbara Kent, Raymond Hatton, Bobby "Wheezer" Hutchins, Walter McGrail, Roy Stewart, John Ince, Jack Quinn, Billy Eagle. ***No Living Witness.*** Mayfair. Director: E. Mason Hopper. Cast: Gilbert Roland, Noah Beery, Barbara Kent, Carmel Myers, Otis Harlan, Dorothy Revier, J. Carrol Naish, Ferike Boros, John Ince, Monte Carter, Broderick O'Farrell, Arthur Millett, James Cooley, Gordon DeMain. ***The Pride of the Legion.*** Mascot. Director: Ford Beebe. Cast: Victor Jory, Barbara Kent, J. Farrell MacDonald, Lucien Littlefield, Sally Blane, Glenn Tryon, Matt Moore, Ralph Ince, Tommy Dugan, Jason Robards, Rin-Tin-Tin, Jr. ***Self-Defense.*** Monogram. Director: Phil Rosen. Cast: Pauline Frederick, Claire Windsor, Theodore Von Eltz, Barbara Kent, Robert Elliott, Henry B. Walthall, Jameson Thomas, George Hackathorne, Willie Fong, Lafe McKee, Si Jenks, George Hayes. **1933: *Oliver Twist.*** Monogram. Director: William J. Cowen. Cast: Dickie Moore, Irving Pichel, William Boyd, Doris Lloyd, Alec B. Francis, Barbara Kent, Lionel Belmore, George Nash, Sonny Ray, Clyde Cook, George K. Arthur, Tempe Pigott, Nelson McDowell, Virginia Sale, Harry Holman, Bobby Nelson. ***Her Forgotten Past.*** Mayfair. Director: Wesley Ford. Cast: Monte Blue, Barbara Kent, Henry B. Walthall, Eddie Phillips, William V. Mong, Dewey Robinson. ***Marriage on Approval.*** Monarch Productions. Director: Howard Higgin. Cast: Barbara Kent, Donald Dillaway, William Farnum, Edward Woods, Dorothy Granger, Phyllis Barry, Leila McIntyre, Lucille Ward, Otis Harlan, Clarence Geldert. **1935: *Old Man Rhythm.*** RKO. Director: Edward Ludwig. Cast: Charles (Buddy) Rogers, George Barbier, Barbara Kent, Grace Bradley, Betty Grable, Eric Rhodes, John Arledge, Johnny Mercer, Donald Meek, Joy Hodges, Lucille Ball, Virginia Reid, Bryant Washburn, Jr., Carlyle Blackwell, Jr., Erich von Stroheim, Jr., Claude Gillingwater, Jr. ***Guard That Girl.*** Columbia. Director: Lambert Hillyer. Cast: Robert Allen, Florence Rice, Ward Bond, Wryley Birch, Barbara Kent, Arthur Hohl, Elisabeth Risdon, Nana Bryant, Thurston Hall, Bert Roach. ***Swell-Head.*** Columbia. Director: Ben Stoloff. Cast: Wallace Ford, Dickie Moore, Barbara Kent, J. Farrell MacDonald, Marion Byron, Sammy Cohen, Frank Moran, Mike Donlin, David Worth, Bryant Washburn. (This film was made in 1933, released in 1935). **1939: *Blondie Meets the Boss.*** Columbia. Director: Frank R. Strayer. Cast: Penny Singleton, Arthur Lake, Daisy (Dog), Danny Mummert, Jonathan Hale, Dorothy Moore, Don Beddoe, Linda Winters, Stanley Brown, Joel Dean, Richard Fiske, Inez Courtney, Joe Coffin, Dick Durrell, Jay Eaton, David Newell, Eddie Acuff, Barbara Kent, James Craig, Robert Sterling. **1941: *Under Age.*** Columbia. Director: Edward Dmytryk. Cast: Tom Neal, Mary Anderson, Alan Baxter, Nan Grey, Leona Maricle, Don Beddoe, Yolande Mollot [Donlan], Richard Terry, Wilma Francis, Patti McCarty, Billie Roy, Gwen Kenyon, Barbara Kent, Nancy Worth.

12

Esther Muir

Esther Muir wanted to talk about regrets and disappointments first, address them, get them over with and to concentrate on her accomplishments. That's how we began.

"The disappointment of my life was failure to play Belle Watling in *Gone with the Wind* [1939]. Some people had written in and suggested me for the part, and David Selznick sent the script to me. I was on cloud nine. I shall never forget the producer saying, 'I have run several of your pictures and admire your work. Every time you play a tough character, however, some sweetness comes through. Someday I will use you.' He sensed my great disappointment. He died before he was able to keep his promise."

By the time I interviewed her in 1990, Muir was accustomed to staring adversity in the face, accepting the hard knocks and turning them to her advantage.

Muir would like to have played Belle Watling, but not getting the part really didn't faze her. She was too busy working in a career that began on the stage in the early 1920s and continued in films of the 1930s and 1940s.

Her roles in almost 70 films ranged from featured parts to near bits. She fared better in independent and B-films, but often fell to the bottom of the cast in big-budget, major studio pictures. "That was another part that ended up on the cutting room floor," she would say.

She might have been a sex symbol of her day—she was blonde and sexy, but she took it in stride that she was taller than most leading men, big-boned and somewhat statuesque. She took what she had and promoted herself, developing a fine career in character parts. She was the alluring siren, the wise-cracking floozie, the overbearing girlfriend and wife.

Who can forget her being covered with wallpaper paste in the Marx Brothers comedy *A Day at the Races* (1937)? Or in an amorous embrace with Groucho in the same film. "Closer, hold me closer," she begs him. "If I hold you

An Esther Muir glamour shot. (Courtesy of Esther Muir.)

any closer, I'll be in back of you." It is the film for which she is remembered, the best work of her career.

Muir was a natural comedienne. She understood the challenges of presenting comedy, getting what was funny over to the audience. Also, she was the perfect foil for comedians like the Marx Brothers and Wheeler and Woolsey.

"A well-developed sense of humor was my foundation for a flair of comedy," she said. "I was born with it. I could always see the funny side of what others deemed a tragedy. My introduction to comedy as a vocation was the explanation of farce by a stage director who impressed me with a statement I never forgot. He said, 'The tin can tied to a dog's tail is funny to everyone except the dog.' It must be played seriously to be believed by an audience."

Muir believed that being versatile in her film opportunities enabled her to enjoy a longer career than if she had been the day's top star or sex goddess. Plus, she said, if she had been a Garbo or a Harlow, the work might not have been nearly as fun.

She was born Esther Muir* on March 11, 1903, in Andes, New York.† One of ten children (seven girls and three boys), Esther remembered her childhood as a bleak one.

"As I look back now, it was a nightmare," she said. "My oldest sisters announced they were leaving if any more brats came into the family. The morning I was born, they made good on their threat and left home to work their way through college. I didn't know them until later in life."

Early on, Muir harbored a desire to be an actress, but had doubts. "I had a very low opinion of myself. I thought I was ugly and that I had no chance at show business, yet I wanted to." A fast learner and a good student, she was granted a scholarship to Vassar College after being named valedictorian of her elementary school graduating class. Her educational ambitions, however, were put aside for two reasons. First, the scholarship did not include expenses; second, the family was broken over the death of Esther's father while she was still a teenager. Her grandmother found she could not properly look after Esther and sent her to New York City to live with a sister.

Escape during those dismal years came in the theaters of New York City. Her sister, who played piano and a Wurlitzer organ for silent films at the Miracle Theater, slipped Muir passes to all the current films. "I was grateful to her, because those passes provided an opportunity to study the acting of my favorite stars, who were people like Mary Pickford and Lillian Gish, and the comedians, Harold Lloyd and Charlie Chaplin."

Her confidence was boosted when she was cast in plays at Morris High School. The maturing Esther also found work as a model. "I did lingerie and stocking ads, which paid double the fees for the latest fashions. I posed in bathing suits in the winter and furs in the summer, because the sessions were six months in advance. It was not conductive to comfort being photographed in a cold loft in swim wear, and the absence of air conditioning made it difficult to look cool in furs."

**She is related to naturalist John Muir, for whom Muir Woods, the national redwood forest just outside San Francisco, is named.*

†Esther's year of birth has been recorded as 1895, 1903 and 1907. She said the 1895 date surfaced when film historian Ephraim Katz questioned her on the year of birth of her first husband Busby Berkeley. He mistakenly used the date for her entry in the 1979 edition of The Film Encyclopedia. *She maintained the year was 1903.*

Muir was still in high school when she secured a small part, thanks to friend and model Dinarzade, in *The Greenwich Village Follies of 1922.* "She told me about the opening in the show. I applied and was given the part. I did my lessons between scenes and missed only one class because of a Wednesday matinee. It was great training." After graduation, Muir shared an apartment with Dinarzade, who later became a Patou model in Paris and the editor of *Vogue* magazine in France.

After high school, Muir had little trouble finding steady employment on the stage. Her comedic skills, she said, bloomed early when she appeared with Charles Ruggles in two plays: *Battling Butler* (1923) and *Queen High* (1926).

She also appeared in *Mercenary Mary* (1925) with John Boles, *Honeymoon Lane* (1926) with Eddie Dowling, *Baby Blue* with Irene Dunne and *International Revue* (1930) with Gertrude Lawrence, Harry Richman and Jack Pearl.

Muir left the cast of *Lady Fingers* at the Vanderbilt Theater, when she took the title role in the sexy comedy *My Girl Friday!* (1929), a play, she said, that "gave me star status and put my name in lights."

When the play closed after over 250 performances, Muir chose not to accompany the play on the road. She was seriously involved with Broadway dance director and choreographer Busby Berkeley, who she had met through columnist Walter Winchell. They married in Baltimore, Maryland, shortly after *My Girl Friday!* closed. Muir, opting for domesticity, decided to give up her acting career while it was at its peak.

The Berkeleys soon packed and left for Hollywood, where Busby had been hired to choreograph and direct the dance numbers in *Whoopee!* (1930) for Samuel Goldwyn. His work kept him on the West Coast.

Once in California, Muir realized the marriage had serious problems: his drinking and his domineering, overbearing mother.

"His mother was widowed when Bus was a little boy, so she kept him on a leash until he married," Muir said. "I was my husband's keeper, but she continued to collect his salary. Her delusions of glamour, with a Park Avenue apartment in New York, a mansion in Dover and Loretta Young's mansion in Beverly Hills, required a Getty income to cover her expenses. I was left with the bills for our little Hollywood apartment and the necessities of life."

A West Coast producer contracted Muir about doing a revival of *My Girl Friday!* in Hollywood. Considering herself retired, she declined. However, since most of Berkeley's income continued to go to his mother, she eventually had no choice (other than to deplete "my stage savings") but to accept the offer. The Berkeleys separated and divorced in 1931.

Muir's start in motion pictures was necessitated by the collapse of her marriage and the need to work. Her early roles were small, and she often went unbilled. Her motion picture debut was in a Buster Keaton film, *Parlor, Bedroom and Bath* (1931), in which she had a small part as one of Keaton's alleged wives.

For the next two years, she continued in feature films in small roles and in two-reel comedies (she made several with Andy Clyde). Her one good role during this period was as Fredric Santley's wife in Columbia's *A Dangerous Affair* (1931), a story about family feuds and missing jewelry.

On the basis of her recent stage work, Muir was signed by Columbia to play opposite the comedy team of Wheeler and Woolsey in *So This Is Africa* (1933). She was billed fourth after Raquel Torres, as a specialist on jungles who falls in love with Woolsey in the wilds of Africa. It was one of the best roles of her career.

She next appeared as Violet with Lionel Barrymore in *Sweepings* (1933). "I remember telling Lionel that I did without lunches in high school to pay the 50 cents for a balcony seat to see him in a play.

"Lionel, who was suffering from arthritis at the time, accepted the part with the promise they would stop work daily at five P.M. The director, John Cromwell, one of the best, came to us one afternoon and asked us to do him the favor of doing one more scene. They wanted to strike the set for another setup. Lionel whispered to me, 'I think you're going to have a few days off.' Then we did the scene where I try to shoot William Gargan, miss him and kill someone else. Lionel dropped his denture in my lap and said to his dresser, 'Make an appointment with my dentist for tomorrow.' It was not a vacation with pay, because I was instructed to sit by the phone in preparation to return whenever Lionel came back to work. I spend three days waiting for the call."

Although 1933 was the busiest year of her career — she turned out 15 films — Muir found time to marry composer and producer Sam Coslow. She excelled during the year at playing floozies and girlfriends, often women from the other side of the tracks. In *Sailor's Luck*, she was the girlfriend of Sammy Cohen and Frank Moran; in *The Bowery* with Wallace Beery and Jackie Cooper, she was billed as "the tart." She was Lucille Weston, a hotel telephone operator and Lola Lane's wisecracking roommate, in *Public Stenographer.*

In *Hell and High Water* (1933), Muir sold her son for $3 and a bottle of gin. "My best scene in the film is where I beg Richard Arlen for the return of my son, after I am released from jail with the promise to abstain from the bottle. I was told later by [Paramount executive] Manny Cohen* that Paramount shelved the film after its Eastern showing, because there were parts of my performance that might offend churches. He complimented me, saying I gave an Oscar-winning performance."

Muir played Lolly, a stage comedienne and Lilyan Tashman's best friend, in the independent feature, *Wine, Women and Song* (1933). Tashman is cast as an actress reduced to performing in cheap vaudeville houses. After a raid, Tashman is jailed and her daughter is taken in by Muir. "Lilyan† lived up to her

**Emanuel "Manny" Cohen (1892–1977), vice-president in charge of production, Paramount Studios.*

†Lilyan Tashman (1899–1934) had been a model and Ziegfeld Follies girl before entering films in the early 1920s. She died in March 1934 (of cancer) just as Wine, Women and Song *was opening in New York.*

A sultry Esther in the early 1930s.

reputation. She was the epitome of a clotheshorse and remained so until her death, not long after the film was completed. She starved herself to live up to her image."

Lew Cody, who appeared as the playboy and showman in the picture, was "a gentleman and scholar," said Muir. "Many of the girls were bragging that he was a wild bachelor who wanted their telephone numbers for his little black book."

Much of Muir's role as a divorcee was cut from the final release of *The Gilded Lily* (1935), which starred Claudette Colbert, but it gave her the chance to work with Fred MacMurray in his first leading man role. "His first scene was with me, and he was so nervous. He vented his fear to me, and I reassured him. Whenever I ran into him later, he always said, 'I couldn't have done it without you,' which drew much laughter from both of us."

Muir continued in small roles throughout 1935 and 1936. She was "a blonde" in Paramount's *Coronado* (1935); a piano player in *Here's to Romance* (1935); Ward Bond's girlfriend in *The First Baby* (1936); a prima donna in *The Great Ziegfeld* (1936); and "the girl in the nightclub" in *Fury* (1936), which was directed by the celebrated German filmmaker Fritz Lang. "Mr. Lang was very easy to work for," Muir recounted. "He would rehearse to see what the actor might have added to the part. If he liked your conception, he would say, 'We'll shoot it that way.' Many directors would not permit your inserting any action not in the script, but he didn't object."

The Great Ziegfeld and *Fury* were both made for MGM, the studio for which Muir was currently under contract. Later in 1936, MGM sent Muir with the Marx Brothers on a road show version of *A Day at the Races.* The gags planned for the upcoming film were tested on audiences during 140 stage performances over a six-week period.

"The wallpaper scene was such a hit from the first performance, that it was a sure thing to be included in the film," said Muir. "We were covered with actual wallpaper paste five times a day. I thought there must be a better way to make a living, even at the good salary I made for one year in preparation and shooting of the film."

Muir appeared on stage and in the film as Flo, the vamp hired to trap

Esther Muir with Groucho Marx in *A Day at the Races* (1937). (Courtesy of Esther Muir.)

Groucho, the chief of staff of a sanatorium, in a romantic interlude. Chico and Harpo (Marx) learn of the plan and, in the famous wallpaper scene, paste Muir to the wall to prevent her from causing Groucho's dismissal.

"We played pranks and had many laughs in spite of the hard and messy work. The Marx Brothers ad-libbed funnier material than the four top writers could concoct for them. It was an unforgettable experience, as well as a lucrative ordeal."

Margaret Dumont,* who played Mrs. Upjohn in the film, provided the perfect foil for the Marx Brothers' antics. "She was a great actress, but was completely devoid of a sense of humor," said Muir. "She was a good example of the tin can tied to the dog's tail I told you about. She added so much to Groucho's scenes with her, and we would have trouble trying to keep from breaking up. She would stop and ask us what we were laughing at. She missed a lot of fun."

Muir gained renewed popularity after *A Day at the Races.* The next year she was billed third in Wheeler and Woolsey's *On Again — Off Again* (1937).

In *Romance in the Dark* (1938), she appeared as an opera diva with Gladys Swarthout, John Barrymore and John Boles. "I had only one scene with Barrymore. He was near the end of his career and couldn't remember his dialogue. He read from a cue card, which I thought was a sad event. [Cue cards] were common in television, but when I was in the movies, an actor was considered senile if they needed them.

"A diva from the Metropolitan Opera dubbed my singing in the film, but when we gathered after the premiere, Barrymore had a hard time believing it wasn't my voice."

Hollywood continued to cast Muir during the latter part of her career as either floozies or vamps. She sang a few bars and danced with Brian Donlevy in *Battle of Broadway* (1938), and appeared in a handful of Westerns: *The Law West of Tombstone* (1938); *Western Jamboree* (1938) and *The Girl and the Gambler* (1939). Her brief parts in MGM's *Three Comrades* (1938) and *Honky Tonk* (1941) were her final A-films.

One of Muir's last good roles was as Betty Blythe's trouble-making girlfriend in *Misbehaving Husbands* (1940), a PRF film with a large cast of former silent film stars: Blythe, Harry Langdon, Gertrude Astor and Mary MacLaren.

Esther returned to the stage briefly in 1940 when she was cast in *Good-Bye to Love* with Joan Blondell. The play folded in tryouts.

She retired from the screen in 1942 following *X Marks the Spot.* "My daughter [Jacqueline] was born a few days after completion of the film, so they shot my scenes as closeups in a taxi," she said. "While in the hospital, after she was born, Sam Wood, who directed *A Day at the Races,* called and told me I was set for the second lead to Ingrid Bergman in *Saratoga Trunk.* I told him that I was retired, that I had given my makeup box to a starlet. Sam replied, 'Why is your baby so important? While we have been talking on the telephone, 20,000 babies have been born in China.'

"I told Sam I had decided to raise my daughter, and that would have been

**Margaret Dumont (1889–1965) appeared in six other Marx Brothers films:* The Cocoanuts *(1929);* Animal Crackers *(1930);* Duck Soup *(1933);* A Night at the Opera *(1935);* At the Circus *(1939); and* The Big Store *(1941). She was also the foil for comedians W. C. Fields, Laurel and Hardy and Jack Benny.*

impossible if I had to drive to the studio at six A.M. and return after she had been put in her cradle for the night."

Her days of playing sirens, hard-boiled dames and prostitutes were over. She was interested in being a mother. Unfortunately, her marriage to Coslow, the father of her daughter, dissolved and they were divorced in the late 1940s.

"The less said about my marriages to Bus Berkeley and Sam Coslow the better," she said. "I spared you the painful details, because of the stigma I suffer at the thought of marriage. I worked hard at it, but failed. I don't talk much about regrets, but my poor choices in husbands were mistakes I would like to have avoided."*

Muir contracted polio in the early 1950s, but made a complete recovery in two years. The illness and therapy depleted her life savings. She found a new career in real estate development. For over 15 years, Muir supervised the building of over 400 tract homes in Southern California. She retired in 1969, when the Los Angeles smog drove her from the region.

Displaying a shrewd business sense differed greatly from her screen persona. "Being underprivileged when I was young provided good training for thrift," Muir said. "It added to my Scottish blood, which produced a keen business sense." At one time, she had homes in Southern California, New York, Arizona and Greece.

Muir never lost her hunger for the college education she failed to receive in her youth. In later years, she took college courses and eventually earned a degree in computer science.

When she died on August 1, 1995, Muir was still enjoying the recognition of having been an actress. One day at school, her grandson† was looking up words in the dictionary when he came across the famous photograph (illustrating slapstick) of his grandmother and Chico Marx in the wallpaper scene from *A Day at the Races.* The teacher and other students gathered around to look at the photo. "My image as a grandmother was ruined," Muir said.

Was the role of Flo in the Marx Brothers' classic her favorite? She shrugged. "I never had a favorite. Supporting the important players was my choice of parts." It never bothered her that she never made it into the starring ranks.

"A superstar is only as good as his or her last film, but character players like ZaSu Pitts could have gone on forever. I was happy that the box office returns didn't indicate whether I would keep working or would join the army of unemployed actors.

"Being versatile had its advantages. Back at the studios, someone made a comment I liked. They said, 'Esther Muir can play anything, including a piano.'"

**Muir's* LA Times *obituary mentioned a third husband, Richard Brown, president of General Time Corporation, a clock manufacturing company.*

†Muir had two grandchildren by her daughter, an actress, and son-in-law, actor Ted Sorel.

FILMOGRAPHY

1931: ***Parlor, Bedroom and Bath.*** MGM. Director: Edward Sedgwick. Cast: Buster Keaton, Charlotte Greenwood, Reginald Denny, Cliff Edwards, Dorothy Christy, Joan Peers, Sally Eilers, Natalie Moorhead, Edward Brophy, Walter Merrill, Sidney Bracy, Esther Muir. ***A Dangerous Affair.*** Columbia. Director: Edward Sedgwick. Cast: Jack Holt, Ralph Graves, Sally Blane, Blanche Friderici, Edward Brophy, William V. Mong, Tyler Brooke, De Witt Jennings, Susan Fleming, Charles Middleton, Fredric Santley, Sidney Bracy, Esther Muir. ***The Deceiver.*** Columbia. Director: Louis King. Cast: Lloyd Hughes, Dorothy Sebastian, Ian Keith, Natalie Moorhead, Richard Tucker, George Bryon, Greta Granstedt, Murray Kinnell, De Witt Jennings, Allan Garcia, Harvey Clark, Sidney Bracy, Frank Halliday, Colin Campbell, Nick Copeland, Esther Muir. **1932:** ***Back Street.*** Universal. Director: John M. Stahl. Cast: Irene Dunne, John Boles, George Meeker, ZaSu Pitts, June Clyde, William Bakewell, Arletta Duncan, Doris Lloyd, Paul Weigel, Jane Darwell, Shirley Grey, James Donlan, Walter Catlett, Robert McWade, Maude Turner Gordon, Rose Dione, Russell Hopton, Betty Blythe, Caryl Lincoln, Esther Muir. ***Madison Sq. Garden.*** Paramount. Director: Harry Joe Brown. Cast: Jack Oakie, Thomas Meighan, Marian Nixon, William Collier Sr., ZaSu Pitts, Lew Cody, William Boyd, Warren Hymer, Robert Elliott, Joyce Compton, Bert Gordon, Noel Francis, Esther Muir. ***Frisco Jenny.*** Warner Brothers. Director: William Wellman. Cast: Ruth Chatterton, Louis Calhern, Helen Jerome Eddy, Donald Cook, James Murray, Hallam Cooley, Pat O'Malley, Harold Huber, Robert Emmett O'Connor, Willard Robertson, Frank McGlynn Sr., J. Carrol Naish, Noel Francis, Sam Godfrey, Franklin Parker, Berton Churchill, Robert Warwick, Harry Holman, Gertrude Astor, Esther Muir. ***So This Is Africa.*** Columbia. Director: Edward F. Cline. Cast: Bert Wheeler, Robert Woolsey, Raquel Torres, Esther Muir, Berton Churchill, Clarence Morehouse, Henry Armetta, Spencer Charters, Jerome Storm, Eddie Clayton. ***Sweepings.*** RKO. Director: John Cromwell. Cast: Lionel Barrymore, Eric Linden, William Gargan, Gloria Stuart, Alan Dinehart, Gregory Ratoff, Helen Mack, Lucien Littlefield, George Meeker, Nan Sunderland, Esther Muir, Franklin Pangborn, Ivan Lebedeff. ***Sailor's Luck.*** Fox. Director: Raoul Walsh. Cast: James Dunn, Sally Eilers, Victor Jory, Sammy Cohen, Frank Moran, Esther Muir, Will Stanton, Curley Wright, Jerry Mandy, Lucien Littlefield, Buster Phelps, Frank Atkinson, Phil Tead, Germaine De Neel, Hank Mann. ***Picture Brides.*** Allied. Director: Phil Rosen. Cast: Dorothy Mackaill, Regis Toomey, Alan Hale, Dorothy Libaire, Harvey Clark, Will Ahern, Mary Kornman, Esther Muir, Mae Busch, Gladys Ahern, Al Hill, Michael Visaroff, Brooks Benedict, Franklin Parker, Larry McGrath, Jimmy Aubrey. ***The Bowery.*** United Artists. Director: Raoul Walsh. Cast: Wallace Beery, George Raft, Jackie Cooper, Fay Wray, Pert Kelton, Herman Bing, Oscar Apfel, Ferdinand Munier, George Walsh, Lillian Harmer, Charles Lane, Harold Huber,

Fletcher Norton, Warren Hymer, Esther Muir, Frank Moran. ***The Warrior's Husband.*** Fox. Director: Walter Lang. Cast: Elissa Landi, Marjorie Rambeau, Ernest Truex, David Manners, Helen Ware, Maude Eburne, Claudia Coleman, Ferdinand Gottschalk, John Sheehan, Lionel Belmore, Tiny Sandford, Helene Madison, Gwen Lee, Esther Muir. ***I Love That Man.*** Paramount. Director: Harry Joe Brown. Cast: Edmund Lowe, Nancy Carroll, Robert Armstrong, Lew Cody, Warren Hymer, Grant Mitchell, Dorothy Burgess, Walter Walker, Berton Churchill, Susan Fleming, Louis Alberni, Lee Kohlmar, Merna Kennedy, Inez Courtney, Harvey Clark, Belle Mitchell, Leon Holmes, Esther Muir, Pat O'Malley. ***Adorable.*** Fox. Director: William Dieterle. Cast: Janet Gaynor, Henry Garat, C. Aubrey Smith, Herbert Mundin, Blanche Friderici, Hans von Twardowski, James Marcus, Esther Muir. ***The Nuisance.*** MGM. Director: Jack Conway. Cast: Lee Tracy, Madge Evans, Frank Morgan, Charles Butterworth, John Miljan, Virginia Cherrill, David Landau, Greta Meyer, Herman Bing, Samuel S. Hinds, Syd Saylor, Nat Pendleton, Esther Muir. ***Public Stenographer.*** Screencraft Productions. Director: Lew Collins. Cast: Lola Lane, William Collier, Jr., Esther Muir, Jason Robards, Duncan Renaldo, Richard Tucker, Bryant Washburn, Al St. John, Al Bridge. ***Broadway Thru a Keyhole.*** United Artists. Director: Lowell Sherman. Cast: Constance Cummings, Paul Kelly, Russ Columbo, Blossom Seeley, Gregory Ratoff, Texas Guinan, Abe Lyman and His Band, Hugh O'Connell, Hobart Cavanaugh, Frances Williams, Eddie Foy, Jr., Barto and Mann, C. Henry Gordon, Helen Jerome Eddy, Lucille Ball, Ethan Laidlaw, Esther Muir. ***Hell and High Water.*** Paramount. Directors: Grover Jones and William Slavens McNutt. Cast: Richard Arlen, Judith Allen, Charley Grapewin, Gertrude W. Hoffmann, Sir Guy Standing, S. Matsui, William Frawley, Charles Knettles, Barton MacLane, Esther Muir, Selmer Jackson. ***The Woman Who Dared.*** Imperial. Director: Millard Webb. Cast: Claudia Dell, Monroe Owsley, Lola Lane, Douglas Fowley, Robert Elliot, Matty Fain, Matthew Betz, Paul Fix, Esther Muir, Herbert Evans, Bryant Washburn, Eddie Kane, Sidney Bracy, Joseph Girard. ***Wine, Women and Song.*** Chadwick. Director: Herbert Brenon. Cast: Lilyan Tashman, Lew Cody, Marjorie Moore, Matty Kemp, Paul Gregory, Gertrude Astor, Bobbe Arnst, Esther Muir, Jesse De Vorska, Bobby Watson. **1934: *Unknown Blonde.*** Majestic. Director: Hobart Henley. Cast: Edward Arnold, Barbara Barondess, Barry Norton, John Miljan, Dorothy Revier, Leila Bennett, Walter Catlett, Helen Jerome Eddy, Claude Gillingwater, Esther Muir, Clarence Wilson, Arthur Hoyt. ***The Party's Over.*** Columbia. Director: Walter Lang. Cast: Stuart Erwin, Ann Sothern, Arline Judge, Chick Chandler, Patsy Kelly, Catharine Doucet, Marjorie Lytell, Henry Travers, William Bakewell, Rollo Lloyd, Esther Muir, Edward McWade, Maurice Black, Nick Copeland, Eddie Baker, Hal Prince. ***Caravan.*** Fox. Director: Erik Charell. Cast: Charles Boyer, Loretta Young, Jean Parker, Phillips Holmes, Louise Fazenda, Eugene Pallette, C. Aubrey Smith, Charley Grapewin, Noah Beery, Dudley Digges, Richard Carle, Billy Bevan, Lionel Belmore, Armand

Kaliz, Spencer Charters, Esther Muir. **1935: *The Gilded Lily.*** Paramount. Director: Wesley Ruggles. Cast: Claudette Colbert, Fred MacMurray, Ray Milland, C. Aubrey Smith, Edward Craven, Luis Alberni, Donald Meek, Claude King, Charles Irwin, Forrester Harvey, Edward Gargan, Charles Wilson, Grace Bradley, Pat Somerset, Tom Dugan, Warren Hymer, Eddie Borden, Rita Carlyle, Leonid Kinskey, Walter Shumway, Rollo Lloyd, Esther Muir, Hayden Stevenson, Samuel E. Hines. ***Racing Luck.*** Republic. Director: Sam Newfield. Cast: William "Bill" Boyd, Barbara Worth, George Ernest, Esther Muir, Ernest Hilliard, Onest Conley, Ben Hall, Henry Rocquemore, Dick Curtis, Ted Caskey. ***Here's to Romance.*** Twentieth Century–Fox. Director: Alfred E. Green. Cast: Nino Martini, Genevieve Tobin, Anita Louise, Maria Gambarelli, Mme. Ernestine Schumann-Heink, Reginald Denny, Vicente Escudero, Adrian Rosley, Mathilde Comont, Elsa Buchanan, Miles Mander, Keye Luke, Pat Somerset, Albert Conti, Egon Brecher, Orrin Burke, Armand Kaliz, Wilson Millar, Jack Mulhall, Esther Muir, Myrtle Stedman. ***The Gay Deception.*** Twentieth Century–Fox. Director: William Wyler. Cast: Francis Lederer, Frances Dee, Benita Hume, Alan Mowbray, Lennox Pawle, Adele St. Maur, Akim Tamiroff, Luis Alberni, Lionel Stander, Ferdinand Gottschalk, Richard Carle, Lenita Lane, Barbara Fritchie, Paul Hurst, Robert Greig, Maidel Turner, Frank Melton, David O'Brien, Robert Graves, Jack Mulhall, Spencer Charters, Wade Boteler, Esther Muir, Iris Adrian, Paul Irving, Nell Craig. ***Coronado.*** Paramount. Director: Norman McLeod. Cast: Johnny Downs, Betty Burgess, Jack Haley, Andy Devine, Leon Errol, Alice White, Eddy Duchin, Jameson Thomas, Berton Churchill, Nella Walker, Jacqueline Wells [Julie Bishop], Esther Muir, Paul Porcasi. **1936: *The Great Ziegfeld.*** MGM. Director: Robert Z. Leonard. Cast: William Powell, Myrna Loy, Luise Rainer, Frank Morgan, Fanny Brice, Virginia Bruce, Reginald Owen, Ray Bolger, Ernest Cossart, Joseph Cawthorne, Nat Pendleton, Harriet Hoctor, Jean Chatburn, Paul Irving, Herman Bing, Marcelle Corday, Raymond Walburn, Ann Gillis, Esther Muir, Mary Howard, Susan Fleming, Ruth Gillette, Virginia Grey. ***Fury.*** MGM. Director: Fritz Lang. Cast: Sylvia Sidney, Spencer Tracy, Walter Abel, Bruce Cabot, Edward Ellis, Walter Brennan, Frank Albertson, George Walcott, Arthur Stone, Morgan Wallace, George Chandler, Roger Gray, Edwin Maxwell, Howard Hickman, Leila Bennett, Esther Dale, Helen Flint, Esther Muir, Clara Blandick, Mary Foy, Arthur Hoyt. ***The First Baby.*** Twentieth Century–Fox. Director: Lewis Seiler. Cast: Johnny Downs, Shirley Deane, Dixie Dunbar, Jane Darwell, Marjorie Gateson, Gene Lockhart, Taylor Holmes, Willard Robertson, Hattie McDaniel, Dickie Jones, Mary Joan Felt, Madeline Holmes, Gloria Roy, Bryant Washburn, Jr., Richard Carpenter, Charles E. Evans, Cyril Ring, Niles Welch, Ward Bond, Esther Muir, Pat O'Malley. **1937: *High Hat.*** Imperial. Director: Clifford Smith. Cast: Frank Luther, Dorothy Dare, Lona Andre, Franklin Pangborn, Ferdinand Munier, Robert Warwick, Esther Muir, Gavin Gordon, Clarence Muse, Downey Sisters, Sonny Edwards. ***A Day at the Races.*** MGM.

Director: Sam Wood. Cast: Groucho Marx, Chico Marx, Harpo Marx, Allan Jones, Maureen O'Sullivan, Margaret Dumont, Leonard Ceeley, Douglas Dumbrille, Esther Muir, Sig Rumann, Robert Middlemass, Vivien Fay, Frankie Darro, Wilbur Mack, Henry Mowbray, Mary MacLaren, Edna Bennett, Hooper Atchley, Dorothy Dandridge. ***On Again—Off Again.*** RKO. Director: Edward Cline. Cast: Bert Wheeler, Robert Woolsey, Marjorie Lord, Patricia Wilder, Esther Muir, Paul Harvey, Russell Hicks, George Meeker, Maxine Jennings, Kitty McHugh, Alec Hartford, Jane Walsh, Alan Bruce, Jack Carson. ***I'll Take Romance.*** Columbia. Director: Edward H. Griffith. Cast: Grace Moore, Melvyn Douglas, Helen Westley, Stuart Erwin, Margaret Hamilton, Walter Kingsford, Richard Carle, Ferdinand Gottschalk, Esther Muir, Frank Forest, Walter O. Stahl, Barry Norton, Lucio Villegas, Franklin Pangborn, Greta Meyer, Albert Conti, Andre Beranger, Ann Doran. ***Under Suspicion.*** Columbia. Director: Lewis D. Collins. Cast: Jack Holt, Katherine De Mille, Luis Alberni, Purnell Pratt, Morgan Wallace, Maurice Murphy, Granville Bates, Craig Reynolds, Robert Emmett Keane, Margaret Irving, Rosalind Keith, Esther Muir. ***Love on Toast.*** Paramount. Director: E. A. Dupont. Cast: Stella Ardler, John Payne, Grant Richards, Katherine Kane, Benny Baker, Isabel Jewell, Luis Alberni, William B. Davidson, Franklin Pangborn, Esther Muir, Arthur Housman, Daisy Bufford, Edward Robins. **1938: *Battle of Broadway.*** Twentieth Century–Fox. Director: George Marshall. Cast: Victor McLaglen, Brian Donlevy, Louise Hovick [Gypsy Rose Lee], Raymond Walburn, Lynn Bari, Jane Darwell, Robert Kellard, Sammy Cohen, Esther Muir, Eddie Holden, Hattie McDaniel, Paul Irving, Frank Moran, Andrew Tombes, Jean Blanche, Jack Pennick, Sumner Getchell, Wesley Barry, Armand Kaliz, Eugene Borden, Edward Earle, Robert Graves. ***Romance in the Dark.*** Paramount. Director: H. C. Potter. Cast: Gladys Swarthout, John Boles, John Barrymore, Claire Dodd, Fritz Feld, Curt Bois, Carlos de Valdez, Torben Meyer, Margaret Randall, Fortunio Bonanova, Esther Muir, Eddy Conrad, Ferdinand Gottschalk, Lois Verner, Janet Elsie Clark, Otto Hoffman. ***City Girl.*** Twentieth Century–Fox. Director: Alfred Werker. Cast: Phyllis Brooks, Ricardo Cortez, Robert Wilcox, Douglas Fowley, Chick Chandler, Esther Muir, Adrienne Ames, George Lynn, Charles Lane, Paul Stanton, Marjorie Main, Norman Willis, Lon Chaney, Jr., Gloria Roy, Brooks Benedict, Delmar Watson, Lee Shumway, Ralph Dunn, Carroll Nye, Wade Boteler. ***The Law West of Tombstone.*** RKO. Director: Glenn Tryon. Cast: Harry Carey, Tim Holt, Evelyn Brent, Jean Rouverol, Clarence Kolb, Allan Lane, Esther Muir, Bradley Page, Paul Guilfoyle, Robert Moya, Ward Bond, George Irving. ***Three Comrades.*** MGM. Director: Frank Borzage. Cast: Robert Taylor, Margaret Sullavan, Franchot Tone, Robert Young, Guy Kibbee, Lionel Atwill, Henry Hull, Charley Grapewin, Monty Woolley, George Zucco, Spencer Charters, Sarah Padden, Morgan Wallace, George Offerman, Jr., Leonard Penn, Priscilla Lawson, Esther Muir, Walter Bonn, Edward McWade, George Chandler, Donald Haines, Norman Willis, Barbara Bedford, Mitchell

Lewis, Marjorie Main, Stanley Andrews, Phillip Terry. ***The Toy Wife.*** MGM. Director: Richard Thorpe. Cast: Luise Rainer, Melvyn Douglas, Robert Young, Barbara O'Neil, H. B. Warner, Alma Kruger, Libby Taylor, Theresa Harris, Walter Kingsford, Clinton Rosemond, Clarence Muse, Leonard Penn, Alan Perl, Margaret Irving, Rafaela Ottiano, Madame Sul-te-wan, Hal Le Seur, Edward Keane, Esther Muir, Priscilla Lawson, George Humbert, Barbara Bedford, Violet McDowell, Willa Curtis, Cora Lang, Irene Allen. ***Western Jamboree.*** Republic. Director: Ralph Staub. Cast: Gene Autry, Smiley Burnette, Jean Rouverol, Esther Muir, Joe Frisco, Frank Darien, Margaret Armstrong, Harry Holman, Kermit Maynard, George Wolcott. ***The Sunset Murder Case*** (a.k.a. ***The Sunset Strip Case***). Grand National. Director: Louis J. Gasnier. Cast: Sally Rand, Reed Hadley, The Henry King Orchestra, Dennie Moore, Sugar Kane, Esther Muir, Vince Barnett, Paul Sutton, Stanley Price, Lona Andre, Frank O'Connor, Bruce Mitchell. **1939: *The Girl and the Gambler.*** RKO. Director: Lew Landers. Cast: Leo Carrillo, Tim Holt, Steffi Duna, Donald MacBride, Chris-Pin Martin, Edward Raquello, Paul Fix, Julian Rivero, Frank Puglia, Esther Muir, Paul Sutton, Charles Stevens, Frank Lackteen. ***The Story of Vernon and Irene Castle.*** RKO. Director: H. C. Potter. Cast: Fred Astaire, Ginger Rogers, Edna May Oliver, Walter Brennan, Lew Fields, Etienne Girardot, Janet Beecher, Rolfe Sedan, Leonid Kinskey, Robert Strange, Douglas Walton, Frances Mercer, Victor Varconi, Donald MacBride, Jack Carson, Ethel Haworth, George Irving, Russell Hicks, Esther Muir. **1940: *Misbehaving Husbands.*** Producers Releasing Corp. Director: William Beaudine. Cast: Harry Langdon, Betty Blythe, Ralph Byrd, Esther Muir, Gayne Whitman, Florence Wright, Luana Walters, Frank Jaquet, Charlotte Treadway, Byron Barr, Mary MacLaren, Gertrude Astor. **1941: *Honky Tonk.*** MGM. Director: Jack Conway. Cast: Clark Gable, Lana Turner, Frank Morgan, Claire Trevor, Marjorie Main, Albert Dekker, Henry O'Neill, Chill Wills, Veda Ann Borg, Douglas Wood, Betty Blythe, Harry Worth, Lew Harvey, Hooper Atchley, Dorothy Granger, Sheila Darcy, Cy Kendall, John Farrell, Esther Muir, Francis X. Bushman, Jr., Eddie Gribbon, Syd Saylor, Harry Semels, Lee Phelps, Heinie Conklin. **1942: *The Mayor of 44th Street.*** RKO. Director: Alfred E. Green. Cast: George Murphy, Anne Shirley, Richard Barthelmess, William Gargan, Joan Merrill, Millard Mitchell, Mary Wickes, Eddie Hart, Roberta Smith, Marten Lamont, Walter Reed, Robert Smith, Lee Bonnell, Kenneth Lundy, Esther Muir, John H. Dilson. ***X Marks the Spot.*** Republic. Director: George Sherman. Cast: Damian O'Flynn, Helen Parrish, Dick Purcell, Jack La Rue, Neil Hamilton, Robert Homans, Anne Jeffreys, Dick Wessel, Esther Muir, Fred Kelsey, Vince Barnett.

13

Anita Page

"I don't care what they say about the other films I did, *Our Dancing Daughters* [1928] was my picture," Anita Page said, tapping the arm of the sofa to emphasize her point. "I say that because I did the acting. Joan Crawford danced her way through it; I acted my way through it."

Page's role was an amoral, hard-drinking flapper who steals Crawford's beau from her and plunges to her death down a flight of stairs. It was perhaps her finest screen performance. It was one to be proud of. Her memories of the film, which provided her big break, are pleasant, but her experiences with Crawford leave her cold.

She continued, "Anybody could have done what Crawford did [in *Our Dancing Daughters*]. I'm not only thinking of when she did the Charleston on top of that table. I'm thinking of any acting she did. She would just pat somebody on the back or she'd look a little sad. She did not seem to be able, in my opinion, to hold an emotional moment."

Sitting in her Burbank apartment in mid–March 1993 beneath a 1929 Hurrell portrait of herself, Anita Page, in the wee hours of the morning, was venting over the exclusive credit she said Crawford was getting with the recent video release of *Our Dancing Daughters.* Only minutes before midnight, she'd returned home from a night on the town with her daughter to find this visitor and a mutual friend, actor Randal Malone, waiting for her. That night was to be a get-acquainted session—it ran until 2:30 A.M., in preparation for an extensive interview later in the week.

Starting as a film extra in New York in the mid–20s, thanks to her actress-friend Betty Bronson, Page studied dance with modern dance legend Martha Graham and modeled with John Robert Powers' agency before joining an independent film company, whose owner had been part of a sensational murder scandal earlier in the century. The company took Anita to her pot of

Anita Page considered this 1929 Hurrell portrait her "Barbara La Marr pose." One of her favorites, this photo was on proud display over her living room sofa. (Courtesy of Randal Malone.)

gold — Hollywood — but soon after arriving, it dissolved in the bright California sun. All associated returned to New York. All, that is, but a determined Anita Page.

After only several months in Hollywood, she signed with MGM. Her brilliant performance in *Our Dancing Daughters*, her second MGM film, caught the attention of her peers. The studio boosted her exposure in an impressive publicity buildup, which sent her soaring in such follow-ups as *Our Modern Maidens* (1929) and *Our Blushing Brides* (1930) and in the studio's first all-talking film, *The Broadway Melody* (1929). She shone bright opposite some of MGM's finest leading men: Lon Chaney, William Haines, John Gilbert, Clark Gable and Ramon Novarro.

Page was a favorite on the MGM lot — she was particularly close to Marion Davies. She insisted that two of her screen lovers, Ramon Novarro and William Haines, both known homosexuals, wanted to take her to the altar. Then again, so did others. She dated Charles Farrell, George O'Brien and Germany's Prince Louis Ferdinand, following his split with actress Lili Damita (later Mrs. Errol Flynn).

MGM's top brass, Louis B. Mayer and Irving Thalberg, appreciating her fiery determination, gave her plum roles until she demanded more money and resisted efforts to remold her into a sex symbol. Then, the studio which had paved her road to stardom punished her with lower caliber pictures, supporting roles and loanouts. It was the beginning of the end.

With her career behind her, she married award-winning songwriter Nacio Herb Brown briefly in 1934, but the union wasn't a love match. She found true happiness when she married a naval lieutenant in 1937. Together for 54 years, they raised two daughters and lived all over the world. They eventually settled in Coronado, California.

For years, Page was reluctant to reminisce about her film career and declined interview requests. Returning to Los Angeles following the death of her husband in 1991, she found herself radiating in the spotlight of film festivals and was eager to tell her Hollywood adventures.

So eager, in fact, that while riding along the Pasadena Freeway on the afternoon of our interview, Page began telling how a movie-struck teenager transformed her dreams of stardom into reality. "After all," she said, "we didn't all come from Schwab's Drugstore."

Nibbling on cheese puffs and sipping champagne, Anita Page, witty, charming and dressed to the nines, tackled a barrage of questions that kept her reminiscing until three A.M. A genuine Jazz Baby still, MGM's "Sunshine Girl," came to life that night in the moonlight, long after the sun sank behind the Hollywood Hills.

The little girl destined for the screen was born Anita Evelyn Pomares on August 4, 1910, in Flushing, New York, to Marino (an electrical engineer) and Maude Mallane Pomares.

Her invitation to join the movie industry came first when she was only six months old. Her mother and an aunt were on a studio tour when a director approached, took one look at baby Anita and asked if he could use her in a film. Mrs. Pomares said no, that if Anita wanted to be an actress, it would be her own decision to make when she is old enough.

Page's decision came when she was only five years old. At a time when most children were thinking about playing outside, Page said she was pondering her future as a movie actress. "Don't ask me how I knew that early. That's one thing I'm grateful for: I had goals. I wanted to be an actress, not on the stage, but on the screen."

She appeared in school plays every chance she got and went often to the darkened theaters, where she concentrated not so much on the scenario but on the flickering images of the gods and goddesses before her. Her favorites were Norma Talmadge ("She was like magic to me") and Wallace Reid. She was not a particular fan of Theda Bara, the screen's first vamp. "There was something about her eyes that gave me the creeps."

When Page was 13, two important events happened to the Pomares family. A brother, Marino, was born, and the family moved (still in New York) three houses down from Betty Bronson, who at that time was in California trying to break into the movies. Not long after their move, Page was sledding one day when she met "a nice-looking boy" who turned out to be Bronson's brother. Page was invited to visit the Bronson home. Her mother said yes to the visit, no to her daughter's pleas to wear rouge for the occasion. Determined to look her best, Page slapped her cheeks until they were red.

By the time Bronson came East to make *A Kiss for Cinderella* (1926), she was a star,* having made her film debut in *Peter Pan* (1924). Page, now a friend

**Bronson (1906–1971) played the Virgin Mary in* Ben-Hur *(1925). Her popularity continued throughout the silent era. She retired from the screen in the early 1930s to marry Ludwig Lauerhass. She returned to the screen in the 1960s as a character actress.*

of the family, was invited to visit Bronson in her suite at the Plaza Hotel. "Was I ever dolled-up," she said.

With the help of Bronson and her mother, Page was offered a bit role in *A Kiss for Cinderella*. Page was elated, Mrs. Pomares, apprehensive. With a little persuasion from her daughter and the assurance that Mrs. Bronson would accompany her to the set, Mrs. Pomares gave her blessing. Page took a week off from school and went to Paramount's New York studios to make her film debut.*

On her first day on the set, Page was excited to be in a studio, but not so caught up in the moment, that she didn't notice "a very attractive man" looking at her. She stared back, and during the week, the two carried on what Page calls "a little flirtation." At the end of the week, the man approached, identified himself as an assistant director and asked her if she would like to play a small role in his next film, *Love 'Em and Leave 'Em* (1926). "Would I?" she answered, without a thought. She said of getting the small part, "Of course, by then, I was already a star in my own mind."

The role was that of a young French girl who flirts with a young American soldier. "So apparently, my flirting with him did very well for me," she said.

The assistant director instructed her to take dancing lessons—"I had the face, but I was a little awkward," she said—and to pose every chance she got. "Come to Hollywood in two years," Page said he told her, "and you'll knock 'em dead."

Heeding his advice, Page signed up for dancing classes at a school where Martha Graham was teaching. "She liked me, and I noticed that she would watch me, but we never talked," she recalled. "I didn't enjoy the experience because we were encouraged to do things exactly like everyone else. That right away ruled it out for me. I wasn't going to sell myself."

She then heard of a modeling school run by John Robert Powers. It seemed to her to be a logical step in her progression as an actress. Powers, however, was reluctant. "Before I could even open my mouth, he said, 'You're not for modeling; you're for the screen.'" Page agreed with him, but said she wanted the experience. He signed her up.

One day in 1927, Powers came to Page with the news she had been waiting for. A small independent studio, Kenilworth† was just opening in the city and was looking for a second lead. Page went for an interview, and after about 15 minutes, she had signed her first movie contract. Her name was changed to Ann Rivers. "I was just thrilled," she said. "I was on my way."

In a week's time, Page had replaced the lead (Suzanne Hughes, the original

**Modern references give* Monsieur Beaucaire *(1924) as Page's film debut. When questioned, she denied appearing in the film. "If I had been in a film with Valentino, don't you think I would have remembered it?" she asked.*

†The company was named after the historic southern mansion of the same name located in Winchester, Virginia.

lead, became the second lead) and was making her debut at the studio. After the picture wrapped, it was decided the company would go to California to market the picture. Kenilworth agreed to pay the expenses of Page, her mother and five-year-old Marino. Page was ecstatic.

The train pulled out of New York en route to Hollywood in December 1927. Page caught a whiff of that sweet smell of stardom toward the West. The scent turned foul, however, when the train pulled into Chicago. The owner of Kenilworth stepped on board to introduce himself to Page and her mother. Page thought her mother, whose color had drained from her face, would collapse.

"We have to get off this train right now," Mrs. Pomares told a horrified Anita. "Do you know who that man is? That's Harry K. Thaw."* The name meant nothing to Page, but to those old enough to remember, Thaw was forever linked to the murder of his wife's lover 20 years before.

Page calmly told her mother they were not leaving the train and they would continue their journey toward what was sure to be her future in the movies. Page told her mother that if they got off the train, the press would write that Thaw had tried to attack them. She convinced her that it was best if they remained quietly in their compartment until they arrived in Los Angeles. Her mother, under the pressure of her daughter's charming determination, agreed.

"They tried to paint Mr. Thaw as erratic and crazy, but I thought he was one of the nicest men I have ever met," Page said. "He was a gentleman who made all the men stand up as we went in to sit down for dinner. That showed his apparent respect for womanhood."

The press, who met the train in California, photographed Thaw with Page and Suzanne Hughes, his two protégée

Page, her mother and brother were taken to the Ambassador Hotel. While Thaw conducted his business dealings, Page went to photographer Edwin Bower Hesser for a sitting and strolled around Hollywood.

"When I got off that train, I knew I was in the most gorgeous place I had ever seen: beautiful palm trees and bright sunshine. It was all I'd ever dreamt it would be," Page reminisced, clasping her hands together. "I had arrived at my mecca."

After a while, Thaw announced that his venture had failed and that he was returning to New York — the picture was not sold and was never released. "I told them that I wasn't going home, that if I did, I would never get out here again," said Page. Mrs. Pomares again agreed with her daughter, and the three took an apartment on DeLongpre Avenue, in the heart of Hollywood. Mr.

**Harry Kendall Thaw (1872–1947), the son of a Pittsburgh railroad and coke magnate, was driven over the edge in 1906 by the affair his wife, actress Evelyn Nesbit (1884–1967), was having with architect Stanford White. In a jealous rage, he shot and killed White in Madison Square Garden. His first trial ended in a hung jury, but he was acquitted at the second trial in 1908 on the grounds of insanity. After spending time in Kirkbride's Insane Asylum in Pennsylvania, he was declared sane and was released in 1915. The film* The Girl in the Red Velvet Swing *(1955) was based on the scandal.*

Pomares, whose job as an electrical engineer was solid, remained in New York to see if Page could establish herself as an actress before he joined his family.

At a New Year's dinner at Betty Bronson's home in 1928, Page was introduced to Harvey Pugh, a Paramount employee who had ambitions of becoming an agent. He set up an appointment for her to meet with a Paramount casting director. Several days later, at the studio, she was told that screen tests were rarely made based solely on photographs, but that her portraits were so exquisite, an exception would be made.

"In those days, the only thing you had was the photography—how you photographed," she said. "You had to have the right bone structure and you had to have the right eyes. You had to have everything in place."

Wearing one of Evelyn Brent's dresses from wardrobe, Page made a test and went home to wait by the phone. After two days, she told her mother she couldn't wait any longer. The two climbed aboard a bus—she like the top level—and rode over Hollywood.

The phone was ringing as they were coming in the door. The man on the other end identified himself as director Malcolm St. Clair.* Thinking it was one of her old beaus playing a trick, Page replied, "Yes, and I'm Mary Pickford." When Harvey Pugh got on the line to explain to her that it was no joke, "I almost fainted," she said. Pugh told her that Paramount was loaning St. Clair to MGM to make a film starring Aileen Pringle and Adolphe Menjou, and that he was interested in testing her the next day for the second lead.

When she arrived at MGM, she was told she was not to see St. Clair as planned, but director Sam Wood† instead. Wood took one look at her, picked up the phone, called William Haines§ and asked him to come and make a test with Page for his next picture, *Telling the World* (1928).

"I had a crush on [Haines] since I was 15," Page admitted. "I thought he had the most gorgeous teeth I had ever seen. He came in wearing riding clothes and we took this test. I was facing the camera and had my arms around his neck. He was going to leave and I couldn't stand it. It was the easiest test I have ever made."

In the meantime, Paramount beckoned and she went out to meet with production executive Jesse L. Lasky, who told her that he had not seen her test, but that he thought the studio might sign her.

**Malcolm (Mal) St. Clair (1897–1952) was at the height of his popularity as a director when Anita arrived in Hollywood. He joined Mack Sennett as a bit player and gag writer in the mid–1910s and began directing comedy shorts for Sennett in 1919. He turned to feature films in 1923. With the coming of sound, the quality of his work declined. He continued directing into the 1940s.*

†Sam Wood (1883–1949) was an actor in two-reelers in 1908 before he turned to directing in the mid–1910s. At Paramount, he directed a number of films starring Gloria Swanson and Wallace Reid. His career flourished in talkies with such successes as A Night at the Opera *(1935),* Our Town *(1940),* Kitty Foyle *(1940) and* Kings Row *(1942).*

§William Haines (1900–1973) was one of MGM's biggest stars near the end of the silent era. He was particularly effective in smart-aleck type roles and college jerks. He retired from the screen in the mid–1930s and became a prominent interior decorator.

Three days later, MGM called her back to the studio, where she waited for half an hour. "It seemed like eight weeks in my mind. Little did I know Irving Thalberg* used to keep them waiting sometimes for two days," said Page.

MGM offered her a contract, then, in a matter of days, Paramount followed with a proposal. However, Paramount, she said, didn't guarantee her as much money, and there were no assurances that she would appear on film. With MGM's promise that they would put her on the screen, Page and her mother signed on the dotted line.

"I was smart enough to know that a lot of little girls would sign up for six months and never get on the screen. Then, they would be let go," she said. "I wanted to go with MGM because they were so good for female actresses. If you ask me, MGM was *the* studio."

Before the ink was dry on the contract, the studio changed her name to Ann Page. However, another actress working under the same name at First National (the wife of director David Kirkland) filed a protest with the Motion Picture Academy of Arts and Sciences. The studio settled on Anita Page.

So far, Page's association with Harry K. Thaw had had no negative impact on her rise to stardom. No one had asked her about it, and she had not volunteered any information. One day, however, as she was getting her clothes ready for *Telling the World*, an MGM supervisor came to her and told her the studio was going to release her.

"They didn't know that I had signed with Kenilworth. They were afraid it would make bad publicity, but I wasn't, because I knew I was innocent," she said. "I went in to see Louis B. Mayer and Thalberg. I cried, I yelled, I screamed. Believe you me, I almost tore down the office. Finally, Mayer turned to Thalberg and asked him what he thought. Thalberg said, 'Give the kid a chance.' So, the kid was in."

The filming of *Telling the World* began, with Page playing a showgirl who is saved from being falsely accused of murder by a reporter (William Haines). By now, Page said she had gotten over her crush on Haines; he was now like a big brother.

Director Sam Wood was eager to show off MGM's newest contract player and encouraged the other MGM players (according to Page), that if they wanted to see "the most beautiful girl in the world," to come over to his set. Ramon Novarro, Marion Davies and Norma Shearer appeared on the set to make their acquaintance. Even Joan Crawford came over for a peek.

The filming was going fine until Page had to do a crying scene, which she found impossible. Wood urged her to use a "blower," a device used to induce tears. Norma Shearer used one, said Page, but *she* said no, explaining that it would take away from her art. "All I could think about was how much money I was costing everybody. Finally, Sam Wood told me that we'd film the scene

**Irving Thalberg (1899–1936), Hollywood's "Boy Wonder," was Louis B. Mayer's vice president and production supervisor. He married (in 1927) one of MGM's most prominent actresses, Norma Shearer.*

later with just the two of us and a cameraman. He kept telling the story and I got caught up in it, and in about ten minutes, I was crying buckets."

By the time the picture wrapped, Page heard the studio was looking for a lead in *Our Dancing Daughters* (1928), the perfect actress to play the part of a fast-living flapper. Page wanted the role so bad, "I could taste it," she said.

Director Harry Beaumont* who thought Anita would never do for the picture, went to Mayer with his misgivings. He told the boss that the film would rise or fall on the part of Ann and that he needed a consummate actress. Mayer, having the last word and remembering Page's outburst in his office several months before, reportedly said, "Take her [Page], she's a Bernhardt."

Our Dancing Daughters marked the beginning of Page's bumpy, rather odd, relationship with the film's star, Joan Crawford.† When Page first arrived on the MGM lot, Crawford went out of her way to gain her friendship. It was written in the early 1990s that Crawford had crushes on not only Page, but also actresses Dorothy Sebastian and Gwen Lee.

"If she did, I would be interested to know," Page said of the rumors. "It might have started when Joan invited me to her home in Brentwood. I remember it was very dark. She also invited me to take dancing classes with her, but my mother wouldn't let me. So, it may have been true in the beginning that she wanted to know me for that reason." Did Crawford make any sexual overtures? "Heavens no, not me!"

Crawford turned sour once filming began. Page was no longer a friend; they were now competitors. Page raised an eyebrow when Crawford came to her one day and told her to be careful not to hurt John Mack Brown§ during their big fight scene. Page brushed off the comments as an attempt to get her to hold back.

"I went straight to Johnny and told him that Joan said I might hurt him. He said, 'I should think not. I've been a football player and I can take care of myself. You give it all you've got.' I did, of course."

With Crawford on the defensive and Beaumont doubtful of Page's ability, Page felt she'd been thrown to the wolves. Then, "that darling Dorothy Sebastian** came up to me and said, 'Anita, I saw the rushes last night. You're going to be great in this picture.'"

**Before coming to MGM, Harry Beaumont (1888–1966) had directed for Essanay, Goldwyn, Fox, Metro and Warners. Before that, he appeared in vaudeville and as a leading man and supporting player in films for Edison. He remained at MGM into the late 1940s.*

†When Joan Crawford (1906–1977) was cast in Our Dancing Daughters *(1928), MGM was giving her the big buildup and had cast her opposite their hottest male stars: Nils Asther, William Haines, John Gilbert, Lon Chaney and Ramon Novarro. The role of Dangerous Diana made her a star and put her name in lights, where it remained for decades.*

§John Mack Brown (1904–1974), an All-American halfback at the University of Alabama, became Johnny Mack Brown in the 1930s and was considered one of the top Western stars of the 1930s and 1940s.

***Dorothy Sebastian (1903–1957) was the second female lead in many MGM films in the late 1920s. The dark-haired beauty starred in B-pictures in the 1930s and appeared in* The Mysterious Pilot, *a serial, in 1937. She was married to actor William Boyd from 1930–36.*

Page's finest scene in the film comes when she shows up drunk to confront her husband (Brown) at a party, makes a spectacle of herself, then falls to her death down a flight of stairs. The scene pumped her adrenaline so much that, in the climax, right before she went down the stairs, Page found herself losing control. Beaumont, with no other alternative, slapped her back into reality. "He's the only man who ever hit me," she said.

For years, she has been asked if it was she who spiraled to the bottom of the staircase. "Honey, if it had been me, I wouldn't be here to tell you." Page fell four steps and a male double did the rest.

Page received rave reviews for her performance. The headlines to Norbert Lusk's column read, "Newcomer is Lauded Highly." He wrote, "Anita Page runs away with the acting honors in what is technically an unsympathetic role, but she brings to it beauty, humor and magnetic unself-conciousness." Thirty years later, Joe Franklin wrote in his book *Classics of the Silent Screen.** "Page's performance was quite the best in the film."

After *Our Dancing Daughters*, Page went right to work on *While the City Sleeps* (1928), which starred Lon Chaney. She was cast as a flapper who falls for Carroll Nye. Chaney played a policeman, quite different from his grotesque portrayals in *The Hunchback of Notre Dame* (1923) and *The Phantom of the Opera* (1925).

"It was fantastic to watch him work. Chaney was such an original," she said. "We had a lot in common about acting. Structurally, we understood and talked about the fact that while you had to have the features to photograph well, the eyes told a lot of what a person was feeling and that you could do a lot of talking through your eyes."

Next, Ramon Novarro† lobbied diligently for Page to appear in his next picture, *The Flying Fleet* (1929). The producers were leery because Page was a bit taller than Novarro. He explained that she was no taller than Joan Crawford, with whom he had worked earlier. The producers conceded, and Page was in.

On the first day of filming, Novarro invited her out, chaperoned by "a young Naval officer," a friend of Novarro's. They continued to court throughout the filming of the picture, always, said Page, with Novarro's friend in tow. Finally, word spread among the crew that Novarro, whose romantic interests were known to lean towards his own sex, was infatuated with his leading lady.

So interested, said Page, that he popped the marriage question to her during the filming of a love scene near the end of the picture. Said Page, "We had this scene coming up and he told me to play it like I really meant it. That's when

*Classics of the Silent Screen *was published in 1959 by The Citadel Press, New York.*

†*Ramon Novarro (1899–1968), one of the silent screen's greatest Latin lovers, was discovered by director Rex Ingram in 1922 and was catapulted to stardom after his appearance in MGM's epic* Ben Hur *(1926). He made a successful transition to sound and continued to play romantic lead opposite such leading ladies as Greta Garbo, Myrna Loy, Madge Evans, Helen Hayes and others, into the early 1930s. Later, in the 1950s, he played bits and character parts. He was murdered by two teenage hustlers in 1968 on Halloween.*

Lon Chaney and Anita Page in *While the City Sleeps* (1928). (Courtesy of Randal Malone.)

he said, 'I love you, will you marry me?' Well, I thought he was good-looking in a very soft kind of way, but frankly I never wanted to marry an actor." Page lightheartedly told Novarro she might consider marrying him on an "off-Thursday."

Novarro's interest in Page was not unusual. During her Hollywood career, she was seen on the arm of several of Hollywood's most eligible bachelors. She went unchaperoned to the premiere of *Show Boat* (1929) with Prince Louis Ferdinand; "He was tall, which was nice, but he wasn't my type. He wasn't very handsome and I like them good-looking." George O'Brien* fit the bill for her, not only because of his stunning looks, but because of his voice. "I could sit and listen to that man talk until doomsday," she said. The pair went on a safari, along with Gary Cooper, and then to the Cocoanut Grove for a night on the town. She didn't hear from him for some time, then learned he was seeing actress Marguerite Churchill.

Then, there was Charles Farrell† whom she dated until it became apparent

**George O'Brien (1900–1985) was rescued from the ranks of a bit player in 1924 by director John Ford who starred him in* The Iron Horse *for Fox. Known for his good looks and muscular physique, O'Brien was linked during the late 1920s with actress Olive Borden, with whom he appeared in* Fig Leaves *and* Three Bad Men, *both in 1926. His performance in F. W. Murnau's* Sunrise *(1927) confirmed his talent as an actor. In the 1930s, he became one of the screen's most popular cowboys. Considered one of Hollywood's most eligible bachelors, he was married to actress Marguerite Churchill (b. 1909) from 1933–1948.*

†Charles Farrell (1901–1990) hit his stride in 1927 with Seventh Heaven, *in which he appeared with Janet Gaynor. The two were, for the next seven years, one of the screen's top love teams. He was married to actress Virginia Valli (1895–1968) from 1931 until her death.*

Ramon Novarro, according to Anita Page, proposed marriage during the filming of *The Flying Fleet* (1929). (Courtesy of Randal Malone.)

to her he wore makeup off the screen—which was not the case at all. "What happened was terrible and I made a big mistake," she said. "When we were together, I saw what looked to me to be eyebrow pencil and I thought he was using makeup. I decided I wouldn't go out with him again. Years later, however, I saw him and realized the man had the same marking there. It was just a scar."

Page's parents wanted her to enjoy her experience in Hollywood and didn't wrap their daughter into a protective cocoon. While Page was not a frequent party-goer, she double-dated from time to time with Betty Bronson and made it a point to attend the parties at Marion Davies' Santa Monica beach house, because the actress was a close friend. Tight production schedules often kept Page's attention focused on the studio.

"I didn't really have time to make friends. My friends were the people I was working with," she said. "I'd get up at five A.M. and be on the set at eight A.M. and then work until six P.M. or later."

She was named one of the 1929 Wampas Baby Stars* and despite a hectic schedule, found time to participate in several Wampas events. "It was just one of the lovely things that was happening to me," she said. It was at a Wampas function that year that she met an up-and-coming Hollywood actress and a soon-to-be fellow MGM contract player. "I looked up and saw this gorgeous figure and that gorgeous platinum hair, and I thought, 'Who's that?' It was Jean Harlow. I wasn't as impressed with any of the Wampas girls there as I was with her."

Page liked to tell a story that presented another side of Harlow, contrary to the sex symbol image movie-goers came to know. One day, Page passed Harlow on the MGM lot without acknowledging her. Harlow, who was testing for the lead in *Red Headed Woman* (1932), told Page later how hurt she was and how she had gone back to her dressing room, put her head down and cried. Then, as she looked up into the mirror, Harlow started laughing hysterically, realizing that Page hadn't recognized her in the red wig she was wearing for the test. "That shows you how sensitive she was," Page said. "She was a lovely person in so many ways."

Page was riding the crest of her career when she was cast in *The Broadway Melody* as Queenie, who, with Bessie Love, are members of a sister act that goes from the vaudeville houses of the Midwest to the bright lights of Broadway. As MGM's first all-talkie, *The Broadway Melody* won the Academy Award for Best Picture and set the tone for a new genre of movie musicals of the 1930s.

Although it was lauded by the critics, the industry and the public, *The Broadway Melody* was never a personal favorite of Page's. With the passing of time, however, her opinion of the picture improved.

She said, "When I was making it, I had to say things like, 'Gee, ain't it elegant?' or 'Ain't it grand?' I loved good English and that just went against my grain. I've noticed in the video they have out now, however, that I'm only saying it twice, so that's not too bad."

The Broadway Melody introduced Page to sound and demonstrated how

**Other Wampas Baby Stars that year included Jean Arthur, Sally Blane, Betty Boyd, Ethlyne Clair, Doris Dawson, Josephine Dunn, Helen Foster, Doris Hill, Caryl Lincoln, Mona Rico, Helen Twelvetrees and Loretta Young.*

rigorous filmmaking could be. The soundproof stages, needed to keep out studio and street noises, made the sets stifling and sometimes unbearably hot.

When Page was filming *Navy Blues* (1929), for instance, an emotional scene was ruined by the opening of a door. "Clarence Brown* was directing—I didn't like working with him because he was worried too much about little effects, while I like the emotion of the work," she said. "Anyway, he wanted one tear coming down my face, and he was making it very tough. We finally got it. At that moment, someone opened the door to the sound stage while a plane was flying over and it blew the shot. We had to do it over again. Needless to say, I wasn't very enthusiastic about it."

By early 1929, when *The Broadway Melody* was released, Page realized sound was not a fad and that the industry would never return to silent films as some believed. "In my opinion, silents were much better than talkies," she said. "One thing you had was mood music, which you could have playing throughout your scene to inspire you. My favorite song was "My Heart at Thy Sweet Voice" from *Samson and Delilah.* I never seemed to tire of it. The trouble with talkies was, they let you have the music, but they'd stop it when you had to talk and it was always a letdown for me."

Conrad Nagel sang "You Were Meant for Me" to Page in *The Hollywood Revue of 1929,* an MGM feature which showed off its contract players. Page was cast again with Joan Crawford in *Our Modern Maidens* (1929) and *Our Blushing Brides* (1930), follow-ups to *Our Dancing Daughters.* "I used to laugh and say that we're going to be 'The Galloping Grandmothers' at the rate we're going with these pictures."

Crawford and beau Douglas Fairbanks, Jr., were courting heavily during the filming of *Our Modern Maidens* and would marry in June 1929. MGM, cashing in on the pairing, cast Fairbanks as Crawford's leading man. The public affections they had for each other were sometimes distracting to other cast members, said Page, who had no time for the love birds' display.

It was about midway through the filming of *Our Modern Maidens* that "my trouble began," the catalyst that became what Page called the "beginning of the end" of her career. In negotiating the renewal of her MGM contract, her agent demanded an increase in her salary.

"I came to realize it wasn't such a good idea, but it was too late; we were already in it," she recounted. "They gave me the money all right, but the thing we didn't ask for and *should* have was the say-so in my parts—like Bette Davis fought for."

In 1930, with a new contract and a higher salary, Page appeared in *Caught Short*—not a particularly good role, she said. It was the first of three comedies

**Clarence Brown (1890–1987), who established his reputation after directing* The Eagle *(1925) with Rudolph Valentino and Vilma Banky, was considered Garbo's preferred director—he directed her in seven films.*

Anita Page (left) with Joan Crawford in *Our Blushing Brides* (1930). (Courtesy of Randal Malone.)

she made with Marie Dressler and Polly Moran (the others were *Reducing* [1931] and *Prosperity* [1932]). "While we were making one of these, Marie told me she had cancer, and in another, she was beginning to get sick," Page said. "She was so brave; she was such a trooper."*

Page found Buster Keaton† "charming" when she worked with him in *Free and Easy* (1930) as a Kansas beauty contest winner who tries to break into films. She later worked with him again in *The Sidewalks of New York* (1931), which Keaton called one of his worst films.

Page realized her career was losing momentum, that the quality of her roles

**Marie Dressler died in 1934 at age 65.*

†Known for his deadpan expression, Buster Keaton (1895–1966) was among the screen's greatest comedians, along with Charlie Chaplin, Harold Lloyd and W. C. Fields. His high marks were made in the 1920s, especially with his masterpiece, The General *(1927). By the time he worked with Anita, he had given up his own studio (along with his artistic control) to work at MGM. His marriage to Natalie Talmadge had failed, and he was slipping deeper into alcoholism.*

was deteriorating. The popularity of the happy-go-lucky flapper and carefree Jazz baby she had recently played so well ended with the Great Depression. In light of its substantial investment in Page, MGM began plans to develop her image into a more sexual one. Page and her parents resisted, due in part to their strict religious convictions.

She refused to pose for risqué photographs showing her in revealing gowns and balked at the studio's request that she appear in public with certain film players strictly for the value of publicity.

Mayer lashed back. "You stand behind what your parents want for you," Page said (quoting Mayer), "instead of doing what I tell you. I'll never lift another finger to help you." Page came to understand soon enough what her boss meant when he told her he could make her a star in three pictures or break Garbo in the same number.

That year, MGM loaned Page to another studio for the first time. The company was Universal and the film was *The Little Accident* (1930) with Douglas Fairbanks, Jr. She considered the project (as well as being loaned out) a bad sign for her future.

At her home studio in 1931, she played Constance Bennett's sister and Clark Gable's wife in *The Easiest Way*.* She liked Gable and he like her, comparing her later, Page was told, to Grace Kelly. Warm feelings, however, didn't carry over into Page's association with Constance Bennett,† who played the glamorous sister kept by wealth. Page was cast in a supporting role as the drab housewife.

"Connie Bennett did one thing that I resented. One day, she came up to me and said, 'Are you wearing makeup? Your closeups are just gorgeous.' With that, she took her hand and ran it down my face. If I had anything on my face, it was just a little talcum powder."

While on the subject of Bennett, Page couldn't resist another anecdote. "I heard this story that she was dancing with this guy at a party, and she asked him, 'Do you know who you're dancing with?' The guy said, 'No.' She replied, 'Constance Bennett.' His response: 'Do you know who you're dancing with?' She said, 'No, who? He said. 'By yourself,' as he walked away."

Page had known John Gilbert for several years before she worked with him in *Gentleman's Fate* (1931). She remembered him once at a party at Marion Davies' beach house, sitting at the feet of Greta Garbo, with whom he had been in love.

"I felt so sorry for Jack. He was so great and kind," she said. "We did this scene where he was lying on this bed and he had to break into tears. He just

*The Easiest Way *was Gable's first film under his MGM contract.*

†*She started in films in 1916 and made many features during the silent era; however, it was in the 1930s, particularly in sophisticated comedies, that Constance Bennett (1904–1966), the daughter of Richard and sister of Joan and Barbara, became a screen favorite. Witty, composed and glamorous, she was the epitome of elegance.*

A 1930 Hurrell portrait of Anita Page. (Courtesy of Randal Malone.)

sat there, and suddenly, the tears just poured. I asked him how he could cry like that. He said, 'Honey, I can do it if the scene plays true.'"

Page was teamed for the final time with William Haines in *Are You Listening?* (1931). They had dated on occasion, as friends. In their four pictures together, they had plenty of love scenes in which Haines, Page said, invariably "held back." For some reason, *Are You Listening?* was different. She explained,

"We were standing outside waiting to go into this room, when all of a sudden, he grabbed me and gave me a big kiss — I mean, he really kissed me. I thought, wow! I was in a daze, kind of surprised. Then his attitude changed. He would come on the set singing, 'Nothing could be sweeter than to see my Anita in the morning.'"

According to Page, Haines proposed marriage. Then, an article appeared in a fan magazine in which Haines told the reporter he was "crazy about Anita Page." Louis B. Mayer, the father figure he was, called Page into his office and, according to Page, said, "You don't want him. Don't you know who that fellow is who's always on the set with him?" To which Anita replied, "Well, Mr. Mayer, Jimmy Shields* seems to have disappeared lately." Nothing came of the relationship, and the two finished the picture as friendly as ever.

Page lobbied diligently for the part of Lil "Red" Andrews in MGM's *Red Headed Woman* (1932). Tests were made and portraits of her in a red wig were taken. It appeared for a short time that she had a chance at the film. Then, Irving Thalberg called her in to discuss the picture.

"I was sitting in his office and he asked me what I was going to do for papa, meaning him, if he gave me the part," Page said. "I told him I was going to give the role all I had and that I would be a great actress in it. He replied, 'Yes, but what else are you going to do for papa if I give you the part?' I got up from my chair and walked out of the office without another word. I knew, of course, when I closed the door, I would not get the picture."†

Page was loaned for the rest of her contract to Columbia for *Soldiers of the Storm*; to Universal for *The Big Cage*; and then, the final blow, the ultimate humiliation, to independent companies Monogram and Chesterfield to make *Jungle Bride* and *I Have Lived*, respectively.

Being reduced to independents was indeed a letdown for Page after her leading roles in major MGM productions. "At the time, I realized what was going on, but there was nothing I could do about it. I just did the best I could." When people asked her about those independent features, she would apologize. Now, after having had the chance to view them on video after so many years, her opinions have changed "I think I did a darn good job in them." Thumbing through one of her scrapbooks, she pulled a newspaper advertisement for *Jungle Bride*. "See," she said, pointing to a clipping, "my name is above the title. I was the star."

After her contract expired, Page said she made a series of tests for Fox Studios and it appeared she would be signed to a contract. She heard nothing for days, then ran into someone she knew from Fox's publicity staff. The girl told her not to quote her or tell that she had given her the information, but that

**William Haines and Jimmy Shields were said to be one of Hollywood's happiest couples. Haines died of cancer in 1973, and a year later, his companion, despondent over the loss, committed suicide.*

†Jean Harlow played the part.

studio executives had lunch with Louis B. Mayer several days before. After the meeting, she said, plans to sign Page were scrapped.

Unemployed, Page signed with producer Billy Rose and appeared on stage back East in *Crazy Quilts.* "I thought I would last about ten weeks. However, I went for seven months doing five shows a day, and I never had a break." Page declined Rose's invitation to take the show south.

Back in California, she went to the Hearst Castle to visit her old pal Marion Davies* for the weekend — she ended up staying five months. During the large dinners at the ranch, Page, at Davies' urging, would help break up tense business conversations between Hearst and some guests by sliding a chair by Hearst and telling corny stories.

Davies' problems with drinking are widely documented. Stories have circulated that to bypass Hearst's tight control on the liquor, Davies would hide her booze in toilet bowls. Page said she never saw her inebriated, and doubted she could have been and still run the house in the manner in which she did. Nevertheless, Page found herself caught in a plan to smuggle liquor to Davies one night after dinner hours, when drinking was strictly forbidden by Hearst.

"Marion asked me if I would go and tell the top steward I had a headache and that I needed an ounce of bourbon," she said. "Well, this man knew me well enough to know I didn't drink straight bourbon. He got it for me and said, 'You'll have to drink it here.' He brought it to me and stood there. What could I do? I didn't dare not drink it, because they would think it was for Marion. So, I had to drink the stuff. I walked back to Marion with this look on my face. She asked me where it was. I pointed to my stomach."

On July 26, 1934, Page crossed the Mexican border into Tijuana and married songwriter Nacio Herb Brown,† who had written the songs for *The Broadway Melody.* She had met him on the set of the film, but had not dated him until years later. Brown was a friend of her father's, who encouraged the marriage, even though Page didn't return his (Brown's) affections. Eight months later, in March 1935, the marriage was annulled, "on the basis that I'd never lived with him as his wife," said Page.

Page accepted a small role in *Hitch Hike to Heaven* (1936), a Chesterfield release, because she said, she wanted to try a new makeup for the screen. It was her last film appearance.

In mid–1936, she and a friend went to a fortune teller. "I see the initials H. H. or K. K. in your life," the psychic told her. "It's not anybody you know

**Marion Davies (1897–1961) came to MGM when Cosmopolitan Pictures, the film company William Randolph Hearst founded for her, merged with the Goldwyn Company in 1924. Although one of the major stars of the 1920s, her career declined after the advent of sound. She rotated in Hollywood's highest circles and lived like royalty with Hearst in a Beverly Hills estate, a 110-room Santa Monica beach house and a castle at San Simeon.*

†The Broadway Melody *(1929) marked the beginning of Nacio Herb Brown's association with MGM. For many years, Brown (1896–1964) composed musical scores and numerous songs, often in collaboration with lyricist Arthur Freed.*

now, but you will know him by the end of the year and will be married to him around the first of next year."

That December, Page met Naval Lieutenant Herschel House. He proposed marriage the next day. The two eloped to Yuma, Arizona, in January 1937. They were married in a Catholic ceremony at her home in Manhattan Beach that March.

House's naval career took the two all over the world. They lived in Coronado (near San Diego) and the Philippines before World War II. After the war, they lived in Washington, D. C., where Page was prominent in society (she was once named the city's Beauty of the Week). Her portraits from that period are striking, but she's purposely wearing much less makeup than her days as a movie player. "That's why I thought Elizabeth Taylor would never make it in Washington,"* Page observed. "She wore too much eye makeup."

Two daughters, Sandra and Linda, were born in the 1940s. As a mother and wife, Page said she was the "happiest woman on earth." Her contacts from her movie days were limited to Marion Davies and actor Wallace Ford and his wife.

Page accepted an offer to play Mother Superior in a film in the early 1960s—"I had always wanted to play her," she said. The news was reported in Hedda Hopper's column. However, after two days, Anita caught the flu and had to bow out of the production.

In 1988, Page made headlines when she fainted in front of the Shrine Auditorium going into the Oscars. She was to appear in a production number featuring a representative from each of the 59 Oscar–winning Best Pictures. The doctors called her illness a combination of heat, exhaustion and excitement. Page said the problems started when her foot got caught under the car seat and she had to rip her shoe free, just as she was to be escorted into the ceremony.

When Admiral House died in 1991, Page returned to Los Angeles, where she enjoyed an active social life. There was an Anita Page Film Festival and other film revivals and conventions. An art deco statue of herself was in circulation.

Page made her first film in 60 years when she accepted a part in *Sunset After Dark* (1996) with friends Randal Malone and Margaret O'Brien.

It was well past midnight by the time the interview drew to a close. Page was as cheerful and animated as ever. She was the center of attention, and nothing could get her down that night. Not even her bitter feelings for Joan Crawford, to whom she finally offered some credit. "While it's true I was no pal of Joan's, I did think she was very good in *What Ever Happened to Baby Jane* [1962]. When she was going down those stairs and trying to get to that phone, I admit I was right there with her. Then, when she goes for the candy

**Elizabeth Taylor was married to U.S. Senator John W. Warner from 1976 to 1982.*

and she can't get it down fast enough, I figured there may have been times in her life when she was that hungry."

Giving it further thought, Page conceded she was pleased to be a part of a group of screen players — yes, that included Crawford — who worked together under the roar of the MGM lion at a time when the studio boasted it had "more stars than in heaven." For her, filmmaking was of a higher caliber then.

"I think most of the films made today are terrible," she said. "Those stars who run around with G-strings on are awful, and I don't admire them at all. I have no wish to see them."

What Anita Page wouldn't turn down, however, was a chance to see herself in one of her own films — her favorite is *Our Dancing Daughters.* "Oh, I love to do that! I'd rather see my old films than any of the new ones today." She added with a wink, "That's natural, don't you suppose?"

FILMOGRAPHY

1926: *A Kiss for Cinderella.* Famous Players-Lasky. Director: Herbert Brenon. Cast: Betty Bronson, Tom Moore, Esther Ralston, Henry Vibart, Dorothy Cumming, Ivan Simpson, Dorothy Walters, Flora Finch, Anita Page, Barbara Barondess. ***Love 'Em and Leave 'Em.*** Famous Players-Lasky. Director: Frank Tuttle. Cast: Evelyn Brent, Lawrence Gray, Louise Brooks, Osgood Perkins, Jack Egan, Marcia Harris, Edward Garvey, Vera Sisson, Joseph McClumn, Anita Page. **1928: *Telling the World.*** MGM. Director: Sam Wood. Cast: William Haines, Anita Page, Eileen Percy, Frank Currier, Polly Moran, Bert Roach, William V. Mong, Matthew Betz. ***Our Dancing Daughters.*** MGM. Director: Harry Beaumont. Cast: Joan Crawford, John Mack Brown, Nils Asther, Dorothy Sebastian, Anita Page, Kathlyn Williams, Edward Nugent, Dorothy Cumming, Huntly Gordon, Evelyn Hall, Sam De Grasse. ***While the City Sleeps.*** MGM. Director: Jack Conway. Cast: Lon Chaney, Anita Page, Carroll Nye, Wheeler Oakman, Mae Busch, Polly Moran, Lydia Yeamans Titus, William Orlamond, Richard Carle. **1929: *The Flying Fleet.*** MGM. Director: George Hill. Cast: Ramon Novarro, Ralph Graves, Anita Page, Edward Nugent, Carroll Nye, Dorothy Cumming, Roy D'Arcy, Sumner Getchell, Gardner James, Alfred Allen, The Three-Sea Hawks. ***The Broadway Melody.*** MGM. Director: Harry Beaumont. Cast: Anita Page, Bessie Love, Charles King, Jed Prouty, Mary Doran, Eddie Kane, J. Emmett Beck, Marshall Ruth, Drew Demarest. ***The Hollywood Revue of 1929.*** MGM. Director: Charles Reisner. Cast: Conrad Nagel, Jack Benny, John Gilbert, Norma Shearer, Joan Crawford, Bessie Love, Lionel Barrymore, Cliff Edwards, Stan Laurel, Oliver Hardy, Anita Page, Nils Asther, The Brox Sisters, Marion Davies, William Haines, Buster Keaton, Marie Dressler, Charles King, Polly Moran, Gus Edwards, Karl Dane, George K. Arthur, Ann Dvorak, Gwen Lee. ***Our Modern Maidens.*** MGM. Director: Jack Conway.

Cast: Joan Crawford, Rod La Rocque, Douglas Fairbanks, Jr., Anita Page, Edward Nugent, Josephine Dunn, Albert Gran. ***Speedway.*** MGM. Director: Harry Beaumont. Cast: William Haines, Anita Page, Ernest Torrence, Karl Dane, John Miljan, Eugenie Besserer, Polly Moran. ***Navy Blues.*** MGM. Director: Clarence Brown. Cast: William Haines, Anita Page, Karl Dane, J. C. Nugent, Edythe Chapman, Gertrude Sutton, Wade Boteler. **1930: *Free and Easy.*** MGM. Director: Edward Sedgwick. Cast: Buster Keaton, Anita Page, Trixie Friganza, Robert Montgomery, Fred Niblo, Edgar Dearing, Gwen Lee, Lionel Barrymore, William Haines, William Collier, Sr., Dorothy Sebastian, Karl Dane, Jackie Coogan, Cecil B. DeMille, Arthur Lange, Joe Farnham, Marion Shilling. ***Caught Short.*** MGM. Director: Charles Reisner. Cast: Marie Dressler, Polly Moran, Anita Page, Charles Morton, Thomas Conlin, Douglas Haig, Nanci Price, Greta Mann, Herbert Prior, T. Roy Barnes, Edward Dillon, Alice Moe, Gwen Lee, Lee Kohlmar, Greta Granstedt. ***Our Blushing Brides.*** MGM. Director: Harry Beaumont. Cast: Joan Crawford, Anita Page, Dorothy Sebastian, Robert Montgomery, Raymond Hackett, John Miljan, Hedda Hopper, Albert Conti, Edward Brophy, Robert E. O'Connor, Martha Sleeper, Mary Doran, Norma Drew, Wilda Mansfield, Gwen Lee, Claire Dodd.
The Little Accident. Universal. Director: William James Craft. Cast: Douglas Fairbanks, Jr., Anita Page, Sally Blane, ZaSu Pitts, Joan Marsh, Roscoe Karns, Slim Summerville, Henry Armetta, Myrtle Stedman, Nora Cecil, Bertha Mann, Gertrude Short, Dot Farley. ***War Nurse.*** MGM. Director: Edgar Selwyn. Cast: Robert Montgomery, Anita Page, June Walker, Robert Ames, ZaSu Pitts, Marie Prevost, Helen Jerome Eddy, Hedda Hopper, Edward Nugent, Martha Sleeper, Michael Vavitch. **1931: *Reducing.*** MGM. Director: Charles Reisner. Cast: Marie Dressler, Polly Moran, Anita Page, Sally Eilers, William Collier, Jr., William Bakewell. ***The Easiest Way.*** MGM. Director: Jack Conway. Cast: Constance Bennett, Robert Montgomery, Anita Page, Hedda Hopper, Clark Gable, Clara Blandick, J. Farrell MacDonald. ***Gentlemen's Fate.*** MGM. Director: Mervyn LeRoy. Cast: John Gilbert, Louis Wolheim, Leila Hyams, Anita Page, Marie Prevost, John Miljan, George Cooper, Ferike Boros, Ralph Ince, Frank Reicher, Paul Porcasi, Tenen Holtz. ***Sidewalks of New York.*** MGM. Director: Jules White, Zion Myers. Cast: Buster Keaton, Anita Page, Cliff Edwards, Frank Rowan, Norman Phillips, Jr., Frank LaRue, Oscar Apfel, Syd Saylor, Clark Marshall. ***Under Eighteen.*** Warner Brothers. Director: Archie Mayo. Cast: Marian Marsh, Regis Toomey, Warren William, J. Farrell MacDonald, Emma Dunn, Anita Page, Norman Foster, Joyce Compton, Judith Vosselli, Dorothy Appleby, Maude Eburne, Claire Dodd, Paul Porcasi, Mary Doran, Murray Kinnell, Walter McGrail. **1932: *Prosperity.*** MGM. Director: Sam Wood. Cast: Marie Dressler, Polly Moran, Anita Page, Norman Foster, Henry Armetta, John Miljan, Jacquie Lyn, Jerry Tucker, Charles Giblyn, Frank Darien, John Roche. ***Skyscraper Souls.*** MGM. Director: Edgar Selwyn. Cast: Warren William, Verree Teasdale, Maureen O'Sullivan, Anita Page, Gregory Ratoff,

Norman Foster, George Barbier, Jean Hersholt, Wallace Ford, Hedda Hopper. ***Are You Listening?*** MGM. Director: Harry Beaumont. Cast: William Haines, Madge Evans, Anita Page, Karen Morley, Neil Hamilton, Wallace Ford, Jean Hersholt, John Miljan, Joan Marsh. ***Night Court.*** MGM. Director: W. S. Van Dyke. Cast: Phillips Holmes, Walter Huston, Anita Page, Lewis Stone, John Miljan, Jean Hersholt, Tully Marshall, Mary Carlisle. **1933:** ***Soldiers of the Storm.*** Columbia. Director: D. Ross Lederman. Cast: Anita Page, Regis Toomey, Barbara Weeks, Robert Ellis, Wheeler Oakman, Barbara Barondess, George Cooper, Dewey Robinson, Henry Wadsworth. ***The Big Cage.*** Universal. Director: Kurt Neumann. Cast: Clyde Beatty, Anita Page, Andy Devine, Vince Barnett, Raymond Hatton, Mickey Rooney, Wallace Ford, Reginald Barlow, Edward Piel, Robert McWade. ***Jungle Bride.*** Monogram. Director: Harry O. Hoyt. Cast: Anita Page, Charles Starrett, Kenneth Thompson, Eddie Borden, Clarence Geldert, Gertrude Simpson, Jay Emmett, Albert Cross. ***I Have Lived.*** Chesterfield. Director: Richard Thorpe. Cast: Alan Dinehart, Anita Page, Allen Vincent, Gertrude Astor, Maude Truax, Matthew Betz, Eddie Boland, Dell Henderson, Florence Dudley, Gladys Blake, Harry Bradley, Edward Keane. **1936:** ***Hitch Hike to Heaven.*** Chesterfield. Director: Frank R. Strayer. Cast: Henrietta Crosman, Herbert Rawlinson, Russell Gleason, Polly Ann Young, Al Shean, Anita Page, Syd Saylor, Harry Harvey, Harry Holman, Ethel Sykes, Lela Bliss, Crauford Kent, John Dilson. **1996:** ***Sunset After Dark.*** Wildcat Entertainment. Director: Mark Gordon. Cast: Tony Maggio, Monique Parent, Randal Malone, Anita Page, Margaret O'Brien.

14

Marion Shilling

Film buffs and historians have asked for decades, what happened to this performer or that performer? What did they do after films and how did their lives turn out?

In the case of Marion Shilling, one might ask whatever happened to Cinderella, after "the end" and the "she-lived-happily-ever-afters" were written.

She dubbed herself a senior Cinderella and said her fairy tale never ended when the Hollywood cameras stopped rolling. The best chapters of her life were to be written after her eight-year career in Hollywood, she insisted. Her career paled in comparison to her happy life off the screen. In fact, she had been a positive and content person for as long as she could remember.

Unlike many fairy tales, there were no wicked stepmothers in Shilling's story. She was raised by loving parents who only wanted the best for their only daughter. She worked on the stage in her father's stock company as a teenager. The company took her to the West Coast in the late 1920s where she caught the attention of MGM executives who negotiated a motion picture contract for her.

In Hollywood, at the birth of sound, a new career was born. For the first three years, she worked at first-rate studios and her career was progressing. Then, it lost its steam following the debilitating illness of her agent.

Virtually on her own, and without the careful planning and guidance, she slipped into low-budget quickies and Westerns. These were hardly ideal working conditions, but they did establish her a place in movie history—Western film fans considered her to be among the finest Western heroines.

With a clear understanding of what she wanted from life, Shilling put her career behind her in 1937 to marry, as she called him, her Prince Charming. She didn't exaggerate when she said they lived happily ever after.

The retired movie actress left Hollywood and, as the years passed, lost all contact with the film colony and her fans. For several years in the 1970s, film

Marion Shilling in the early 1930s. (Courtesy of Marion Shilling.)

historian Roi Uselton searched unsuccessfully for Shilling in connection with his article "The Wampas Baby Stars" which was published in *Films in Review*. With persistence, he located her living quietly in the San Francisco area.

This rediscovery led to several appearances at film festivals during the 1980s, fan mail and a new legion of fans, who, thanks to video, enjoyed her work. She called Uselton her Christopher Columbus, the hero who "rescued me from oblivion. It's like he waved a magic wand over my life. I'm no longer just mama and grandma, but a former movie actress."

Marion Shilling and I met in San Francisco in 1993 and conducted our interview during much correspondence and conversation. A very modest individual, she would never bring up the past (she was too content in the present, much involved in the lives of her children and grandchildren) unless questioned and then she would offer a thoughtful and straightforward response.

I was a guest in her home over a weekend in December 1994. That Saturday, it happened to be her birthday and I accompanied her and her son on their weekly two-hour walk. We returned home, our exercise completed, and she wondered what we would do next. Why not watch a Marion Shilling movie on video, I suggested.

She shuddered at the thought. "Oh, please, Michael, let's not ruin a good day." I didn't press the matter. We simply talked about the film and moved on.

It pained her to view those early films; she felt, with the experiences of a lifetime, the results would have been different if she were able to return to those days.

"I would relish the chance to return to the studios and try it all once more, in an endeavor to give a more polished performance. How I wish I could create a time warp and return as my present self to enlighten and guide that unripe little girl I was in the 1930s."

Her attitude slowly improved over the next few years. After convincing her to allow me to send her copies of *Lord Byron of Broadway* and *Shadow of the Law*, I received a letter in which she said I had bestowed upon her the gift of self-esteem.

"I had felt such a disgust for that wishy-washy girl on the screen," she wrote. "But in viewing *Lord Byron* I realized that I had been assigned that role many times. A shallow person who moons over a man. The man — understandably — lured away from her by a more sexy gal, but in the end he finally returns to Miss Milquetoast ... I tried to do my best. I've completely forgiven myself."

Although she became the actress of the family, Marion (born Marion Schilling Dec. 3, 1910, in Denver, Colorado) was not the first in the family bitten by the acting bug. It was her father Edward, who, since childhood, had been enticed by the theater.

While he was waiting for his theatrical goals to materialize, Mr. Schilling worked in a Denver bank, first as a teller, then as an officer in charge of the new business department. Ironically, he didn't have to go after his dream; It came to him.

One day, Margaret Fealey, the owner of a Denver acting school and mother of early film actress and stage performer Maude Fealey, came into the bank. She told Mr. Schilling she was bringing Clyde Fitch's *Her Own Way* to the Denver stage and that she had cast every role except a ten-year-old girl. Mr. Schilling couldn't wait to introduce Marion to Fealey, who thought her perfect for the part. The play marked Marion's theatrical debut.

Then in 1922, a customer entered the bank, met Mr. Schilling and introduced himself as O. D. Woodward, a leading stock company producer. In the course of the conversation, Woodward disclosed his plans to start a new company in St. Louis, Missouri. Sensing Mr. Schilling's enthusiasm for the theater, Woodward offered to make him part of his organization.

Leaving Denver behind, Schilling moved his wife Kathryne and 11-year-old Marion to Missouri and set out to throw some light on his blind ambitions. First, they went to New York where the two businessmen assembled a company of actors and lined up a group of new plays. The Schillings settled in St. Louis and the company opened there in September 1922. Successful for six years, the company eventually expanded to Kansas City and Cincinnati.

Having a production company in the family was the launching pad Marion needed for her career. She appeared in the stock company's productions of *Miss Lulu Bett, Rebecca of Sunnybrook Farm, Daddy Long Legs* and *Penrod.*

In high school, Marion's studies took precedence over her theater work, as she had plans for college and a journalism career.

But in January 1928, several months after she graduated from Central High School, her plans took the theatrical route, leaving her collegiate ambitions ditched. The company secured the West Coast rights to the play and the original production of *Dracula,* which had done record business in New York with Bela Lugosi in the title role.

The family left immediately for California, stopping briefly in Denver to see old friends and family. *Dracula* opened mid-summer at the Biltmore Theater in Los Angeles.

In addition to the small role Shilling had in the production, she was required to scream backstage at each performance. "I developed such a bloodcurdling scream that later on in the movies, I was frequently called upon to dub for other actresses," said Shilling. "I screamed for Constance Bennett and for Pola Negri, a high moment for me. During her heyday, Pola was my idol, my great screen crush."

Lugosi was beginning his long legacy in horror with *Dracula.** The cast

**Hungarian-born Lugosi (1882–1956) first appeared on the stage in 1901 and in films in 1915. He immigrated to the United States in 1921, where he continued working on the stage and screen. His role in* Dracula, *which he filmed in 1931 for director Tod Browning, was the signature part of his long career.*

found him easy to work with. "He was a warm, kind, guileless and straightforward person, not remotely weird and eerie like his stage and screen persona," Shilling recalled.

Scattered throughout audiences at the Biltmore for the run of the play were motion picture actors and executives. One was the "It" girl, Clara Bow. "There was a much-publicized romance between her and Lugosi," said Marion. "She would sometimes come over to the theater directly from her beach house clad in a fur coat over her bathing suit."

Shilling's association with *Dracula* afforded her the opportunity of meeting many associated with the movie industry, and in June 1928 she met MGM casting director John Lancaster. He showed an immediate interest in the 17-year-old actress and kept in touch with her throughout the play's run. After *Dracula* closed, after playing for ten weeks in Los Angeles and San Francisco, he offered her an MGM screen test.

In late May 1929, Shilling reported to the MGM studios to test for a role in the upcoming production of *Wise Girls* (1929), based on the hit play, *Kempy*. She competed with six other young hopefuls, one of whom was actress Doris Hill. "I was rushed to the hairdresser with a script in my hand. While three girls worked on my hair, I studied the part and learned my lines."

That day, Shilling tested until seven P.M. Then, two days later, MGM called her back and signed her to a long-term contract.* The next day, the cast went into rehearsal and, a week later, filming began. The picture was completed in about ten days.

Shilling credited the film's director, E. Mason Hopper, with putting her at ease on the set of her first film. "I can still remember vividly some of his early suggestions. 'Keep your head above the tide.' 'Be on your toes.' 'Hold your head high.' 'Act like the queen of the studio.' Those were wonderful words to a new, green girl, numbed by all that was suddenly happening to her."

MGM was the studio that boasted it had more stars than there were in Heaven. During her first days at the studio, she remembered Joan Crawford going out of her way to make her feel welcome. "Every morning in the hairdressing room, she put the curling iron to her hair, while the professional was doing mine. She would chatter away with me on completely equal terms."

Lord Byron of Broadway (1930), her next picture, was expected to be a blockbuster musical for MGM, but it turned out to be a disappointment for the studio and a blow to Shilling. In spite of its great musical numbers, the film flopped for several reasons: the public's unfamiliarity with leads Charles Kaley and Ethelind Terry (imported from New York for their Hollywood debuts), the thin story line and the ongoing struggle with dialogue and music in films.

**In* Wise Girls, *Marion was billed as Schilling, her real surname. However, with the rise of Hitler in the early 1930s, studio brass thought an English-sounding name, rather than a German-sounding one, was appropriate. Therefore, the "c" was removed and she became Marion Shilling.*

Midway through the filming of the picture, director William Nigh was replaced by Harry Beaumont. Then the stock market crash in October 1929 blew an even darker cloud over the production. Producer, Harry Rapf,* returning from New York where he had lost a fortune, viewed the rough cut of the original picture. Ordinarily, he was a "gloomy, unsmiling person," said Shilling, but the disappointing result of his latest film plunged him deeper into despair.

Rapf initiated a series of austerity measures to save money. With the cutbacks and box office flop of *Lord Byron*, Shilling was released from her contract in the fall of 1930.†

Shilling's brush with unemployment didn't last long. In the winter of 1931, producer Phil Goldstone, to whom she'd been introduced by John Lancaster, signed her to a personal contract at a much higher salary than she was earning at MGM.

Goldstone secured her a supporting role as a factory worker in *The Swellhead* (1930) with James Gleason, Johnny Walker and Natalie Kingston. Gleason, said Shilling, was a "doll," but it was the picture's director James Flood for whom she held the fondest memories. Late one night, Flood decided he didn't like the way a certain scene was written. Gleason, an accomplished playwright, quickly composed a page of dialogue, most of which Shilling was to deliver. "I was a fast study, memorized the scene in a few minutes and we did the scene in one take. Mr. Flood put his arms around me and said, 'You g.d. little trouper.'"

After *The Swellhead,* Shilling spent many weeks in the winter of 1930 helping test actors with Goldstone for a film based on Tolstoy's *Resurrection*. When a suitable leading man couldn't be found, the project was shelved and Marion was again looking for work.

That spring (1930), Lancaster introduced her to Paramount executives, who tested, then signed her for the lead opposite William Powell in *Shadow of the Law* (1930). The studio also negotiated a long-term contract.

In the picture, Powell escaped from prison and set out to clear his name. In the meantime, he became the manager of a North Carolina mill and fell in love with the owner's daughter (Shilling). The story ended on a high note, but not before he was blackmailed by Natalie Moorhead, the only person who could clear his name so he could marry.

Since Powell had portrayed villains during the silent era, Shilling expected he would be a "self-satisfied, smug, smart-alecky sort of person." Much to her surprise, he was the opposite. "Self-effacing, deferential, exceedingly thoughtful of other people, he was one of the kindest human beings I have ever met," she said of her leading man. "He sensed that I was in awe of him so, from the start, he did what he could to put me at ease."

**Harry Rapf (1882–1949), a film producer since 1915, is credited with discovering Rin Tin Tin — he produced the dog's popular movies — and Joan Crawford, whom he brought to MGM's attention in the mid–1920s.*

†Charles Kaley and Ethelind Terry returned to the New York stage after Lord Byron.

After her appearance in *Shadow of the Law*, Shilling was not assigned to, nor even tested, for another film at Paramount. She reasoned, "I suppose there were so many young girls under contract at Paramount at that time that there weren't enough parts to go around."

Still, the studio profited from Shilling's services, as she was loaned to other studios. First, she appeared at Fox with Irene Rich and H. B. Warner in *On Your Back* (1930). Making the film enlightened her to the workings of studio politics. Shilling's character, who was in love with Rich's son, was a stronger and more sympathetic part than Rich's so "from the very first day I sensed that the odds were against me. I breathed an unfriendly atmosphere."

Shilling had a role of substance, some powerful scenes and juicy dialogue. She was so good, in fact, that her work, when studied in a preview showing, caught the attention of Irene Rich, who realized that Shilling dominated much of the film. After the first showing, changes were ordered and made. Key scenes were re-shot and in the final version, the entire film was manipulated to favor Rich.*

"For instance," said Shilling, "the climactic scene of the film was one in which I, Irene's victim, at last had a chance to tell her off. My speech, to which I gave all the power I was capable of, covered an entire page of script. In the final version, how was the scene presented? Throughout the speech I was shown with my back to camera in a long shot. At frequent intervals, during my outpouring, the camera cut from my back to a huge idealized closeup of Irene."

While Rich was aloof, H. B. Warner was "charming," full of anecdotes about the stage and screen, as well as advice, particularly about the "danger threatened by men." "Just below the skin," Warner told her, "we're all animals."

In December 1930, while filming *Beyond Victory* (1931), Shilling celebrated her 20th birthday. In the World War I anti-war drama, she played the sweetheart of Lew Cody. The director surprised her with a cake and the cast and crew gathered around for the celebration that evening.

It was on the set of *Young Donovan's Kid* (1931) that Shilling met director Fred Niblo† who would later become a close friend. "One of the reasons for his success as a director, certainly, was that he had been an actor himself," Shilling said of Niblo. "He could empathize, see and feel a scene from an actor's viewpoint. He never talked down to us. He was a lovely human being."

In the film, Shilling and young Jackie Cooper influenced the reformation of a violent gunman (Richard Dix). Riding high in the saddle, Dix, fresh from his success in *Cimarron* (1931), had "great star" written all over him, said

**Irene Rich (1891–1988) had been a leading lady in silent films — her career began in 1918 — usually in refined, society roles. By the coming of sound, Rich was being cast in more maternal roles. She retired from the screen in 1932, but returned later in the decade in character roles.*

*†Fred Niblo (1874–1948) gained stature a decade before by directing lavish costume dramas starring Rudolph Valentino [*Blood and Sand *(1922)] and Douglas Fairbanks [*The Mark of Zorro *(1920)] and [*The Three Musketeers *(1921)]. It was his work on* Ben Hur *(1926) that Niblo reached his directorial peak.*

William Powell and Marion Shilling in *Shadow of the Law* (1930). (Courtesy of Marion Shilling.)

Shilling. "What a contrast to such unassuming souls as Fred Niblo, William Powell and Lew Cody. Dix made his entrance to the set each morning followed by a parade of retainers. Secretary, stand-in, valet, and even two musicians, who put him in the proper mood."

Boris Karloff, cast as a villain who crept from a darkened alley to mug the virtuous Shilling, gained success that year as the monster in *Frankenstein* (1931). She had the opportunity to talk with Karloff at length between scenes and found a "perfectly mannered, English gentleman" beneath his heavy makeup and ragged attire.

During the spring of 1931, Shilling worked in *The Common Law* (1931), another RKO-Pathé film, with Constance Bennett, Joel McCrea and Lew Cody. The plot revolved around the makeups and breakups of Bennett and her two suitors, McCrea and Cody. While Shilling admired Bennett's grace, sophistication and self-assurance, Bennett was cool and unapproachable to everyone on the set, except McCrea, whose complete attention she jealously monopolized. "She had a mad crush on Joel McCrea. The rest of us were just pieces of furniture to her. The minute the director yelled cut, Connie would yank Joel to her portable dressing room, bang the door and not reappear until they were again called to the set."

H. B. Warner, Marion Shilling and Irene Rich in *On Your Back* (1930). (Courtesy of Marion Shilling.)

RKO-Pathé in 1931 launched a series of Westerns starring Tom Keene, formerly George Duryea. In the first, *Sundown Trail* (1931), Shilling was cast as a city girl who inherits a ranch. It was the first of her many Western films.

The cast spent ten days in July 1931 filming in and around Mojave Desert's Victorville. When the cameras weren't rolling, Shilling found herself being constantly teased by Keene, Nick Stuart and Cliff Edwards. Their risqué remarks and antics kept her giggling and blushing. "A bit later in my life when I became more hip, I thought of some great comebacks, but as with so many marvelous afterthoughts, it was too late, alas, too late."

To get them through the hot desert days, the cast had to depend on the flamboyant director Robert F. Hill* whom they dubbed "Bring 'Em Back Alive." "Immaculately groomed, he wore riding pants and pith helmet, and everything he said was with emphasis," said Shilling. "His booming voice and the way he dashed about left no doubt to onlookers as to who was directing the picture."

Although she had ridden burros as a small child in the Colorado Rockies, it

**Director Robert F. Hill's career, which included acting and screenwriting, spanned from 1916 to 1941. Hill (1886–1966) directed numerous serials, including Elmo Lincoln's* The Adventures of Tarzan *(1921).*

Joel McCrea, Constance Bennett and Marion Shilling in *The Common Law* (1931). (Courtesy of Marion Shilling.)

was in *Sundown Trail* that she first learned to ride horseback. She was "nervous, very nervous, at first," but with experience, she became a good rider, a skill she'd need later in her long string of Westerns.

Shilling was directed by Roscoe "Fatty" Arbuckle* in the six *Gay Girls Comedies* (1931). "That sweet, dear Roscoe Arbuckle. He was one of the finest human beings I have ever known. And what a clever director. So relaxed and altogether considerate of everyone."

1931 was a good year for Shilling's career and her future looked promising. Under the careful guidance of John Lancaster, who was now her agent, she had secured some quality film roles. Shilling worked steadily for Pathé, had the promise of several plum roles and was told of the possibility of being teamed with Joel McCrea (it never happened). Then, she received the high honor of being named a 1931 Wampas Baby Star.†

**Arbuckle was tried three times for the 1921 death of Virginia Rappe. The first two ended in a hung jury, and he was acquitted in the third. The scandal ruined his career, but he later directed films as William B. Goodrich, the pseudonym he used for the* Gay Girl Comedies. *He died in 1933 at age 46.*

†Other actresses named that year were Frances Dee, Sidney Fox, Joan Marsh, Rochelle Hudson, Frances Dade, Judith Wood, Constance Cummings, Joan Blondell, Anita Louise, Marian Marsh, Barbara Weeks and Karen Morley.

For a while, it looked as if there was only one way to go: up. In late 1931, however, John Lancaster suffered a devastating heart attack from which he never recovered. His illness left him virtually inactive and, "there was no one to look after my interests," said Shilling.

Lancaster had been the push behind Shilling's career. "He was a dynamic, influential go-getter of an agent." Fierce loyalty to the man who had discovered her three years earlier prevented her from leaving his office.

There were other agents but, "it never occurred to me to desert him," she said. After Lancaster's death, she signed with agents Lichtig and Englander, but "they weren't in Mr. Lancaster's class."

It was also during Lancaster's illness that RKO took over Pathé, leaving any plans to promote Shilling's career by the wayside. After a year at Pathé, her career took the route of independent productions.

In late 1931, Shilling was signed by Monogram to appear with Rex Bell in *Forgotten Women* (1932), a Hollywood tale tracing the successes and heartaches of several actresses trying to succeed in the movies. Bell was seriously involved with Clara Bow during the filming of the picture and would tie the knot in December 1931. "It was no wonder that Clara Bow was so wild about him," said Shilling. "He was a lovable guy. So easy and pleasant to work with. Once during the filming of *Forgotten Women*, Bell happened to overhear the producer say some favorable things about me. On his way home, Rex drove considerably out of his way to stop by our house and pass on the good words to my folks and me."

Shop Angel (1932), a quickie made in January 1932 for Premier, was an easily forgettable film, but for Shilling it was more. On the set of the picture, she met her future husband Edward Cook. It happened thanks to Cupid's emissaries Morris Schlank (the producer) and his wife Bess, a dress designer.

The Cooks, Edward and his parents, were spending their winter in Southern California. Bess Schlank, who made many of Mrs. Cook's clothes, invited them to the set of *Shop Angel* to introduce Marion and Edward. They met and hit it off, but it was months later, after a bout with the flu and following the filming of *The County Fair* (1932), that Shilling was available for a date.

In the meantime, Edward sent flowers and telephoned. He was so entranced by the young actress that he proposed to her while dancing one evening. Being devoted to her parents and still fond of California, she declined. He courted her persistently, however, and in 1937, once her film career was over, she accepted.

A Man's Land, in which Shilling inherited a ranch, was the first of two films she made with cowboy Hoot Gibson. Working with Hoot was pleasant and the two were "good friends." Hoot started in films as a stunt man, but once a star, he left dangerous work to doubles. Said Shilling, "During our filming, he'd be photographed mounting a horse and later getting off. Stunt men doubled for him in between. It was vital that the star not be injured and thus hold up production."

Shilling finished 1932 with two forgettable quickies: *A Parisian Romance* and *Heart Punch*. Shilling had scenes in the latter with Mae Busch, whose career stretched back to the early 1910s. "She was a real trooper," said Shilling. "Toughened and seasoned with life."

Work in films in 1933 was skimpy, primarily because Shilling was making commercials—"more commercials than I could possible count," she said. Frequently, she appeared in Technicolor ads with Cullen Landis and Jack Mulhall. She also did a two-reeler advertising Norge refrigerators with Russell Gleason.

Then, there was the Lucky Strike commercial she made with Genevieve Tobin in 1933. The director called for them to ride up to a palatial mansion in Holmby Hills, dismount and light cigarettes. Shilling handled the skittish horses with ease; however, Tobin, who had no background in Westerns, was "pale with terror," said Shilling. "She was too good a trouper and went on. Since neither of us smoked, I'm certain we didn't make many converts to Luckies."

Shilling was busy in Westerns during most of 1934. *The Westerner*, which she made that year with Tim McCoy, was not released until 1936. "Tim McCoy was an urbane intellectual, quite unlike his cowboy image. He was very sweet and we dated for a awhile, but Tim was a bit of a fast worker for me."

After making a Western with Reb Russell, Shilling signed to do the first of her two serials: *The Red Rider* (1934) with Buck Jones. Not long after the contracts were signed, Fred Niblo offered her the role of Helena in Max Reinhardt's stage production of *A Midsummer Night's Dream*. She had no choice but to decline—for the present. She concentrated on the serial.

The Red Rider was shot in about seven weeks at Universal and on location in the studio's wooded hills north of Hollywood. Shilling's recollections of making the serial could fill many pages. "All through the movie, there was a bit part played by an Indian, a stolid old fellow who was usually seen sitting in a quiet corner by himself. One day Buck said, 'Marion, there's someone I want you to meet.' So Buck took me over to the old Indian in the corner. 'Marion,' Buck said, 'may I present Jim Thorpe.'* My shocked surprise and delight must have been well apparent as a wide smile broke out on Jim's face."

Buck Jones was a "star presence" on the set, said Shilling, but he was "kind and helpful to everyone. A great wit and a marvelous sense of humor. After all these years, Buck still has me chuckling."

While Shilling was filming *The Red Rider*, Niblo kept in touch and when the picture wrapped, he signed her for *A Midsummer Night's Dream*. The company, with its stars, Olivia de Havilland† and Mickey Rooney, went East and toured in late November 1934 and the winter of 1935.

**Jim Thorpe (1888–1953), an Indian athlete, won the pentathlon and decathlon in the 1912 Olympics. He entered films in 1931, playing chiefs and renegades in scores of B Westerns.*

†Olivia de Havilland (b. 1916), while still in high school, appeared in a stage production of "A Midsummer Night's Dream." After "Dream," Warner Brothers signed her to a seven-year contract. She was later loaned to Selznick to portray Melanie in Gone with the Wind *(1939). De Havilland won two Best Actress Academy Awards for* To Each His Own *(1946) and* The Heiress *(1949).*

The company opened Thanksgiving night in Chicago to a sold-out Auditorium Theater. Then on to Milwaukee—another story. "A big barn of a theater, bitter weather and lukewarm audiences," said Shilling. The company went to St. Louis, where Marion "had a grand time" seeing old friends and former school teachers.

The tour was a highlight in Shilling's career. She was again on the stage and working with de Havilland and Rooney, both professionals. "Olivia was warm, vivacious, intelligent, bursting with talent. We had adjoining dressing rooms and I had the privilege of becoming close friends with both Olivia and her mother."

Lilian Fontaine (the mother of Olivia and actress Joan Fontaine) was a strong presence in Olivia's life and kept a watchful eye on the developing relationship between her daughter and the actor Leif Erickson, said Shilling. "I'm certain that Mrs. Fontaine accompanied Olivia to prevent her from doing something foolish. Her mom strongly implied to me that she feared Olivia might elope with Leif. I'll always remember her very words. 'Marion, a woman never fully recovers from the pain of a divorce.'"

Mickey Rooney, whom Shilling knew before as Mickey McGuire, was the life of the *Dream* company, the hit of the show. "Despite colds and fatigue, Mickey never failed to bolster our spirit," she said. "All of us—and the critics—loved him. So friendly. Nearly every evening he'd come into my dressing room and hold the hair dryer over my curls while I applied my makeup."

The play's producer, Max Reinhardt, spoke no English, but conveyed all of his suggestions and direction through his longtime assistant Felix Weissberger. Said Shilling, "Reinhardt, one of the theater's greatest geniuses, was a slightly built, sweet, modest man."

According to Marion, *Dream* was scheduled to open at New York's Center Theater in January 1935, but because *The Great Waltz* was such a success, those in charge were reluctant to cut the run. An expensive production such as *Dream* took an entire train to transport the cast, crew and scenery; its producers could not afford to wait on the road until a suitable theater was available in New York. "We were awakened from our 'dream' and returned to California," Shilling recalled.

In Hollywood, big plans lay in store for the play. Warner Brothers was planning to bring *Dream* to the screen. Rooney and de Havilland were retained in their roles; however Jean Muir, under contract to Warner Brothers, was cast in Shilling's role, Helena.

Shilling signed to do *The Keeper of the Bees* (1935) with Neil Hamilton and Betty Furness. Christy Cabanne directed. The film was a pleasant experience. Cabanne, she said, was easy to work with, and she especially got along well with Betty Furness, who always knitted between scenes, a hobby she learned from Joan Crawford.

Shilling continued working steadily in Westerns and with some of the screen's most durable cowboys: Reb Russell, Buck Jones, Guinn "Big Boy" Williams and Tom Tyler. In *Rio Rattler* (1935), Tyler was pleasant enough—"a handsome, macho fellow with a magnificent build"—but he carried on little conversation with his co-star off the set. His attentions focused instead on his current flame, Marlene Dietrich. "She was enamored of him at the time and kept him busy after hours. He was quiet to me, probably tired from his evenings with Marlene."

Working with cowboy Fred Scott in *Romance Rides the Range (1936) was* another good, rich experience for Shilling. "Fred was an unusually high-grade, well-educated and talented man," she said. "He and his wife Mary were about to be married and the entire set glowed with their happiness."

The serial *The Clutching Hand* (1936) boasted a cast of actors whose careers extended back to the beginnings of motion pictures: Jack Mulhall, William Farnum, Rex Lease, Mae Busch, Bryant Washburn and Robert Frazer. Shilling was in awe. "I had been an ardent fan of silent pictures. I had a grand time getting my old favorites to reminisce. It didn't take much encouragement."

Ralph Forbes, with whom Shilling appeared in *I'll Name the Murderer* (1936), was another long-established actor who relished talking of the old days. "He was polished, gracious and exceedingly affable. "He was well aware of his charm and, like Richard Dix, luxuriated for lengthy periods while his valet brushed him off."

I'll Name the Murderer was Shilling's final picture. She hadn't planned it that way, but, over the past four years, her ambitions had been changing. "The nesting urge had become pretty strong in me and I thought it was time to yield to Edward's entreaties," she said.

Following her last film, she made some Technicolor commercials and enrolled in a creative writing class; however, she was comfortable with the idea that, after she married, her career would be over. Her future husband saw all her films, but "did not encourage me in my career," she said.

On December 4, 1937, six days short of her 27th birthday, Shilling became Mrs. Edward Cook. It was a small ceremony—only their parents and Bess Schlank, who introduced the two, and the judge were present.

After the marriage, in the spring of 1938, the Cooks went East, then returned to California the following winter for the birth of their son, Edward ("Ned"), in February 1939. That April they returned to Pennsylvania and lived there until after World War II, when they returned to and settled in California. A daughter, Frances, was born in March 1941. ("Fran" lost her battle with cancer in 1995.)

In California, while her husband fulfilled a lifelong ambition of doing graduate work in physics, Shilling devoted herself to being a mother and wife and had little thought of her bygone career. She was involved in various fund raisers, the PTA, the League of Women Voters and Recording for the Blind.

Long ago, Shilling's husband called her "the frustrated college student" because of her love for reading and studying. She became deeply involved in metaphysics, finding the meaning of life—"as though it were possible." Her bookshelves held a collection of books on the great mystics, saints and philosophers.

Shilling felt her role in *Wise Girls* (1929) was her finest performance; however, no director (her favorites were Fred Niblo, Edward H. Griffith and Richard Thorpe) was able to "assist me in realizing my full potential, the best I was able to be at that period in my life," she said.

Her favorite of all the screen actors she appeared with was Lew Cody. "He couldn't have been more kind and helpful."

About her Westerns, she said, "They were fun to make, an utter joy. Camaraderie and much kidding, but we had to keep on our toes and do a scene right the first time so Westerns were excellent training. The cowboys without exception were 'regular' fellows. I can still smell the crisp air of those early mornings, and galloping over the wildflower-covered hills was a thrill indeed."

Happy with her career, yes, but Shilling felt the course of action was a bit out of sequence. "I wish I could have had the benefit of all that training in Westerns and low-budget films—that superb experience, and then gone to the big studios, with their better opportunities," she said.

She said she would appreciate the chance to re-do it all. "One more opportunity to do a better job, with the advantage of the experience I've gathered, the seasoning, the higher sense of self I've been able to gain. To know how to avoid all of those stupid mistakes I've made, all in all to give a more polished performance of Marion."

She pondered the idea, then quickly added a condition. She would only opt to live it all again, if the ending of her "fairy tale" remained the same.

"My real-life story has been more exciting and romantic than any movie or stage role I ever played." That in contrast, she said, to "many of the prominent actresses whom I may have envied at the time who are finding comfort these days only in their scrapbooks."

Filmography

1929: *Wise Girls.* MGM. Director: E. Mason Hopper. Cast: Elliott Nugent, Norma Lee, Roland Young, J. C. Nugent, Clara Blandick, Marion Schilling [Shilling], Leora Spellman, James Donlan. **1930: *Lord Byron of Broadway.*** MGM. Directors: William Nigh and Harry Beaumont. Cast: Ethelind Terry, Charles Kaley, Marion Shilling, Cliff Edwards, Gwen Lee, Benny Rubin, Drew Demarest, John Byron, Rita Flynn, Gino Corrado. ***Shadow of the Law.*** Paramount. Director: Louis Gasnier. Cast: William Powell, Marion Shilling, Natalie Moorhead, Regis Toomey, Paul Hurst, Richard Tucker. ***Free and Easy.*** MGM. Director: Edward Sedgwick. Cast: Buster Keaton, Anita Page, Trixie Friganza, Robert Montgomery, Fred Niblo, Edgar Dearing, Gwen Lee, Lionel Barrymore, William Haines, William Collier, Sr., Dorothy Sebastian, Karl Dane, Jackie

Coogan, Cecil B. DeMille, Arthur Lange, Marion Shilling. ***The Swellhead.*** Tiffany. Director: James Flood. Cast: James Gleason, Johnny Walker, Marion Shilling, Natalie Kingston, Paul Hurst, Freeman Wood, Lillian Elliott. ***On Your Back.*** Fox. Director: Guthrie McClintic. Cast: Irene Rich, H. B. Warner, Raymond Hackett, Marion Shilling, Ilka Chase, Charlotte Henry, Wheeler Oakman, Arthur Hoyt. **1931:** ***Beyond Victory.*** RKO-Pathé. Director: John Robertson. Cast: Bill Boyd, ZaSu Pitts, Marion Shilling, Lew Cody, James Gleason, Theodore Von Eltz, Mary Carr, Russell Gleason, Fred Scott, Frank Reicher. ***Young Donovan's Kid.*** RKO-Radio. Director: Fred Niblo. Cast: Richard Dix, Marion Shilling, Jackie Cooper, Frank Sheridan, Boris Karloff, Fred Kelsey, Richard Alexander, Wilfred Lucas. ***The Common Law.*** RKO-Pathé. Director: Paul Stein. Cast: Constance Bennett, Joel McCrea, Lew Cody, Marion Shilling, Robert Williams, Hedda Hopper, Yola D'Avril, Walter Walker. ***Sundown Trail.*** RKO-Pathé. Director: Robert F. Hill. Cast: Tom Keene, Marion Shilling, Nick Stuart, Hooper Atchley, Stanley Blystone, Louise Beavers. **1932:** ***The County Fair.*** Monogram. Director: Louis King. Cast: Hobart Bosworth, Marion Shilling, Ralph Ince, William Collier, Jr., Otto Hoffman, Snowflake, Kit Guard. ***Forgotten Women.*** Monogram. Director: Richard Thorpe. Cast: Marion Shilling, Rex Bell, Beryl Mercer, Virginia Lee Corbin, Carmelita Geraghty, Edna Murphy, Edward Earle. ***Shop Angel.*** Premier. Director: E. Mason Hopper. Cast: Marion Shilling, Holmes Herbert, Anthony Bushell, Walter Byron, Creighton Hale, Dorothy Christy. ***A Man's Land.*** First Allied. Director: Phil Rosen. Cast: Hoot Gibson, Marion Shilling, Ethel Wales, Skeeter Bill Robbins, Robert Ellis, Charles King, Hal Burney. ***A Parisian Romance.*** Allied. Director: Chester M. Franklin. Cast: Lew Cody, Marion Shilling, Gilbert Roland, Joyce Compton, Yola D'Avril, Nicholas Soussanin, George Lewis, Helen Jerome Eddy, Bryant Washburn, Luis Alberni. ***Heart Punch.*** Mayfair. Director: B. Reeves Eason. Cast: Lloyd Hughes, Marion Shilling, George Lewis, Wheeler Oakman, Mae Busch, Walter Miller. **1934:** ***Curtain at Eight.*** Majestic. Director: E. Mason Hopper. Cast: Dorothy Mackaill, C. Aubrey Smith, Paul Cavanagh, Sam Hardy, Marion Shilling, Russell Hopton, Natalie Moorhead, Hale Hamilton, Ruthelma Stevens, Jack Mulhall. ***The Westerner.*** Columbia. Director: David Selman. Cast: Tim McCoy, Marion Shilling, Joseph Sauers [Sawyer], Hooper Atchley, John Dilson, Wade Boteler. ***Inside Information.*** Stage & Screen. Director: Robert Hill. Cast: Rex Lease, Marion Shilling, Tarzan (dog), Philo McCullough, Charles King, Victor Potel, Henry Hall. ***The Red Rider.*** Universal (serial). Director: Louis Friedlander [Lew Landers]. Cast: Buck Jones, Marion Shilling, Walter Miller, Grant Withers. ***Thunder Over Texas.*** Beacon. Director: John Warner [Edgar G. Ulmer]. Cast: Guinn "Big Boy" Williams, Marion Shilling, Helen Westcott, Philo McCullough, Claude Payton. ***Fighting to Live.*** Principal. Director: Eddie Cline. Cast: Reb Russell, Marion Shilling, Gaylord [Steve] Pendleton, Eddie Phillips. **1935:** ***Blazing Guns.*** Marcy. Director: Ray Heinz. Cast: Reb Russell, Marion Shilling,

Joseph Girard, Lafe McKee. ***Stone of Silver Creek.*** Universal. Director: Nick Grinde. Cast: Buck Jones, Noel Francis, Niles Welch, Marion Shilling, Murdock MacQuarrie, Grady Sutton, Peggy Campbell, Rodney Hildebrand, Harry Semels. ***A Shot in the Dark.*** Chesterfield. Director: Charles Lamont. Cast: Charles Starrett, Robert Warwick, Edward Van Sloan, Marion Shilling, Doris Lloyd, Helen Jerome Eddy, James Bush, John Davidson. ***The Keeper of the Bees.*** Monogram. Director: Christy Cabanne. Cast: Neil Hamilton, Betty Furness, Emma Dunn, Edith Fellows, Hobart Bosworth, Helen Jerome Eddy, Marion Shilling, Barbara Bedford, Lafe McKee. ***Gun Play.*** Beacon Productions. Director: Albert Herman. Cast: Guinn "Big Boy" Williams, Marion Shilling, Frank Yaconelli, Wally Wales, Charles French, Tom London. ***Society Fever.*** Invincible. Director: Frank Strayer. Cast: Lois Wilson, Lloyd Hughes, Hedda Hopper, Guinn Williams, Grant Withers, Marion Shilling, George Irving. Sheila Terry, Lois January. ***Captured in Chinatown.*** Consolidated Pictures Corp. Director: Elmer Clifton. Cast: Marion Shilling, Charles Delaney, Tarzan (dog), Philo McCullough, Paul Ellis, Robert Walker, Bobby Nelson, John Elliott. ***Rio Rattler.*** Steiner. Director: Franklyn Shamray. Cast: Tom Tyler, Marion Shilling, Eddie Gribbon, Tom London, Slim Whitaker, Lafe McKee. **1936:** ***Romance Rides the Range.*** Spectrum. Director: Harry Fraser. Cast: Fred Scott, Cliff Nazarro, Marion Shilling, Buzz Barton, Robert Kortman, Theodore Lorch, Jack Evans. ***Cavalcade of the West.*** Diversion. Director: Harry Fraser. Cast: Hoot Gibson, Rex Lease, Marion Shilling, Adam Goodman, Nina Guilbert, Earl Dwire. ***Idaho Kid.*** Colony. Director: Robert Hill. Cast: Rex Bell, Marion Shilling, David Sharpe, Earl Dwire, Lafe McKee, Lane Chandler, Dorothy Wood. ***The Clutching Hand.*** Stage & Screen (serial). Director: Albert Herman. Cast: Jack Mulhall, Marion Shilling, William Farnum, Rex Lease, Mae Busch, Ruth Mix, Bryant Washburn, Robert Frazer, Gaston Glass, Yakima Canutt. ***Gun Smoke.*** Willis Kent. Director: Bartlett Carre. Cast: Buck Coburn, Marion Shilling, Bud Osborne, Benny Corbett, Henry Hall, Roger Williams, Philo McCullough, Lafe McKee. ***I'll Name the Murderer.*** Puritan. Director: Raymond K. Johnson. Cast: Ralph Forbes, Marion Shilling, Malcolm McGregor, James Guilfoyle, John C. Cowell, William Norton Bailey, Agnes Anderson, Mildred Claire, Gayne Kinsey.

15

Lupita Tovar

She was known in Hollywood Society for years as Lupita Kohner, a prominent hostess and the wife of agent Paul Kohner. As Mrs. Kohner, she was content to live in the shadow of and provide quiet support to her husband and children, actress Susan Kohner and producer Pancho Kohner.

Before she was Mrs. Paul Kohner, she was Lupita Tovar, a young girl from Mexico who, near the end of the silent era, left school in her native country for Hollywood.

It was okay that she couldn't speak English in silent films, but talkies threatened to send her packing for Mexico. Then she was sent to Universal, where she met producer Paul Kohner and played leads in the studio's Spanish-language versions of its English-language films *The Cat Creeps* and *Dracula.* During her career, which consisted of over 30 films between 1929 and 1945, Lupita also appeared opposite some of Hollywood's most popular Western heroes: Buck Jones, George O'Brien and Gene Autry.

When she and Paul Kohner married, her appearances in films became sporadic. They lived in Europe until the mid–1930s, when the rise of Adolf Hitler in Germany threatened their safety.

Back in the states, Tovar worked only when necessary to support her family, while Kohner, no longer secure at Universal after President Carl Laemmle's departure, struggled to establish his talent and literary agency.

Tovar was known as the sweetheart of Mexico after starring in the country's first talking film, *Santa* (1931), considered the *Gone with the Wind* of Mexico. Her native country honored her in the 1980s with an Ariel for her work in *Santa* (the equivalent of an Oscar) and by issuing a postage stamp on which her likeness appeared. Her performance in *Santa,* she said, was her best work in motion pictures.

Recognition in the U.S., however, came slow. The resurgence in her

A Max Autrey portrait of Lupita Tovar during her Fox contract, about 1929. (Courtesy of Lupita Tovar.)

popularity both in the U.S. and in Spanish-speaking countries came in the early 1990s when the Spanish version of *Dracula,* considered by some to be superior to the English-language version, was re-released. She made appearances with the film in festivals across Mexico, Spain and the United States.

Our conversation took place (in March 1994) in her rambling, Spanish hacienda-style home in fashionable Bel Air, where she continued to live following the death of her husband in 1988. Diego Rivera paintings of her children adorned the walls of the living room, and her awards and family photos were on display on the piano. On the way to the den, in which she spent much of her time, we passed her husband's study, which had remained as he left it: Portraits of his famous clients on the walls, and on his desk, his Rolodex, holding addresses and phone numbers of a Hollywood's Who's Who.

The home surrounded by lush vegetation was quite and peaceful, much like Tovar herself. There was a sense of serenity and calmness in this woman who had lived a full, rich life. One could see it in her face and in her eyes.

Her successful professional and personal life did not go ignored by her peers, who reminded her occasionally how fortunate she was.

"I remember one evening when Lupe Velez was here," Tovar said. "We were sitting just about where we are now. I remember her exact words. She said, 'Lupita, I envy you, because you have everything, a wonderful husband and two beautiful children.' 'Lupe,' I said, 'you have nothing to envy me for. You've had a wonderful career.' It wasn't long after that she killed herself. I was so sorry for her."

Velez had reason to wish for the happiness Tovar experienced throughout her life, for professional contentment and domestic stability often eludes those who called Hollywood their home.

"I have been very lucky in my life," Tovar said. "I can only say I had a guardian angel who guided me, even as far back as a little girl in Mexico.

Born Lupita Tovar in Tejuantepec, Mexico, on July 27, 1910, she was the oldest of nine children. Her mother was Irish (born in Mexico of Irish parentage), her father Mexican. In 1918, the family moved to Mexico City. Her father worked for the National Railroad of Mexico. Her education began in a convent. There was no room for show business ambitions. "My family was very, very strict," she said. "You don't think about being an actress when you are going to a school of nuns. We didn't go to the movies much, only once in a great moon, when we would get permission from my grandmother Sullivan."

When she was 16, Tovar switched schools, where her lessons included dancing and gymnastics. "I loved the change," she said. "You didn't have this with the sisters. From then, I thought I would be a dancer. I didn't think of being an actress. My earliest ambitions were to dance.

Tovar was in dance class performing a routine the day director Robert Flaherty* visited her school. It was 1928, and he was in Mexico testing young

**Robert Flaherty (1884–1951) combined his passion for exploration with the art of movie making to become the father of the film documentary. His expedition of the Hudson Bay and his filming of every day life of the Eskimos became* Nanook of the North *(1922). For MGM he co-directed (with W.S. Van Dyke) a documentary feature film,* White Shadows in the South Seas *(1928). At the time he met Tovar, he had joined Fox Studios to make a film about Pueblo Indians (the deal fell through). He then worked with F.W. Murnau on* Tabu *(1931) and shot his much-acclaimed* Man of Aran *(1934), a documentary about the life of an Irish fisherman. He later collaborated with Zoltan Korda on a fictional film,* Elephant Boy *(1937), starring Sabu.*

hopefuls for possible work at Fox Studios in Hollywood. Screen tests were made of Tovar and some 60 others who had show business ambitions. She took first prize and was subsequently offered a contract.

Representatives from Fox took the contract to her father, who adamantly declined the offer. "He was completely surprised," said Tovar. "'You won, that's fine ,' he said, 'but the contract goes back.' The next morning, he sent the contract back. A second one soon arrived, and they again came to his office and asked him what it was he wanted. My father said I was a schoolgirl, that I hadn't been out of the house, out of the family and that he just couldn't send me.

"Fox said my father could send a chaperone, that as long as the contract ran, I would have a salary. They talked and talked with him. Finally, a letter came from the Mexican consulate from Los Angeles saying it was a great opportunity for a young girl to represent Mexico. His friends told him it was a chance for me to learn English, that if it didn't work out, I would be back in six months. I think that convinced him."

After Tovar signed the seven-year, $150-a-week contract,* Fox announced they were casting her as the lead in *The Black Watch* (1929) and that she would begin work upon her arrival in Hollywood. Tovar never forgot her first impressions of Tinseltown.

"It was like arriving into a fairy tale," she said. "There was an aura of mystery and glamour around the actresses. They were something out of a fairy book, so beautiful and well dressed." The first stars she met in Hollywood were those under contract to Fox: Charles Farrell, Virginia Valli, Olive Borden, George O'Brien, Marguerite Churchill and Janet Gaynor.

After she settled at the studio, Tovar learned her role in *The Black Watch* would be given to Myrna Loy, and that she would play a much smaller part. "Of course I didn't know anything about acting. I had never put on lipstick or anything like that. They taught me how to make myself up, and they made lots and lots of tests."

Tovar appeared at Fox in small roles in *The Veiled Woman* and *Joy Street* with Lois Moran. "I liked Lois a lot. She thought it was cute that I couldn't speak English. I was trying so hard. I had an interpreter who told me what I was supposed to do. Since it was silent films, they told me to say whatever I felt like, so I did.

"Silent films were wonderful, because you didn't have to worry about your dialogue and could say anything. We had music on the set. It was absolutely marvelous."

Tovar busied herself with English lessons when not at the studio. She also took dancing lessons from Eduardo Cansino, who along with his wife, Volga,† became Lupita's close friends.

**The studio also paid her grandmother, who was fluent in English, $25 a week for accompanying Lupita to Hollywood.*

†Eduardo and Volga Cansino were the parents of Margarita Carmen Cansino, who later became Rita Hayworth.

Not long before her first six months with Fox were over, Robert Flaherty dropped by her home to discuss two issues: the problem he had experienced at Fox that was prompting his departure from the studio, and her career and future with Fox. He told Tovar the studio was not using her talent to its full potential and thought she would be perfect for a film he was planning to direct in the South Seas. Because of the inactivity in her career, it was believed she would be dropped by the studio after the first six months. He asked her to test for the part early and to be ready to start his new film when she was contractually free from Fox. Tovar agreed, and during the evenings she went to a studio in Hollywood where she made a series of screen tests for the director.

"On the last day my option was to be taken, at five o'clock to be exact, I got a call asking me to come to the studio. When I got there, the casting director asked me to sign my option. I looked at him and said, 'I thought you had nothing for me.' 'We'll find something,' he said. They had found out that Flaherty was testing me, and to get even with him, they renewed my option."

Tovar was frustrated over the political games, but soon faced another dilemma — sound. Not long after her first option was exercised, the talkie revolution erupted in the industry.

"First I was concerned, because I had been sending all my money home to my parents, just keeping enough to live on," she said. "Second, although I had been trying hard, I could hardly speak English. The requirements for acting were suddenly different, and I knew I wasn't trained."

The studio was also doubtful about her future in talkies. Casting director Jimmy Ryan called her into his office to discuss the situation. "He said, 'Lupita, I am very afraid that your next option will not be taken, because we are bringing in people from the theater for talking pictures. That is a shame, because I think you have a very bright future.' He was so very nice about the whole thing."

Ryan informed the actress that Universal was developing a foreign department for making films in different languages. He gave her a letter of recommendation and sent her to the studio. When she arrived, Tovar was taken to a room where she waited for hours. The only interaction came when someone stopped and offered her $100 to accompany them to a party. She declined, saying she didn't go to those functions.

During the day, she noticed a man walking from office to office, taking every opportunity to leer at her through a crack in one of the doors. Tovar feeling uncomfortable, decided she had waited long enough for nothing. She gave her letter to one of the secretaries and left the studio. That afternoon, she was summoned back to the studio. This time, Mrs. Cansino accompanied her, as Tovar was afraid to return alone.

"They had made me very uncomfortable," she said. "I didn't like being stared at."

Back at the studio, the casting director asked Tovar if she knew Paul

Kohner. She did not. Kohner, she was told, was head of the foreign film department and the one she would meet next.

"We walked into his office, and there stood the man who had stared at me, the one who made me feel so uncomfortable. He stood up, and with very nice manners said, 'Miss Tovar, we have met before.' 'Never,' I said."

After discussing some of Tovar's film work, Kohner asked to take the two ladies to dinner that evening. They declined, but arrangements were made for them to return the next day to view some of Tovar's work.

"The next day, we ran one of the pictures I made," Tovar said. "I noticed he was not looking at the screen, but at me. I said, 'You look at the screen or you'll miss me.'"

Seeing her potential, Kohner offered her a job dubbing films in Spanish at $15 a day. Her first work was introducing on film *The King of Jazz* (1930) to Spanish-speaking audiences.

Discouraged with her current assignment, Tovar decided to give up her career and return to Mexico. "I realized this was tough work, because I couldn't depend on two or three days of work here and there. That was not enough to pay the rent and support my grandmother. I had just about run out of money, and I had free passes for the train back to Mexico." She broke the news to a disappointed Kohner. He considered the situation and begged her to delay her decision until he would meet with her the next day.

During the 24-hour period, Kohner met with Carl Laemmle and explained his concept of the studio producing Spanish versions of its films. A big chunk of business, the Latin-American customer bloc, was being lost due to the advent of sound. He explained the enormous market for foreign versions and the cost effectiveness of shooting simultaneously with the English versions, using existing sets and equipment.

He reminded Laemmle that, in three weeks, filming would begin on *The Cat Creeps* (1930), a remake of *The Cat and the Canary* (1927). Why not produce a Spanish-speaking version? Laemmle asked about casting. Kohner told him there were available actors and actresses working as extras at Universal, in addition to one in particular (Tovar) he had in mind for the lead.

"Paul convinced Laemmle, and two days later, I was on my way downtown to sign a contract," Tovar said. "I had no idea what they were paying me — I didn't ask. I was so excited to get the job."

Two weeks later, Tovar was being directed by George Melford* and playing opposite Antonio Moreno in *La Voluntad del Muerto*, the Spanish version of *The Cat Creeps*. "Antonio Moreno was very, very popular, and I was his leading

**George Melford (1889–1961) began his career on the stage and screen as an actor before switching to directing in the 1910s. Although his career extended into 1960, his most prolific work was done in the silent era (he directed Rudolph Valentino in* The Sheik *[1921] and* Moran of the Lady Letty *[1922]). He later returned to acting, appearing in such films as* My Little Chickadee *(1940) and* The Ten Commandments *(1956).*

lady. I never thought I would meet him, and here I was playing opposite him. It was terrific."

After the picture wrapped, the studio planned a premiere on the Universal lot. "Everyone was in tuxedo, and I was told to get a new dress for the occasion. I spent a week's salary on it. That night, Paul made a speech. I remember his exact words. He said, 'This young lady you're going to see tonight, a complete unknown, could walk out of here a star.' When the lights went up, everyone was congratulating him. He (as producer) had made a success."

Acclaim also came to Tovar. The day after the screening, she received a call from the studio asking her to accompany the film to Mexico for personal appearances. She jumped at the chance to return to her homeland for the first time in two years.

"I thought I was just going to see my family. I still didn't think of myself as an actress," she said. "When my train arrived in Mexico, there to meet me were my schoolmates, my teachers, my family and representatives from Universal in Mexico. I looked back, and on the engine was a banner reading, 'Here travels Lupita Tovar.' It was November 20, 1930, and it was the biggest day of my life."

Her father was disgusted at the attention the film brought his daughter. He could not accept his daughter being in show business, the center of attention. His family, while not as extreme, also wondered about her activities in Hollywood. "During my trip to Mexico, we paid a visit to my aunts. They had a publicity photo of me dressed in skimpy clothing on display, but had draped it in lace. It was very funny."

What was not humorous to Tovar, however, was her father's behavior following the first screening of *The Cat Creeps.* "After the showing, he led me out by the hand. He couldn't stand all the publicity. He had no understanding of it."

After making five other appearances at screenings around Mexico City, Tovar was preparing to return to Hollywood when her father demanded she give up her career and return home. "He said I couldn't go back to Hollywood. A representative from Universal came to talk with him about it. He asked him if he could pay the studio what they had invested in me. This was business, he explained, and the studio would sue. My father finally said I could return.

"I went back to Hollywood with my eyes swollen from crying. My father was absolutely furious. He was a very stubborn man, and whatever he said was law. I knew I couldn't go back to Mexico under his rule after having my independence."

Back in Hollywood, Lupita played Eva in the Spanish version of *Dracula* (Helen Chandler played the equivalent part, Mina, in the English version). It, like *The Cat Creeps,* was filmed at night (after the regular cast had gone home) on the same sets that director Tod Browning did.

"It was very, very difficult," Tovar said. "I needed my sleep, usually 10 hours a night. It was a complete change, because I had to sleep during the day. We started shooting about eight P.M. and broke for dinner at midnight."

Lupita Tovar and Carlos Villarias in the Spanish-language version of *Dracula* (1931). (Courtesy of Lupita Tovar.)

To get into the role of Eva, Tovar arrived an hour early every evening and wandered around the *Dracula* sound stage. "I was actually frightened by the sets. They were very dark and eerie, but I would sit there in the dark and try to concentrate. In *Dracula*, we had wonderful actors — most of them came from the stage and were very well-known. I had to keep up with them."

Although he could not speak Spanish, director George Melford handled the cast with ease, she said. "I called him Uncle George. What a sweet man he was. He would say, 'You understand what I mean?' I would say, 'I think so.' He said, 'Not you think so — yes or no!' We usually had one take of a scene — that was it. We could not afford to waste as much film as in the English version. We rehearsed once and took the scene."

Barry Norton* who had the role of John (Juan) Harker, played by David Manners in English version, was a constant source of kidding and laughs on the set. "He used to say that Dracula was going to have a hard time carrying me around if Paul Kohner continued to bring me boxes of candy on the set. He was so full of mischief."

Although Tovar said Kohner "had his eye on her," there was nothing in his actions that would prompt anyone to say the two were yet an "item."

One of the many comparisons made between the English and Spanish versions was the costumes worn by the actresses. In the Spanish version, Tovar was allowed to wear revealing gowns, unlike the actresses in the English version. "My father really got upset over those, but I had no approval of anything. They thought Latin American countries wanted something more sexy."

During the first half of 1931, Lupita was busy making Westerns and Spanish versions of Universal films. Her first oater was with Richard Talmadge, but it was *Border Law* (1931) opposite Buck Jones that was particularly memorable to her. "They asked me if I could ride a horse. I never said no when asked if I could do something, because I was afraid they would fire me. I said, 'Sure, I can ride a horse.' The horse ran away with me on it. I was hanging on for dear life, and Buck dragged me off onto his horse. That's when I decided to learn how to ride."

Because of her popularity in her country after the release of *The Cat Creeps* and *Dracula*, Tovar was selected to star in Mexico's first talking film, *Santa* (1931). Antonio Moreno directed the movie (a remake of a 1918 silent film) based on the story of a woman who became the most famous prostitute in Mexico.

The film was a sensation. "I tell you I could not walk on the streets when *Santa* came out," she said. "People tore my dress for souvenirs. It was something."

While Tovar was in Mexico for the filming of *Santa*, Paul Kohner had

**Barry Norton (1905–1956), a native of Argentina, was particularly memorable for his roles at Fox:* What Price Glory *(1926);* The Lily *(1926);* The Legion of the Condemned *(1928); and* Four Devils *(1929).*

gone to Europe to visit his ailing father. It was during the separation, Tovar said, that her feelings for Kohner deepened. "I knew then that I was in love with him. He called me in Mexico when he returned to Hollywood and said he wanted me home before Christmas [1931]. I told him I had to finish filming. When it was over, I didn't wait to see the rushes. I was back in Hollywood by New Year's Eve."

Another separation came later the next year when Universal sent Kohner to Europe to produce films in Germany. The night before he was to leave, he gave Tovar a ring which she immediately returned. "I thought he was going away and that I would never see him again. Maybe he would meet somebody else. He went to my grandmother and gave her the ring and told her to keep it for me, that I didn't understand why he couldn't make a commitment."

Finally, as Tovar was getting ready to begin work on a Western at Columbia, Kohner called from Germany and proposed marriage. He also had arranged for her to star in the upcoming German film *Ecstasy* (1933). She immediately made plans to leave the country, then went to break the news to Columbia boss Harry Cohn. "I said, 'Harry, I am very sorry that I cannot make this film for you. I am going to Europe to be married.' He was absolutely furious, such a roughneck. He said, 'Do you know you'll never work in this studio again?' I said 'I don't think I will.'"

Two weeks later, she was in Berlin, and on October 30, 1932, the two were married by a rabbi in the home of Kohner's parents in Czechoslovakia.

During Kohner's stay in Berlin, before Tovar joined him, he had shared her publicity portraits with German director Gustav Machaty, who would soon be directing *Ecstasy*. Tovar said she was set to play the lead until she got to Berlin and Kohner told her he had changed his mind.

"Paul said he didn't want his wife, me, running around in the woods without a stitch of clothing," she said. "A month or so after we married, we went to the set to meet Gustav Machaty. He walked over and said, 'Is this the girl? How could you do this to me? You gave me her pictures and told me she was on her way and then you say she'll not do the work.' All this while Hedy Lamarr* was sitting right there on the set hearing it all. That's the way it was. Paul didn't want me working."

In 1934, the Kohners traveled to England for the opening of a Universal film. As they walked into London's Dorchester Hotel during their visit, they met Buster Keaton, producer Sam Spiegel and director Adrian Brunel sitting in the lobby. "There's my girl," Keaton said when he saw her. In the ensuing conversation, the Kohners learned the three were planning to produce *The Invader* for the screen. Keaton wanted Tovar as his leading lady; Kohner said no, explaining that his wife was retired and had only accompanied him to see London.

*Ecstasy *brought Hedy Lamarr (b. 1913), who played the leading role, international fame. The plot of the film centered around an impotent man, his young bride and the young gentleman who spies her swimming in the nude. Lamarr's first work in Hollywood was* Algiers *(1938), but her biggest commercial success came as Delilah in* Samson and Delilah *(1949).*

After the weekend, they returned to Berlin, where several days later, Spiegel followed, continuing his campaign to woo Tovar back to the screen. Her husband reluctantly gave his approval.

"*The Invader* was not one of Keaton's best films," she said. "It was at the very end of his career. He was drinking heavily, always in a stupor. They watched him very closely, but somehow he got the liquor."

The one scene that Tovar never forgot took place aboard a yacht, from which she was supposed to fall into the water below and be rescued by Keaton.

"I'm not a good swimmer, and Keaton, who had been drinking, thought it all very funny. As I would come up for air, he would push me down. I was struggling with him. Finally one of the electricians saw I was in trouble and jumped in and pulled me out. They then had to pull Keaton out and start working on him. The next day, after they repaired my costume, we went back to the set. Keaton said, 'I'm sorry, kid.' I told him it was okay. We never talked about it again."

After the film wrapped, Tovar tried to forget the disastrous experience. She never saw the movie.

By the mid–1930s, the Kohners were becoming increasingly concerned over conditions in Germany with the rise of the Nazis and the suspected persecution of Jews. "We didn't yet know about the death camps, but I saw people being beaten on the subways by the Nazis. It was horrible."

The Kohners' decision to leave Europe in 1935 came after a brush with the Nazi police at the border of Germany and Czechoslovakia. They were on their way to visit Kohner's parents.

"After they asked for our passports, they took our luggage and sent us to separate offices. They ripped off my fur coat and hat and took off all my clothes. After they went through my luggage, they came back in and threw my clothes at me. I was taken to another office and saw everything I had all over the floor. Then they asked me to sign a paper that I had been treated with courtesy. I said I wouldn't, that I wanted to phone my ambassador. They replied, 'People can disappear and no one ever hears from them again.' So I put my name on the paper."

Tovar said they allowed them their freedom to continue across the border only after coming across a photo in Kohner's briefcase of a ceremony at Universal (in Hollywood) in which Carl Laemmle and staff— Paul was in the group — welcomed a high-ranking German official to California.

Once in Czechoslovakia, the Kohners decided against returning home to Berlin. They telephoned their maid to pack their belongings and send everything to his parents' home. They traveled to Paris and London, then crossed the Atlantic, arriving in the United States in April 1935.

Back in Hollywood, Kohner found himself having to virtually start over professionally. He still worked at Universal, but was less stable at the studio after Carl Laemmle lost control in 1936. Tovar was allowed to work only because they were financially strained.

George O'Brien and Lupita Tovar in ***The Fighting Gringo*** (1939). (Courtesy of Lupita Tovar.)

She made a handful of films in her native country and had nice roles in several Westerns, among them *The Fighting Gringo* (1939) and *South of the Border* (1939). For the most part, however, her roles diminished to little more than bits ([*Blockade* [1938], *Green Hell* [1940] and *The Westerner* [1940]).

Tovar insisted, however, the size of the role mattered little to her, although she had been featured and starred earlier in the decade. "I didn't feel it was a comedown. Money was very important to us, because we didn't have anything. When we put down on this house in 1936, we had nothing, not even furniture. So, it was no longer the idea of gaining control in a film, it was solely for the money. I was Mrs. Paul Kohner, and that was what was important to me."

Not only being a wife, but also a mother, was at the top of her list. Susan was born in 1936, and Paul, Jr. (Pancho), in 1939.

Paul Kohner established his agency in 1938. Director John Huston was one of his first clients. Their association has been called the longest agent–client relationship in Hollywood history, lasting until Huston's death in 1987.*

Tovar continued to work sporadically into the 1940s. She tested for the part of Humphrey Bogart's mistress in *Casablanca* (1943). "It was a French girl with a French accent. Michael Curtiz, the director, saw I couldn't do it. Maybe not then, but now I could," she laughed. She retired from films in 1945 (after *The Crime Doctor's Courage*) at the urging of her son's pediatrician, who indicated her absence from home during her work possibly contributed to Pancho's asthma condition.

Being the wife of an agent, however, was almost like working again. "I was with him every minute. We went out a lot in those days. You have to be nice to the clients whether you like them or not. Actors are very neurotic, and the way you treat a client is very personal. You have to know a lot about human nature. Some of them are wonderful, but they are not all nice. Lana Turner, for instance, was a very difficult woman."

As his clientele continued to grow over the years, Kohner handled the careers of the some of Hollywood's biggest stars and directors: Charles Bronson, Billy Wilder, David Niven, Greta Garbo, Yul Brynner, Liv Ullmann and others.

During World War II, Kohner helped place exiled authors, writers, composers, directors and actors with Hollywood studios. He was also instrumental in the formation of the European Film Fund, which financially assisted industry professionals in coming to and establishing them in the United States.

As her children grew older, Tovar supported their interest in show business. Susan, whose professional debut came on the stage in *The Girl in the Via Flaminia* at age 14, eventually became a leading lady in films in the late 1950s

**Kohner's association with Huston, as well as his extraordinary life, is chronicled in* The Magician of Sunset Boulevard: The Improbable Life of Paul Kohner, Hollywood Agent *(Morgan Press, 1977), written by Paul's brother Frederick.*

A 1930s glamour portrait of Lupita Tovar. (Courtesy of Lupita Tovar.)

and early 1960s. She appeared on stage with Tyrone Power in *A Quiet Place* and was nominated for Best Supporting Actress for her performance in *Imitation of Life* (1959).*

Pancho intended to study international law in college, but married and moved to Spain, where he worked as an assistant director to John Huston, and as the production manager for a series of big-budget films. As a film producer, he worked frequently with Charles Bronson.

The recognition Lupita Tovar received in the early 1990s came at the right time, she said. "After my husband died in 1988, I said, 'This is it. My life is over,' because I lived for him. I was in mourning for a long time. I only regret that he is not here to see the resurgence in the popularity of *Dracula,* because it [the Spanish version] was his idea."

The last thing she expected was to receive awards and recognition for work she did over 60 years ago. Surprised, indeed, but grateful.

"It's like a dream being invited to all of these festivals and showings of my films. Was that really me up there on the screen? I had almost forgotten I was an actress. It has been absolutely wonderful how people have been so nice. Usually people die and then they get an award, but to be alive and receive this honor is fantastic!"

Filmography

1929: ***The Veiled Woman.*** Fox. Director: Emmett Flynn. Cast: Lia Tora, Paul Vincenti, Walter McGrail, Josef Swickard, Kenneth Thomson, Andre Cheron, Ivan Lebedeff, Maude George, Lupita Tovar. ***The Black Watch.*** Fox. Director: John Ford. Cast: Victor McLaglen, Myrna Loy, David Rollins, Lumsden Hare, Roy D'Arcy, Mitchell Lewis, Cyril Chadwick, Claude King, Francis Ford, Walter Long, David Torrence, Frederick Sullivan, Richard Travers, Pat Somerset,

**Susan retired from the screen after her 1964 marriage to fashion designer John Weitz.*

David Percy, Joseph Diskay, Lupita Tovar. ***Joy Street.*** Fox. Director: Raymond Cannon. Cast: Lois Moran, Nick Stuart, Rex Bell, Jose Crespo, Dorothy Ward, Ada Williams, Maria Alba, Sally Phipps, Florence Allen, Mabel Vail, Carol Wines, John Breeden, Marshall Ruth, James Barnes, Allen Dale, Lupita Tovar. ***The Cock-Eyed World.*** Fox. Director: Raoul Walsh. Cast: Victor McLaglen, Edmund Lowe, Lily Damita, Lelia Karnelly, El Brendel, Bob Burns, Jeanette Dagna, Joe Brown, Stuart Erwin, Ivan Linow, Jean Bary, Solidad Jiminez, Albert Dresden, Joe Rochay, Lupita Tovar. **1930:** Lupita introduced on film the Spanish-speaking version of ***The King of Jazz.*** ***La Voluntad del Muerto.*** Universal (Spanish version of ***The Cat Creeps***). Director: George Melford. Cast: Antonio Moreno, Lupita Tovar, Andres de Segurola, Roberto Guzman, Paul Ellis, Lucio Villegas, Agostino Borgato, Conchita Ballesteros, Maria Calvo. **1931:** ***Dracula.*** Universal (Spanish version). Director: George Melford. Cast: Carlos Villarias, Pablo Alvarez Rubio, Lupita Tovar, Barry Norton, Eduardo Arozamena, Carmen Guerrero, Manuel Arbo, Jose Soriano Viosca. ***Santa.*** Compania Nacional Productora de Peliculas. Director: Antonio Moreno. Cast: Lupita Tovar, Carlos Orellana, Juan Jose Martinez Casado, Donald Reed, Antonio R. Frausto, Mimi Derba, Joaquin Busquets, Rosita Arriaga, Sofia Alvarez, Raul de Anda. ***East of Boreno.*** Universal. Director: George Melford. Cast: Rose Hobart, Charles Bickford, Georges Renavent, Lupita Tovar, Noble Johnson. ***Yankee Don.*** Richard Talmadge Productions. Cast: Richard Talmadge, Lupita Tovar, Gayne Whitman, Julian Rivero, Sam Appel, Alma Real, Victor Stanford. ***Border Law.*** Columbia. Director: Louis King. Cast: Buck Jones, Lupita Tovar, James Mason, Frank Rice, Don Chapman, Louis Hickus, F. R. Smith, John Wallace, Lafe McKee. ***Carne de Cabaret.*** Columbia (Spanish version of ***Ten Cents a Dance***). Director: Christy Cabanne. Cast: Lupita Tovar, Ramon Pereda, Rene Cardona, Carmen Guerrero, Soledad Jimenez, Aurora del Real, Maria Calvo, Nancy Torres, Ralph Navarro, Juan Duval, Felipe Flores, Mary O'Keefe, Rodolfo Hoyos. ***El Tenorio Del Harem.*** Universal. Director: Kurt Neumann. Cast: Slim Summerville, Lupita Tovar, Tom Kennedy, Manuel Arbo, Eduardo Arozamena, Jose Pena. **1934:** ***Vidas Rotas.*** Inca (Spanish). Director: Eusebio Fernandez Ardavin. Cast: Lupita Tovar, Maruchi Fresno, Enrique Zabala, Candida Losada, Jose Isbert. **1935:** ***Alas Sobre del Chaco.*** Universal (Spanish version of ***Storm Over the Andes***). Director: Christy Cabanne. Cast: Jose Crespo, Lupita Tovar, Antonio Moreno, Romualdo Tirado, Julio Pena, Barry Norton, Juanita Garfias, Juan Torena, Jose Rubio, Luis Diaz Flores, Francisco Maran, Anita Camargo, Paco Moreno, George Lewis, Jose Caraballo, Lucio Villegas, Alma Real. ***An Old Spanish Custom*** (***The Invader/The Intruder***). British & Continental Films. Director: Adrian Brunel. Cast: Buster Keaton, Lupita Tovar, Esme Percy, Lyn Harding, Webster Booth, Andrea Malandrinos, Hilda Moreno, Clifford Heatherley. **1936:** ***El Capitán Tormenta.*** Grand National (Spanish version of ***Captain Calamity***). Director: John Reinhardt. Cast: Lupita Tovar, Fortunio Bonanova, Juan Toreno,

Movita, Romualdo Tirado, Jose Luis Tortosa, Roy D'Arcy, George Lewis, Barry Norton, Paco Moreno, Agostino Borgato, Jose Pena, Rosa Rey, Alberto Gandero. ***Mariguana.*** (Mexican). Director: Jose Bohr. Cast: Lupita Tovar, Barry Norton, Rene Cardona, Angel T. Sala, Alberto Marti, Sara Garcia, Emilio Fernandez, Manuel Noriega, Carmelita Bohr. **1938** ***El Rosario de Amozoc*** (Mexican). Director: Jose Bohr. Cast: Emilio Tuero, Carlos Orellana, Augstin Insunza, Daniel Herrera. ***Blockade.*** United Artists. Director: William Dieterle. Cast: Henry Fonda, Madeleine Carroll, Vladimir Sokoloff, Leo Carrillo, John Halliday, Reginald Denny, Robert Warwick, Fred Kohler, Sr., Carlos De Valdez, Peter Godfrey, Nick Thompson, Rosina Galli, William B. Davidson, Lupita Tovar, Katherine DeMille. **1939** ***The Fighting Gringo.*** RKO. Director: David Howard. Cast: George O'Brien, Lupita Tovar, Lucio Villegas, LeRoy Mason, William Royle, Glenn Strange, Slim Whittaker, Mary Field, Martin Garralaga, Dick Botiller, Bill Cody, Sr., Cactus Mack, Chris-Pin Martin. ***Tropic Fury.*** Universal. Director: Christy Cabanne. Cast: Richard Arlen, Andy Devine, Beverly Roberts, Lou Merrill, Lupita Tovar, Samuel S. Hinds, Charles Trowbridge, Leonard Mudie, Adia Kuznetzoff, Noble Johnson, Frank Mitchell, Miburn Stone. ***South of the Border.*** Republic. Director: George Sherman. Cast: Gene Autry, Smiley Burnette, June Storey, Lupita Tovar, Mary Lee, Frank Reicher, Duncan Renaldo, Alan Edwards, Claire Du Brey, Dick Botiller, William Farnum, Rex Lease. ***Maria.*** (Mexican). Director: Chano Urueta. Cast: Rodolfo Landa, Lupita Tovar, Josefina Escobedo, Mimi Derba, Eduardo Arozamena, Miguel Arenas. **1940:** ***The Westerner.*** United Artists. Director: William Wyler. Cast: Gary Cooper, Walter Brennan, Doris Davenport, Fred Stone, Paul Hurst, Chill Wills, Charles Halton, Forrest Tucker, Tom Tyler, Arthur Aylesworth, Lilian Bond, Dana Andrews, Roger Gray, Trevor Bardette, Lupita Tovar, Julian Rivero, Lucien Littlefield, Jack Pennick, Arthur Mix, Helen Foster, Connie Leon, Charles Coleman. ***Green Hell.*** Universal. Director: James Whale. Cast: Douglas Fairbanks, Jr., Joan Bennett, John Howard, Vincent Price, George Sanders, Alan Hale, George Bancroft, Gene Garrick, Francis McDonald, Ray Mala, Peter Bronte, Lupita Tovar, Bob Fischer, Noble Johnson, Julian Rivero, Yola d'Avril, Nena Quartaro, Kay Linaker. **1941:** ***Two-Gun Sheriff.*** Republic. Director: George Sherman. Cast: Don "Red" Barry, Lupita Tovar, Lynn Merrick, Fred Kohler, Jr., Jay Novello. **1943:** ***Resurreccion.*** (Mexican). Director: Gilberto Martinez Solares. Cast: Lupita Tovar, Emilio Tuero, Sara Garcia, Eugenia Galindo, Elena D'Orgaz. ***Miguel Strogoff*** (***El Correo del Zar***). (Mexican). Director: Miguel M. Delgado. Cast: Lupita Tovar, Julian Soler, Julio Villarreal, Anita Blanch, Miguel Arenas. **1944:** ***Gun to Gun.*** Warner Brothers. Director: Ross Lederman. Cast: Tom Tyler, Lupita Tovar, Robert Shayne, Pedro De Cordoba, Harry Woods. **1945:** ***The Crime Doctor's Courage.*** Columbia. Director: George Sherman. Cast: Warner Baxter, Hillary Brooke, Lupita Tovar, Jerome Cowan, Robert Scott, Lloyd Corrigan.

16

Barbara Weeks

What a relief it was in 1932 to be free of her contractual obligations to Samuel Goldwyn. She detested the sight of the man, and considered any alternative better than being bound professionally to the legendary producer. Then along came Harry Cohn.

The boss of Columbia placed her under contract and promised her career advancement. She thought perhaps she might be one of the few lucky ones who would be spared the legendary wrath of Cohn. The association, however, soon turned sour, and it did not surprise her.

After she brushed off his romantic overtures, Cohn spewed his venom, setting out to rid himself of his latest acquisition. Her punishment, she soon learned, was being loaned to other companies and being assigned to Westerns at her home studio.

Being in show business for half a decade, she knew how to play games too. She kept quiet, never letting on that, while some actresses considered Westerns to be the professional skids, she found them to be among her most enjoyable film experiences. Moreover, she considered her best film to be one of the independents originally meant to humiliate her.

While it was serious back in the 1930s when the drama was unfolding, 60 years later, in her first interview since retiring from the screen in 1940, Barbara Weeks laughed over the studio politics that derailed her career. From the vantage point of the 1990s, Cohn's treatment of her rated no more than a shrug, the same indifference she had for most of her show business career.

As a teenager, Barbara Weeks was saddled with considerable responsibility when her mother, after concluding she was not the success she had hoped, put Weeks to work on the New York stage. An exceptional dancer, she caught the attention of Broadway producer Florenz Ziegfeld, who hired her as a showgirl in

Whoopee. When the legendary showman went west to Hollywood in 1930 to put the Broadway musical on film, he took Weeks with him.

Barbara Weeks was one of the 1931 Wampas Baby Stars.

She remained in films (mostly at Warner Brothers and Fox) under a personal contract to Ziegfeld and Samuel Goldwyn. After Ziegfeld's death in 1932, she signed with Columbia Pictures, where she worked until her retirement from the screen in the late 1930s.

A versatile actress (she could handle Westerns, musicals or drama with equal ease), Weeks spent her teenage years in theater dressing rooms and in cramped hotel rooms and her young adulthood on sound stages. Being the sole breadwinner for the family, she never had time to realize, until her teenage years were over, that she had missed her childhood and the normal life teenagers are supposed to lead.

After eight years and 40 films in Hollywood, she was relieved when it was over. For the first time, she lived her life for herself. She opted for marriage, the only way she knew to finally break free of her mother's dominance.

She established another vocation for herself and lived a quiet life free of any publicity about her former life as an actress.

While Weeks made an effort to forget Hollywood over the years, she admitted it will never completely leave her. Her movie memories, she has found, usually invade her privacy during the late, late show. 'I will recognize someone in an old movie and I'll think back, 'Oh, I knew him or her way back when.' Then, I start remembering Hollywood."

From as far back as she could remember, her life was anything but normal. She was born Barbara Weeks on July 4, 1913, in Somerville, Massachusetts, just outside Boston. Her parents divorced when she was only nine months old.

Throughout her life, Barbara's mother had ambitions of being a stage actress. When Barbara was still quite young, her mother sent her to live with her grandmother while she followed her dreams to New York. There was enough ambition for everyone, however, including Barbara.

"My mother decided I had talents she didn't have and decided she was going to do something about it," said Weeks. "I took dancing lessons and all sorts of things to become that great something or other."

As time went by, her mother realized she would never be the success she hoped. Deciding she didn't have the talent required for the profession, she abandoned her career only to ignite what she thought was her second chance at fame: her daughter. In 1926, when Weeks was 13, her mother decided it was time to test her daughter's talents and potential for success. Mrs. Weeks brought her to live in New York.

Within three months of her arrival, Weeks had made her professional debut in a musical show. She then had a small role in *Ringside*, a 1928 play about boxing. Finally, her big opportunity came.

An acquaintance of Mrs. Weeks called her at dancing school one afternoon and invited her to drop by and meet some friends of hers. One of them was in a Ziegfeld show. Weeks, as instructed, danced for the woman, who realized the talent the youngster possessed and arranged an appointment with Florenz Ziegfeld.

"I was scared to death," said Weeks of meeting Ziegfeld. "His office was an oblong room and you had to walk and walk to get to his desk. He was seated behind his desk, where on top were an assortment of toy elephants. I'll never forget that meeting."

Ziegfeld was charmed by the youngster and signed her as a showgirl for his stage show *Whoopee*, which opened in December 1928 at the New Amsterdam Theater. She appeared with Ziegfeld as Bobbe Weeks (Bobbe was a childhood nickname). Once in Hollywood, she used her real name, Barbara.

The meeting began a friendship that lasted until Ziegfeld's death in 1932. He kept an eye on her advancing career and allowed her at times to sit in his theater box for performances of *Show Boat* (with Helen Morgan) and other shows.

If Ziegfeld had watched that closely over Weeks' budding career, he might have realized the stress the 13-year-old was under. With her job in *Whoopee*, Weeks became the sole wage earner for the family. Her situation was aggravated by the fact that, like many other young hopefuls, she had an ambitious mother in the wings. It was not a normal life for a teenager.

Rather than going to a classroom, tutors either came to the theater (on matinee days) or to the Weeks' apartment. Out of the bright footlights of the New Amsterdam, it was a rather dull and lonely life. Mrs. Weeks did not encourage her daughter to be a normal teenager and she did not allow friends to divert her daughter's attention from what were her own ambitions.

"My mother was with me constantly, telling me what to do and what to say and how to look. I wasn't living my life, my mother was. She really didn't allow me to have any social life at all. I resented it later on, but at the time, I didn't know any better."

The strain was not only emotional, but physical as well. "*Whoopee* was very demanding because, not only was I a dancer in it, I also had to go to dancing school, where it was nothing but dancing."

Through her work, Weeks often met others in show business. She liked and enjoyed working with Eddie Cantor in *Whoopee* and remembered Buddy and Vilma Ebsen* being in the show's chorus. It was through James Cagney that Weeks met Joan Blondell, who would become one of her closest Hollywood friends.†

After *Whoopee!* closed on Broadway in November 1929, the show was taken on the road. It played in major cities such as Washington, D.C., Baltimore, Philadelphia and Cleveland, where it closed. Weeks found the diversity of cities refreshing. "We had a lot of fun," she recalled. "It was quite different from New York. We were in a different hotel in a different city every three weeks or so. I really enjoyed that."

Ziegfeld had recently been making motion picture deals to bring some of his shows to movie audiences. In 1929, he and Samuel Goldwyn entered into a partnership and formed the Z & G Productions. They would use the company to co-produce *Whoopee!* in Hollywood.

Harboring a desire to break into the movies, Weeks was thrilled at the possibility of going to Hollywood. Ziegfeld, however, had other plans. "I wanted to be in the movies and Mr. Ziegfeld wanted me to stay on the stage. He said he was going to put me in more shows in New York. In time, however, as the negotiations continued, he told me I could go along."

Signed to a personal contract to both Ziegfeld and Goldwyn, Weeks made her motion picture debut in *Whoopee!* (1930). Eddie Cantor and Ethel Shutta recreated their roles for the film, and Eleanor Hunt§ was promoted from show girl to ingenue.

"I didn't think Eleanor Hunt was such a good casting choice," Barbara admitted. "There were lots of people interviewed for the part. She got it, and I don't know how. I couldn't have done it anyway. I was too young."

Weeks said she was the sole chorus girl brought from New York to appear in the film. Once in Hollywood, she was joined in the chorus by up-and-coming Virginia Bruce and Betty Grable. "Betty's mother was a cripple, and I can remember she used to come to the studio when we were filming *Whoopee!* In between scenes, she would have Betty practice on an empty sound stage. I liked Betty. She was an awfully nice girl, but her mother was a real tough cookie."

**Buddy and Vilma Ebsen were then a brother/sister act on the stage. He later entered films and scored hits on television in* The Beverly Hillbillies *and* Barnaby Jones.

†The silent film actress Madge Bellamy (1899–1990) was another of Weeks' friends. "She was a doll," she said. "When Madge was going back to New York, she was selling all of her furniture. We were over at her house one day and people were coming and going, buying furniture. She had this Chinese cabinet that I fell in love with. I bought it and I still have it today. She was lots of fun, and what a marvelous sense of humor that gal had."

§Eleanor Hunt (1910–1981) continued working in films into the late 1930s, but her claim to fame was her role in Whoopee!. *Numerous film references erroneously give hers as the real name of actress Joyce Compton.*

Weeks also worked very closely with Busby Berkeley,* whom Goldwyn hired to direct the dance numbers. "Being in the New York production, I already knew the routines. Though Busby Berkeley got the credit, I was the one who put them on."

Despite his strictness, Weeks got along well with the choreographer. "Yes, he was very demanding; I remember that about him. He was understanding, however, and he didn't push us too hard. I liked him very much; he was a nice man."

The *Whoopee!* film shoot, like the stage production, was a strenuous project. In addition to Ziegfeld and Goldwyn's constant squabbles over control,† the necessity for airtight and noise-proof sound stages took its toll on the dancers.

"We just about died from the heat," Weeks said. "The lights they had were so hot. Now and then, they'd have to turn them off to give us a break. There was no way they could open a door or anything like that when filming was going on or it would ruin the scene."

With the merging of four gifted professionals (Ziegfeld, Cantor, Goldwyn and Berkeley) and Technicolor, *Whoopee!* couldn't go wrong with critics or audiences. It turned out to be a smashing success, grossing over $2 million and helping to establish the trend for the musical genre of the 1930s.

Weeks, however, felt the stage hit didn't translate effectively on film. "The audience has a lot to do with it," she said. "When you are on the stage, every audience is different. Filming is very tiresome and boring, and it doesn't give you the enthusiasm you get from the stage. That was evident in *Whoopee!*, the film."

When the production wrapped, Weeks and her mother convinced Ziegfeld to allow her to stay and work in Hollywood. During the production of *Whoopee!*, the two lived at the Hollywood Hotel. After it was decided they were in town permanently, they rented an apartment and eventually bought a house on Beachwood Drive, just under the HOLLYWOOD sign.

Under contract to both Ziegfeld and Goldwyn, Weeks went to work immediately in the studios. At Warner Brothers, she made five films in rapid succession. In *Man to Man* (1930), her next film after *Whoopee!*, Weeks had her first speaking part. "My mother, after seeing the picture, told me the acting was okay, but I had terrible clothes." Weeks liked Allan Dwan as director and enjoyed working with Phillips Holmes, who lived around the corner from their apartment.

*Whoopee! *brought Berkeley from New York to Hollywood, where he had been a stage actor and later a dance director. The film marked the beginning of his seemingly magical techniques in Hollywood musicals of the 1930s: the overhead shots, successive closeups of show girls and the symmetrical arrangements of routines.*

†*Weeks remembered Patricia Ziegfeld, the daughter of Florenz Ziegfeld and Billie Burke, and one of her earliest Hollywood friends, telling her of the creative battles between Ziegfeld and Goldwyn during the making of* Whoopee!.

Working at Warner Brothers with Barbara Stanwyck in *Illicit* (1931) was also a treat for her. "She was a darling to me, such a pleasant, fun kind of person," Barbara said. "She was very down-to-earth."

Weeks appeared in her first Western, *Two Fisted Justice* with Tom Tyler in 1931. Her frequent horseback rides through Central Park in New York and owning her own filly (Flapper), in California, prepared her for this and other Westerns. While she enjoyed working with Tyler, she found him to be an "ignorant kind of guy, a good-looking dumbbell."

Eddie Cantor was instrumental in securing Weeks her first big role and one of the best of her career: the ingenue in the musical/comedy, *Palmy Days* (1931). Cantor was again working with Goldwyn and Berkeley in this film about phony psychics. Charlotte Greenwood, the actress known for her high kick, played an instructor and George Raft, a hood.

"Charlotte was charming and could be as funny off the screen as on when she wanted to be," said Weeks. "She was one of those Christian Scientists, but she still had a twinkle in her eye. She was a fun person to be around." George Raft was another story. He once asked Weeks for a date. It didn't take her long to realize that one night on the town with him was enough. "He was a womanizer, and that always did it for me. I sound as if I was an angel, but I can assure you, there are times when you just can't stand people like that. He was a bad boy."

Weeks said the film's director, Edward Sutherland, was her favorite director. "No doubt, he was the best, a very fine man."

It was on the *Palmy Days* set that Weeks learned she had been named a 1931 Wampas Baby Star, with friends Joan Blondell and Joan Marsh. Although she considered it an honor to be chosen, her shooting schedule (she made seven pictures in 1931 and 11 in 1932) kept her from some appearances.

Being named a Wampas Baby Star for her potential as an actress was encouraging and she believed Ziegfeld was guiding her advancing career. It was through him that she met some of the most influential members of Hollywood society. It wasn't long after her arrival in California that Ziegfeld introduced her to William Randolph Hearst and his companion Marion Davies. Weeks considered her frequent visits to San Simeon (the Hearst Castle) and Wyntoon to be among her most treasured memories of Hollywood.

That first invitation to visit the "Ranch" came when she was home from the studio recovering from double pneumonia. "Mr. Hearst had his secretary call to see if I was interested in recuperating in San Simeon. I was so amazed I almost dropped the phone. We, my mother and I, took the train from Glendale to San Luis Obispo, where he had limousines to take us to the castle. I'll never forget the sight as we were driving along the coast, we could see the castle all lit up. It was absolutely beautiful and so fascinating. I had wonderful times there."

She became such a regular — while in films and after she married — Weeks was assigned her own room, one of the three suites called the Cloisters. "In that room, there was the most beautiful rug I have ever seen," she said. "I have never again seen anything like it in my life. It was a royal blue, and in one corner, there was a golden dragon with a pink rose in its mouth." She marveled at the museum-quality treasures Hearst had collected over the years. "He took me down into the cellar once, and you have no idea the priceless things he had in storage there."

Hearst, she remembered, was a "fabulous" personality. "I liked Marion, but I liked Mr. Hearst better. I have seen him when he was so furious, but he was such a smart man and so intelligent. Marion, you see, was an alcoholic. When she got plastered, she would begin to stutter. As soon as she would start stuttering, it would make him so mad, he would get up from the table and walk away."

Weeks said it was obvious that Davies' "niece," Patricia Van Cleve, was actually her (Davies') love child with Hearst.* "Patricia was drunk at a party one night and told me so. You couldn't help but notice. She looked exactly like him, with that long face and blonde hair. There was an awful lot of that going on in Hollywood."

Weeks was saddened and dismayed when Ziegfeld died suddenly in July 1932 from pleurisy and pneumonia. Not only was she despondent over losing a close friend, she had considered him to be at the helm of her career. After his death, Weeks was under exclusive contract to Samuel Goldwyn.

"Mr. Ziegfeld was a protector of me, and when that was gone, I had to fight my own battles. Believe me, it wasn't pleasant." That included fighting off Goldwyn's sexual advances. "It was rather personal, but let's put it this way. After Ziegfeld died, Goldwyn didn't waste any time in chasing me around his desk. I disliked him immensely."

Weeks confided to her mother, who intervened and demanded Goldwyn dissolve the contract. He had no choice but to agree.

When news of the release leaked out, Columbia head Harry Cohn approached Weeks with an offer. Signing on the dotted line, she entered the final phase of her career — her contract with Columbia Studios.

Her association with the mogul turned out to be a turbulent union. "Everything you've heard about Harry Cohn is the truth, take my word for it. He was a horrible man and so crude. He didn't have anything, no education, no manners, no anything." Not long after her arrival on the lot, she began to witness his cruelty. "I was invited with many other people to have luncheon in one of his conference rooms. One of the chairs was connected to an electrical current — if you sat on it, you had a shock. I didn't have to sit on it, but I saw another girl who did, and I was so embarrassed for her, I could have killed him."

Any hopes Weeks had for career advancement at the studio were squelched

**Patricia Van Cleve (1923–1993) was raised as the daughter of Marion Davies' sister Rose and George Van Cleve. Near the end of her life, Patricia confessed the truth of her parentage in a series of tape recordings. The story is recounted in an article, "San Simeon's Child," in the April 1995* Vanity Fair.

Barbara Weeks and Thomas Meighan in *Cheaters at Play* (1932). (Courtesy of Roi Uselton.)

when she refused Cohn's blunt sexual advances. "He was a terrible womanizer, and when he didn't get very far with me, he wanted to get rid of me." Part of his retaliation, Weeks soon learned, involved assigning the first-rate projects to other actresses, while she was cast in Westerns.

"Cohn, however, never realized how much I liked being in them," she said. "He considered Westerns punishment, but naturally I never mentioned it to him. I just enjoyed myself."

At Columbia in 1932, Weeks was the leading lady opposite cowboy Buck Jones in three films: *White Eagle, Forbidden Trail* and *Sundown Rider.* She found Jones, one of the film idols of her youth, "a charmer and wonderful guy to work with." She had far different feelings for Lambert Hillyer, the director of all three films. "He was a slave driver. I can remember in one of those movies, we were out in the desert in the middle of August. I had to wear a heavy woolen riding outfit. I nearly fainted from the heat. Hillyer would say something like, 'Oh, she's all right.' Finally, I said, 'To hell with you,' and I just sat down. The prop men brought chilled, ice-cold pails of water to put my hands in to cool me off. I didn't like Hillyer at all."

In one of the films she made at Columbia, *Deception* (1932), Weeks was cast as Nat Pendleton's fiancée, while Thelma Todd played Leo Carrillo's mistress in the story of fixed wrestling matches. Weeks remembered little of the picture; it was the cast that stuck in her mind.

"I knew Thelma Todd quite well. She was a delightful gal. What a ham

Barbara Weeks and Buck Jones in ***Forbidden Trail*** (1932). (Courtesy of Roi Uselton.)

Nat Pendleton was. He emoted all over the screen. Leo Carrillo I liked. He was a happy-go-lucky guy."

Cohn used Weeks in several more Columbia programmers (she appeared as Tim McCoy's leading lady in 1933's *Rusty Rides Alone*), and then loaned her to Fox for three features in 1933–34. In *She Was a Lady* (1934), the cast, which included Helen Twelvetrees, Donald Woods, Ralph Morgan and others, went on location to the High Sierras. "I did a lot of riding in the picture, which I enjoyed making. I had worked one other time with Helen Twelvetrees (in *Now I'll Tell* [1934]) and found her to be a nice girl, a rather petite person and kind of introverted."

Weeks kept quiet as Cohn continued loaning her out, thankful that they kept her far from his clutches. She didn't rebel when he assigned her to what others considered the ultimate humiliation: loanouts to independent companies (Chesterfield, Liberty and Goldsmith).

Ironically, Weeks considered her role as a gangster's moll in Goldsmith's *Woman Unafraid* (1934) to be the best role of her career, though she never saw the finished product. "I liked the part, and I especially enjoyed jumping through a window, which in those days of moviemaking was made of something like spun sugar."

For about a year in the mid–1930s, Weeks was in New York, where she modeled, did commercials and appeared on the stage in *Satellite*. "Noel Francis was also in the cast, but it was a screwy thing. It opened and closed in one night. It was terrible, but I got good reviews."

It was on a flight back to California in 1936 that she met Lewis Parker, a test pilot for Lockheed. They courted seriously and soon planned to marry. Shortly after their return to the West Coast, however, Lockheed sent him to Japan for a year. Weeks continued in films.*

Back at Columbia in 1937, she appeared with Charles Starrett in three Westerns: *Two Fisted Sheriff*, *One Man Justice* and *The Old Wyoming Trail*. "I liked Charlie Starrett very much," she said. "He had a darling wife and kids."

By 1938, her career in films was disintegrating. She appeared in small roles in *Paris Honeymoon* and *Dramatic School*, as one of the many students. When she married Parker on December 4, 1938, she (with the encouragement of her husband) decided to retire from the screen.

"I was pretty fed up with Hollywood, and he didn't like the idea. My mother blew her top, but I didn't give a damn. We went to Yuma, Arizona, and got married quickly. She didn't like it at all. What the heck, I had enough

**Her relationship with Parker was her first serious romance, she said. During her years in Hollywood, Weeks dated many people associated with the industry, from directors and cameramen to actors. She was seen on the town with Phillips Holmes, Paul Page, William Bakewell, Donald Dillaway and Guinn Williams, to whom she was reportedly engaged to be married in 1934. "Guinn and I were not really engaged," she said. "It was strictly publicity stuff. We went out about three or four times, but there was never a great moment there."*

Barbara Weeks and Charles Starrett in *One Man Justice* (1937). (Courtesy of Roi Uselton.)

of it." Her marriage earned her freedom from her domineering mother and it was only then, Weeks said, that she was able to discover the real person inside her. "For the first time, I was free. It was like night and day."

When Parker's work carried him to Australia for what was originally planned to be six months, Weeks followed. They ended up living there a year and a half. When it was learned he was married to an ex–Hollywood film actress, an Australian director called to ask if she might be interested in the role of the female menace in his next picture, *Dad Rudd, M.P.* (1940). The project got her out of the apartment and gave her something to do while her husband worked.

"It was a terrible picture, and the Australian studios were way behind us in technology, but I had fun with the part."

Back in Los Angeles in the early 1940s, Weeks had little contact with the film industry. She and her husband continued to be guests at San Simeon, however, and it was through her husband that Weeks got to know Bette Davis. Arthur Farnsworth, Davis' husband at the time, and Parker had attended Harvard together.

"They used to come to our house for dinner, and we'd go to theirs. My husband was a great pianist and 'Farney' a marvelous violinist. The two of them would get the Scotch bottle out and play all evening long."

The night before Farnsworth's accident (August 1943), in which he fell along Hollywood Boulevard, he and Davis had been guests in the Parker home. "She was responsible for Farney's death," Weeks said. "The doctors told her he had a clot on the base of his brain [due to the accident] that had to be removed. She, being a Christian Scientist at the time, wouldn't allow it. It could have saved his life.

"I couldn't stand Bette. She was a marvelous actress, but a very unpleasant person. She treated Farney like dirt. I never forgave her for it. I couldn't speak to her after his death."

After World War II, Parker left Lockheed and took a job with Phillips Oil as a commercial flyer. He was on his way to Egypt, where the company had oil wells, when his plane disappeared over the North Atlantic. He was never heard from nor seen again. "It was worse than a tragedy," Weeks said. "It took me years to get over that."

During the 1940s, Weeks did some fashion modeling while in New York. She had a short-lived marriage to William Cox, a lumberman, in April 1949. The union produced a son, Schuyler, her only child, in 1950.

Saddled with the responsibility of raising a son alone, Weeks, who had no work experience other than modeling and show business, had to learn a new vocation. After teaching herself to type, she became a secretary. Over the years, she worked at an aircraft company and a college in Northern California, where she retired in the 1970s. She was recognized occasionally as *the* Barbara Weeks of the movies. "I asked them not to say anything because I didn't want any publicity about having been in show business. I put it behind me and tried to forget it."

Due to an obituary in *Variety*, some of her fans, film historians and contemporaries believed she passed away in 1954; however, it was another Barbara Weeks, a stage and radio actress, who died. Weeks said she used to receive her mail and once had to prove to a doubting Screen Actors Guild that she was still alive.

Film historian Roi Uselton's patient and dedicated search for Weeks extended over a ten-year period. He finally located her living in Northern California in 1977.

When interviewed about her career in films in September 1996, Weeks still lived very quietly in California and said she rarely gave much thought to her film career.

Although she expressed an overall dissatisfaction with her career, she said she would alter very little of it if given the opportunity. On second thought, her life might have been different, she said, had she not had "such a bossy, dictatorial mother." How so? "I would have been able to express myself better than I did. When someone is constantly at you, you get to the point to where you hide many of your thoughts and moods from that person. Finally, it gets to be a habit."

The happiest time in her professional life came when she was on the stage in *Whoopee,* not on any of the Hollywood sound stages. "The stage is tiring and it's hard work, but movies are boring to make. They just didn't give me the enthusiasm I got from the stage."

Weeks expressed regret that in her 40 films, producers and directors never tapped into her true talents as a performer.

"I had talents they didn't bother to find out about. I tried it but it just didn't work," she said. "I just wasn't cut out to be a Bette Davis or a Joan Crawford. I didn't have that 'I'll die for' attitude. I had the talent, but I didn't care to kill myself just because I was in the movies."

FILMOGRAPHY

1930: *Whoopee!* Samuel Goldwyn/United Artists. Director: Thornton Freeland. Cast: Eddie Cantor, Eleanor Hunt, Paul Gregory, John Rutherford, Ethel Shutta, Spencer Charters, Chief Caupolican, Albert Hackett, Walter Law, Marilyn Morgan, Jeanne Morgan, Virginia Bruce, Barbara Weeks, Georgia Lerch, Betty Grable, Betty Stockton. ***Man to Man.*** Warner Brothers. Director: Allan Dwan. Cast: Phillips Holmes, Grant Mitchell, Lucille Powers, Barbara Weeks, Otis Harlan, Russell Simpson, Dwight Frye. **1931: *Men of the Sky.*** Warner Brothers. Director: Alfred E. Green. Cast: Irene Delroy, Jack Whiting, Bramwell Fletcher, John St. Polis, Edwin Maxwell, Otto Mathieson, Armand Kaliz, Frank McHugh, Barbara Weeks. ***Fifty Million Frenchmen.*** Warner Brothers. Director: Lloyd Bacon. Cast: Olsen and Johnson, William Gaxton, Helen Broderick, John Halliday, Claudia Dell, Lester Crawford, Evalyn Knapp, Charles Judels, Carmelita Geraghty, Vera Gordon, Bela Lugosi, Barbara Weeks. ***Illicit.*** Warner Brothers. Director: Archie Mayo. Cast: Barbara Stanwyck, James Rennie, Charles Butterworth, Joan Blondell, Natalie Moorhead, Ricardo Cortez, Claude Gillingwater, Barbara Weeks. ***Men in Her Life.*** Columbia. Director: William Beaudine. Cast: Lois Moran, Charles Bickford, Victor Varconi, Donald Dillaway, Luis Alberni, Adrienne D'Ambricourt, Barbara Weeks, Oscar Apfel, Hooper Atchley. ***Party Husband.*** Warner Brothers. Director: Clarence Badger. Cast: Dorothy Mackaill, James Rennie, Dorothy Peterson, Joe Donahue,

Donald Cook, Helen Ware, Paul Porcasi, Mary Doran, Gilbert Emery, Barbara Weeks. ***Two Fisted Justice.*** Monogram. Director: G. A. Durlam. Cast: Tom Tyler, Barbara Weeks, Bobbie Nelson, William Walling, John Elliott, Gordon De Main, Yakima Canutt. ***Palmy Days.*** United Artists. Director: Edward Sutherland. Cast: Eddie Cantor, Charlotte Greenwood, Barbara Weeks, Spencer Charters, Paul Page, Charles Middleton, George Raft, Harry Wood, Arthur Hoyt. **1932: *Stepping Sisters.*** Fox. Director: Seymour Felix. Cast: Louise Dresser, Minna Gombell, Jobyna Howland, William Collier, Sr., Stanley Smith, Barbara Weeks, Howard Phillips, Ferdinand Munier, Mary Forbes, Franklin Pangborn. ***Cheaters at Play.*** Fox. Director: Hamilton MacFadden. Cast: Thomas Meighan, Charlotte Greenwood, William Bakewell, Ralph Morgan, Barbara Weeks, Linda Watkins, Olin Howland, William Pawley, James Kirkwood. ***The Devil's Lottery.*** Fox. Director: Sam Taylor. Cast: Elissa Landi, Victor McLaglen, Alexander Kirkland, Ralph Morgan, Paul Cavanagh, Barbara Weeks, Beryl Mercer, Herbert Mundin, Halliwell Hobbes, Lumsden Hare. ***Hell's Headquarters.*** Mayfair. Director: Andrew L. Stone. Cast: Jack Mulhall, Barbara Weeks, Frank Mayo, Phillips Smalley, Fred Parker, Everett Brown. ***Discarded Lovers.*** Tower. Director: Fred Newmeyer. Cast: Natalie Moorhead, Russell Hopton, J. Farrell MacDonald, Barbara Weeks, Jason Robards, Roy D'Arcy, Sharon Lynn, Fred Kelsey, Robert Frazer. ***By Whose Hand?*** Columbia. Director: Benjamin Stoloff. Cast: Ben Lyon, Barbara Weeks, William V. Mong, Ethel Kenyon, Kenneth Thomson, Tom Dugan, William Halligan, Nat Pendleton. ***White Eagle.*** Columbia. Director: Lambert Hillyer. Cast: Buck Jones, Barbara Weeks, Ward Bond, Robert Ellis, Jason Robards, Jim Thorpe, Robert Elliott. ***The Night Mayor.*** Columbia. Director: Benjamin Stoloff. Cast: Lee Tracy, Evalyn Knapp, Eugene Pallette, Warren Hymer, Donald Dillaway, Vince Barnett, Astrid Allwyn, Barbara Weeks, Gloria Shea, Emmett Corrigan, Tom O'Brien, Wade Boteler. ***Deception.*** Columbia. Director: Lew Seiler. Cast: Leo Carrillo, Dickie Moore, Nat Pendleton, Thelma Todd, Barbara Weeks, Frank Sheridan, Henry Armetta, Hans Steinke, Greta Granstedt. ***Forbidden Trail.*** Columbia. Director: Lambert Hillyer. Cast: Buck Jones, Barbara Weeks, Mary Carr, George Cooper, Frank La Rue, Wallis Clark, Tom Forman. ***Sundown Rider.*** Columbia. Director: Lambert Hillyer. Cast: Buck Jones, Barbara Weeks, Pat O'Malley, Wheeler Oakman, Niles Welch, Bradley Page, Ward Bond. **1933: *State Trooper.*** Columbia. Director: D. Ross Lederman. Cast: Regis Toomey, Evalyn Knapp, Barbara Weeks, Raymond Hatton, Matthew Betz, Edwin Maxwell, Walter McGrail, Lew Kelly, Don Chapman, Eddie Chandler, Ward Bond. ***Soldiers of the Storm.*** Columbia. Director: D. Ross Lederman. Cast: Anita Page, Regis Toomey, Barbara Weeks, Robert Ellis, Wheeler Oakman, Barbara Barondess, George Cooper, Dewey Robinson, Henry Wadsworth. ***My Weakness.*** Fox. Director: David Butler. Cast: Lew Ayres, Lilian Harvey, Charles Butterworth, Harry Langdon, Sid Silvers, Irene Bentley, Henry Travers, Adrian Rosley, Mary Howard, Irene Ware, Barbara Weeks, Susan Fleming,

Marcelle Edwards, Marjorie King. ***Olsen's Big Moment.*** Fox. Director: Malcolm St. Clair. Cast: El Brendel, Walter Catlett, Barbara Weeks, Susan Fleming, John Arledge, Maidel Turner, Edward Pawley. ***Rusty Rides Alone.*** Columbia. Director: D. Ross Lederman. Cast: Tim McCoy, Silver King, Barbara Weeks, Dorothy Burgess, Wheeler Oakman, Edward Burns, Rockcliffe Fellows, Clarence Geldert. **1934: *The Quitter.*** Chesterfield. Director: Richard Thorpe. Cast: Charley Grapewin, Emma Dunn, William Bakewell, Barbara Weeks, Hale Hamilton, Glen Boles, Mary Kornman, Lafe McKee, Aggie Herring. ***Now I'll Tell.*** Fox. Director: Edwin Burke. Cast: Spencer Tracy, Helen Twelvetrees, Alice Faye, Robert Gleckler, Henry O'Neill, Hobart Cavanaugh, G. P. Huntley, Jr., Shirley Temple, Ronnie Cosbey, Ray Cooke, Frank Marlowe, Clarence Wilson, Barbara Weeks, Theodore Newton, Vince Barnett. ***When Strangers Meet.*** Liberty. Director: Christy Cabanne. Cast: Richard Cromwell, Arline Judge, Lucien Littlefield, Charles Middleton, Hale Hamilton, Sarah Padden, Maude Eburne, Barbara Weeks, Sheila Terry, Ray Walker, Vera Gordon, Luis Alberni, Arthur Hoyt, Bryant Washburn. ***She Was a Lady.*** Fox. Director: Hamilton MacFadden. Cast: Helen Twelvetrees, Donald Woods, Ralph Morgan, Monroe Owsley, Irving Pichel, Doris Lloyd, Kitty Kelly, Halliwell Hobbes, Mary Forbes, Paul Harvey, Jackie Searl, Barbara Weeks, Karol Kay, Harold Goodwin. ***The Crosby Case.*** Universal. Director: Edwin L. Marin. Cast: Onslow Stevens, Wynne Gibson, Warren Hymer, John Wray, Edward Van Sloan, Skeets Gallagher, Alan Dinehart, J. Farrell MacDonald, William Collier, Sr., Barbara Weeks, Harold Huber, Harry Seymour, Mischa Auer, Wade Boteler, Arthur Hoyt. ***Woman Unafraid.*** Goldsmith. Director: William J. Cowen. Cast: Lucille Gleason, Skeets Gallagher, Lona Andre, Warren Hymer, Barbara Weeks, Laura Treadwell, Ruth Clifford, Eddie Phillips, Jason Robards. **1935: *School for Girls.*** Liberty. Director: William Nigh. Cast: Sidney Fox, Paul Kelly, Lois Wilson, Lucille LaVerne, Dorothy Lee, Toby Wing, Dorothy Appleby, Lona Andre, Russell Hopton, Barbara Weeks, Kathleen Burke, Anna Q. Nilsson, Purnell Pratt, Robert Warwick, William Farnum. **1937: *Two Fisted Sheriff.*** Columbia. Director: Leon Barsha. Cast: Charles Starrett, Barbara Weeks, Bruce Lane, Edward Peil, Sr., Ernie Adams, Claire McDowell. ***One Man Justice.*** Columbia. Director: Leon Barsha. Cast: Charles Starrett, Barbara Weeks, Hal Taliaferro, Jack Clifford, Mary Gordon, Edmund Cobb. ***The Old Wyoming Trail.*** Columbia. Director: Folmer Blangsted. Cast: Charles Starrett, Barbara Weeks, Donald Grayson, Dick Curtis, Edward Le Saint. ***Pick a Star.*** Roach-MGM. Director: Edward Sedgwick. Cast: Patsy Kelly, Jack Haley, Rosina Lawrence, Mischa Auer, Lyda Roberti, Stan Laurel, Oliver Hardy, Charles Halton, Tom Dugan, Russell Hicks, Cully Richards, Spencer Charters, Sam Adams, Robert Gleckler, Joyce Compton, Johnny Arthur, James Finlayson, Walter Long, Wesley Barry, Benny Burt, Barbara Weeks, Brooks Benedict, Wilbur Mack. **1938: *Dramatic School.*** MGM. Director: Robert B. Sinclair. Cast: Luise Rainer, Paulette Goddard, Alan Marshal, Lana Turner, Genevieve Tobin,

Anthony Allan, Henry Stephenson, Gale Sondergaard, Melville Cooper, Erik Rhodes, Virginia Grey, Ann Rutherford, Hans Conried, Rand Brooks, Jean Chatburn, Marie Blake, Cecilia Callejo, Margaret Dumont, Frank Puglia, Dorothy Granger, Esther Dale, Maurice Cass, Dorothea Wolbert, Gino Corrado, Barbara Weeks, Valerie Day. **1939:** ***Paris Honeymoon.*** Paramount. Director: Frank Tuttle. Cast: Bing Crosby, Franciska Gaal, Akim Tamiroff, Shirley Ross, Edward Everett Horton, Ben Blue, Rafaela Ottiano, Gregory Gaye, Luana Walters, Alex Melesh, Victor Kilian, Michael Visaroff, Keith Kenneth, Raymond Hatton, Evelyn Keyes, Barbara Weeks, Albert Dekker, Ethel Clayton. **1940:** ***Dad Rudd, M.P.*** British Empire (Australian). Director: Ken G. Hall. Cast: Bert Bailey, Barbara Weeks, Connie Martyn, Yvonne East, Fred McDonald, Alec Kellaway, Frank Harvey, Grant Taylor.

Index